EUROSTARS
EUROCITIES

Studies in Urban and Social Change

Published by Blackwell in association with the *International Journal of Urban and Regional Research*.

Series Editors: Neil Brenner; Linda McDowell, Margit Mayer, Patrick Le Galès, Chris Pickvance and Jenny Robinson

The Blackwell Studies in Urban and Social Change aim to advance debates and empirical analyses stimulated by changes in the fortunes of cities and regions across the world. Topics range from monographs on single places to large-scale comparisons across East and West, North and South. The series is explicitly interdisciplinary; the editors judge books by their contribution to intellectual solutions rather than according to disciplinary origin.

Published

Eurostars and Eurocities: Free Movement and Mobility in an Integrating Europe
Adrian Favell

Urban China in Transition
John R. Logan (ed.)

Getting Into Local Power: The Politics of Ethnic Minorities in British and French Cities
Romain Garbaye

Cities of Europe
Yuri Kazepov (ed.)

Cities, War, and Terrorism
Stephen Graham (ed.)

Cities and Visitors: Regulating Tourists, Markets, and City Space
Lily M. Hoffman, Susan S. Fainstein, and Dennis R. Judd (eds)

Understanding the City: Contemporary and Future Perspectives
John Eade and Christopher Mele (eds)

The New Chinese City: Globalization and Market Reform
John R. Logan (ed.)

Cinema and the City: Film and Urban Societies in a Global Context
Mark Shiel and Tony Fitzmaurice (eds)

The Social Control of Cities? A Comparative Perspective
Sophie Body-Gendrot

Globalizing Cities: A New Spatial Order?
Peter Marcuse and Ronald van Kempen (eds)

Contemporary Urban Japan: A Sociology of Consumption
John Clammer

Capital Culture: Gender at Work in the City
Linda McDowell

Cities After Socialism: Urban and Regional Change and Conflict in Post-Socialist Societies
Gregory Andrusz, Michael Harloe and Ivan Szelenyi (eds)

The People's Home? Social Rented Housing in Europe and America
Michael Harloe

Post-Fordism
Ash Amin (ed.)

Free Markets and Food Riots
John Walton and David Seddon

Fragmented Societies
Enzo Mingione

Urban Poverty and the Underclass: A Reader
Enzo Mingione

Forthcoming

Cities and Regions in a Global Era
Alan Harding (ed.)

Urban South Africa
Alan Mabin

Urban Social Movements and the State
Margit Mayer

Social Capital Formation in Immigrant Neighborhoods
Min Zhou

Networked Disease: Emerging Infections in the Global City
S. Harris Ali and Roger Keil (eds)

Servicing Bodies
Linda McDowell

EUROSTARS AND EUROCITIES

FREE MOVEMENT AND MOBILITY IN AN INTEGRATING EUROPE

Adrian Favell

© 2008 by Adrian Favell

BLACKWELL PUBLISHING

350 Main Street, Malden, MA 02148–5020, USA
9600 Garsington Road, Oxford OX4 2DQ, UK
550 Swanston Street, Carlton, Victoria 3053, Australia

The right of Adrian Favell to be identified as the author of this work has been asserted in accordance with the UK Copyright, Designs, and Patents Act 1988.

First published 2008 by Blackwell Publishing Ltd

2   2009

Library of Congress Cataloging-in-Publication Data

Favell, Adrian.
   Eurostars and Eurocities : free movement and mobility in an integrating Europe / Adrian Favell.
      p. cm. – (Studies in urban and social change)
   Includes bibliographical references and index.
   ISBN 978-1-4051-3404-0 (pbk. : alk. paper) – ISBN 978-1-4051-3405-7 (hardcover : alk. paper)
1. Emigration and immigration–Research–Case studies. 2. Nationalism–Europe.
3. Transnationalism. I. Title.
   JV6013.5.F38 2008
   304.8'4—dc22

                                        2007026740

A catalogue record for this title is available from the British Library.

Set in 10.5/12 pt Baskerville
by SPi Publisher Services, Pondicherry, India.
Printed and bound in Singapore
by C.O.S. Printers Pte Ltd

The publisher's policy is to use permanent paper from mills that operate a sustainable forestry policy, and which has been manufactured from pulp processed using acid-free and elementary chlorine-free practices. Furthermore, the publisher ensures that the text paper and cover board used have met acceptable environmental accreditation standards.

For further information on
Blackwell Publishing, visit our website at
www.blackwellpublishing.com

Contents

Series Editors' Preface

The Blackwell *Studies in Urban and Social Change* series aims to advance theoretical debates and empirical analyses stimulated by changes in the fortunes of cities and regions across the world. Among topics taken up in past volumes and welcomed for future submissions are:

- Connections between economic restructuring and urban change
- Urban divisions, difference, and diversity
- Convergence and divergence among regions of East and West, North, and South
- Urban and environmental movements
- International migration and capital flows
- Trends in urban political economy
- Patterns of urban-based consumption

The series is explicitly interdisciplinary; the editors judge books by their contribution to intellectual solutions rather than according to disciplinary origin. Proposals may be submitted to members of the series Editorial Committee:

Neil Brenner
Linda McDowell
Margit Mayer
Patrick Le Galès
Chris Pickvance
Jenny Robinson

Preface

Observing Europe today is like a Rorschach test. Look at the continent one way and Europe is still divided up into distinctive nationalized societies: coloured blocks on a map, political nations, each with its own system and culture; everything in its right place. A continent defined by national rivalries, memories of conflict, cultural distinctions, patriotic identities. This is the way most Europeans still see it; the primary world in which they make sense of their lives; the countries in which they remain rooted. This is an old and familiar continent.

But look at Europe another way and something remarkable appears to be happening. A European Union has been built. European economies, legal systems, and political institutions are integrating. A European society seems to be in the making. Alongside the familiar patchwork of nation-state-societies, new forms of cross-border mobility, networks, and exchanges have emerged. Freedom of movement, in particular, has given the opportunity to millions of EU citizens to move effortlessly across borders: to forget roots, change lives and careers; to go look for work in a foreign city; to shop, study, buy second homes, or retire in a foreign land. For those that do move, horizons change. The old nation-state-society no longer appears so inevitable as one's ultimate identity, or the framework in which to live out your life. Those who move to live and work abroad go looking for a new Europe, a different horizon. One perhaps that is finally coming out from the shadow of the past – the dark continent of the twentieth century.

These old and new Europes coexist, and for all the talk of European integration, the "stayers" in Europe still vastly outnumber the "movers". One of the interviewees I talked to in the making of this book, Laure, a French media manager working in London, spoke of the kind of archetypal upbringing of average middle-class children in continental Europe as "la jeunesse dorée" ("the golden youth"). A safe and secure family base, school and college friends you will keep for life, maybe a little socially conservative, but enlightened and well educated. This was a life she had left behind for a risky career abroad. She compared her life, and the cross-border mobility on which it was based, with the stable lives of the friends she left behind. They had stayed close to home, and followed their parents' footsteps into a similarly comfortable affluence, rooted in the city or region in which they were born and structured by reliable and familiar social institutions.

European nationals may notionally all be European citizens today, but it is worth remembering that, historically in Europe, it is the nation-state-society that has underwritten this promise of the good life to its citizens. Premised on the territorial loyalty of its population, the pastoral welfare states of Europe have, since the end of the nineteenth century, more or less exclusively managed, coordinated, and overseen the long and winding path of their citizens from the cradle to the grave. The nationalized welfare state is supposed to be in terminal crisis, but it is a model that can still be found working.

I am writing the last parts of this book from our flat in Århus, Denmark. A child born here today, in this society, still has a lot to look forward to – as a Dane. I look out the window. It is a nice street, near the port; a few minutes easy walk or cycle to the city centre. There is an internet café on the street corner, and the flat looks across to a big park, that is in fact a cemetery. A few doors up the street, there is a brand new four-storey crèche: an impressive glass construction, that lights the street at night, colour coded by floor level for different age groups. During the day it is a hive of kids running around, drawing stuff, playing with Lego. Morning and evening, I count the elegantly dressed Danes, pushing their children in buggies or on the back of bicycles up and down the hill. This is the welfarist dream come true: in which a rich, individualistic society can still afford the luxury of universal childcare and generous maternity and paternity leave for well-off middle class parents in their twenties and thirties. The young mums and dads of Århus look like a blonde royalty: sitting in futurist cafés, sipping caffè lattés and reading glossy catwalk magazines, while little Rasmus or Helle sleeps in the baby carriage. Half the town seems to be self-employed as a freelance designer, artist, journalist, or architect – and everyone has a child or two. Pretty much everything that happens here, in the local newspaper, on TV, or over dinner with your family, is conceptualized, narrated, and understood in terms of what it means for Denmark or being Danish. Everybody is singing the same song – a proud national anthem. Europe is barely ever mentioned.

The Danes are not alone among the citizens of Europe in rarely looking to the EU to take care of their everyday needs, or as the horizon against which their lives will be constructed. They may well be drinking Italian style coffee or enjoying fine French wine, but a Europe without borders, if they think of it at all, is associated with the short-term benefits of tourism, business travel, or buying property abroad, not the kind of unmoving, stable benefits to which long-term membership – national citizenship – in a nationalized welfare state entitles you. Paradoxically, though, the rather egalitarian affluence they enjoy has, in the postwar period, been largely built on a process of European Union that has piece by piece dismantled the economic and political independence on which proud nation-states, such as Denmark, have built their societies. This European Union is built on freedom of movement: of capital, goods, services, *and* persons. In terms of trade and financial interdependence the effects of this European integration have been extraordinary, even in Denmark. Yet the same logic apparently does not work for persons. A Dane is also a European citizen, with rights to live and work wherever they want in the European Union. Mobility could – and perhaps should – be a big part of their future lives.

The theorists and advocates of European integration sing a very different song; a song for Europe. In the EU Commission's European Year of Worker's Mobility 2006, European citizens on the move were projected as the key population heralding the building of a new Europe beyond the nation-state.[1] After more than fifty years of institutional construction and legal development, the visionaries of Europe await the sociological proof of a new highly Europeanized population. Economists project models of growth and dynamism based on higher numbers of scientific, technical, and professional talent on the move.[2] Lawyers take up their cases in the European law courts, while political and social theorists speculate about the future of postnational citizenship and cosmopolitanism with these movers as their heroes. The limited intra-European mobility of West Europeans is also proposed as the guideline and model for the mobility of East Europeans opened up by the EU enlargements of 2004 and 2007. One might well ask: Who are these people being touted as the "new Europeans", the "pioneers of European integration"? What do their experiences tell us about the Europe of today, hamstrung between the old and the new? How do their lives compare to those of the vast majority who stayed home? Very little research has ever been done on them.[3]

These are the questions and themes explored in this book. My interview with Laure was one of 60 such interviews I made to profile the small but symbolically powerful population at the heart of these questions. In fact, in sheer numerical terms, migrant West Europeans are in fact not so easy to find. They are the exception among Europeans: less than 2 percent live and work abroad in the continent. Due to the temporary, often highly mobile modes of living across borders, they also often do not show up in official statistics (and percentages) of foreign residents, or even in the phone books of the countries they live in. If you go looking for them, you have to do it ethnographically, and you have to construct your population one by one, as it were, through life histories and subjective narratives rather than any rigid sampling procedures. Identify the pioneers as ideal types, exceptions to the rule, one-off cases illustrating individual mechanisms that might someday aggregate into a trend, a pattern, even a structure – a Europe that is changing, perhaps. Or maybe not. Maybe interviewing these would-be pioneers – and finding out what happens to them – one might instead find out why so many of their classmates and colleagues back home never left in the first place.[4]

Eurostars and Eurocities

Finding this population – the *Eurostars* as I call them – always seemed like an interesting challenge. But I make it easy on myself. I go looking for the pioneers in the most obvious places: those big, rich *Eurocities* in the Northwest of Europe – global cities, too – which are known, despite the immobility, to be hubs of European free movement, with significant foreign West European populations: Amsterdam, London, and Brussels. Other locations might have been chosen – Paris, Berlin, Munich, Copenhagen, Geneva, Zurich, Vienna, Barcelona, or Milan, for example – but each of my chosen cities has, in its own way, a claim to be the quintessential European capital. For methodological reasons, I limited myself to considering West Europeans from the pre-2004 EU15 member states. In theory, they should face none of the formal barriers and subtler forms of prejudice that still restrict Europeans from more recent East and Central European member states, as well as (obviously) non-European immigrants. To capture their experiences, I opted for in-depth, oral history style interviews with the resident foreign West Europeans in each of the three cities: both men and women, younger and older, single and married, of various professions and nationalities. For reference, a summary and index of the interviewees is included in the appendix material to this book, as well as a note on methodology.

Piecing together and juxtaposing these interviews, I tell the stories of the various individuals and families I met, against the ethnographic setting of the three Eurocities they live in and the backdrop of a still highly nationalized Europe of nation-states. Between each of the short chapters, interviews appear as extracts in their own right, letting a chosen few narrate their own stories as illustrative interludes to the main text. The voices of others are woven into the main chapters, set against the broad flow of a narrative that runs from the idea of freedom and the experiences of mobility, to the more complicated issues of settlement, participation, and integration in the three cities. Throughout, sections focusing on the microlevel experience of individuals are interspersed with broader macrolevel reflections on political legal frameworks, historical background, urban dynamics, or social structural change in Europe. But this is not a conventional work of social science, and I am tempted to suggest to those wishing to read the book as it should be – from start to finish, like a novel – that they should look away now, in case it spoils the plot.

Chapters one to four present the three cities as extraordinary hubs of the new European migration, each with its own international appeal and profile. I also explore the idea of freedom of movement and its political origins. The next four chapters then pose conventional questions from the sociology and human geography of migration, about why and how people move: looking at the new forms of social and spatial mobility emerging in the continent, and the European scale of the movers' everyday lives. The key to whether this mobility prefigures a more dramatic change in the number of Europeans leaving home lies in how well movers manage the transition from sojourner to settler in their chosen countries of residence. It is here that the cities vary dramatically. Chapters nine to fourteen tease out the difficulties of creating a truly cosmopolitan, denationalized lifestyle, detailing the forms of nationally specific exclusion that even the most global of cities can impose on these otherwise privileged foreign residents. Down the road it becomes clearer why so few Europeans live and settle abroad, and why these new Europeans are the exception not the rule in the European Union. The excitement and professional opportunities of the younger movers in the open, cosmopolitan cities they first encounter, can be contrasted with the growing sense of unease and practical difficulties of their older peers, as they come to terms with the consequences of their chosen lifestyle – particularly where it involves issues of quality of life, long-term financial planning, childrearing, and health care. But no individual story is a deterministic one. With such a diversity of people and places, there is no single outcome or answer to the question of Europe as seen through their eyes. One by one, rather, the stories add up to a portrait of the potentials and pitfalls of free movement in Europe at a human level; a portrait of a remarkable generation (or two) of people who, with Laure, stepped off the national path to follow an uncertain future in an integrating Europe.[5]

Roll the Credits

After such a painfully long time, it is hard to recall the appropriate credit for every little dab of paint on this canvas.

First, my thanks to the Eurostars themselves. Although masked behind pseudonyms and blurred personal details, and portrayed in brief snapshots that might have changed, I have tried my utmost to stay true to their voices and experiences. They represent the real people that should populate all social theory and social science treatises, but so rarely do. I hope at least that I do some justice to these remarkable lives, and apologise for any errors of interpretation and narrative.

I am very grateful to the generous cooperation of several corporations, who responded to me without any material incentive. Thanks to Geoff Williams, Martin de Jong, Fiona Mills, and Tammy Bernard at Unilever; Elena Larrea and Esther O'Hallaran at Pret; Frank Heemskerk at ABN Amro; Simon Payne at Expatica; Pascale Zoetaert and John Miller at *Bulletin*; Martin van Schieveen at *Expat* magazine. At the European Commission, thanks to Jimmy Jamar, Ivone Kaizeler, Els van Winckel, and David Bearfield. I offer the book as a sincere contribution to the tireless struggle of actors in Brussels and elsewhere for a better, brighter Europe.

A brief word about the locations in which the book was conceived. It is written in memory of nights out at those classic long lost Brussels clubs of *Le Sud* and *Planet Claire*, and of long hours spent at so many great bars and cafés: *L'Amour Fou*, *L'Ultime Atome*, *Bazaar*, *Monk*, and *Café Belga* in Brussels; *Café Krull*, *De Jaren*, and *Het Schuim* in Amsterdam; *Lynfabrikken*, *Englen*, and *Fredes Flyvende Tallerken* in Århus; *Chango* and *Silverlake Coffee Company* in LA. A special word for the *Vikingeklubben* in Risskov – there is simply no better way to start the day – and the *Shimizu-yu onsen* in Omotesando for keeping me sane during the final editing. It would be churlish also not to mention easyInternetCafé, Ryan Air, and the Eurostar train without which none of this mobility would have been possible.

Then there are the many friends who participated in the research in some way or other. Thanks (and hello – wherever you are!) for help in Amsterdam, to Maaike, Juliette, Jeroen, Joannet, Beate, Stefaan, Lorraine, Boris, Gaby, Shanta, Marleen, Julie, Markus, Elena, Damian, Saskia, and Hans; in London, to Sara, Eiko, Robert, Marianne, Andrés, Laetitia, Francisco, Susana, Mike, Lavan, Rick, Lucy and Franck for the bed and fine dining in Hoxton, Nick, Aurélie, Blanca, Krisztina, Dave, Claire, Dan, and Rob; and in Brussels to Alan, Sophie, Magali, Tom, Angelique, Steve, Anna, Martin, Marta, Marcel, Seppo, James, Maggie, Sarah, Heidi, Jerôme, Diederik, Nadya, Francesca, Katarzyna, Annemieke, Kristel, Alisdair, Isabelle, Ann-Christina (who taught me Danish), Joanne, and Isabel. *Lang leef Eurostars!*

In the Netherlands, I am also grateful to: funding from the UK-Netherlands Partnership Programme in Science, Kees Groenendijk, Tessel de Lange, Michèle de Waard, Dirk Koppes, Ted Badoux, Karen Phalet, Philip Muus, Robert Kloosterman, Don Weenink, and colleagues at the University of Utrecht. In London: to Kirsty Hughes, Patrick McGovern, Richard Stanton, Hari Kunzru, Andrew Gimson, Elspeth Guild, and John

Salt; in Brussels: to the Region of Brussels which funded my initial report through the Research in Brussels program, Marc Swyngedouw who made the initial project possible, Hassan Bousetta, Koen Abts, Irina Zinovieva, Inge Giovaere, Marco Martiniello, Philippe and Sue van Parijs, Franziska, Maria and Bernd at Academic Cooperation Association, Nadia de Beule, François-Xavier de Donnea, Caroline de Gruyter, Bart Aerts, "The Voice of Brussels" (whoever he/she is), Annelore Isaac, Alain Verstandig, Richard Hill, Ixelles commune, Frank Hoornaert, Jo Buelens, Unna Lassiter, Roland Demarcke, Carlo Luyckx, Gideon Rachman, Olivier Guilbaut, Vinciane Jacquiez, Leo Verhoeven, Ilse Thienpont, Rik Jellema, Alain Maskens, Kris Deschouwer, and invaluable research assistance from Eli Kvamme.

I thank Science Po, Paris for the very kind invitation to be visiting scholar in Winter 2006 at the Centre d'Études Européennes. My thanks and regards to Renaud Dehousse, Pascal Perrineau, Nicolas Jabko, Sylvie Strudel, Andy Smith, Charlotte Halpern, Patrick Simon, and Sophie Body-Gendrot, and thanks with great appreciation to Sophie Duchesne – I hope I've finally written something about mobility worthy of the many discussions we have had on the subject. *Et j'embrasse fort* Valérie, Romain and, of course, Pascal for being such good friends there.

I am grateful to academic debate and discussion with Eleonore Kofman, Paul Kennedy, Mike Savage, Tim Butler, Mabel Berezin, Harlan Koff, Ari Zolberg, Anja Weiss, Irene Hardill, Chris Rumford, Jeff Checkel, Gary Marks, Liesbet Hooghe, Peter Katzenstein, Giovanni Peri, David Plane, Siain O'Riain, Caitriona Ni Laoire, Ulrich Krotz, Kathleen Thelen, Ash Amin, Deborah Cohen, Martin Kohli, Alison Woodward, Dominic Boyer, Marion Fourcade, Barbara Hobson, Paul Statham, Klaus Eder, Michael Bommes, Christian Joppke, Hans Jörg Trenz, Doug Holmes, Steven Lukes, John Lie, Andreas Glaeser, Michèle Lamont, Saskia Sassen, Dorte Martinsen, Ian Manners, Ruud Koopmans, Phil Rees, Julie-Anne Boudreau, Colleen Thouez, Olivier Kramsch, Helen Wallace, Jon Beaverstock, Darren Smith, Brad Blitz, Willem Maas, Elizabeth Bernstein, Ödül Bozkurt, Yasemin Soysal, Sin Yi Cheung, Frédéric Mérand, and Niilo Kauppi.

I am also grateful for invitations to present the book as work-in-progress at various seminars: at the Universities of Sussex and Stockholm, UC-Berkeley, UC-San Diego and UCLA, Cornell University, the Sorbonne and Science Po, Paris, the Vrije Universiteit Amsterdam, Humboldt University Berlin, Carleton University Ottawa, European University Institute Florence, Australia House and Royal Holloway College, London, GRIPS and Hitotsubashi University, Tokyo; and in conference at the Sektion Soziale Ungleichheit und Sozialstrukturanalyse of the German Sociological Association, the Council for European Studies, the European Union Studies Association, the European Sociological Association, the American Sociological

Association, the European Consortium for Sociological Research, and the International Conference on Population Geographies.

My thanks to the University of Sussex for sabbatical time in 2001. My regards to Russell King – he will recognize this as a Sussex Migration product through and through. I owe something to all my friends and colleagues there, but particularly Tony Fielding, Richard Black, Mick Dunford, Ralph Grillo, Jeff Pratt, Jenny Money, Simon Rycroft, Paul Taggart, and Bhavna Sapat. At the other end of the project, in late 2006, I must also thank colleagues at the Danish Institute for International Studies, Copenhagen for such an enjoyable and productive stay.

This is also very much a UCLA product. I thank the institution for generous funding support and sabbatical time, and salute my outstanding roster of colleagues. Among these, I must thank Roger Waldinger, who has been a wonderful mentor, along with Rogers Brubaker, Jack Katz, Andreas Wimmer, Gail Kligman, Mick Mann, Ron Rogowski, Ivan Berend, Françoise Lionnet, John Agnew, Michael Storper, Jenifer Abramson at the library, our graduate students in the international migration working group, the UCLA International Institute global fellows forum, and all the members of our working group on "The Human Face of Global Mobility". Thanks for research assistance to Kristin Surak.

A few special thanks are needed. I owe gratitude to all my PIONEUR colleagues for their collective and individual contributions to the parallel quantitative survey that I draw on throughout. I detail their contributions in the section on methodology. My work in Amsterdam and Brussels would have been utterly impossible without the advice, friendship, and hospitality of Ben Crum and Dirk Jacobs, respectively. Neil Fligstein, Juan Diez Medrano, Neil Brenner, Virginie Guiraudon, Damian Tambini, Ettore Recchi, Javier Moreno, and Ann-Christina Lauring Knudsen also provided extraordinary close readings at the crucial final stage; and thanks to Harvey Molotch and the series editors for advice at an earlier stage. Patrick Le Galès has been immensely supportive of this project at various key stages along the way, and thanks to everyone at Blackwell, especially Jacqueline Scott, for their patience and unwavering support for the book.

A special word of thanks to Pat and Michael for being the best of friends in California, and Michael for being such fun to work with; to Beth and Simon who have shared so much of the Euro-American experience with me; and to Helen and Damian, who have so often provided an idyllic refuge in England, and who perceptively suggested the three works that proved the best stylistic models – albeit obliquely – for my writing: Richard Sennett's *The Corrosion of Character: The Personal Consequences of Work in the New Capitalism*, Anna Funder's *Stasiland: Stories From Behind the Berlin Wall*, and John Steinbeck's *The Grapes of Wrath*.

Grazie mille to Ettore for understanding every word and for guessing the title of the sequel: "Children of the Revolution".

Finally, an exhausted hug of thanks to all my family in England and Denmark; and with love to Stine, still my favourite of all the Eurostars I know.

The book is dedicated to everyone with the Wykes gene out there –
to the memory of Charlie and Gwen.

1

Freedom-Vrijheid-Liberté

Consider freedom of movement *qua* freedom. What is it? What is this new kind of freedom in Europe today? Here are a few examples.

You take a train. The station looks modern, the train fast. The two of you have been looking forward to this for a long time. The train departs, and rolls out through the city. You both laugh as local commuter trains overtake it. The announcements come in three languages – English, Dutch and French, with distinctive, slightly false accents. They are apologising for the delay. The train eventually enters a long tunnel, and suddenly it is travelling fast. When it comes out, the landscape is different, flashing by. Twice as fast. You arrive in the heart of a new city in less time than it would have taken to get out to the airport and pass through security in the first. You take another fast train. The cities and countries spin by in a blur, while you talk, station-to-station, trans-Europe express. The world outside is familiar, but strange. The new currency you hold can be used everywhere. You arrive in another new city. European modernity rises up around you ... You feel liberated. Eurostars.

You finish your undergraduate studies and decide to leave home. You throw all your things into a ruck sack, and say goodbye to your parents and home town – an affluent small city in the provinces of continental Europe. You take a cheap airplane, with a one-way ticket that flies you direct to a small, modern airport, miles out from the city. When you arrive in the big city – the capital of European finance and media – you find a job a couple of days later, making BLT sandwiches every morning for the biggest chain of lunchtime cafés. This is a means not an end. At nights you study English and follow courses for an MA in graphic design or business studies. You live in a damp £100–a-week dorm, with three other young Europeans. One of them works as a sandwich-board guy for the West End bargain computer shops, while his girlfriend is handing out leaflets for language schools round the corner. Someone else just got a job making coffee for the commuters on the trains. There are parties most nights, and you meet new friends every day … You feel liberated. A free mover.

You finish work early and head down to the Irish pub near the international institutions to meet up and chat with friends of ten different nationalities. Everyone speaks English, but it's a new continental version, no longer defined by the Queen of England or the BBC (which you still watch on cable), and certainly not the President of the United States. You love listening to all the different European accents, and charming hybrid grammatical inventions. Everyone seems to be enjoying the way you can step in and out of national identities in this place. Someone suggests a Greek restaurant, and the evening spills on into a lively salsa bar near the centre. Later, you wander the streets, before finding an underground night club in a bombed-out building, that serves up lemon vodka and hip hop, until 5 in the morning … You feel liberated. A denationalized European.

You decide to quit your job with the company, and start afresh. Some friends abroad are offering you a chance to go it alone. You fly out to see them, and over a few beers, the deal is done. They agree to be your first clients. You set up the company, work out the red tape. There are no barriers to service provision here. Work conditions are good, and the business starts rolling in. It's fun to be in a new city, a new country. There are tax breaks, and other associates who have cashed in the same way. The lifestyle is good, the quality of living even better. The city feels open, tolerant, and liberal. You are a foreigner, but your international connections bring in the work. You wonder why you never did this before … You feel liberated. A cross-national entrepreneur.

You retire from your job, and sell your home where you have both lived for thirty years. You put everything you own in a car and drive south. You leave your country. There are no passport controls, and the grass now grows over checkpoints that once marked out the military borders of nations. One country, then another. The weather improves, and the air gets warmer. You reach the ocean, and smell the olive trees. You arrive at your new white-washed house, silhouetted against an azure sky. At the small town down the road you can collect your pension from your offshore account, arrange to see a doctor, or draw money on an international credit card. You eat and sleep well, and begin to forget the stresses of your old life, the cold damp mornings on the commuter train. You like your new life as citizens of nowhere ... You feel liberated, sexy beasts. The new barbarians.

These are the stories to expect. Everyday lives, simple stories, banal even, but stories revealing trajectories nevertheless unique to this new Europe in the making. Freedom of movement of persons may just be the most remarkable achievement of the European Union, and its slow fifty-plus year progress towards integration, enlargement, and unity.

Individuals can now build lives – careers, networks, relationships, families – beyond the nation-state containers that once defined personal identity and personal history. This freedom of movement is not a global phenomenon; it is regionally defined, and specific to Europe. There is nothing else quite like it on the planet. If you are American, you cannot just move to London and get a job. If you are Australian, you still have to line up in the foreigners' channel at the airport, fill out a landing card, and get your passport stamped. If you are Indian, you might be able to live permanently in Britain, even vote in the general election, but every time you travel abroad within Europe, you have to get a visa. These kinds of migration restrictions are still the norm in a world of nation-states, a world of national identities and bounded citizenships. This world certainly still exists, but something else exists within the integrating space of the European Union. European freedom of movement is a unique legal and political construction in the modern world, in which one has the right to move, travel, live, work, study, and retire without frontiers. In which any invocation of national boundary to restrict these opportunities for European foreigners is considered discrimination.

This distinctive new form of freedom, European freedom, deserves to be explored. How does one experience this freedom? Can one really live out and fulfil it? If so, where? Is it really freedom? What are its downsides? If you ask those who appear to be the most free, what do they say?

You Are Free

The train rolls into Centraal Station, Amsterdam. *Natuurlijk*. When you step off the train, here, you know you've arrived in Europe. You step over the junkies and out the hall, and there it is: perhaps the most well-known square mile of freedom in the Western world. Ahead, stretching up the waterside, lies the sordid strip up Damrak to Damplein: past sex museums and kebab shops, tacky stores selling souvenir dildos and clogs, boats crowded with sweaty tourists. Take a left, follow the smell, and you're straight into the red light zone. You rub shoulders with leery stag weekend groups and naïve frat boys, all in search of the rowdy coffee shops and supermarket-style brothels that make this place famous. Every few seconds, an edgy drug pusher catches your eye, whispering an inventory of mind altering substances as you pass by. This is everyone's first idea of Amsterdam, the place where everything is permitted.

So let's start here, as so many do. For instance, Ray from Ireland, who runs a successful transportation business in the city:

> *Soft drugs … was my main knowledge of it. I hadn't spent a huge amount of time on mainland Europe. All I really knew about Amsterdam was that it was small, everybody spoke English, they had a red light district, and you could smoke a joint without too much hassle – which nine years ago seemed* [smiles] … *reasonably OK. For someone of my situation … Being single* [laughs].

This much is no different to the American frat boy's idea of freedom, of course, with the red light zone in Amsterdam a must-do on any quick EURAIL tour of the continent. Only here, in old Amsterdam, the frat boys can kiss and hold hands, and nobody seems to mind. It's only a start, but it feels good. *Free.* Ray, again:

> *The premise* [here] *is that you can do what you want as long as it doesn't bother anybody else. If you want to wear a bikini on roller-skates going down the Herengracht that's up to you. Try doing that in Dublin and you're in a padded cell* [laughs].

If you stay awhile, you learn to stop being a tourist, and start (trying) to be a resident. You get a job, look for a flat, and start taking part in city life. You realize that the red light zone and toleration towards soft drugs and sex work is only a part of how the place works. The city in fact offers much more appealing types of freedom. Susan, a young English woman, who works for a bank:

> *Amsterdam is so diverse, so many different cultures. It brings out the best in all worlds in some ways. What annoys me is people base their idea of Amsterdam on the red light district, which is absolutely the wrong thing to do. It's not representative. Like Leidseplein, another big touristy area … I can understand why they're there, I'm sure that's where we went when we visited the first time, but … You kind of forget it's there when you've been here awhile. When you live here …*

You start getting annoyed rather than flattered that the Dutch respond to you systematically in perfect, albeit strongly accented English. You start trying to take on board some of their distinctive habits: milk with bread and cheese for lunch; abusing pedestrians who get in your way in the cycle lane; joining clubs with strange mottos or initiation rites. As you get to know it, Amsterdam begins to feel less weird and unique, more like it's the quintessential European city. Behind it, the Netherlands takes shape as the prototypical, model European society; if only because its contours are so clearly drawn, its self-contained social system so distinctive, so constructed, so vividly *Dutch*. It's not the only way of being European, or even the most European, but it sure is European. Europe at its best, perhaps? A lot of the foreigners who move here think that when they arrive. Such as Valerio, from Italy, who works as a costume buyer for a theatre:

> *Let's say when I was a student, everything was different. I was attending* [expecting to find] *people who had the same interests that I had ... It was a kind of fairy country.*

What is this freedom that Amsterdam embodies? Is it just freedom from the state, the dream of anarchists everywhere? Spaces in society that escape the state's penetrative gaze, its will to legislate and control, tell you what you should and shouldn't do? Yes and no. For sure, Amsterdam outscores any city in Europe in terms of its liberal appeal. Its historical tradition of religious tolerance and asylum, and famously liberal attitudes, make it a magnet for all seeking a refuge from conservatism. American progressives, in particular, who despair about their own society, love it here. So is it in the coffee shop where we find freedom? In a haze of smoke? Or in legalized sex for money? Is that it? Not quite. The freedom here is, in fact, all legislated, regulated, controlled. These Dutch freedoms are organized spaces carved out of a society otherwise not so permissive in its attitudes. The Dutch even have a word for it: *gedogen*. To overlook, to ignore, to pretend it's not there. There is a set place for everything.

But there *is* more to it than that. Amsterdam, Dutch society, *does* seems to embody some of the most open possibilities of progressive modernity. There are, for example, gay people in all levels of society. Guillaume, a French freelance journalist and activist, explains why this makes you feel free:

> [When I arrived] *many people were gay and it was not an issue. Like you have brown hair or black hair, it was nothing special. Wow! It felt very impressive ... In the gay life* [here] *half of the people are foreigners, and 50 percent of the reason they came here was to be free. They don't come because it's a gay city, that's a mistake. They come because it's non-homophobic, which is really not the same thing. They come here to be able to be normal. Here nobody cares. You are just human.*

This city, like others, is seen as a *refuge*: from the provinces, from the intolerant, the xenophobic, the small-minded. From persecution. From ingrained tradition, hierarchy, privilege, thoughtless social reproduction. From other people's norms. From where you've come from. As Guillaume stresses, it's the place to be yourself, to be *human*. The freedom of experiencing cities like this also teaches you things. Ingrid is a Danish European Union *fonctionnaire*, nearing retirement after more than thirty years in Brussels, a city in which she feels completely at home:

> *I'm for opening, and the understanding of different people. Tolerance is a really important element in everyday life. If you don't have tolerance you can't live in peace with yourself. You learn that also in a city like Brussels ... In an international job, you see that people are very different. It's fortunate to live and work in an environment like that.*

This urban atmosphere in turn can be the key to one's own well-being and happiness. Sandra, a Germanophone artist from Luxembourg, resident in London, puts it this way:

> *I love London. I think it's a very beautiful city. I think the people [here] are very tolerant ... Once they accept you, they accept you the way you are. You can unfold your own creativity, whatever you want to do, without being criticized. When we lived in Germany – in Germany I'm a foreigner as well – the Germans are much more critical about everything. Here you can really be your own self. I never had the feeling of claustrophobia in London.*

Within these quintessential international cities, there are local spaces where the intersection of cultures and diversity is even more intense. The easiest way to find them is to look for multi-ethnic gentrifying neighbourhoods, in which old locals, new ethnic minority immigrants, and a cosmopolitan sprinkling of foreign urban professionals intermix. Some have developed now into highly affluent areas, such as the Jordaan in Amsterdam, Islington in London, and Châtelain in Brussels. Others are still in development: De Pijp in Amsterdam, Shoreditch in London, Sint Katelijne in Brussels: exciting, protean places where the cosmopolitan brew of Eurocities best comes together in a specific locale.

London, Brussels, and other Eurocities share these dimensions, but Amsterdam might be thought of as emblematic. It helps us remember that freedom is a cultural thing too: it is, as John Stuart Mill would say, about lifestyles, diversity, and experimentation as much as anything else. Freedom must, of course, be economic and political too, as is more commonly stressed. Amsterdam, of course, is a free and open city – like London and Brussels – partly because of globalization and all that: of historical free trade, of its being a centre of global networks, of the flows and mobilities of the modern world in which it is a node. The freedom to move money and things across borders, as well as people. Amsterdam is a free society, like others, because liberal society has embraced the wisdom of giving people rights to do these things. A society in which transactions do not end at the borders of a nation-state. A society not embedded in the inertia of rooted national traditions, or singular cultures. A society built on the promise of some cosmopolitan future, not one based on ideas about the natural, national order of things.

In a sense, this is what the Dutch Enlightenment was all about. Creating a modern society, free from history, from nature, from the impossibility of an inverted land, in which the sea level is higher than the land on which the people live. As the Dutch never cease to remind you: this society, this city, is a man-made miracle. Rational, modernistic, organized down to the last brick, and thus emboldened in its defiance of nature. God might have made the world, but human hands and minds built the Netherlands. Amsterdam is a city built on stilts, with tall buildings sitting on soft mud and water, and oceans penned back behind *dijks* and the system of land-reclaimed *polders*. I remember my rapt discovery of the wonderful embossed diagram in the *stadhuis*, when you realize for the first time just how low Schiphol airport is relative to the city. It lies several meters below sea level. All of this, of course, was the fruit of the first golden age of globalization, the Dutch seventeenth century.

Amsterdam might then represent modernity – European modernity – at its best. Where freedom from tradition – from old Europe – is also freedom from where you came from, from how you were socialized. For those that move across the new Europe, this aspect of freedom is crucial: it is freedom from the nation-state, the most insidious and persistent source of identity in the modern world; the power of national culture to mould us in each other's image, as citizens belong to this nationality, this culture, and no other. The way society disciplines our behaviour as a set of standardized, nationalized norms. For some, particularly young women, this might take the form of freedom from your family and their expectations. Anastasia is a young Greek woman, who chose Amsterdam for this reason:

> *There is a freedom here, a sort of a freedom we don't have in Greece. They are not so attached to the family here. They don't have to make such compromises. I don't know a lot of Greeks here, because Greeks don't move* [abroad]. *I felt free not to compromise on all this. You have to marry, you have to have kids, have to have things and make things, prove yourself, like having a good job, a nice husband, a good family. Everybody feels they can exercise control on you. You can go on a bus and the lady next to you can make remarks to you. Here, because I'm a foreigner, nobody cares what I'm doing.*

Once you move away from home, your family, things change. You get a new deal. If you are Belgian, for example, London or Amsterdam might provide this. Saskia, who works in finance in London:

> *The thing is, my father is a quite well known figure in Belgium: the head of* [a major nationalized company]. *Belgium is a small country, you are always known as*

the daughter of someone else. If I'm at a wedding, I get asked, if I am connected [professionally] *to him. It's interesting that my sister is in Luxembourg, and I'm here* [in London]. *It's nice to know that when you get a job it's really what you do and not what your father did.*

This is freedom from parochialism, from the old-boy network of home. If you are a German woman you might find what you are looking for in Amsterdam or London. Nina came to "relaxed, very laid back" Amsterdam to get away from working in a patriarchal German law firm. Freedom for her was symbolized by buying a little nutshell boat with her German partner, and being able to drink a bottle of wine out on the canals. If you are an English woman, the same thing might be found in Brussels. For example, Janet, a trade journalist. For her, it is the multinational quality of the place, that defines the space it allows her:

It's because of the distinct lack of Belgian nationality, there isn't a strong stamp. You can make a space [here]. *In Paris, it would be harder, you would have more of a French* [context] ... *Brussels allows you that space to create your own life, that is semi-attached to the expat life, semi-attached to the Belgian life, kind of floating in-between.*

Belgians describe going to the Netherlands in terms of escape from a conservative culture, or nationalist politics. Amsterdam feels like a liberation. But a Dutch person in Brussels can feel the same way about their relation to home. Joannet, who is working as a political consultant on Dutch-Belgian affairs in Brussels, puts it in terms of "quality of life":

The one thing I like is that I have the feeling here of freedom. In the Netherlands, there are all these rules. They have this character thing where you always control what other people are doing. People are always giving their opinion, even if you don't ask them. With the Dutch, if eating goose is in then it's goose for everyone, if it's too hot with the window open, then it's too hot everywhere ... That goes for clothes, the movies you like, the books you read, what you do and what you don't do generally in life ... I feel much happier here. I don't have this idea that I should do something because its in or everyone is doing it.

The short move to Brussels enabled her to escape the national norms, and see her own country in a new light – something of great practical use in her daily work.

I get angry about Dutch issues. I'm not always proud to be Dutch. I went further away [from the Netherlands] *but I got closer involved. It's true I find it much easier to criticize the Netherlands now: whether it's the political system, or our businesses, or the people, or a consumer organization, or how the house sale of my mum is handled … The Netherlands is a really really small world. I sometimes find that hard to understand. I'm a bit impatient there.* [I think] *come on guys! Let's be bigger than that, be a bit a more flexible!*

What everyone is talking about here is freedom from the nation-state, a *denationalized* freedom: in both the spatial (economic) and cosmopolitan (cultural) sense. You are free to move, to leave your country and live and work abroad. And you are free to benefit from this distance it gives to be self-critical, and to play around with ascriptive national identities that hitherto might have felt fixed and stamped for life. When I talk to Bernhard, a German lawyer in Brussels, about his national identity, he pinpoints another dimension of this freedom.

Do I think about it? From time to time, of course. [Before] *it was clear, but after two years in Brussels it is changing. In relation to my friends back in Germany, they live in another world somehow. I realize that I'm slowly moving out of that context. That makes it quite interesting. I don't ask about it, I just observe. I'm German, but it's great fun being European and making fun of your nationality and other nationalities. That's a game with the identities that you can observe a lot around here, which I like a lot.*

Nicole is a web designer in London on a modest income. She gives another spin on this theme:

I'm two hours from Lille. I feel French in England, and English in France. I love that. Being abroad, being a stranger, being different [here]. *And I love going back to France, and being different. I have a little more.*

It's a common refrain among the French in London. Nathalie, who works for a retail company, says:

It's a pity that most people are not sometimes a foreigner somewhere. I am much more free [after this experience]. *I realize I am "me", not French, not English.*

This is freedom with an almost existential quality. Ray, the businessman in Amsterdam, eventually settled down, but he didn't become Dutch.

I've never had any problems with being a foreigner. I enjoy being a foreigner. I'm a professional foreigner wherever I go. I consider myself not to fit in. I have the same thing back in Ireland. I feel no different to how I feel here. The only difference is I kind of fit in more over there. They don't notice. They think it's because my accent is kind of like theirs, that I know what they're talking about. But I'm lost in their conversations as well. Yes, I couldn't imagine [now] *I would feel anything other than a professional foreigner. I can't imagine it.*

This attitude is equated in Ray's case with personality: the wish to not be part of one's ascribed group identity – often one of the hardest things to avoid as a stereotyped, nationally labelled "expat".

When I first came here, my circle of friends was through work, or other Irish people I met in The Tara [a well known Irish pub in Amsterdam]. *It's an acceptable way to be a complete stranger, and make some friends in an evening. Not now. My circle of people tend to be of mixed African/Portuguese descent* [his wife is from Angola], *as opposed to Irish in fact. In fact, I have no Irish friends in Holland. I'd hate to think I missed one* [smiles], *but no I don't think I have any Irish friends. Among the Irish* [here] *there is fairly strong "paddyish" club, lots of people. I'm not part of that. I'm a family man, not interested in anything very much outside my wife and daughter.*

As Ray suggests, family remains important in these lives, even if nationality does not. You want some space and freedom, but not too much. This provides the other key aspect that European mobility allows. Saskia, in London, has also worked in Boston, Massachusetts, and Luxembourg. Neither felt right.

There is a certain freedom that comes with being a foreigner somewhere. There are not that many expectations, and if people expect things from you and you don't do it, you always have this escape. I've grown used to it, to really like being a foreigner somewhere. When I was in Luxembourg, it was like being back in Belgium. I was still a foreigner there, but I was not perceived as one. I was expected to be back in the group, which I really hate. Here, I'm a foreigner, I'm perceived as a foreigner, it's OK. But, unlike in the US, I'm very close [to home]. *I really enjoy going back,* [but] *I'm not sure I could live in Belgium.*

Saskia has the professional freedom of the globe, the desire to be mobile, and the open-minded attitude to make it work. But living and working in London, she is close in space and time to home, to family, to the key reference points in her life. European mobility is sometimes all about regional movement over small distances separated by large national boundaries. With this, another key element of this distinctively European freedom falls into place.

The open, integrating space of Europe still has many such boundaries; so many distinctive national and regional cultures, ways of being. With so many boundaries to transcend, rights of free movement in hand, and transportation getting easier, the sheer number of potential border crossings and self-transformations means that the kind of freedom available is rapidly exponential. Maria is a high-flying Portuguese lawyer, working for a major Dutch bank:

> *For me, it's incredibly important to know new people, to travel, with different languages, different places, cultures. It's amazing the way we are. So far, I'm just completed 26, and I've lived in four different countries* [all in Western Europe]. *It's quite an experience! I can't say that average Portuguese students do this.*

The European *movers* thus open up dimensions in their life, inaccessible to the national *stayers*: the people back home whose lives are immersed and contained in their own national culture. Move even once, and it has consequences; it changes you. You can never really go back. The liberating feeling can even get to be quite addictive. You might keep chasing it. It could even hold the key to the deepest freedom of all: freedom from your *self*. Jeroen, a Dutch scientist working in the pharmaceuticals business in London, puts it this way:

> *I've never been so comfortable with the label of being Dutch. There are all these habits I'd never thought of. I thought I did everything different than my parents, but still there are a lot of things. I do like to know this. To do stuff consciously, to wonder where it comes from, what motivates me. That helps you get some form of freedom, I guess. To be free floating* [in this way].

Eurostars in Eurocities enjoy all these possibilities. The distinctive freedoms of European modernity. Surely the most enticing fruit from fifty years of European integration and European free movement rights.

A Management Consultant's Tale

David is living with his partner Pete in a classic Amsterdam apartment, overlooking a canal. He is one of the very few Eurostars I find with homes in this kind of location. It isn't so easy to get set up like this here. The flat's entrance is a stone's throw away from Reguliersdwarsstraat, the centre of the city's male gay social life. It is a flat high in the roof, the ceiling's a bit low, but – wow! – the view is great. David is ready to talk. It was he that approached me for the interview, and he is very reflective, autobiographical and – eventually – confessional. He has much better theories about the Netherlands than me, and knows a lot more about this society. A near-perfect Dutch speaker, and now a successful independent consultant working with Dutch businesses, he is about as close as you can get to an acceptable foreigner here. He is the model of integration. Still, when I arrive, he offers me a cup of tea.

A Management Consultant's Tale—cont'd

Initially, I moved around a lot. My partner, Pete, had been in Holland since he was ten. We met at Cambridge University. It came to a certain point where he was finishing some piece of research, and we had a choice to stay in the UK or move to Holland. For lots of reasons there wasn't much to make us stay. The intention was that Pete would continue with the Dutch part of his research, and that I would find a job here.

It took a long time initially, because I couldn't speak Dutch. For the first year, we moved around, staying a few months with his family, then an appartment we couldn't afford. I saw an advert for a job as a English teacher in a college of Higher Education, and that seemed like a good idea. It wasn't something I wanted to do, although I had done it as a student, but it was the obvious thing to do. So I applied and got it. It was quite a difficult year from arriving to actually starting in that job. We didn't have any money. Pete had unemployment benefit for one person, because I officially wasn't allowed to be here. It was a job in Leeuwarden, in Friesland, the north of Holland. At the time, I naïvely thought Holland is such a small country, it won't matter where you are. Anyway, later we found out ... We ended up living there for about five years. About eight years ago we moved to Amsterdam.

Did you decide these moves together?

No, he followed me. Eight years was a long time in Friesland! It took two years to find my feet. After that we started getting itchy feet ... At the beginning it was easy for me to find a job because of my knowledge of several languages, even though I didn't speak fluent Dutch. The easiest way to get a job over here was to know at least English, then use your other languages to work with companies that have trade with others abroad. Especially in customer services.

I started working for an American management consultancy firm in Amsterdam. I had a job as a communication specialist, so I had to work with the consultants, check presentations, research proposals and other things. I'm in the process of going freelance now. Shortly I'll be going to three days a week, and sell my three days back to the company or work on a three day contract. It's a good moment to do it. I've built up quite a broad network. People often don't stay in consultancy companies for long. Eventually so many people were calling me that it was obvious there was enough work to live on. It has worked out very successfully ... It's now general management consultancy. I'm working for Phillips, KLM, etc., improving production processes, reducing costs – you know, improving profits, whatever [laughs].

David and Pete saved up, found a house in a dream location after enduring years out in a much less glamorous suburb.

We never intended to stay there, to be honest. We always thought we'd buy [in central Amsterdam] *as quickly as possible, but we stayed out there for five years, a long time. Our salaries kept rising, and we thought the longer we wait the better – until we realized that house prices were rising a lot faster than our salaries. So we looked around and found this place.*

We always wanted to live on a canal, but the quite simple reason why we live right here is that the bars we go to are just two minutes' walk. My gym is a two minute walk in the other direction, and I just liked being in physically beautiful environments. I studied in Cambridge, I lived in a beautiful farm in Friesland, now we live here. You've got to be able to afford it. If you can afford it, you can do it [live in the centre as a foreigner].

In Friesland, we rented a farmhouse. Then one of the farmer's sons wanted to move in. There was a lot of resentment – that was a case of competing for scarce resources, just

A Management Consultant's Tale—cont'd

like it is in Amsterdam. When we moved to Amsterdam, we didn't particularly know how the system worked. We didn't know anybody who knew of anything we could move into, so we ended up getting something that happened to be available, renting on the free sector. It was a new housing estate, that had just been completed. It was also quite expensive, on the edge of Amsterdam, in Osdorp, on the way to Schiphol. There was a lot of families with young children, and one particular family who didn't like us, who was always very hostile. I could never figure out quite why. Whether it was because we were foreign or whether it was because we were two guys living together … We lived there for about five years, commuting or driving to work, or a long tram ride into the centre of Amsterdam. It was a 15 minutes' walk to the last tram stop. There were a lot of foreigners there, a lot of immigrants. If ever you got a taxi, that was one thing that the taxi drivers always used to point out. They often used to make us get out and walk the last part.

There are other neighbourhoods in Amsterdam, such as the Bijlmermeer, the infamous area of south Amsterdam, that are similarly off the map for most West Europeans and white Dutch in the city.

Personally I never found it so dramatic [there]. *The houses are quite big. The particular one we lived in was all new. I never felt threatened there, I never felt outnumbered. It's only maybe to do with me and my history …*

We talk about the complex strategies native Dutch use to get housing. It requires long-term planning.

I know how some people get houses because they know someone, or they rent from some-one who is officially there. Personally I wouldn't feel comfortable doing that [subletting is illegal], *but I know a lot of people who do that. We didn't have that network of people who might help us out. Social networks are one of the main reasons we moved to Amsterdam. We thought – rightly so – that we would meet people. First of all, people at our educational level – which there were very very few of in Friesland – and secondly, people who were gay. There are very few of them in Friesland, and that was actually the main motivator in coming to Amsterdam. That certainly worked out as we hoped it would.*

David now begins to retrace his own personal mobility story, a story deeply linked to his sexuality.

When you change countries, there are always things pushing you to leave, and things attracting you to where you end up. In my case, it was quite clear. I thought there was a very unpleasant atmosphere [in Britain]. *I was 21, 22, and I felt that I could develop much more self-confidence in Holland than I ever could there. I think I probably have. Friesland is not intolerant. People were always very friendly. We went to village parties, for a drink at New Year. I was very touched by that when I arrived in Holland. I certainly could not have expected that in the UK in a similar place.*

Cambridge was quite an easy place to be, but I'd grown up in the north of England. It was the late 80s, the heyday of Thatcherism, and people had lots of irrational fears about AIDS. It was very difficult to find somewhere to live. We were refused somewhere because we were gay, and my family weren't comfortable with it. Then, in contrast, whenever I came to Holland, people accepted it as a banal fact … In a conversation in Holland, the first question is "Have you got a girlfriend?" and if you say no, they ask "Have you got a boyfriend?" just in the next breath. Pete's family were British, of course, but they always accepted me

A Management Consultant's Tale—cont'd

in a way that I didn't feel accepted by my own family. I just felt I would have better chances here, and that I would learn to love myself more being in Holland.

One thing I felt in the UK, was that the police would never protect me if I needed it. Quite the opposite. I had this fear that if ever they found out I was gay they might beat me up or whatever. Or if I got bashed up for being gay, I didn't believe for one minute the police would be interested. So really I had this fear for my physical safety. Whereas in Holland I've never had that. I've never had to test it, but I always thought that the police wouldn't treat it as an issue that I'm gay, if anything ever happened.

Our talk turns to how he deals with cultural differences.

I've been here long enough here now really to not notice the difference between Dutch and British cultural practices. I tend to notice the difference when I go back [there] than when I'm here. In actual fact, I've spent all my working life in Holland. People who don't know I'm English, don't know that I'm not Dutch. They might hear something strange and wonder what strange corner of Holland I come from. But they wouldn't realize that I'm not Dutch. In any case, the one identity doesn't cancel out the other. By assuming a Dutch identity, it doesn't cancel out my British identity. It's something you add on.

That requires a very high level of know-how and linguistic competence. High enough to allow you the freedom to decide yourself.

Yeah. Most of my friends are Dutch, and a few of them are foreigners. Most of them are well integrated. They speak Dutch, live here permanently. I speak Dutch with most of my friends. Then there are one or two Americans, that's a clique that does not speak Dutch. That's a closed crowd. If you get into that crowd, it's all expats. But all of them, they've all been attracted to Amsterdam because of the gay life you can have here.

That seems like a special dimension to the city, even when its an expat experience. You would probably tolerate the environment a lot more if you were here for that. Maybe it would not be the same for a straight couple?

Yeah, I think if you are gay, you might put up with more things because the benefits are greater.

So where is home?

Home? This place suits me best. I may end up living somewhere else for certain periods, but I'd always like to have a place in Amsterdam. I'd be quite happy to grow old here. I like travelling a lot, but it's always nice to come back to Amsterdam ... Put it this way, if they ever say to me "Are you Dutch?" I'd hesitate, but if they ask, "Are you an Amsterdammer?", I'd just say "Yeah!", straight out.

Would an Amsterdammer, born and bred, agree?

Yeah, I think they probably would!

2

New Amsterdam

If Amsterdam can, for the moment, stand in as the ideal European city – the New Jerusalem of European modernity, built by hands and minds (and the occasional joint) – it might well be asked next what an ideal Europe might look like. With so much cultural diversity, so much history and local inter-cultural hostility threatening to spoil the party, what kind of theoretical model might be proposed that everyone could agree on as a framework? How do you build "unity in diversity"?

Games Without Frontiers

One of the great, false clichés of critical European commentary – particularly since the debate over the so-called "democratic deficit" has grown to domi-nate all discussions – is that if only the founding fathers were to do it all again, they would have begun with defining a common culture. *Si tout était à refaire, on commencerait par la culture,* Jean Monnet is alleged once to have said. But thought about as a theoretical question, this is patently not so. A complex, sprawling, and wilfully diverse phenomenon like "European society" calls for a very trimmed down theory; a parsimonious model to help conceive how the whole might work. A constitution of simple principles and assumptions; not an epic, all encompassing narrative, or thick cultural stew. The ambitious social engineers of a new Europe would start off as they did – and as they still do – with the same rationale that has always underlain the European project. Theorize how the EU might work economically, first, before considering all the multiple political, social, and cultural dimensions that might embellish the project.

Some such logic lies behind the European Commission's own "official" theory, that has driven its progress from customs union, to single market, to single currency. This is the Theory of Economic Integration. In an ever integrating world of competing economies, the imperatives of efficient production, economies of scale, and growth through international trade and investment, push smaller nations to enter into regional groupings with their neighbours, that enable greater collective returns within a common market. National barriers to trade – such as customs tariffs and the restrictions of imports – are broken down. Piece by piece, this leads to the building of a complete internal market, culminating in a common currency – to eliminate all transaction costs – and the emergence of a supranational economic space, over which new institutions regulate the functioning of a fully formed regional market.

The underlying goal of this construction, of course, has been eminently political: to overcome centuries of civil war between European nations, by enforcing tight economic interdependence, and to create allegiance to a European project by building a successful European economy. A successful economy might also enable a unity that transcends cultural diversity, while preserving and drawing upon it. As the construction has grown, political and cultural questions at the European level have, of course, arisen as part of a debate about the building of stable legal and political institutions to structure the market and preserve its achievements. Issues about democratic deficit, constitutions, security, and so on, also derive from this, but the single most important legislative activity of the European institutions, and the one that has the most impact on the everyday lives of Europeans, is the enabling and enforcement of free movement in all the different sectors of the economy.

Crucially, in distinction to other regional integration projects around the world – such as NAFTA or ASEAN – freedom of movement in the EU has also included since the 1950s the freedom of movement of persons, alongside that of capital, goods, and services (which includes the freedom of business establishment across borders). This is the idea of Europe as an open labour market. The idea was initially associated with the significant mobility of worker populations from the South to the North in the 1950s and 1960s, and was essentially established to support this. Surplus labour in one part of the Union would respond to market signals and move to other parts where work was to be found. This would lead to a re-equilibrating of the inequalities between places, as well as being a basic source of economic dynamism, since all factors of production would be free to move to the most efficient location. In many ways, this was indeed the case. Large mobile worker populations from Italy and elsewhere fuelled the economic growth of many of Europe's richer nations in their respective "golden ages" after World War II. When the demand dried up, and Europe's peripheries themselves became less differentiated economically, mobility of this kind also dried up. Much of the EU's regional and structural policies have in fact been dedicated to an opposite redistribution, to even out inequalities in the European space (and hence the need for movement); the demand for immigrant workers increasingly shifted to external non-EU sources. But the theory about the positive effects of internal mobility continues to be held, especially among advocates of European enlargement. In a monetary union, mobile labour is seen as the security valve that will cushion asymmetric shocks to the system. Moreover, less negatively, increased intra-European mobility is still seen as a proactive source of dynamism and growth, in an otherwise dangerously sclerotic Europe, especially if it encourages the professional and the highly skilled to move. For new and poorer member states, it is seen as a key mechanism of development, encouraging new business transactions across borders. Freedom of movement is also always rated the most valuable right of European citizens, whenever they are asked.

As the jurisprudence of freedom of movement has been developed by an activist European Court of Justice, its provisions have been extended well beyond the basic economic logic. Rights for workers have been extended to spouses, to families, to students, to retirees, and now basically to anyone willing to move and take up to six months in a foreign member state to look for work. The logic thus is now couched in educational, professional, and experiential terms – as a way of positively building cross-national interchange and European identity, as well as allowing talent to circulate and maximize its potential within a common European space. With borders down, grass growing over the customs posts that used to keep populations contained in formal territories, and cars and trains speeding through the continent without any kind of border control, there is much to be said for this being the EU's most striking and extraordinary achievement. Not least, because it seems to reverse and break down two to three centuries of onward, consistent nation-state-society building in Europe.

The upscaling of European nation-states into a bigger denationalized Europe also has a cultural payoff. Cross-national interdependence of this kind is increasingly seen as the route to enlightenment, the cosmopolitan ideal – in a continent more famous than not for its tendency to self-destruct in pursuit of such goals. Prior to the twentieth century, republicans, nationalists, and liberals alike tended to think it was the nation-state-society which would best serve these liberational goals. Transcending the nation, however, became the guiding ideal in the late twentieth century, building upon the political achievements of European nation-states in this regard, while mindful of their chauvinistic and martial failings. The nation-state-society is now seen as particularistic and regressive in the light of an integrating Europe, in better tune with the human rights and individualist freedom claimed by global citizens today. The trajectory of European modernity – the legacy of Enlightenment cosmopolitanism – thus became essentially post-national.

Why did the founding fathers hit upon this particular theoretical model for building Europe? The answer lies, like many things, across the Atlantic. The EU was a creation sanctioned and inspired by the US. American Marshall Aid funds poured in to rebuild Europe, neutralizing hostile nations, and encouraging the building of a free economic space, that would provide the foundation and appropriate scale for a self-sustaining European economy in the future. In defiance of geography, Britain initially opted out – mainly because of an illusory notion of self-sufficiency born of empire. But Europe, too, became inevitable for Britain. It too, along with other non-members and periphery onlookers, has eventually become integrated into the European economy, as trade among European nations has grown dramatically and interdependency on every level has deepened.

The federal idea of Europe is clearly also inspired by American history, in which the US overcame its own civil wars and barriers of state independence in the late nineteenth century, during a dramatic era of state and institution building. This culminated in the "progressive era" of Teddy Roosevelt, that broke monopolies, regulated corporate control, and created the federal economic and political union of the twentieth century. The core of this, as with an integrating Europe, was the breaking down of legal and political barriers to mobility between states, and the creation of a single, large-scale economic space – an economy that would provide the foundation for a nation-state-society that grew to dwarf all others in its capacities and dynamism. Within this space, the American way of life is dramatically mobile on all levels. Regional cities function as more-or-less interchangeable nodes in an economy of limitless opportunities, with competitive relations between cities and regions encouraging mobility at all levels. Americans routinely move across states four or five times in a lifetime. Not just lower-level workers, but *all* middle and upper-class professionals see this kind of mobility as part and parcel of their careers. American cities, especially for these people, always offer easy and open settlement. American society is conceived by all as a flattened space, in which barriers to mobility have been removed. The US economy's dynamism in fact owes as much if not more to this extraordinary *internal* migration and mobility potential, as it does to its highly visible external immigration for which it is more famous.

America thus provided the model. America of the 1950s and 1960s was, for Europeans, freedom incarnate. It was the ideal, and the only game in town, after their own pitiful orgy of self-destruction. The flame of modernity passed across the Atlantic post-1945 – and not just because America had all the firepower. Europe got what it needed, as well as a lot of things it hadn't bargained for. It got Bogart and Bacall; it got Jackson Pollack; it got Elvis; it got Civil Rights, Easy Riders, Woodstock, and Flower Power; it also got freeways, malls, downtowns and unbridled development, drive-in burger bars, miles of fries, and coca-cola just like vintage wine. An old Europe emerging from the ruins could only look to this with awe. The scale; the dynamism; the self-confidence. Just as the EU was an American invention, the American ideal was the route out of the mid-century dark continent: via individualism, consumer power, human rights, capitalist growth, affluence, optimism, and the appeal (however rose tinted) of an open society built on multiple cultures, racial diversity, and migrant/immigrant-led dynamism. Europeans might well compare the land of opportunity over there with their lands of oppression, class distinction, aristocratic privilege, parochialism, and prejudice. All the clichés about America and Europe are here: old Europe versus the new world. But it would be naïve to think that none of this appeal remains – especially among average European consumer populations, who still feel America is a better guide to the future than Europe's dark past.

European free movers, especially those in the highest flying corporate careers, often self-consciously think of the US as a model, as well as sometimes the next step in their outwards and upwards spatial and social mobility. American ideals are written all over the EU's formulation of the four freedoms, and its relentless promotion of mobility. They seem to imagine Europe can come to resemble as a regional space the globalist's vision of a "flat world" in the American image. But is the American model really the right one for Europe? The automatic association of the European Union with the federal United States of America although powerful is in fact mismatched in several ways. Unlike the US, Europe is not a well defined geographical space. Its borders are ambiguous, spilling out over into the Mediterranean, and eastwards across the Urals. Europe has a long, complicated history, and cannot simply conceive itself ideologically as a blank slate, as in the American ideal. It is not (only) a continent of immigrants, but of longstanding populations ingrained in territories and distinct national and regional cultures. European territoriality is thick, place-related, localistic, spatially defined, apparently "rooted" – at least more so than it is in North America. European notions of government and governance, law and welfare are also deeply divergent.

Free movement, in fact, turns out to be two quite different things in the two continents. Americans can move freely internally, because they are moving within a single, largely undifferentiated, but wholly *nationalized* space. This space is a container that defines all other migration experience *into* the space as a nationalizing, Americanizing one. When you move to the US as a temporary foreign worker, everybody – from red-white-and-blue republican to progressive-minded liberal – welcomes you and expects that you are coming to stay. Stay any longer, and a green card is a *permanent* residency; not a

temporary work permit. Whether you like it or not, you are an "immigrant" –
and thus a presumptive American – following the classic immigration path.
Freedom of movement in Europe is different. It is an *inter*national move; a
move *out* of the nation-state, not *into* a nationalizing Europe. Becoming more
European, in this sense, means *becoming* post-national, psychologically at
least – while continuing to retain your national passport and primary
national identity as a source. To put it another way, free movement in
Europe leads to you becoming less British, French, Danish, etc. It is a negative
freedom; a freedom *from* the nation-state-society you have left. The opposite
happens as a free (global) mover arriving in the US. You find very quickly
you have your national identity stamped on you as "ethnicity". You become
"English", or "French", or "Italian", even if you felt you were more "European"
or "global". The ethnicizing process itself is part of Americanization: a first
step towards hyphenization, and becoming an American citizen.

Ambitious students and career minded professionals continue to drain
across the Atlantic – as the European Commission is painfully aware. They
feel they have to compete on the same terms, and are sparing no effort in
trying to lure Europeans back.[1] Not surprisingly: they are some of the continent's most talented individuals. But there is a sense in which Europe is not
comparable to the US on this question. Europe is not a nation-state-society
like the US. It does not "own" the fruits of a migrant's labour, in the way the
US seeks to possess its new residents, stamp them American, and hold them
up as avatars of the American dream. That is what modern nations have
always done with their citizens: seeking to capture and contain for the nation
all the output of an individual's life. This is the OECD vision of the world:
a world divided up into national "teams" who like at the Olympics compete for
gold medals in terms of their GDP, rates of growth, freedom ratings, number
of patents, etc. The image of self-contained populations, competing for their
nations as citizens, is actually the antithesis of the Europe of the Eurostars.
Their Europe is one *beyond* such frontiers, a post-national space, in which
individuals are building lives using their rights *against* the nation – an extension of the logic of human rights. This surely would be a *real* space of individual
freedom, quite different to the intensely nationalized idea of freedom held by
Americans. The prescriptions of American modernity might not so accurately
square with the imperatives of European modernity any more, if ever.

The European Union of 27 already dwarfs the US in terms of population,
and is comparable on many other vital statistics. A United States of Europe – if
it were ever to exist – would have taken over much of the US's successful
postwar philosophy, having improved it with a post-national conception of
freedom, closer to cosmopolitan ideals than the American dream. On a
good day, the trajectory of European modernity promises this. On a good
day, that is. Everyone knows that sunny days are few and far between in
Brussels, London, and Amsterdam. Southern European residents never fail

to mention this in interviews. To think this way, then, is to think counterfactually. The actual European Union of the first decade of the twenty-first century is far from "united in diversity". It is threatened by rejection in many member states, dominated by nationalist politicians, who talk only of national interests to a national audience, reported on only by exclusively nationalized medias. It is plagued by dubious constitutional and democratic issues. The EU, on most days, looks rarely more than an uncomfortable patchwork of proud, sometimes cranky nation-states, held together by an ever closer economic and political union, but undermined by the very diversity that gives it its greatest resources. The apparently successful currency union and enlargement process mitigate the cracks, but even the most fervent Euro-optimists have been feeling queasy lately.

As the founding fathers knew well, if European Union is to work, ultimately it will be built from below, by the fulfilment of European ideals in the lives and practices of individuals: their work, their experiences, their relationships, their children. If there is such a thing as the European dream, it has to be found in the stories of real people. America has played a crucial role in the lives and professional trajectories of several of the Eurostars I spoke to, in terms of freedom and self-development. For Saskia, a London high flyer working in the City, it was a "wonderful place to start a career" and the place where she got her first break in the music world, invited to join an influential board in Boston in her twenties. This was something that would "never happen" in continental Europe, she says, where you'd have to be old and grey – and male. For Stefan, an architect in Amsterdam, New York was the liberating, multicultural place where he was allowed to "question everything", and where he developed all his ideas as an architect. But they both came back. Saskia saw a close friend, a fast track banker in his twenties, abandoned overnight by the US health care system after he had a stroke. "Not everything can be bought and sold", she says. There are some things society should do for its citizens, and welfare coverage is so much better in Europe. Stefan, meanwhile, could not deal with the low quality of life in a society where working conditions are extreme and childcare impossibly expensive. He was looking for a place where he could still enjoy that sense of freedom and a multicultural environment, but also really build things; and a place where he and his family might live a manageable, sustainable lifestyle, with social benefits – a "combination of different things". Stefan, like other free movers, came looking for Europe at its best. He chose Amsterdam.

Safe European Home

First, a memory. Amsterdam never looks better than in the rare times – that only happen once every five years or so – when the city freezes up long enough for all the canals to go solid white. I remember it was the day the whole country was going crazy about the possibility that this year they might finally be able to hold the *Elfstedentocht* skating race up in Friesland. They'd had seven solid days of deep freeze, and it looked like they were about to announce the race, which they had been unable to hold for several years. It was midnight, and I was walking back, with my Dutch friend Ben, to his flat, on the iced up Jordaancanal. We were walking on water – under the same humped-back brick bridges that, years before, I had ridden over with another Dutch friend, Juliette, sitting on the back of her bicycle. She showed me Amsterdam for the first time; now Ben was showing me it again. The city was magical. That was the day I decided to move to the Netherlands.

I still like to picture Amsterdam this way. Who could fail to be seduced by this Venice of the North – by the Jordaan in Old Amsterdam – on a night like this? Looking for Europe at its best, Amsterdam appears to be a great match. Most obviously, it is easy to get a job here, and to get a good job, with excellent benefits, working conditions, and career prospects. Axel, from Austria, works in the telecommunications business. He points out how 70 percent of the management in his multinational corporation are American, English, or from somewhere else. A lot of people from Britain, Ireland, and elsewhere seem to be trying Amsterdam out, seeing the Netherlands as an open, appealing option on the continent. Susan, who is a personnel manager in banking, explains that the Dutch often cannot source good skilled employees from within the Netherlands and often have to look outside. This applies especially to specialisms that are in high demand: IT, e-commerce, finance, law, human resources. There are more opportunities because there are fewer people going for jobs or vying for promotion.[2]

One very attractive factor is that foreigners, including EU citizens, can get a 30 percent "expat" tax break if they are only employed in the Netherlands on a short-term basis of 2–3 years. This makes a huge difference for Susan, who also appreciates the high level of benefits, the "extra month" holiday salary, and outside factors like low commuting costs in a well organized city. She reckons she is making about 50 percent more than she would have earned in Britain, although she points out it is critical to get a good entry package because after that promotion scales are very rigid. Anastasia confirms this picture, pointing out the benefits of having found a job in a then booming sector – telecommunications – which led rapidly to interesting work and promotion. She thinks it would have taken her much longer to achieve this in her native Greece.

This employment openness is not unique to Amsterdam. Most European global cities now offer a comparably healthy range of employment – usually English-language based. But Amsterdam has other comparative advantages. For some, it is explicitly because it is *not* London. Paris, meanwhile, is explicitly ruled out by several people as not open or international enough. The

French are said to be "very nationalist", the Dutch not. Mainly this is because the Dutch "all speak English".[3] This plus Amsterdam's humane size is frequently mentioned. London is equally international and open, but lacks Amsterdam's intimacy and scale. David underlines this as a key factor in establishing the city as a great place for gay people to live. In London, the gay lifestyle is "much more diluted". Ray likes the fact it is smaller than London, but still "sophisticated and cosmopolitan".

Part of the attraction of freedom Dutch-style is how well organized the society is. The Dutch know how to organize freedom like nowhere else in the world. The spatial mathematics are daunting. How do you square a country with Bangladeshi-style levels of density, with Scandinavian-style quality of life? The equation is even more daunting considering that a large proportion of this population is concentrated in the hub of the Randstad, much of which is reclaimed from the sea. Part of the man-made miracle of the Netherlands is the extraordinary infrastructure that makes this society possible. Positive organized freedom of this kind is quite the antithesis of the negative, "anything goes" freedom of unfettered free market capitalism let loose in the American flat world, and is something that foreign residents of the Netherlands positively embrace.

The quality of life this affords is affirmed time and time again as crucial in the balance between work and private life. Maria, a corporate lawyer, is very career oriented, but is clear that this aspect of the Netherlands is a huge plus. It is perhaps on this point that the Dutch corporate environment stands out internationally. Working in London is always seen in negative terms, by comparison, a city where quality of life is notoriously low. Maria complains about how law firms in London expect you to work 12-plus hours a day. The distinctive social organization of the Netherlands, rather, hinges on very clear distinctions between work and outside. Business is explicitly organized to be dynamic and efficient, but not bleed into private life or personal time, or upset things like childcare. Organized and paid holiday time – a dramatic contrast with the savage working schedule of US-style employment terms – is seen as central to the effectiveness of companies. Maria says her boss is constantly nagging her to take a vacation, and when she did he congratulated her. Maria, who is ambitious and self-motivated, in fact chooses to work late most nights, and skip vacations. Her hobbies take a second place to her career. Good personnel management, it seems, might actually lead to higher productivity.

The Netherlands in fact compares favourably to all of Europe on these terms. It shares with Scandinavian countries a willingness not to compromise on the thoroughly socialized nature of work life. Nina is sure her native Germany would be tougher for a corporate lawyer. Her friends there work longer hours, and face much more hierarchical work relations. She feels the Netherlands too is better for her as a woman, in terms of childcare or working part time. These aspects of corporate governance tend to be maintained even in American-owned companies based in the Netherlands. To some extent, the mix of styles can lead to an even better corporation. Axel is a manager at one such company. He complains that workers can be slower with their jobs, and quicker to assert their employment rights; but the mix of job security and American-style management, he thinks, works as a good combination.

American progressives have long idealized the Netherlands (and Scandinavian countries) as liberal exemplars in this sense. Aspects of this idealization – particularly on questions of moral tolerance – often fail to understand the complex social system in which such toleration is embedded. The Netherlands is most certainly not a society where anything goes. Everything, including soft drugs and sex work, is organized, regulated, and has its defined place. But its distinctive corporate organization – the legal institutional framework that governs the way corporations and the market work – does underline viable alternative ways in which capitalist enterprise can be organized. Foreign residents who choose to live and work in the Netherlands are, on the whole, very happy with the balance struck.

Amsterdam is also a graphic reminder that a global city does not infrastructurally speaking have to be a sprawling mess like Los Angeles, or be endowed with a public transport infrastructure or road system on the permanent verge of collapse such as London. Its spatial organization positively facilitates international life. As Stefan, the architect, points out, Schiphol airport is close to the city, and it boasts excellent, well connected high speed train links to France and Germany, that give it a European centrality that London does not have in the same way. On the face of it, these aspects add up to secure the city its enormous international prestige and appeal: the "combination" of all the best things that brought Stefan and so many others to the city.

Yet all of this leads on to a huge puzzle, when broader trends in internal European migration are brought into the picture. The Netherlands is routinely ranked by business observers as the most open global national economy in the world.[4] Yet the number of foreign resident Europeans in the country turns out to be dramatically low. Less than 200,000 West Europeans have been registered annually as living in the Netherlands during the last 20 to 30 years – around 1.5 percent of the total population, and only a quarter of the total of around 800,000 foreigners totally, the rest of which are mainly Turkish, Moroccan, African, and other nationalities.[5] Despite its almost universal appeal, and a wide open labour market, the Netherlands has far fewer West European residents, in both percentage and absolute terms, than Belgium, France, or Germany. This is a particularly striking contrast to Germany, where over 3 percent of a population five times as large are West European (around 2 million people). Arrivals every year in the Netherlands, on the other hand, would appear to be high. Anecdotally, there seems to be almost a flood of young Germans, British, Irish, and other nationalities in the city. But the numbers of residents simply do not bear these figures out.[6]

Why is this? The puzzle of low figures for resident foreign Europeans in the Netherlands is in fact a heightened example of a puzzle about European free movement generally. Despite an economic union premised on free movement and increasing kinds of mobility, official population statistics have consistently reported that a very low percentage of West Europeans migrate and settle permanently in other European countries. Since South-to-North guest worker migration ended in the early 1970s, numbers have not altered dramatically with any of the big steps taken in European integration, such as the Schengen Agreement on open borders (1985), the completion of the Single Market (1992), or the introduction of the euro (2002). And although the recent enlargements of the EU in 2004 and 2007 have led to some short-term changes in East-West mobility patterns, previous enlargements in fact suggest greater return migration and temporary circulation than people moving to resettle as foreigners. The percentage of West Europeans is, with the exception of Belgium and Luxembourg, well under 5 percent in all countries, and well behind percentages of non-West European migrants everywhere. In fact, a minority of less than 1 in 50 such Europeans lives and works abroad.[7] Compare this to the economic system that provides the European free movement with its inspiration – the US – and the issue becomes even more stark.[8] Discounting within these figures the ongoing but small-scale working-class migration from the South, and a growing retirement migration to the South, and leaving aside the new East-West migration which has a very different dynamic, average working-age middle class Europeans show a remarkable propensity to stay put in their native countries. One can only conclude that the European economic and social system – on the question of free movement of persons, at the very least – must function in ways that scarcely resemble at all the premises of its founding principles.[9]

The obvious answer to this puzzle that everyone cites is, of course, "culture". Academics and ordinary folks alike refer to culture as an explanation when they are gesturing to the mass of reasons why people do things that don't seem to boil down to self-interest and "rational" economic-style calculations. Customs, habits, know-how, ways of doing things; of being one of "us" rather than one of "them". And language, of course, the primary means of communication. From a cultural point of view, the puzzle of free movement is no real puzzle at all. This is the argument essentially that "people don't move ... because they don't move". People, on the whole, they say, prefer to stay where they belong – where they come from, immersed in their home culture – rather than confused and excluded, in the midst of strangers.

The Theory of Economic Integration, the theory on which everyone could rationally agree, here hits the challenge of another view of Europe – one in which the continent is divided up into a patchwork of stable national and regional cultures each preserving its space and identity in the whole, by maintaining barriers of distinction from its neighbours. More mobility would cut across and damage this. The EU has worked tirelessly to break down formal barriers to free movement of workers: both in terms of legal reform (on discriminatory practices, recognition of qualifications, access to benefits) and in terms of "citizen" information and advice services. It even has in its sights very deeply rooted practices like the monopolistic national organization of certain professions, and the non-transferability of pension funds around national welfare state systems.[10] But still there seems to be more: any number of other hidden or informal barriers to successful free movement at a societal or cultural level. Even the most casual traveller around Europe quickly understands that the continent today remains a Babel of national distinctions, local customs, and regional peculiarities, which demand of any European an extraordinarily high level of nationally specific know-how and local knowledge to feel comfortable living and working outside their country of origin. Could this be the underlying reason for the lack of intra-European migration?

The answer must lie with those who have, one by one, embodied the economic model in their lives and practices. The free movers: the prototypical Eurostars, who have taken up the legal and social opportunities offered to them by freedom of movement in Europe, yet who might still encounter other more subtle impediments to their successful implantation in foreign soil. The odds have been loaded in their favour: the ones I interviewed live in the most international, cosmopolitan places, work in the most open, international careers, and face the least overt barriers. The thinking goes: if they can't achieve freedom of movement *here* – in places like Amsterdam, London, or Brussels – then they are hardly likely to have more success in, say, Groningen, Bristol, or Bruges. Their experiences will enable an adjudication between these two apparently contradictory ideas of Europe: the economic versus the cultural model of how Europe works.

A Logistics Manager's Tale

Haarlemmerstraat, Amsterdam. Take a right at Centraal Station, head along parallel to the tracks and water, towards the Jordaan. Past coffee shops, letting agencies, and kebab houses. I find Helen in a small bar. *Gezellig*. There is a smell of dope in the air. We try not to inhale. She's just back from work, around the corner from her flat, and dressed for the gym a bit later. She looks to be in her mid to late thirties, and is brisk and energetic, even after a busy day at the office.

I work for a major US logistics company, for five and a half years now. I started working at the head office in Brussels, but work 30 miles away from Amsterdam now. I am a

A Logistics Manager's Tale—cont'd

client manager, responsible for the business we get. It's a managerial type role, responsible for a warehouse employing 55 people. Another 25 people elsewhere. Before that I was employed in the UK.

Logistics and distribution companies such as Helen's quite literally provide the infrastructure for today's hypermobile, global world. They enable it to move, oil the wheels. The logistics branch of the firm provides the services too for the even larger heavy transportation and machines company of the same name, as well as a network of other similar companies.

We have our own distribution network. For machines, spare parts and so on. Plus we sell its services to other clients, to other machine-based companies. Any item of high value that is time sensitive will go through our centre. They want it next week, or delivery the next day, we do it. We've even got our own train every night from Almere to Grimbergen, which then gets a free ride on the larger network. It's a fun division to work in. It's young, been there since 1987. The transportation part of the company has been there since 1925. That company is even more American in style; we are quite European. There's just me and lots of Dutch people. My boss is Flemish. It's still very American in some ways, but the atmosphere is very Dutch at work, even more in its style, I think.

I ask her where she's come from. It's an average, provincial, middle-class background, like so many of the people I talk to.

Northern Ireland. A small village in County Tyrone, then we lived near Derry. Moved house once. My mum was a legal secretary, then worked part time as a civil servant. Father was managerial, worked for the same company all his life. They are very proud I live here. It's very unusual for my family, they hadn't travelled. They come here to see me. It's getting easier, flights for €50 each way. I left home when I was 18. I was a language student: a course linked to professional interpreting. Did a year abroad, teaching in Spain, and lived in South America. That's becoming very trendy now. Then three years in Spain. It changed me a lot. What you want, your perspective. Less of a professional thing, more personally.

Her mobility experience in Europe now – although definitely *not* the US – is linked to her being a *bona fide* world traveller.

I've never really planned anything. I knew when I left college, I wanted to travel and work in other countries. I don't think about it too much, I can't really imagine how. I think about all the moments when you made a decision or a decision happened. You just take it.

Helen is an ideal type free mover. She is an also an ideal interviewee for me, having lived in Brussels, Amsterdam, and London. On Brussels, she is positive, but with mixed feelings.

Yes, but not so much when I lived there! I miss it now. When I went there I never thought I'd settle down, that it would be home. Brussels is a transient place. I knew a couple of Belgian friends, but the rest you think, in three or four years they are not going to be there. Here, I don't feel it's the same. I thought I'd find somewhere and settle down a bit. In Malaga, I knew the three other non-Spanish people, but you just didn't meet other foreigners. I never took any notice of the English and Irish [holidaymakers or retirees] around there, and in Malaga city they just weren't there. I got invited out into the Spanish atmosphere. When I travel I don't want to be an expat, what's the point?

A Logistics Manager's Tale—cont'd

The move to Amsterdam, effectively, was a local move.

Although I did really want to go to Italy or South America, on the other hand I loved being in Brussels because I'd built up quite a good social network, and Almere was not so far away from that. So I can keep my friends in Brussels, it's two to three hours, and it's easy to get home to Northern Ireland. If I want to stay … I knew Amsterdam would be a pretty busy place to be, less of a culture shock. I can go to South America another time.

Where I live the neighbours are very social. There is a patio, the Dutch sit outside, and are open to have a chat with you. It's the same as in Ireland. I love the fact here people I meet here don't have cars, and they work part time. One guy I know has just given up accountancy job, and is retraining in the police. He just wants to do something useful. I get the feeling in Britain that people don't do that, that people put such an importance on what you earn and what sort of car you have. I appreciate things, locally, like the dance class at my squash club, with two excellent dance teachers. How you can get this combination of having a house and sports near your house. Then you come home on a Tuesday, its half past six, and there's people outside the bars, taking boats out. You feel like you are on holiday every week night. Working is only part of your week. It's very good for you, you know. I really find it weird going back to the UK. It just reminds me of a more stressed job and environment. When I go back now [to London] *the stress takes the life out of me. I think I have a better quality of life here.*

What about your social networks?

They are foreigners mainly, but I found it the place with the least barriers to somebody who wants to make an effort [to have Dutch friends]. *I get annoyed with all the Dutch people who say it's so difficult to learn Dutch. It's not, people just don't make the effort. It's the difference between the expat who travels, who is always moving, who doesn't bother because they are always moving in expat circles, and others … I'd feel very uncomfortable if I couldn't speak Dutch.*

"I am not an expat!" This is the perpetual protest of the Eurostars. Helen is in fact quite highly integrated for someone whose employment scenario is more like the typically mobile expat profile. She seems to have found the key to Dutch sociability.

My social networks are around the sport that I do. I play squash and climb. It's also connections through friends of friends of friends. I find I don't socialize with people in work, because I'm a manager and they're family people. I don't go to typically foreigner places. Here people have similar kinds of lifestyles [to me], *that has been a way in. The Dutch are really big into clubs, and I think like that as well. I went to a choir, found all the right contacts. It was a women's choir.*

One of the other secrets of Helen's success is that she is on a very lucrative MNC deal, that pays all the differentials linked to her mobility – and hence for a beautiful and very expensive flat in the Jordaan. Getting access to this kind of housing at the top end of city scale is simply not possible for most foreigners in the city.

I live on Brouwersgracht, in this converted warehouse. I only pay the same as I would have paid in Brussels, for the same square meters, the company pays the rest. I found it by going through some estate agent. It's very difficult in Amsterdam once you get to a certain level.

A Logistics Manager's Tale—cont'd

The rent is €1,600, and I pay half. I never see any of the money. You are really exploited here, it couldn't be paid by a Dutch person. It's extortionate. There was some Dutch guy going to Italy for a sabbatical. He was asking for twice my rent. Who is going to pay that? Well, after two weeks they'd found some company willing to pay this.

What about your future plans? Can you see yourself getting attached to a place?

That's a bit scary sometimes. I got quite attached to Spain, but I knew going back there it would be very difficult to recreate what I had. I do like it here, the details of my life make me feel really good here. I'm at home here. It's not about the money. I've got a brilliant place to live, I've got friends, it's easy to get around. I want to do an MBA. I'd love to have that on my CV. I like my work, but I'm not really that into my career. It just gives me another thing to move on to. It's not that I'm wildly ambitious. The MBA gives me more resources, because after two years they are really looking to move you again.

Do you identify with Amsterdam?

I don't know. It's very Dutch. Weird and wonderful. I feel a bit of a visitor, but then I'm part of it too.

Are you a migrant?

Migrants are … [laughs] … I think I am, but it sounds too amazing. [Reflecting some more] No I don't, but I suppose I don't know many other people like me, so I don't really think of myself in that category. I never think about it … Migration is packing up and going to Australia, America, but I guess in a sense I am. Packing everything and taking your life with you. I guess I never had the life together like that. I always went with a ruck sack or something. Even now, I could bring all that I owned, it's not much. I think of a migrant as someone who is making one big move.

Helen might just be the most independent kind of free mover: a single woman, with a career, a flat, and life of her own.

I maybe shouldn't say this, but I'm a very lucky person in life, I'm never really sick. I've just been a cat always landing on its feet … I don't need anybody around me that much. On the one hand you do want to move on, it's what you like doing. On the other hand, it's a big emotional upheaval. Each time you do it, you become a little more jaded. You are not married, so you are in it by yourself.

Now and again you get lonely, and you think, gosh, you know. You see others … I'm quite jealous of friends who still have old school friends back home, things like that. I don't have much in common with mine. They left school, no university, had children right away. I guess that's what I really miss. Having friends in one place, because they are all over … I suppose that's the downside. But I wouldn't have it any other way. This is what I want.

3

London Calls

Amsterdam has its attractions, but it is not the brightest beacon in Europe's landscape. For those in search of fame and fortune, the Eurocity of choice turns out *not* to be one with punctual trams running in the streets, bars that stay open all night, ice cream parlours on every street corner, or great bottled beer in sprawling streetside cafés. It certainly does *not* have efficient well run municipal facilities, cheap public transport, or immaculately cleaned sidewalks. You can't spend euros there (yet), and a lot of the natives don't even think they are European. Yet Eurocity it is, the capital of Europe in many ways: London.[1]

A quiet and unstoppable *European* invasion of England took place in the latter half of the 1990s. Always a global hub for immigration of all kinds, London became increasingly *the* target of mobile young continental Europeans; in fact, the prime destination of European free movement for this particular generation. It started with West Europeans – from France, Spain, Denmark, Germany, Italy – and in the new millennium extended, with enlargement around the corner, to a new wave of East Europeans. With stagnant economies elsewhere, no other city has been able to compete with London's global cultural cool or economic clout, or its access to the English-language business, media, and cultural worlds.[2] In part, this only confirms London's global centrality; officially, Britain is eurosceptic in its attitudes, mid-Atlantic in its mindset. But there is another side to being a regional hub of migration. London has become the key stage in the life-course trajectories of a vast number of European citizens. The relatively stable social systems of temporary and permanent migration to and from the continent make London a Eurocity every bit as Europeanized as Amsterdam, Paris, Brussels, Munich, Barcelona, or Vienna – whether the natives like it or not.[3]

London is certainly connected like no other city in Europe. Its long history of immigration and asylum is second to none, something only deepened by the distinctively postcolonial multiculturalism that has developed in the post-war period. Moreover, in the liberal 1990s, London's labour market for foreigners expanded dramatically, with an unprecedented rise in undocumented immigration from all over the world. London is also often seen as the image of the polarized city, characterized by its dominantly service-based industries at both top and bottom ends. London is thus embedded in all kinds of global networks: whether transatlantic, pan-Asian, or postcolonial. But all of this only underlines the more locally immediate fact that its growth has also enhanced its role as a Eurocity, of central importance to the regional economic system in Europe. Though this is well apparent in the macrolevel economic data, it is much less well documented at the microlevel: at the level of individuals, their mobile lives and experiences, their transactions in and through the city.[4] Anecdotally, they are everywhere to be seen. Go anywhere in the city, you will hear many French, Spanish, Danish, German or Italian accents – and since the mid-2000s many Polish and Romanian accents too. Working in pubs is no longer the exclusive province of Australians and New Zealanders on holiday visas. And young Americans have been squeezed out by visa and work permit restrictions which favour European free movers over the so-called "special relationship" with the USA. The visible effects on the city's population are patent: London is more European than ever.

Ten Thousand Holes

London has been calling the young and ambitious of the continent since at least the 1960s (see Giulia's tale, pp. 78–82). Fast forward to the late 1990s and early "noughties" – to borrow author Jonathan Coe's delightful phrase – and the stories and city have not changed that much. Nowadays, though, you don't need to marry to stay or get a work permit. Flying in (or out) on Ryan Air and easyJet is a whole lot easier than the interminable ferries and night trains that were still my first memories (in the early 1980s) of foreign travel. The closeness of regional movement in Europe, in this sense, makes a big difference. Academics theorize endlessly about "global networks" and the "space of flows" linking London to the wide world. Yet in real life physical distance matters, and bodies have to be actually moved through time and space. Forget social theory: short of a *Star Trek*-style teleporter, the notion of time/space compression is always quite likely to retain a certain academic quality. Two or three hours door to door is always going to feel a whole lot better than another sleepless night and eight hours jet lag on a packed transatlantic flight. This closeness makes living in London so much more accessible to Europeans. Above all, this is an effect of the Eurostar train. Cross-channel travel this way makes arriving in London – or leaving England – feel like you've just taken the underground tube across town, but somehow by magic arrived in a foreign land. Using any of the airports for a short-hop flight to Paris or Brussels – or even Cologne or Amsterdam – is now not worth it in terms of the commute, check in, and security. The offence to Little Englanders of this particular hole in the ground is obvious. Yet while the British press fumes about a handful of bedraggled asylum seekers who manage to creep in through the Channel Tunnel, and has got increasingly anxious about folks with visible Slavic or Balkan origins, it casts a complete blind eye to the thousands of as-yet-unemployed young West Europeans pouring into Britain, on the Eurostar train and cheap network airlines, with the all their belongings in backpacks. The vast majority head for London.

The Mayor's office certainly talks the talk of Eurocities in all its official documentation. Ken Livingstone has been very pro-Europe, with London portrayed in dynamic, regional European terms. Fraternizing with colleagues from Stockholm, Paris, or Madrid is an important way of emphasizing the shaky political autonomy of the city from national politics. What is remarkable is just how little this office – and London generally – knows about the large numbers of Europeans in its midst. Ever present, yet invisible, they are a crucial part of the city's dynamo, yet largely uncounted. Most cities know something about their populations. The EU-sponsored Urban Audit – an immense database on the 300 largest cities in Western Europe – has done wonders in compiling data on the foreign populations across European cities.[5] However, the Dutch project manager, Lewis Dijkstra, shrugs his shoulders and laughs when asked about data on the foreign European population of London. The city didn't know. Trying to investigate the question myself, I found out little more. Very helpful and informative demographic officers in the Mayor's office passed me around their colleagues for an hour or so, in search of somebody who might have a clue. Regional development officials, ethnic minority specialists, all came up blank. They have good numbers for Senegalese or Algerians, as well of course as all kinds of information on Bangladeshis and West Indians. East Europeans have been counted through a registration scheme. But West Europeans, it seems, are invisible.[6]

Getting a handle on numbers is not easy. Official census statistics are not going to be much use, given that much of the migration is short term and often not registered.[7] When you go to the national consulates in question, the numbers given as registered are massively below real figures. Anecdotal evidence suggests that the clear majority of European residents in Britain never even thought of registering with their consulate, explaining that it only becomes necessary if you need to obtain a new (European) passport without going home, or you lose your driving license. Britain is exceptionally porous in this sense. There are so many holes in this economy and society – and perhaps that is its secret. Settling in quickly is generally easy in London because bureaucratic start-up questions are seen as much easier to deal with than in other countries. It is easy to register with a GP (General Practitioner), and to the surprise of some it also proves easy to claim benefits if you are unemployed or looking for work. Several interviewees had experienced a period of unemployment and had not felt pressured to give up and go home. Housing benefit helping to cover rent in these circumstances can be quite generous, and they were very positive about the lack of barriers faced by foreigners claiming these rights. This porousness impacts severely the state's ability to count how many foreign Europeans are resident. This is uniquely so among Northwest European states, which are generally highly conscious about checking people in and (especially) out of watertight welfare state systems. There is no way you can get away with this kind of thing in the Netherlands, for example. But Britain is extraordinarily flexible about residence. It all suggests that official figures way underestimate the numbers of foreigners resident in the country.[8]

Faced with this official lacuna, the best thing to do is to talk to service providers – i.e. organizations, magazines, or websites for expats in London – and employers. These are people who generally have a much more practical, hands on, commercially based knowledge of these mobile populations in question: because they want to sell something to them. For example, among the most striking London stories has been the relocation there of a new generation of talented and entrepreneurial young French people, especially women. The official consulate figures cite around 40,000 French in London, and the Labour Force Survey counts little more than 50,000. But on service provider websites the numbers discussed are more in the order of 200,000 French in London and the Southeast, and some media cite 300,000. This leads on to the somewhat hyperbolic idea that London might be now the fourth largest French city after Paris, Lyon, and Marseilles.[9]

London Belongs to Me

The French in London, particularly the young women I interviewed, numbered among the most prototypical of the free movers I met. A lot of this is explained by Britain's – and London's – specific "offshore" relationship with the economy and distinct welfare systems of continental Europe. With unemployment running at 12 percent in France in the early 1990s, compared to 5 percent in Britain, the reasoning behind a move was not difficult. I ask Nour, a successful journalist, why there were so many talented, educated young French people in London:

> *There was a big recession in Europe, especially France, and a boom in London. People would come and accept more menial jobs in London. At what cost, that's another issue. Bad working hours, less social services, but still you had a job.*

Others, like Nicole or Valérie, a former broker in her early thirties (see her tale below, pp. 182–5), stress the opportunities they associate with the "Anglo-Saxon" mode of working and flexible labour market. This proto-typical migrant reasoning is supplemented by employment factors specific to particular sectors, such as finance and media. Laure (see below, pp. 165–8) sought out work in the nascent cable TV industry in the early 1990s. Nour moved back to London from the US to work in cable television, after weighing up Paris as an option. She cites the more dynamic work atmosphere, with more career opportunities.

All these respondents recognize certain aspects of Parisian life as better. They can cogently enumerate the comparative benefits of Paris, particularly in terms of quality of life. Yet ambitious executives like Philippe, a fast track manager at Unilever, had little doubt professionally or personally that a spell in London was going to be better for him and his partner than heading straight to the metropolitan centre.

> *If I remember well, I think in 2000, the fact that England, London, was the place to be, probably in the world. It was thriving, booming, exploding. It was all over the place. And we were really really happy that the position we were offered was in the UK.*

One organization dedicated to promoting French relocation to Britain is La France Libre d'Entreprendre. Led by the vocal young French exile Olivier Cadic, it has promoted the idea of Britain as a low tax business environment for ambitious French business entrepreneurs fed up with social security payments and a 35 hour week.[10] Many have offices clustered around the Eurostar train terminal in Ashford, Kent. With high unemployment and a growing social discontent in France throughout the last decade, the economic reasons for location became imperative for many. Although mostly ignored in Britain, the phenomenon has received quite a bit of press in France. The Euro-economists at least should be pleased. This is movement entirely in concord with the Theory of European Integration. The young, mostly provincial-origin French, did indeed "get on their bike" and move – as economists would predict.[11] The benefits for Britain, though, have been underestimated. The British economic "miracle" of the last few years has in fact been partly fuelled by these European economic dynamics, building on Britain's strategic economic positioning and tax incentives, and its ability to bleed the brightest and the best from its European neighbours.[12]

The irony of this mass migration of Eurostars to Southeast England is that they are the systematic refutation of all the negative arguments about migrants bandied about by commentators. Britain's offshore place in the EU is a comfortable one. It creams off the benefits of membership, while not having to share in the costs. Translate the economic theory into actual people – the population that embody this – and it turns out that one of the main conduits for the boom economy between 1995 and 2005 were the floods of young Europeans coming to live and work in Britain.

Anti-immigrant arguments tend to rest on three assertions. The first is that immigrants bring unwanted cultural and racial problems to stable, culturally unified nations. This is a staple of nativist politicians. The second is that immigrants are a parasitic burden on the welfare state, because they are not fully participating members of society. This is used by the same politicians, but also more widely argued by moderates and some scholars. The third is that open migration policy and open labour markets tend over time to cause the selection of migrants – in terms of their quality and thus the benefits that can be extracted from them – to head downwards. This is because as mobility becomes more open, economists argue that you attract an increasing proportion of poorly educated "mass" migrants, instead of the "exceptionally" mobile, most talented, most educated migrants, who might be happy to work below their level in return for citizenship.

Eurostars' migration into London systematically contravenes these three arguments. There are in fact very few cultural or racial issues raised by these close European neighbours. Britain remains fixated on more "exotic" forms of cultural difference as a threat, whether it is radical Islam, the great unwashed of Roma invading the country, too many Polish workers, or people-trafficking from China and Southeast Asia. Nobody notices or complains about well-spoken French, Italian, or German kids working in cafés, trains, hotel lobbies, or bargain airlines. They are unproblematic, and no politician or policy maker need ever make a fuss. European residents also are certainly not a burden on the welfare state. All of them always maintain medical and dental treatment back home, and they are working and paying taxes and national insurance in Britain towards pensions from which they will never see the benefit. They are also more often than not temporary and short-term migrants, who will not be looking for childcare benefits, schools, medical treatment, or retirement care in the long run. Finally, the British economy gets an almost free ride on the back of the superior state school systems and cheaper universities of its neighbours. These well brought up, highly educated young Europeans come to Britain with degrees in hand, only to work in snack bars and menial office jobs. They are motivated, dynamic, and ideal employees; but they are willing to take a cut in pay and quality of life, just to be in London. The city and the national economy pockets the difference. They are, in other words, the economic theorists' dream immigrants: Gordon Brown's babies.[13]

Other nationalities can feel the same way as the London French. Jaime remembers his excitement when he found that he could stay after studying for a degree in graphic design. Graphic excitement:

> *I was fixated with the idea of getting into the big town, and working here. You know* [makes amazed face] *"London, England"!* [I had] *a few interviews. I was thinking of giving myself a couple of months until my money runs out. Two days before I decided to go back to Madrid, I got a job.*

He remembers how amazed he was that he could compete equally for a job with "natives" – and get it.

> *Actually, I was very lucky to get that job. It was more like a fluke than an opportunity. Anyway, you are very happy about it. Jumping for joy, over the moon!*

Jaime is typical of one of the carefree younger migrants who came to London and liked it. Another highly indicative particularity of Britain's wide open labour market is that there are not even barriers to European foreigners working in sensitive "national" professions, such as the civil service. This again is in contrast to state practice in other countries.[14] Isabel works as a Home Office economist and has found neither language or know-how a barrier. Only work for the Foreign Office, or involving confidential national matters, is ruled out. These openings lure older people to stay, after an initial taste as a student or after graduation.

One particular company stands out for its deliberate policy of targeting young Europeans as prospective employees: Pret (*Prêt-à-Manger*), a hugely successful London-based sandwich chain. This company actually has a recruitment policy tailored around these new EU free movement dynamics. They have capitalized on this talented and highly available workforce, by targeting young Europeans as they arrive. Pret's recruitment office is in fact found on platform one at Victoria Station, the historical gateway to Europe. Their personnel manager, herself a young Spanish Basque woman who had been in London for seven years or so, confirmed the scale of this commitment and the smartness with which the company has benefited from it. All of the young West Europeans arrive ready and able to work, with no visa restrictions. Many are university educated, but willing to take simple service sector work to be in London. Pret thus creams off a workforce high in human, social, and economic capital, but willing to work for a modest wage in return for congenial hours, a sympathetic corporate ambiance, and above all a great social life. Pret openly encourages relationships and networking between employees, organizes parties, publishes a magazine for them, and promises a structured career development plan without longer-term ties.[15] Again, this is rational European integration theory at work – impacting the London economy in very direct ways.

Liberation

Of course, London seduces with many other quintessential urban attractions. In cultural terms, it basks in an almost universally accepted awe of its liberating and cutting edge sense of style. The turn of the century saw London's cultural caché – packaged ubiquitously as "cool Britannia" – at its highest ever. London calling has thus offered Europe's most appealing and challenging rite of passage, notably – as it always has done for the armies of frustrated suburban youth who have moved there in search of the city lights – as a refuge from dull provinces, limited horizons, or overly protective family environments. It offers the "outsider" freedom of not belonging yet feeling at home, a place of comfortable anonymity. These contours of the classic city of modernity, the "sentiment de liberté", as Valérie puts it, are echoed by Nicole:

> *London is definitely more open minded, more flexible than France, at work and in general. Since I was a teenager, I had this feeling of frustration. It's not open minded in France, it is not encouraged. On TV, in education, anybody who is trying to be open minded is looked at as someone eccentric. Stupid things like clothes. My French friends* [when they visit] *stare at people here, they have a more conservative style. They don't have a positive image of being eccentric. It could be fun, creative, but still it is something that means you are too different.*

Others cite London's manifold cultural attractions, both popular and high culture at its best. Carmen and Franz don't get to meet many English people, but the cultural dimension of the city makes them feel at home. London's art world is seen as internationally unmatched in Europe for practicing artists such as Sandra. For Saskia, meanwhile, London's cultural reputation means classical music. She plays and goes to concerts. She says moving here was "like being a kid in a candy store".

London's open, fluid social world is thus a great attraction for the younger Eurostars. This really is the great libertarian city, and the possibilities for meeting people are endless, even if many will probably be foreigners too. Nicole reminisces about her first arrival in the city, following the trail as many have done to the cheap hostels in Bayswater or Kensington:

When I first came, I used to sleep in a hostel in Bayswater, which is a brilliant place to meet people. You have people from everywhere around the world. They are just like you, have been here for two weeks, they don't know how long they are going to stay, and they're very excited because they've just got a job ... Everything you do is new, so it's full of energy, you are never alone, you eat together and share everything ... After six months I couldn't stand it anymore, but the first three months were wonderful.

London work life also makes socializing easy. Nicole had no problem doing as provincial newcomers to London have always done, using social contacts inside and out of work to structure your new life in the city. This does not happen in France. Nicole's social life improved after she no longer had a French boyfriend, and joined in the usual after-work social life that is common in many companies.

After office drinking can be fairly superficial, but it is the basic social lubricant and the way the city works – for allcomers. The international social world in London socializes and parties in pretty much the same way as the natives do, although the two worlds do not necessarily intersect. London, also, is apparently welcoming as an identity. When I ask her if she considers herself a Londoner now, Valérie tells me of an email that has been going round the office: "The 100 things that make you a Londoner". Most of these refer to becoming used to the extortionate price of cinema tickets, sushi, or rent, the terrible weather, the lack of clothes worn by clubbers in winter, or paying council taxes, etc. No barriers to foreigners there. It would seem a city uniquely open to this rapid self-identification. Most do indeed think of themselves as Londoners, but it is no guide to their integration. Sandra is a long-term committed resident, and as fully integrated as you get as a European foreigner. She certainly is one, and responds enthusiastically to the question. But ask the same question of Carmen and Franz, who are among the least rooted and most critical, and they too see themselves in these terms. Being a Londoner is just *being there*, working, enjoying and enduring it like everyone else. It is nothing specific. Part of the city's secret is its capacity to accommodate all kinds of different communities that can thrive quite happily, although they may never intersect. The young Spanish community is a case in point. Jaime offers me a guide, describing how they socialize together, in order to get around their frustrations with early closing and British eating habits. Remarkably, many of them arrive in London barely speaking a word of English.

London's liberational feel is also linked to its long, accomplished history of open immigration and asylum. This goes a lot further back than the very visible postcolonial multiculturalism of the postwar period, that spills out into the streets of Notting Hill every August, in Europe's biggest street party. Nineteenth-century London was the most important European city of empire, after its dramatic expansion and emergence during the late seventeenth and early eighteenth centuries. A famous drawing of London of the World Exhibition of 1851 shows London as the first urban sprawl, although the extent of the city then was not much bigger than the central core of Brussels or Amsterdam now. Immigrants have always fuelled these dynamics, alongside a highly mobile British population cramming in towards the centre. Germans, Slavs, Poles, and Southern Europeans in the nineteenth century joined Jewish and Huguenot refugees of various earlier eras. Many generations of immigrant London can be seen in the urban architecture, particularly the churches and markets of London's East End: the traditional point of arrival for many immigrants.

Without doubt, London's multiracial, cosmopolitan allure today is still a great part of the attraction for foreign European migrants. It certainly appears that Londoners are more comfortable with celebrating this heritage than some places. The French are often very positive on this point compared to back home, linking it to their feeling of not being discriminated against. Contrary to the poor image of British state schools, Laure, for example, has found great satisfaction getting involved in a typically multicultural London school. One thing everyone realizes, though, is that London is *not* the rest of Britain. Multiculturalism in Britain remains a highly concentrated urban phenomenon, rooted in a handful of major cities only. The academic image of multi-ethnic Britain is largely based on ignoring the fact that most of the country is decidedly *not* multicultural in its population make-up, culture, or attitudes. Like true Londoners, the foreign European residents usually have hardly ever stepped out of the capital. There is nothing unusual about this: all residents there tend to find their lives sucked wholly into the urban scene. The only getaway is usually when they take cheap air flights to catch some sun, or go somewhere "continental" for the weekend. The annual *Time Out* directory of short breaks – based on the destinations you can fly to for cheap – looks like a directory of medium sized European cities. The same cities the foreign European residents fly to when they are going home.

This Is Not America

But what has Europe got to do with all this? The perception is often that London is special not because it is arguably the capital of Europe, but in fact because it is more like a generic American city: a hub of industry, capital, networks, and global culture, that just happens to be better embedded in world networks than its European rivals. Another Atlanta, for example? This appears to be the suggestion behind the global cities analysis based on financial flows and networks. Derived from this, geographers and spatial economists have prophesied the "fading charm of European cities". They argue that efficiencies of scale will cause capital, trade, and population to concentrate in an ever smaller roster of world cities. It's bad news for the regional European city. There's too many of them, they are not big enough, and they are too close together. Most will decline and only a few major concentrations – the global cities – will survive as major hubs. The laws of mobility in a flattening world – of flows of capital, goods, services, and persons – appear to dictate that. And London for them is the model of this isomorphic future – making it the farthest outpost of the American empire in the West.

The virtual networks may be real, the global connections all there, but this flattening, homogenizing vision of London as a generic global city is denied in flesh and blood by each and every one of the foreign European residents in the city. The laws of mobility apparently may work for virtual ciphers and economists' models, but they apparently don't work that well for real people. Even the most mobile of people like to live in locations that are still region-ally connected; they also like to live in distinctive, esoteric places, not just abstract space and time. Some of America's flat world ideals can be true: freedom, mobility, being a pioneer, an individual. But mobility is so much better if you can live in a global city that feels European in its urbane, cos-mopolitan attractions; and that is close enough to where you come from that you can still pop home at the weekend. London, in other words, offers some of the attractions of the US, except that it is squarely located in Europe.

London also offers the allure of American-style business and flexibility. Only the London business world turns out to be an economy embedded in a "thick" social environment: of personal networks, human ties, and a social life that bears little resemblance to the uniform suburban dullness, conserva-tism, and protestant work ethic of the US. This is the British version of "soft capitalism", the interpersonal secret of its success. London is also sometimes thought to be more American than European because it was the first subur-ban city, driven to expansion as all twentieth-century "edge cities" have by centripetal, exurban forces. Could not London's sprawling development just be transposed to the archetypal, soulless, American edge city, with new deserts and green fields on which to build ever new housing tracks, com-mercial units, freeways, and shopping malls? Eurostars for sure don't think so. Unlike native Londoners who do eventually move out of the city for an exurban life, the suburban option for Eurostars is not appealing. They want to live in the city and be part of the city. The desperate compromises that housing prices force on residents ensure many of them have to work very hard to live in an urban way there. But their efforts are helping to keep London alive as a Eurocity, with its own distinctive qualities of life as in any other European city.

Traditionally, since the 1960s, when they went through their own waves of hipster re-gentrification, the Georgian town houses and apartments of

Kensington, Earls Court, and Chelsea have been the most international parts of the town. This is by now an interchangeably international neighbourhood, not a European one, with many Australians, Americans, and Arabs among the few native English and foreign European residents. A later generation of European movers into the city have sighted Islington as the new cosmopolitan neighbourhood of choice, that at least a few years ago was still accessible to their rather more modest price range. Pedro, a Spanish banker, bought in Islington for this reason, after having lived in the more expensive Kensington. In ten years, the redevelopment of Angel tube station, countless new bars and restaurants, and a clientele of affluent yuppies, have pushed Islington beyond most people's range again. The younger Eurostars seeking to buy in London are now having to look elsewhere. The problem is not financing. A mortgage generally costs no more than rent, and getting one is easy enough for foreign Europeans in London's overheated property market. As Norbert, a German research economist, says, there is "no barrier other than price". The problem lies in finding somewhere urban and central that you can still afford. Isabel and Saskia got lucky following the Metropolitan line north to West Hampstead. Close to town, on a tube line, a cosmopolitan feel, with nice pubs and restaurants. All the best things about London as a European city. A certain villagey quality of life, green spaces nearby, and the city still at your feet … Don't bother looking there now, you're too late! There are actually very few of these affordable places in zones one or two. Yet it is crucial to settling in London that residents manage to effect this change to a more localized type of life in the city – while preserving the urban lifestyle that brought them there in the first place.

Jeroen found a similar pocket not far from Paddington. At his flat for the interview, I say it seems a nice neighbourhood.

Yeah, they're doing it up. Georgian houses. It makes a difference [living here]. *If you walk past the restaurant, they say hello, things like that. There's a little bit of artistic snobbery, plus it's a mixed neighbourhood culturally. The carnival is not far away. It's a mix of rich people and not. One needs that in an area. It has to have some heart … I lived* [further out] *in Shepherd's Bush in the beginning. That was not quite so good. Much more generic. McDonald's, cheap tourist hotels, loud, people going to drink. You wouldn't meet anyone if you went into the pub … I made a lot of effort to go back toward the centre.*

Jeroen had looked beyond the edge of cosmopolitan London, towards the suburbs, and he didn't like what he saw. All of these residents are living in a different, congenial urban London, in which none of the qualities of a European style of life have been sacrificed (yet) for the generic McSuburbs. Their London is not its American version, but one they are recreating every day as a European place. Most of this is related to the little everyday things that keep the city a historically vibrant Eurocity, with its own unique charm and dynamism – the feeling of diversity, of being near people, and being near the continent. The Eurostars in London are proud and defensive of that. This is not America.

A Data Analyst's Tale

One doesn't necessarily think of London as a city of skyscrapers, but it certainly has a few spectacular towers of glass and steel of its own. So when visiting the City in these anxious, terrorized first years of the twenty-first century, it's hard to ignore what a huge target they – and you – represent while walking among them. The day before I'd sat with Saskia – the risk assessment specialist from Belgium – in a wine bar deep under Canary Wharf, and it was hard not to think of ground zero. Today, I'm meeting Donatella for lunch outside her office in the International Finance Centre, Tower 42, near the London Stock Exchange. I suppose we'll have a great view from here if the sirens sound and it all comes tumbling down. Donatella is in her thirties and comes from Puglia, in the south of Italy. She is perhaps the best prototype of European mobility I've found. Better even than Maria, the blue chip lawyer in Amsterdam (see below, pp. 63–4), because her family were not middle class like many of the other Eurostars, but southern Italian farmers from a poor region. Now 38, she is frank, to the point, and knows exactly what she wants. She mentions a relationship, but she talks and thinks like a single woman. London was her dream, but it may only be a step in a global search that might still take her ... well, anywhere.

I work for the second rated insurance company in the world. I am an information specialist. I work in the knowledge centre. It's a global service: whenever from each location they need information, they come to us and we try to help. We do research, about the impact on our business of emerging trends, technologies and so on.

She has been in London five years now.

In the Italian environment, it's not that easy to move forward, change your career. I wanted an international experience, and I wanted to learn English. So I thought: what's the best opportunity to do both? Here I know the environment is much more flexible – and it turned out to be exactly as I thought. It was absolutely easy for me to come, learn the language, to study, and to change my career. So I started everything again!

This was a remarkable move to make, age 33. After a year of language study, she took a masters degree in information science and then got a job in the City. Just like that.

Yes. I did university in Italy. I studied economics, then I worked in a polling company doing consumer and political research. After that, I was a bit tired, I wanted a change. Of course it's not easy at this age. You are a junior again, even though I had accumulated some experience there in Italy. It was a late move, yes. My Italian friends say: this is unusual, this [moving to a city like London] *is something you do just after graduation, because it's not easy to find a good job in Italy. Mainly they come to work in investment banks here. But for me it hasn't been like this at all. I just felt unhappy and I felt that I didn't want to do*

A Data Analyst's Tale—cont'd

that job anymore. You can't just switch. In Italy, the system is much more inflexible, either the education system or the business environment. You want to change your life but you can't. Whereas here you can get every qualification very very easily.

What about your hometown?

It's a small village in the Southeast of Italy. Then I moved to Milan. That was a big change from the South to the North, to study at Bocconi [Milan's famous business school]. *That was already a big change.*

When you left home, did everyone else move?

No, I was the only one, then the following year my sister followed. All my friends actually studied locally in the South, or they went to Rome, Bari, Pescara, Lecce. I was the only one to go to Milan. Because of my studies, Milan is the best city to pay it off. It gave me a lot of experience, change, but I didn't really like Milan, so I'm much happier here in London.

Although it is highly international, Milan still seems quite a closed city for outsiders.

Yes, and they mainly come from the rest of Italy! [laughs]. *No, the environment is not international at all. It's quite provincial, I might say. The image, the* [international] *reputation is too high. Everybody can tell you that every Milanese guy who studies at Bocconi dreams of leaving and coming to London. That tells you about the place.*

Was it easy to meet locals here?

No. [My friends] *are about 20 percent English, 20 percent Italian, 60 percent international. Exactly like me. Expatriates. They stay here for a few years, and of course they are willing to make new friends, eager to meet expats like you. They have to because they haven't got a lot of background. I really didn't have many friends when I arrived here.*

The age group thing is difficult. As soon as people get a bit older, they get a bit more settled, harder to meet …

Exactly, and I wasn't so young [laughs]. *Other foreigners had friends from university, and they mainly had a much more international background than me. For me this is the only experience. We meet through friends of friends, parties … Not clubs, but going to the theatre, cinema, language courses …*

The foreigners come together through a mutual need to deal with the city. London must be quite a tough place to live in some ways?

Oh, I'm doing OK. You have to become very good at money management. You buy a smaller flat that you would do normally. You see very high earning people, and that makes a lot of pressure on you, of course. But the bureaucracy is quite easier. Everybody has got a space. So even though it's very competitive, it's still open for everybody. It's very good, yeah!

But would you ever describe yourself as a Londoner?

[Laughing] *NO! No, no. I define myself as an expat. But I see this as very positive. I'm free to live with foreigners, free to choose my own life … Sometimes I had the feeling English people may resent that you come here. Your English is not so good, you might earn more money than them, because you are better qualified. Sometimes I felt resentment and in this way I felt less integrated than I would like to be. But then as a society* [to live in], *it's not so suffocating. If you felt "integrated", you would have created exactly the same environment as* [you left] *in Italy. Whereas, no, here I benefit from being not too much integrated, I can see things from outside.*

A Data Analyst's Tale—cont'd

What about your relationship with home, Italy?

I follow Italian politics. I was very engaged in the past, and I still follow it. I vote when I can go back, yes. In truth, thanks to internet you can follow quite a lot. I also have satellite TV … The connection is still strong. I have been there for too many years, you can't just cut off. The first thing I do in the morning on the internet is look at the Italian news, and only after do I look at the English news, or the international news. Even though for work I have to follow what happens here and internationally for research reasons. But if I have time on my own, the first thing is the Italian news.

What about your family?

My holidays are very limited. They come to visit, but I have to choose parents or holiday. It's not enough, for three or four days. It's getting easier, cheaper. I had the same problem in Milan, but I had more holidays. Sometimes I feel guilty. They feel very well [fine] about it, they are very open. Also my brothers and sisters. But they all went back to live locally.

Many of the Italians I have talked with seem to have an idea they are going to go back one day, a kind of "sunset clause" on their mobility …

They want to go back? It's not my case. You are talking about people from the North [of Italy]. I'm sure they dream to go back. I can understand. They come from rich provinces. They have a job to go back to, it's dead easy for them. For me I wouldn't go back to this small village, there wouldn't be any job for me. I would have to go back to Milan, and I don't want to go back to Milan. I don't have many options … It's not easy.

I can see myself in another place outside Italy, which is not Italy, but not going back to Italy. Actually at the moment I'm buying a flat here, but in London this is not a huge commitment. You can sell it, in two years. It's not a problem.

Are you a migrant?

No, no! This is something I felt a little bit more when I was living in Milan, because coming from the South people there make you feel more like a migrant – even though I was a kind of intellectual migrant. No. I see myself as an expatriate – not a migrant, not at all. It depends on your perspective. If your perspective is global, then you are not a migrant. You are a mover, your mobility is much higher.

A note of regret creeps into her voice.

Since I left home at 19, I always said I would never go back. Once you move from your own village … Sometimes I go back to see my friends – who are very well settled, I have to say, with good jobs, childrens – and I wonder: have I done the right thing? I've had much more experience. I've seen much more than them. But there's something that's missing anyway. The fact you feel unrooted, this is the bad side, the thing I resent a bit. It's the drawback of this life, this international life.

We pause, and listen to a jumbo jet flying high over the city. The talk brightens up again, as I ask about the future. She has it planned out.

I'm thinking, not in terms of timescale, but in terms of work experience. I'm thinking I will leave London when I have accumulated a certain work experience in my job, and I know I can easily move to another country, and get a very good job easily. Only if the job perspectives were very good, otherwise it would not be worth it. Maybe Hong Kong, Singapore,

A Data Analyst's Tale—cont'd

New York ... although [laughing] *I'm scared to go to the US ... Once you are used to the nice life, the easy life in Europe. Even England was a shock and adjustment! ... Maybe Paris, that's a good combination. It has a much better standard of life ... After that, I think I would like to move again, have more challenging experiences abroad. Perhaps in less developed countries. Perhaps in NGOs, or the non-profit sector. Somewhere I could apply these skills. This is my idea, my dream.*

4

Brussels-Brussel-Bruxelles

The train now stops in Brussels. The multilingual announcements say it all. Brussels-Brussel-Bruxelles, *la cosmopolite*. First impressions are not good. This scruffy, shabby-looking and much despised conurbation has none of the tourist marketing charm of Amsterdam or Paris, none of the urban cred of London or Berlin. Yet this mixed-up crossroads at the heart of Northwest Europe is in fact the great underrated European city, a cosmopolitan haven largely undiscovered even by many who pass through it regularly. For all its importance as the political capital of Europe, Brussels remains a city chronically misrepresented and misunderstood by those travellers and outside observers who bother to comment upon it. Researchers and journalists covering EU politics rarely cast more than a sideways glance at the city and the social context in which all this political activity is located. The image is underlined and extended in the frequently cynical comments in media coverage about corruption, bureaucracy, and – after the Dutroux child kidnap scandal of the late 1990s – depravity in Belgium by foreign journalists. The fact that most of these commentators have failed to take a look outside the grim, office bound avenues of the Schuman and Leopold quarters, or have little or no idea about the diversity, range, and quality of cultural life in the city, has not prevented this image from spreading as the one that most non-residents have. And, given that Brussels is identified with Europe and the European Union – as its beating heart and symbolic capital – Euroscepticism only feeds on this ignorance.

By any standards, the international composition of the Brussels population is extraordinary. Everyone knows of course about the *fonctionnaires* – the so-called "eurocrats" – who work for the European Commission and a range of other European and international organizations, such as NATO. As a major site of (for example) pharmaceutical, food production, and distribution companies, Brussels also has its fair share of corporate "expats". But to this knowledge needs to be added a much wider range of urban professionals living and working in the city, who have chosen the city as one of the key hubs of Europe. The other side of this presence – linked to but by no means exhaustively explained by the locations of international organizations and multinational corporations in the city – is the fact that Brussels offers an exceptionally conducive context for their lives here. Not only does Brussels rate highly as an emergent "global city" – in terms of its corporate and political networks – but it offers a historical context of rare diversity in Europe.

First, it is unusually multinational as a capital city. It sits at the intersection of the French, Dutch, German, and English-speaking worlds, influenced and inflected by each, but not exclusively defined by any. Because of its location, a multinational European history has flowed through the city, in ways rather different to the heavily nationalized histories of the capitals of other, larger European nations. Secondly, linked to this, it is a rare example of a state capital which is not the capital and centre of a single dominant national society. Belgium exists as an entity, but it is difficult nowadays not to think of the country as two relatively distinct national societies somehow still coexisting within one federal state. Brussels-Region is in fact a third, independent administrative entity, alongside the Flanders and Wallonia regions. The Belgian state also attributes administrative powers to three non-territorial linguistic communities (Flemish, Walloon, and German), of which the Flemish choose to locate the capital in Brussels, even though it lies outside the territory of Flanders. Brussels is not the Walloon capital, although its Belgian national population is thought to be about around 85 percent Francophone and 15 percent Dutch speaking – many *Bruxellois* and *Brusselaars* are in fact bilingual. Since its creation in 1989, Brussels-Region has emerged as a separate political entity within Belgium, asserting an international identity and cross-cultural face. In this context, the legendary communal tensions between Walloons and Flemish over the city are not only zero-sum in nature; they can also be creative. The complex, cross-cutting federal, regional, linguistic, and communal competencies of the Belgian state create a uniquely multileveled or nested scenario for Brussels in Belgium and Europe. As well as politicizing the minutiae of nearly every aspect of everyday life in the city, the structures create a context in which many spaces have opened for social action and social change. This feeds into a third dimension of diversity, overlaying the state structure and national geopolitical history: the large-scale immigration of the last few decades, that covers the full range from guest workers and colonial migrants (from Spain, Portugal, and Italy; then the Congo, North Africa, and Turkey), through refugees, to highly skilled professionals of all nationalities.[1]

Given these dimensions, diversity thrives alongside the many social tensions and problems to which immigration and cultural pluralism can lead. Brussels is quite simply unique as a multinational, multilingual, multileveled, and multicultural city. The last twenty years have also seen something of a return to the late nineteenth-century cosmopolitan inheritance of the city: the short golden period before the collapse of the European international system, famously recounted by Karl Polanyi in *The Great Transformation*. For a while, Brussels was the heart of it all. From 1880 to 1910, no city in Europe saw a more spectacular boom period of industrial, commercial, artistic, and colonial wealth. Brussels became the historical crossroads of Europe in the age of empire, a European economic capital between the great powers. It is exactly this that was destroyed in the international collapse of the early twentieth century. Brussels paid a high price from the military fallout of Germany, France, Britain, and Italy. Re-emerging politically at the heart of a European Union, that would now allow small states a bigger say in curbing the nationalist ambitions of larger ones, it was to be dismembered first by rampant American-style modernization and suburbanization – again, more dramatic than almost anywhere else in Western Europe – and then an industrial decline that shattered the heart of the city. A once grand city became a shell, particularly in areas in and around the downtown. Weak urban governance led to uncontrolled development, a peacetime destruction worse than anything that happened during the two world wars. A freeway was blasted through the historical centre, and a beltway ring was gouged out that severed the downtown from surrounding communes. Many beautiful art deco buildings were pulled down to make way for tower blocks. In the new Schuman quarter, concrete was poured and plastered over several distinctive neighbourhoods to house the EU.

The discordant, mostly ugly infrastructure, overlaid onto such diversity and cultural heritage, perhaps accounts for why it is such a strange place, with little continuity and only hidden appeal. At first sight it is an alienating place, as foreign to most Belgians as it is to the foreign visitors expecting the tidy, packaged experiences offered by the more nationalized cultures of touristic Paris or Amsterdam. As the city declined in the 1950s and 1960s, middle-class Belgians moved out in droves, vacating a ravaged urban landscape. When immigration and international populations then refilled the city, it thus had an effect much more transformative than other major cities that were never so renounced by their native populations. Brussels now has a foreign and immigrant population that far outstrips the percentages found in London, Amsterdam, or Paris and, even more strikingly, the autonomy and independence of these immigrant communities marks large sections of the city.

The overwhelming air of negativity that hangs over external foreign perceptions of Brussels is shared by many provincial Belgians towards their capital. The fact is that nobody likes Brussels, except true *Bruxellois*. You have to *live* there to understand this. A city of surrealist, multicultural anarchy; a city of multiple decentred communes, with beautiful, undiscovered neighbourhoods, still full of glorious late nineteenth-century town houses; a city of idiosyncratic cafés, fabulous restaurants, world-class beer, chocolate, and *frites*; a city of extraordinary night life, hidden away in the bombed out buildings and abandoned streets of the downtown and surroundings. Many of the Eurostars discover this after a first taste of life in neighbourhoods such as the one centred on Place Fernand Coq in Ixelles, the most obviously cosmopolitan commune of the city. This is, of course, the city of the *Zinneke*, well known to *Brusselaars*, but unknown to so many others who pass through. *Zinneke* is the term used by residents to refer affectionately to the hybrid "mongrel" identity of the "true" people from Brussels, who have a tangled mix of Flemish, Francophone, and other origins. The name was adopted by the successful *Zinneke* parade of May 2000, which celebrated Brussels' multicultural diversity during the European Year of Culture. The parade has run successfully every two years since then.

There is always one highly diverse group missing from the party: Brussels' resident Eurostars. This more recent international European population is not seen by many Belgians as part of the multicultural tapestry of the city.[2] Belgians tend to dismiss them all as remote and temporary eurocrats and expats – with a probably exploitative relationship to the city – but these are false and limited stereotypes.[3] The city's own myths about the European population need to be deconstructed, along with those imposed upon it from the outside. Lately, negativity towards these European foreigners in the city has only grown. Their number is expanding, with the EU accession process bringing ever more foreign residents to the city, from an even broader range of nationalities. This of course only means even faster changes to the urban fabric, more obvious practical accommodation problems, more visible diversity in the streets, bars, restaurants, and shops. Yet, despite concerns, Brussels still has some way to go to get back to its optimal size, given the many decades of population decline and real estate neglect. Moreover, the attitudes of the new *Bruxellois* do not conform to this negative image. The majority are committed to the city, engaged with its qualities and very positive about their lives there. Indeed, for all its problems and tarnished image, Brussels can be seen to offer these international residents an extraordinary standard and range of social and cultural life: something always discussed in terms of its superior quality of life. What gives it an advantage over other Eurocities is that this quality of life is exceptionally accessible to foreign residents, and not monopolized by locals or the global rich, as it often is elsewhere.[4]

Found a Job

The secret of Brussels' attractiveness as a destination begins, as it does with Amsterdam and London, with the labour market. Brussels offers an extraordinarily open range of short-term jobs and longer-term career opportunities for free-moving EU nationals.[5] The informal, word-of-mouth way in which foreign European residents seem to find and change jobs, particularly in the orbit of the European institutions, is remarkable. For those young and flexible enough, unemployment rarely proves to be a long-term hurdle, even though contracts can be short. It also accounts for why so many who come with very short-term plans end up staying for years. The opportunities are well known – and it largely explains why people come to the city. They do not come because of the fame of Brussels' nightlife, its restaurants, or the multicultural ambiance. These are things that are discovered with surprise and pleasure later. This is sharply different to why people move to Amsterdam or London. These cities also offer abundant opportunities, but are also famously attractive for cultural and historical reasons.

To take just one example, Bernhard, who works in lobbying for a religious NGO, is making it up as he goes along. He has a three year contract and "no specific plans", estimating he has enough on his CV to easily get work in the lobbying world. At some point he intends to take the *concours* (EU recruitment competition) for a full-time position in the Commission. For sure, he'd like to stay in Brussels a few more years, probably in the NGO world. As an international hub linked to the fast-moving dynamic of the EU, Brussels offers many such short-term openings in both the public international sector, as well as with the private corporations drawn to the city as a European capital. Belgian businesses too are adept at drawing on the talented international pool of labour present in the city. From the employee point of view, you can find challenging career opportunities in this dynamic environment but, crucially, escape the downsides of larger capitals like London or Paris. Rob and Rachel, an English couple who have been in Brussels seven years, had coordinated their careers in the private and public sectors, respectively. They just "don't fancy" the "rat race" of London. Rob summarizes that he thinks Brussels is unique among European cities in what it has to offer: "the combination of geographical location, cross-section of the population, property, and work opportunities." Jonathan, a former Londoner who lives in Brussels with his wife Ellen and three children, had turned European work experience in agricultural lobbying into working for himself as a consultant. For him, too, there was no looking back. He emphasizes how it is a great place for families to live. According to the Irish in Brussels, too, the work and living environment compares favourably on expense, lifestyle, and stress to Dublin, another boom city of a similar size.

It is important to remember that unlike EU *fonctionnaires* and career expats, individual free movers have a very free and open choice whether to remain in the city. Employment possibilities being good elsewhere, it is an open question why many of them in fact settle in Brussels. It is certainly not because Belgium has a high reputation internationally. It is surely the most "uncool" major city destination in Europe. Why people stay has to have more to do with just the structure of the job market or career satisfaction. The people in question are *not* really high-flying elites – who would be predisposed in fact to move on because of career opportunities. Rather, they are more like averagely successful professional middle classes back home, people who aspire to average middle class satisfactions. The main focus in the question of settlement, then, is on how the city enables or restricts their achievement of a satisfactory "shape" to their lives. Decisions like this are rarely dictated by career alone. They have as much to do with the domestic and leisure quality of life issues. That is, they discover very quickly that Brussels is a city with manifold attractions beyond any they expected on arrival. And that the kind of disposable income they receive here offers them a quality of life that would be absolutely impossible in rival cities.

The Euro Village

The aspect of discovering by surprise the city is a big part of Brussels' charm. When I ask Andreas, a Norwegian think-tank economist, if he identifies with the city after a couple of years' happy professional and married life in the city, his response is typical:[6]

> *Yeah, you could say so. It sounds a bit silly … but it is turning into my city in a way. It's a lot nicer to live here than to visit as a tourist, it grows on you.*

European foreign residents in fact participate above averagely in the cultural life of the city.[7] Much of the nightlife, cinemas, restaurants, and other attractions probably depend on the presence in the city of European residents with disposable income, and highly sociable lifestyles. For younger newcomers in the city, one of the great discoveries is Brussels' easy and open nightlife. What Brussels has to offer, it is true, is seen as less spectacular than London, Paris, or Amsterdam, but at the "alternative" end nightlife can be a lot more idiosyncratic and original. The formerly run down Sint Katelijne near the centre has become a buzzing, multinational hub of bars and cafés, centred on Saint Géry. For quiet nights, meanwhile, there are clusters of effortlessly cosmopolitan cafés in Ixelles. This would be one of the few evenings when there *isn't* one of the numerous, huge-scale *stagiaire* (EU intern) parties going on. Imagine several hundred young, affluent Europeans, chatting away in dozens of different languages, dancing, drinking, and copulating to Eurotrash music in some enormous old ballroom or disco – or a rampant all night house party at a friend's (or friends of friends) place.[8]

Discovering the charms of Brussels might be a challenge, but everyday life is easy. There are obvious things – such as the superb restaurants. Everyone mentions the restaurants. They are rated as high on quality, but much better value, less pretentious, and just as diverse than either Paris or London. Amsterdam, where kitchens close notoriously early, and where Dutch cuisine is austere at best, is simply not a great food destination. Again, Brussels is underrated on this score. Food and eating well is a Belgian obsession, and many diehard Parisians secretly travel up to the city to eat, where there are numerous Michelin starred restaurants, and prices are much cheaper. People eat out more and better because it is affordable and has the best of several European (and non-European) traditions. Brussels also scores highly on other cultural offerings: notably music, film, dance, and art. There are countless annual festivals, and the city is an affordable base for many younger, creative new artists and cultural entrepreneurs – especially in the fields of dance and theater.

The key to all this is the relation of size and population to what is going on. In this sense, Brussels rates very positively to bigger cities like London and Paris, and as easily comparable to the legendarily cultured Amsterdam. Numerous interviewees mention the village-like feel of the city, despite its size. Rachel, who is English, elaborates on this accessibility, by pointing to how being part of the "Euro" group they are circulating within a fraction of the city's population, so that you are "always bumping into people". They can in fact not be very integrated into Belgian life, while feeling fully integrated into the life of the city. For Southern Europeans, the charm is also villagey. They narrate Brussels as a respite from the cities that they might otherwise live in, comparing it favourably to "pazzesca [crazy]" Rome, the "total hysteria" of Milan, or the "stress" of London and Paris.

The Crossroads

Brussels is really a carrefour [crossroads] *where you meet people you haven't seen for ages, because so many people come here.*

Bernhard, German NGO lobbyist

Over and over again, these highly mobile people stress the location of the city as a huge factor in their happiness with the city. It is easy to drive around, easy to get to the airport, easy to take a train to Paris, Amsterdam, or London. And it is easy to fly to any destination in Europe or further afield from Zaventem, one of Europe's major hubs. In a couple of hours you can drive to France, the Netherlands, or Germany. The ever-improving train connections are a central part of the appeal – Brussels is at the heart of the emerging European high-speed train network.[9]

Above all, for Eurostars, Brussels is the place where their ideal of a multinational European life can be truly lived – as an effortless, everyday fact of life. Just as transport connections link the place to everywhere in the continent, it is also the place that the continent passes through. Andreas echoes Bernhard, in affirming a key dimension in their sense that this must be the place for them. Life in a genuinely multinational environment is liberating – and gets to be quite addictive. The typical image given is of a Brussels dinner party, with great food and drink, and the buzz of different languages around the table. Both Joannet, from the Netherlands, and Janet, from England, mention exactly this. Janet says how it is common to find yourself around a restaurant table with seven or eight nationalities – something that is hard to find in other cities. Joannet adds:

> *You organize a party, and people are from all over. Everyone here is very used to that. You sit at the dinner table and start in English, and go via German into French, while that part of the table speaks Italian ... It's very interesting, very colourful. It gives me lots of energy* [compared to] *the Dutch perspective ...*

Bernhard, from Germany, was able to compare it directly to Paris, where he lived before – right in the center in St. Germain. Choosing again to live in the center of things, he was disappointed at first. But it didn't take long for the multicultural charms of the city – "this multitude of people, cultures" – to grow on him, not least because he was living in Sint Katelijne, one of the most dynamic gentrifying neighbourhoods. It is particularly notable that the English in Brussels – who come from a country often said to be the most multicultural in Europe – also appreciate the rather distinctive form of multicultural life afforded by this city. Rob finds it is the multinational, multilingual aspect that makes the difference. Rachel, meanwhile, compares it favourably to multinational Switzerland, where her Italian-origin father had worked. Switzerland, she finds, is not a very open society in comparison, despite the similar multinational composition. Plus it is outside the EU, so she and Rob would have working permit hassles. In comparison, Brussels was more attractive.

> *It seemed to be a good option. So we thought, "Belgium is on the doorstep, we know people there, we'll give it a go". And yeah, we've had kind of a nice life here.*

Where the Streets Have Two Names

Much of the negative stereotyping of foreign Europeans in Brussels criticizes them for not "integrating" into Belgian life. Rachel describes their happy life there as "living in the bubble". Yet look closely and the idea that Europeans are not integrating into Brussels is wholly wrong. Brussels, in fact, is special because it is, uniquely, an almost wholly denationalized space. Their lives can be integrated, in a sociological sense, but whatever they are integrating into, it is not Belgium.

Bernhard has also thought a lot about these things because he is involved in lobbying questions on immigration, and chose to live in one of the heavily immigrant neighbourhoods of the city. Immigration debates in Europe today are dominated by moralizing about how immigrants should behave in order to "deserve" the citizenship of the nations they have chosen to live in – especially on issues such as learning the language, or adopting Western norms in schooling or gender relations. Bernhard speaks French and Dutch, likes Belgium, but feels there is something missing from the typically nation-centred focus of these integration debates. Modern technology in future will let you live in two or more societies – Brussels has a large range of multinational television channels that prove the point.[10] And here he works with Europeans of all kinds. He just doesn't meet Belgians regularly. When he went to a friend's mother's funeral, he found it was one of the rare occasions when he was really in Belgian society. It takes involvement in one of society's key rituals to bring home just how peculiarly integrated you are; for the Eurostars, things like funerals happen somewhere else, somewhere you are not living.

The peculiar mode of integration enabled by Brussels is something that many underline. They identify with the city, feel "at home" – while knowing few Belgians. But they are also people who have made lives out of mobility and not putting down roots. At the same time, they often seek to avoid the obvious expat services and institutions. Caterina puts it nicely. She says, "I am integrated as much as I ever integrate." For her and for others in the mid-30s–40s age range, Brussels is the place where they can make sense of their self-consciously denationalized lives. Other longer-term residents in Brussels, such as Jonathan and Ellen, have made lasting connections in various ways with local life – for example, through involvement as parents in the schooling of their children – but stressed that this involvement had not especially led to making new Belgian acquaintances. Though they did have a few Belgian friends, their social world still revolved around people of other (various) nationalities. In measuring their "integration" here (which was otherwise high), it was irrelevant whether or not their friends were Belgian. They did not need this to have a full and richly social life. Brussels facilitates this kind of "structural integration" and allows residents to avoid the mistaken cultural idea of integration that lies behind national worries about this population and their "euro-ghettos". The trajectories of the oldest foreign residents in the city underline this. Those I interviewed (in particular Ingrid and Richard) were individuals who had totally settled in the country. Brussels was home, but they were never going to become Belgian. One might expect, after twenty or more years living in the city, that these would be the most integrated people. Yet it is in fact one of the remarkable qualities of Brussels that residents can live in this international city and never need attempt to integrate as a national of the country.

The problem with the Belgian integration discussion, then, is that it equates the functional integration of these individuals in the "society" they are part of – a modern, differentiated, increasingly virtual and deterritorialized entity – with ideas about integration dominated by the nation-centred idea of immigrant integration that prevails today within European nation-states. This is the idea that nation-state-societies can become more multicultural, and absorb to some extent a wide variety of "foreign" cultures, *only* if immigrants also "integrate" into the national culture. This idea is dubious at best for the Netherlands, France, or Britain where it predominates in official thinking. In Belgium, the idea simply does not work, even for non-European immigrants. It is peculiar and highly paradoxical that indigenous Belgians expect foreign non-European immigrants to become prototypically "Belgian" when in fact Belgians themselves – sharply divided between Flemish and Walloon cultures – are not even themselves "integrated" into a single national society. Since so much of the conflict in Belgium is about actors at different levels trying to claim their context or scale of politics as the preeminent one, the ambiguity of the Eurostars in the city, whose lives cut across these levels, is one that unsurprisingly sets off tensions.

One of the ironies of Brussels is that the space for the participation of foreign Europeans has emerged largely from their self-conscious avoidance of the often impenetrable and always unpleasant Francophone-Flemish tussles over the city and its surroundings.[11] When Dave, a businessman, first moved to Brussels, he lived in a Dutch area within a French-speaking commune. As he puts it, after taking one look at the kind of squabbles that dominate intra-Belgian relations, he thought it wiser not to take sides. He stuck to English. Caterina, from Italy, summarizes the situation well:

I feel the tension from the Flemish and Walloons. There is this sort of immolistic dimension [to it]. *You hear things like – if there's something wrong with someone – they'll say, "Oh, he's Flemish!" Stupid things like that. I know all these things, but I think everyone does after a while.*

Yet the reality is that the cross-national struggle in Belgium, particularly in the context of the region of Brussels, in fact can be as enabling as disabling of the European population there. It is one of the reasons that Brussels in a sense does not belong to anyone, and so has space for everyone. The smart route as a long-term resident strategically is to play off the sides against each other, make contacts on either side, as a neutral observer. There are many tragicomic aspects to the Belgian break-up from a Belgian point of view. But from a foreign European resident's perspective, it is this evolving, unfinished struggle which most creates the denationalized social spaces in which the Eurostars thrive. For some, particularly the Germans and British I interviewed, playing this game in context means identifying with the Flemish minority, who are typically younger and more progressive in their cultural tastes than both the native Walloons and the Flemish in Flanders. An example among my sample is Annelis and Marc, who returned there from Amsterdam. This is because they see themselves as a self-consciously multicultural vanguard in the city, who have chosen to live as a minority in the capital to escape the exclusionary ethnic politics of their home region. In a way, they too live as European foreigners in the city; and so the common allegiance is not surprising. Brussels – a uniquely multileveled, nested entity – allows these residents to combine at once a sense of living at all scales, as a route to urban freedom: the city as neighborhood, metropolis, region, community, as well as euro- and global city.[12] This is the "integration" that can be achieved there: the life perhaps of the true cosmopolitan, at home at all levels, all at once.

The New *Zinneke*

The fact is that some of the most hybrid and thus most typically *Bruxellois* people in the city are those European foreigners who have settled in Brussels and made it their home. They are the new *Zinneke*, even if not yet recognized as part of the underlying multicultural tapestry of the place by most Belgian residents. None of these people had attitudes about Brussels that correspond to the stereotypes.

Bent, a 50-year-old Danish management consultant – and Brussels landlord – has been in the city for 20 years. Surprising as it may seem, he rates the overall quality of life better in Brussels and Belgium than Denmark. He thinks Belgium has fewer rules, and he can no longer deal with the "Danish mentality", particularly on tax. Bent has for all practical purposes gone native. He shares the same Belgian frustrations as other citizens: the high taxation on business "independents", the inefficiency of the hyperfederalized system, the self-destructive politics, the unequal communities. But he also appreciates it as a place where he feels at home. Education and the health service are two things he points to as better in Belgium. He has long realized that this must be the place where his life works for him, that bit freer and easier. When I ask about any plans for leaving, he is adamant it will not be back to Denmark. They are thinking about the South for retirement, but he thinks they will always have a base in Brussels.

Despite certain common negative themes, the overwhelming opinion of European foreign residents towards Brussels as a city is positive. Towards Belgium, opinion is much more ambiguous. It is perceived very positively as a country that is underrated and perceived unfairly by those that do not know it. European residents are wonderful ambassadors for fine Belgian products abroad, such as its chocolate and beer, or its art and architecture. But it is also perceived as a country that is constantly shooting itself in the foot: with a political system riven by infighting, an economy whose basic wealth is being squandered, and an alarming ethnocultural political struggle over the future of the country that had led to the emergence of unpleasant nationalist politics. For them, Brussels incarnates the good things about Belgium; but it also defines itself as the contrary of many of the negative aspects of Belgian society outside. Ironically, this is the reverse mirror image of how most Belgians outside the capital perceive Brussels.

Saïd is another fine example of the new *Zinneke*, a quite unique character on the Brussels scene. Tall, wordy, and charming, he is from Marseilles: a Frenchman of North African origin, who works for an international charity organization. He eloquently summed up the unique sense of freedom he felt here. Providing you stay out of the way of the police, he said, there was an infinite amount of creative, unusual things going on in all the spaces left unoccupied in this porous capital city. None of the usual national pressures applied. In this, he says, Brussels is so different to Paris, where the weight of unavoidable "Frenchness" can be felt pervasively in every aspect of social and cultural life in the city, however "global" it became. Brussels also compared favourably in this respect to London, Amsterdam, and Stockholm, another city he knew well.

It's perhaps no surprise that native Belgians in Brussels don't really see or understand this quality of the place – or only see it in negative, threatening terms. I put some of these typical comments about Brussels from the Eurostars to Saskia, a Belgian who lives in London:

> *To me the international side of Brussels is completely foreign, because it's completely detached from the Belgian world … It's funny, their perception of Brussels is so different to mine. If I knew that side of it, I would probably like it a lot more than I like it as a Belgian.*

She should talk to Dario, the Italian architect. Of all my interviewees, he has perhaps the most articulate vision. It would surely help if Belgians were able to get to meet and talk to more Eurostars like him. There are many things that Belgians don't appreciate enough about their capital city.

An Architect's Tale

I would be hard pressed to find a better ideal type free mover than Dario. European Commission brochures could be written about him and his striking career move. He is an Italian architect who has done the impossible: made it as a successful freelance architect in the rather parochial Belgian architecture world. It is an inspiring story. Like many people, I'm vaguely envious of people who make a living as architects. My idea of the profession is a silly romanticized mix of Le Corbusier – rational-socialist urban planning creating the liveable communities of the future – and Ayn Rand's *The Fountainhead* – the rampant individualist dream of erecting monuments to power and freedom up in the sky. I don't elaborate on these rather embarrassing notions while we talk. We meet over a glass or two of *Jupiler* in one of the cafés on Place du Châtelain in Ixelles, itself a consummate example of "Eurogentrification" in the city. The interview takes place in a mix of English and French.

I'm an architect, from Milan. I'm 37. I came here ten years ago. I finished my studies in Italy, and I was already working as a lot of architects in Italy do – because while you are studying you are all the time working – so I had enough experience to go abroad. I already had my own office, with a few projects. I had the occasion to get a foreign research grant. My contacts proposed me to come to Brussels, where they had contacts. "It would be easier for me to make a research in a smaller town, and they don't have the foreign researchers in Brussels" – people in Milan told me this. My first intention was to go to Paris – as anyone can understand [laughs]. *I thought Paris for six months would be great. So I tried to go there, and it was very difficult to get access to the institutions or people. When I came here to meet people, I met a lot in a few days. They were very nice, enthusiastic to have someone coming from Italy to do the research.*

What was your image of the city?

I'd been here once before. I had a imagined it as a strange city, a place in movement, with a lot of problematic urban situations – that are still there. But it was interesting because it was easy to understand there were a lot of things to do [for an architect], *a lot of opportunities. Also I had here some friends, working for the European institutions or European offices, and they were enthusiastic. They said they had a very easy going and fun life, and the rhythm of the work wasn't hard. The price of the appartments and cost of living was very low, and there was a night life. It was very full of things. There is a another very important element. Brussels is in the middle of things geographically. It is very easy to move to Paris, to London, to Frankfurt, and to Amsterdam, naturally.*

I arrived here and already I knew 30 people [laughing]. *It's amazing. I think in Paris, no way. There was a sort of enthusiastic situation because everybody was there for a short time, so they wanted to live the experience to the full. I understood a lot, very fast. The particularity of life here, and I think the quality of life here. For instance, friendship, contact with people is very easy. When you go to a party, you don't have to be invited. Everybody is welcome, you just go. Coming from Italy, where there is a different attitude with social rules, it was very different and really fun.*

An Architect's Tale—cont'd

Were there other people like you here?

No. At that moment, I was quite unique in architecture here. Brussels, for most architects, it was not very interesting. There is no really modern or contemporary architecture, and people here are very conservative. They have a fear of new expression. Not in their way of life, but in terms of architecture and urbanism. I went to some offices, asking just to work part time to get some experience. It was a period in which all the agencies were looking for architects. It was very easy to find a job, I just had to choose which one.

Some friends in Italy asked him to write for an architectural magazine back home. While doing research for a piece on the restoration of old industrial era buildings, Dario had a chance meeting with some architects working on another project, restoring the house of the famous comics authors Schuiten and Peeters. Their comic *Brüssel* allegorizes the destruction wrought by developers on the postwar city. These architects were also teachers, and they invited him to do some teaching at the city's architectural school. This led to another job offer.

Yeah, everybody wanted to meet me. Because I was different, from a different culture, with a different attitude, a different way of seeing things. In Italy, when you are a young professional, you are not paid for teaching. You are just there for something for your CV [laughs]. So I ask them, "Do you pay me for this job?" They look at me, as if I was a strange person. "But it's normal, every job is paid!" I knew it was an important decision. It meant to cut off from Italy for a certain time. I didn't know for how long. I thought, "Why not, if I feel better staying here?" So I ask to a lot of friend in Italy, to my family, my professor, and everybody was enthusiastic. They told me, "Try it, it's a very nice opportunity. Why come back here to do what everybody else is doing already? That's not so interesting for you. You can make and find the way on your own this way." So I accepted.

One thing led to another. Dario picked up book contracts to write about classic art nouveau architect Victor Horta for an Italian publisher, then started collaborating with a Flemish colleague on another project about Belgian domestic architecture of the 1950s and 1960s, which led to a prize-winning exhibition and film. He also continued to work as an architect for an agency.

It was great, we created something from nothing. It is difficult, because people treat us like we are 15 years [old], like we are really young people. But it was a very good experience. It gave me the opportunity to meet a lot of people, architects, journalists. It offered me a kind of notoriety. It was a hard life, a lot of hours every day, but I was having a lot of fun. I do things in a very instinctive way. I don't plan the next year, it's not my character. With the agency I have a deal that I just do the projects I like. I'm working on a house in Switzerland currently. Architecture is a strange discipline, and people have a strange idea of what is to be an architect. But here in Belgium, there is the possibility to do what I'm doing. A lot of things: to write in newspapers, to be an architect, a teacher …

Belgium sits on a treasure that they don't know about, or don't want to know. They have a country, a proportion of people, internal production and activities, the geographical situation,

An Architect's Tale—cont'd

infrastructure, culture … Everything is here to give this country a very high position, if they only knew it. It's strange [all the negativity] *… I have often met Belgians who pose this question, "What are you doing here?", and I respond to it twelve, fifteen times a year. They have a story in mind* [that you are temporary, passing through], *and yet you've been here some time. After ten years, they still have this impression … But it's in this sense, that I find that Belgium is really lucky. On the fact that here* [in Brussels] *you are a foreigner, but it is not difficult. Finally, you can work, do things well. As long as you don't play the conqueror. You are not here to invade Belgium. I think not many people among the* [foreign] *Europeans are here as conquerors. They are here because they are working, because there is a demand. That gives a quality to the city, this place.*

How would you compare yourself to your peer group back home?

I don't think it would be like this in Italy. When I think about my colleagues in university, I wasn't the best student for sure. But when you retrace the line of my story, you see I had some opportunities, I created some myself, and I took them. [In Italy] *I saw some friends doing really hard work, trying hard to attain something. It was terrible for them. When I go to Milan, I see everyone living in the same way, with their homogenous ways of talking and thinking. It's very conventional, behavior like this and like that. I'm horrified, I don't want to live like that! I find Belgium is much more simple. I'm at ease with it.*

They were following the standard path?

Yeah. I have a nice social life here, because I can choose what I want to do. Now I have a lot of Belgian friends. I have strong relations with all my friends and family in Italy. I go five or six times a year in Milan … It's changing now that people are settling down. I'm not settled, I'm starting to feel the difference. It's not hard, but sometimes it becomes difficult. I had some stories with girls here, but I never finalized to a point to get married or have children. That's life. But I think that what is strange and amazing in Brussels is that I realize there is a lot of people living this kind of life, so it's not so heavy. You don't have the social pressure on you. You don't have this pressure that you have in Italy to sistemarsi [roughly, "to settle down and get a regular life"]. *I have some friends* [in Italy], *who got married, got children. It's like their life is over. They don't have projects, they don't have aims. For them I'm like a spaceman! This difference leads us to find each other very curious.*

Have you thought about moving on?

Yes, I thought about Spain, Portugal – also Argentina, although Argentina is a very weak country. When you arrive there, you have to choose: or you are rich or you are poor. There is no middle, and without a middle class, you just can't be a European. In a certain way, we are all middle class in Europe. Belgium is a country where you can have security, even if you don't have a very strong situation.

How would you make it work in these places?

It would be an experiment. I really don't plan. I prefer to be like I am. Creating opportunities, situations where they can happen. I try to see what is possible. I think it's a more fun way of living. I want to continue to do all the things I like to do, and if I can do it, I can survive. I'm not a very "global" or "new economy" guy, but in another way, I am very "new economy", very "global".

An Architect's Tale—cont'd

As an Italian, do you have a strong idea of home?

Well, I'm Jewish, so already my parents are not really Italian. My parents were born in Egypt, my mother was an Italian national. We don't have two generations that have stayed in the same country [laughs], *so I'm relaxed about that. I'm an Italian, I think of Italy as my country, really, but apart from that, I don't have any problem if tomorrow I go to France or Spain. Perhaps other Italians are more attached … Well, I see lots of Italians here who like very well the idea of continuing to live abroad. They like it. This feeling of being a foreigner. It gives them enthusiasm, energy. They want to discover things. You just feel better.*

Do you think of yourself as a migrant?

[Simply] *Yes … Not a nomad, but I am a migrant, certainly. Especially since I could migrate somewhere very quickly. I wouldn't have any practical problems, and I wouldn't have any problems in my head about moving. I see myself as 100 percent a migrant, totally.*

The majority of people I talk to don't recognize themselves with this word, even if they are having a "migrant" experience …

I think it's a psychological block. Once you've lived a certain number of years in a place, you have to pass this barrier and think of yourself as a migrant. Psychologically, there should be no problem going anywhere else, to continue to move around ["continue à tourner"]. *You won't be especially looking for some roots. Voilà. I'm going to stay here. Perhaps in the end, I'll find out that I do stay in Belgium. Have two children with a girl here, finally bring them up here. I don't know.*

5

Migration

The attractions of Amsterdam, London, and Brussels are manifold, and young, highly mobile Europeans can be found in significant numbers on their streets. Yet the aggregate figures for EU free movement keep saying that Europeans don't move (much). Why is this? Are the Eurostars I found really the exception to an immobile continent, or are they, rather, pioneers of something that is still to come? One strategy for answering this is to follow a textbook deductive approach to understand the reasoning behind their migration, and piece together the increasingly complex factors shaping individual mobility decisions. The premise of the European Commission is that increasing economic incentives to move (for professional and career reasons) should first lead "rational" middle class Europeans to move abroad. Starting off with a rather narrow, economist's idea of the calculation at stake in a migration decision, it is possible to then relax the assumptions associated with this model, and bring in other less rationalist considerations to account for the increasingly more nuanced inductive examples. The point of using rational actor theory as a starting point is heuristic. Following this theoretical logic will help generate a profile of who the ideal type European migrants are, what motivates them, how they vary, and why others – less ideally placed – might not have felt that the opportunities and benefits were sufficiently attractive to move. The logic goes from explaining why some people did move, towards why most people did not.

Prototypes

The most obviously rational of the European free movers in these terms are the young professionals from the South of Europe. Growing up in countries where advancement is seen to be blocked by hierarchical, nepotistic, or arbitrary career paths, they pursued an alternative route abroad. The decisions were individualistic, clearly calculated, and articulated in these terms. Issues to do with family, friends, or their preference for the Southern way of life were discounted against the benefits of a career move to a dynamic Northern city, particularly in terms of human capital enhancement. The decision is recounted in these terms, and the calculation is still ongoing. Most of them reckon on cashing in their move some day and going home.

These are the prototypes, the "heroes" of this study; the archetypal Eurostars. You know a free mover when you meet one. Maria, from Portugal, is 26. She works as an international law specialist for the bank ABN Amro. I meet her in her high rise place of work. Slightly built, impeccably smart, she is the model of the overachieving young executive in the outsized corporate office. Having studied law in Portugal, she quickly realized the frustrations she would have in pursuing a career there. Instead, she took the high road of master's studies in three different European countries – one of the many new Euro-inspired cross-national programs – before putting herself and her CV on the market age 24 to the applause of numerous blue chip corporations. ABN Amro gets the nod, a progressive, internationally minded company that is one of the biggest employers in Amsterdam. Her studies have been homologous to her lifestyle: she works in international law, dealing with the translating of deals from one national legal framework to another. Her boyfriend is from South America, and is also so multi-talented in international tax law that all employment barriers, visa restrictions, and racial prejudice simply melted in front of an all-conquering CV. This is how the international labour market is *supposed* to work.

Above all, Maria is crystal clear about her career plan, motivations, and the costs and benefits that have brought her there. She is thrilled with her career but misses Portugal deeply, especially the idyllic-sounding world of family and friends back home. But she is very focused on what she had to get away from in career terms. Above all, Portugal lacked in opportunities: there are too many law students, and it is riven by nepotistic practices. She rails about the irrationality of it.

I don't believe at this point that Portugal is as sophisticated as I would like it to be ... If I stayed in Portugal I would be a number, one more looking for a job.

Moving abroad means you stop being just a "number" and start being valued accurately (by the "market") for your own individual talents and achievements.

Very similar quotes could have been taken from numerous other interviews: with Donatella in London (Italian data analyst, see pp. 42–5), Anastasia (Greek telecommunications administrator) in Amsterdam, Federica (Italian social worker, see pp. 96–9) and Caterina (Italian, science project manager) in Brussels, Isabel (Spanish, economist) in London. It is no accident the prototypical rational free mover in Europe is in fact a young single woman from the South of Europe who moves north for career reasons. Imagine a Europe populated with Marias and Donatellas. Fearless, focused, overachieving, hypermobile. Imagine what the economy would look like as an aggregate of their productivity. Essentially, this is how the European Commission sees it. Perhaps because many of its own high flyers in the corridors of Brussels are rather like these women.

The bottom line for the Italians and Spanish I met in all three cities – shared equally by the young French women in London – was that they moved because of career frustration at home. Nicole, the website builder, summarizes this attitude:

> *The Latin countries are absolutely not flexible on the work market. You are just young, so your opinion doesn't count. They say you don't have any experience – even though you have! – and I was working crazy hours, and being paid peanuts, no rewards.*

Nicole points out how just getting away from Paris was enough to make the move justifiable: "the opportunities were in London". So, despite not knowing anyone, having no connections, and having thought first of other places like Amsterdam and Canada, she moved to London. Reasoning like the model rational migrant here, London *ceteris paribus* was the best destination.

The *ceteris paribus* reasoning works, as it should do, for the other cities. Susan, the personnel manager in Amsterdam, "took out great steps in her career ladder" going there, although she knew little about the place. Caterina in Brussels found advancement easy, although she didn't know much about the place to begin with. The argument in fact stands out most sharply for the foreign language student abroad – Helen, Janet, Ellen, Rachel – individuals who moved to make use of the languages they studied at university. This path is heavily gendered. Nearly all language students – a declining breed in England – are women, and all move abroad wherever they can to not lose what they have invested in their education.

Naturally, rational actor explanations work for men too. Pedro works as a broker in London. He comes from Galicia, a peripheral region in the Northwest of Spain. He hated his job and wanted to change completely. Raoul, a research scientist in Brussels, also left his "small village" in Northern Spain. His move to Brussels was typical of rational mobility within specific science fields. In science, more than any profession, you go where there is an international specialism, regardless of borders – in his case, aeronautical engineering. Also, although it helps, one doesn't have to come from the South of Europe to be a rational actor. Even a German can be one. For example, Franz in London, who also works in the finance sector. Rationality for him was to pursue distinction: to move in order to give his career greater value:

> *Why are people moving? My first move was from Frankfurt to Paris. I was looking for a job in Paris, because it would mean I'm not number 15,907 in Germany* [looking for a job as a banker] ... *I think I was quite unique* [in Frankfurt], *to say, listen I quit my job now, I take my little car and go away and see what I can do ...*

His wife, Carmen, who is Spanish and also working in banking, says that none of his friends and family "expected that that he would survive so long". The point here, as with Maria, is that if everybody moved like this it wouldn't have the same value. This adds a little wrinkle into the argument that moves are rationally interchangeable. Yes, anybody in that position could have made the move, but only a few do; and it's the fact it's *only* a few which makes the move a "rational" success. The low numbers of free movers might be critical to the attraction of free movement.[1]

A rational movement can also be initiated by an opportunity, arising at a particular moment, that coincides with a lack of other constraints. Alan, who is an entrepreneurial businessman, talks about himself as an almost accidental mover, although he now runs a successful transportation company near Amsterdam:

> *I always say I just came here for the weekend. It's fifteen years now! Over a weekend and a few beers I was offered a job, a salary, company car, an expense account, all that. It really wasn't that difficult to say yes ... After two years, I got bored, I was wondering what to do. A customer said, "Why don't you start your own company? You can have our account for starters." I had a friend who was English, in the computer software business, a salesman. He knew nothing about my trade. I knew nothing about starting a company. But we got together and started it.*

The possibility of accident and timing coming into the picture also brings in the factor of risk and personality. Relaxing the assumption that all actors are the same, some might be thought to be psychologically predisposed to movement. Jaime, the young Spanish graphic designer in London, is a good illustration. He came to London because he correctly perceived his career would get a head start there:

> *In Spain, at the university level, there are just the traditional careers. They are not very innovative. It's set in its ways, like France or Italy. You have to study law or*

engineering, much more traditional roles. Here they've got like twenty different design careers, so many options to choose from.

Jaime came with a friend – who had the same reasons – but it was something about his exceptionally open, risk-taking personality that made the difference. His friend went home. A special kind of mentality is needed, as Maria in Amsterdam points out:

> *Because families are very tight, people can't imagine to go away from the family for one year. I lost this thing of fear. For some young girl from Portugal, one year in Holland, they would think that they were losing their life or something, endless time. Now for me one year, it is reduced to almost nothing. I don't have any problems, moving around, I think.*

Speaking of the Dutch in London, and why the internationally mobile Dutch seem so distinct from those that stay at home, Jeroen the scientist thinks there is a selection bias at work:

> *The people who go … are fairly intelligent, sharp, they have more a adventurous attitude. That's what brings them … Obviously bankers are an exception to that!* [laughs]

Thus far, the accounts given do not deviate greatly from a typical rational actor model. The movers here have indeed reasoned as individuals, a first assumption that would be made; and they have been able to weigh up material, emotional, and other costs and benefits, as well as ordering them as preferences, a second key assumption. A third typical assumption – that the information they had to hand would be perfect – is not so clearly substantiated.[2] Many had fairly sketchy ideas about their destination and its consequences for their lives. Many apparently saw the move as a short-term "shot in the dark", rather than a long-term investment; and they were willing to take risks, different from most of their peers, in choosing to go abroad. Among younger migrants, this kind of low-cost "whatever happens" calculation appears to be a dominant reasoning.

Students

Education is the crucial vector for young migration of this kind. The impact of the EU's Erasmus/Socrates student mobility program has been enormous: 1.4 million students moved internationally between 1987 and 2005.[3] This in effect represents an *institutionalization* of this migration – the extension of opportunity structures, that would otherwise have to rely on individual initiatives. In setting up these schemes, the EU is proactively trying to alter the incentive structure faced by young Europeans, who will at least be able to "give it a go" for a year or two of their college education.

Among my interviewees, numerous got their first taste of going abroad through Erasmus/Socrates. This simple first mechanism can then lead to further migration, via a series of different paths: additional study, seeing new professional opportunities, getting a taste for difference or foreign countries, or, of course, romance. Nicole got her first taste of going abroad in Pontypridd, Wales, which was followed by an unhappy year in Paris. Stefan got his first taste of international architecture this way. Many people in his office had done international fellowships of one kind or another. Anastasia left Greece to go to Lille in France, and immediately fell in with a multinational group of Europeans, who sound an awful lot like the cast of the charming French film about Erasmus students, *L'Auberge Espagnole*. The students Europeanize themselves as they date each other in multiple dual national combinations. She then moved to the Netherlands with a Dutch boyfriend, while other friends moved on elsewhere. Valerio first came to Holland to study fine art. It gave him the idea of later mobility for work, putting in mind that he'd always like to come back after a nice, albeit short, first experience of the life and work here. Guillaume, similarly, went to Utrecht, tasting gay liberation for the first time.

When I went back to Strasbourg I had a nervous breakdown. Like half of my school actually, because they all went abroad and they realized how cool it was – especially those that went to England, Germany, America. They really felt the difference. I decided not to stay in France, and try another year in the Netherlands.

Claudia and Miguel, who are respectively Italian and Portuguese, and are now long-term settled in Brussels, managed to do all four paths cited above. Both came to do postgraduate studies at Louvain-la-Neuve for just one year. They met, did further studies there; then found work in IT and lobbying, respectively, in Brussels; then got married and bought a house. Brussels offered professional opportunities and a quality of living not necessarily attainable in the South.

The education channel to movement is not limited to the Erasmus/ Socrates program. Many other young Europeans have taken the bolder decision to simply do their degree abroad. All European universities are beginning to compete for undergraduate – and especially masters students – but Britain undoubtedly leads the way. As is well known, the British education system is now largely servicing Europe with vocational and academic degrees, MAs, MBAs, and so on. Europeans pay the same fees as domestic students, and find university admissions officers sympathetic to their sometimes difficult-to-compare home country qualifications. In London, the young Eurostars often find themselves outnumbering their British counterparts. Valérie completed a degree a couple of years back in IT and Finance at Westminster University:

> *Well, I thought I'm going to college in Britain, I'm going to meet English people ... No ... It was strange, the first people I met were an Italian girl, a Russian, Czech, Spanish, another from Algeria ... The English who were there were all Hindus, so among the* vrai vrai vrai *English there, was only two* de souche anglaise [of English roots] ...

Again, Southern Europeans are the typical example, but Germans and French also decide to do degrees in Britain, cashing in on the education time differential (three straight years, instead of five-plus at the time) as much as its allegedly world-class universities. In fact many "universities" in Britain are far from that: just former polytechnics and technical colleges with fancy prospectuses and websites. As Jaime says:

> *I was amazed. I thought, wow, do they really have so many careers? Or is it only a marketing trick to lure you there?*

Some of these same young Europeans go on to people PhD programs that might otherwise collapse due to the impossibility of recruiting comparably qualified British students. Anniken came from Norway to do a PhD at the LSE. Isabel, an economist in the British civil service, came from Galicia, Spain to do an Economics PhD at the University of Essex – on the mobility of labour, no less! Economics programs in Britain have a terrible time finding non-existent British economics postgraduates, so the programs are full of Southern Europeans, Turks, South Americans, Asians, and others.

Ironically, now, many departments in Britain find their best applicants for faculty positions from among European foreigners applying to Britain's famously open university system – a rare model of free movement practice in continental Europe's often stiflingly immobile academic world.

The only comparably specific choice to British MAs and PhDs that lead on to work in the City, as these mainly have, are those that opt to do specific "Euro" courses as a route towards working in European international organizations. The most famous is the Collège d'Europe in Bruges, a veritable finishing school for eurocrats. Ellen, who worked for years as a political consultant in Brussels, was an early British pioneer there in 1981. She was a *stagiaire* in the DG for Social Affairs, then went on to a private consultancy firm, then redundancy in 1996. Now she was combining some independent work with three children. This quite typical Brussels trajectory is echoed by many who have worked a way into the Euro-world orbiting the Commission and European institutions. The other famous European college, the European

University Institute in Florence, is meant to be exclusively academic, but there are numerous examples of PhDs there who instead opted to go into the European institutions using its networks. Others go on to fast-track careers in international banking and international organizations. Other universities are now trying to emulate these tempting career pathways. For example, the Vrije Universiteit Brussel (VUB), where Joannet, another political consultant in Brussels, left Groningen, in provincial Netherlands, to follow a Euro-law course.

Couples

In some of these examples, the individualistic, economistic core of the starting assumptions is beginning to blur. Romance and relationships are playing a role in decisions, alongside career factors.[4] It can be hard to disassociate factors, or pinpoint the locus of reasoning. Can the aspect of romance – or adventure – be quantified into the calculus of career benefits and long-term payoffs? Relaxing the economism of the rationale, other differentials may indeed come into play, although they may still be factors that migrants can rank or prioritize. Subjectively, it looks like something "beyond the rational" is providing the mechanism for the rest of the reasoning to fall into place. Objectively, Anastasia's decision to go to Amsterdam and stay there, against the wishes of her family, certainly still looks a rational European move. But the key mechanism that triggered everything was her Erasmus romance. They "splitted", as she says, but she had a job and (crucially) an appartment, so decided to stay. Falling out of love can also be the mechanism. Bernhard in Brussels equates his own past international moves, or lack of them, with the fluctuations of the relationship he had back home as a student in Germany. He wanted a career in the diplomatic service, but his girlfriend at the time "would never have joined him on that trip". Later, when they finished, the idea of international mobility came up again. As in *L'Auberge Espagnole*, the French hero of the film – played by the brilliant young actor Romain Duris – only begins to discover the romance of living abroad when things fall apart with the girlfriend back home. Ironically, in its international version, the film is packaged as if it stars Audrey Tatou (the heroine of the hit film *Amélie*), who plays the annoying stay-at-home French girlfriend in a very small cameo part. She is cruelly satirized as the uninitiated stayer, who has no access to the fun and sexy new world her boyfriend discovers in Barcelona with his Erasmus friends.

Nina in Amsterdam certainly also came with "rational" reasons, in her case prioritized by the conditions of work in the Netherlands and career opportunities. But the crucial mechanism here was the possibility of coordination with her boyfriend, also German, who was also in a good position to find work there. She didn't want to go back to Germany after a "liberating" stay as a law intern in San Francisco; and work in Germany for him would have meant work in the provinces. Amsterdam was a good compromise, "a place where we could both work, and a bit more cosmopolitan". Bent, the Dane in Brussels, is of a much older generation, a veteran migrant in the city. Yet he is also prototypical. From a family background in farming, in Jutland, he moved in the early 1980s as an engineer, as a "conscious decision" to "gain experience outside of Denmark", at a time when he was at the end of a contract. "It was just an opportunity that came up", he says. He married someone from Iceland, had children. Twenty years later, he is immersed in an international family life, with a second wife, who is Spanish, and children from both marriages. It is Brussels, as a coordination point and site of romance, that has made this possible.

It is possible to model the decisions of married life (or co-habitation) as a kind of rational coordination. In doing so, however, it relaxes the individualistic assumption of migrant reasoning. It is hard to doubt, for instance, that Claudia and Miguel weighed up the benefits of their choosing to study in Belgium, and then choosing to stay on and work in Brussels, rather than heading home. However, the crucial enabling factor was their joint decision to settle *there*, and not try Italy, Portugal, or somewhere else. Brussels provided the ideal career and personal coordination point for them – "neutral territory", as they put it – as well as providing the opportunities and quality of life. This "third country" reasoning is very typical of young couples of mixed nationality. It usually has both specific career and spatial aspects, in that both job opportunities and practical family arrangements – i.e. staying in touch with home, visiting families equally – are important issues. It also requires a distinctly international city, something that makes the situation rather different to similar coordination choices that young professional American couples routinely make. Brussels and London, especially, are seen this way. Isabel stayed in London with her Mexican boyfriend for these reasons. This is ironic given that they both speak the same language, and might reasonably choose to live in a Hispanic environment. Joannet gives one of the major reasons she lives in Brussels with her husband as "very personal", because she is "married to a British guy, and Belgium is a neutral territory". They can go home and complain to each other about the "weird" foreign things around them – and understand each other. This would be very different if one of them were in their home country.

The process of finding a third country can be quite systematic. Andreas, from Norway, and his Italian partner, took time and rational method (in this case, a kind of "pre-commitment", i.e. "tying yourself to the mast") to find the right place in Europe. Like Stefan, Jeroen, Caterina, and Saskia, they were self-declared "Europeans" moving back into international jobs after a short experience of work in the US, in their case, Washington, DC. They subsequently got married in Brussels, and have moved on mentally from a short stay to something longer.

We decided on a couple of cities … We say, "OK, we try only there." We go together. We made a rule: the first to find something they really wanted, then we would go there. We decided beforehand to avoid disputes, and I was the first one to get something.

Brussels turned out to be the right move, for two reasons. First, neither of them were handicapped linguistically. And second, it is equidistant between their home cities, and extremely well connected to both. London or Scandinavia were possibilities, but they now appreciate that Brussels was a better compromise. What starts out "merely" as a rational coordination about location begins here to take on meaning in a specific "place", as Andreas and his wife become prototypical, denationalized Eurostars in the classic political Eurocity. It becomes hard to see how the couple – who speak English with each other and have careers in the orbit of European institutions – could live anywhere else.

The City in London becomes a similar sort of environment for European couples working in finance and insurance. When Franz, the German banker from Frankfurt, met Carmen, from Spain, in Paris, it was love at first sight. They get to London, via Paris, then Madrid, and nearly Frankfurt.[5] "First I moved for the job, then the job moved me", he says. They were engaged, and the bank offered him Asia or Spain. He wanted to learn Spanish, so this choice was obvious, "a personal and professional move, combined, a lucky move". But then, with the euro coming up, the bank no longer wanted people in every country, and because he was German, asked to move him to Frankfurt. This could be good for Carmen, they thought, and it was all planned and decided. Carmen picks up the story:

Carmen: *When Franz came to Spain, he immediately got used to everything. Before that he couldn't say a word in Spanish.*

Adrian: *That was a major investment.*

Carmen: *A major risk! Big one. Then, when they offered him a position in Frankfurt, that was a big risk for me. I said, "OK let's try that." We did the whole moving company and everything. We were supposed to take the plane to Frankfurt, but then Franz was called to London for a meeting. He came back and said he'd been offered another position in London, and we have to choose. I was frozen, of course. London is better for me because of English, because of the City, professional opportunities. But on the other hand, I had been preparing myself for months to go to Frankfurt. The furniture was already on its way! We had to make the decision in 24 hours that was going to change our whole life … Professionally, it has been fantastic for me.*

This step-by-step reasoning, following a complicated path, in which the personal and professional decisions are interwoven, yet still slightly fatalistic, is echoed by many of the couples. The international Eurocity at least provides a good enough endpoint to tie up the loose ends of personal narrative in one single convincing destination. Where things get a little more complicated is when children too are involved in the situation. The third-city option can work for couples with children, but it requires a peculiar scenario.

Anniken came from Norway to do her PhD, and her French husband Dominic is employed at the London Stock Exchange. London works for them, not only professionally and because they like it, but also because Anniken has a rather jaundiced view that socialization as a French boy might have on her son, if they were to do the obvious thing and move to France to make the linguistic situation easier. As it happens, as for Andreas, Norway is now very distant in her mind. Our conversation is repeatedly disrupted by the little four-year-old, Matteo, shouting in the microphone.

> Anniken: *We have a very intelligent son who speaks Norwegian to me, French to his Dad, English to everyone else, although obviously, he has created a vocabulary for himself in Norwegian. He understands whatever language you talk to him. It would be easier for me not to be responsible for [his] English, but I would be more responsible for his happiness if I dragged him to Norway.*
>
> Adrian: *Is the attraction of London because it is a "third" city, a "neutral" place …?*
>
> Anniken: *We are home [here] for a bit, then we'll see. For me this has always been an issue, between France and Norway. If we were in France, I would have to go on nagging about the French all the time. For me it is important, if we had to move back to Paris, that he has lived a couple of years abroad and that he understands what it is to be a foreigner. I think I would have problems being the mother of a Frenchman! If we were there, it would be even more important to stress the Norwegian side of living.*
>
> Adrian: *Why's that less important here?*
>
> Anniken: *The only Paris I know, is one of Frenchmen … You are just a Frenchman's wife [there]. You are supposed to know the culture, the language. I was always disadvantaged.*

In France, the home of one of the parents, paradoxically, Anniken would end up perhaps more of a typical expat wife. She would have to "naturalize" herself, and yet stress more about being Norwegian to her son. The family would be less international, and the domestic balance would change. The situation in London works for Anniken and Dominic because there are, remarkably, quite a few couples like them living there.

We met them through babies. Yeah, we are definitely in an environment where loads of people are like us, mixed couples.

Another version of the third country rationale is the quite common pattern of couples from the same country who decided to go somewhere as a change, or escape from where they come from. Nina and her boyfriend in Amsterdam are a German version of this, but it is most striking among Europhile British couples, who opt out of Britain in search of a more cosmopolitan, continental life. Again, this is often linked to language studies. Rachel and Rob followed this route when, after university in Manchester, they threw everything in a car and headed to Brussels. They knew people there who could help them, and it was a feasible place for Rob to find work as an English speaker. He was able to temp for companies like Proctor and Gamble, before landing a job in logistics, "a million miles apart from what he'd been doing". I ask if they knew a lot of people who just moved like that, on spec.

Rachel: *I don't know. We did it a stage when we had nothing to lose anyway, we'd just graduated. We had no long-term plan, no jobs to give up, no woe if it all went wrong … We gave ourselves a three month time limit. If it doesn't work out we'll just go back.*

Rob: *There was no mortgage to pay … I think there was also a decision, if we don't do it now, it's now or never, so we just took the plunge, and did it. But it's not as daunting, looking back. Some people said "Whoa! It was really brave", and all that, but it wasn't any more drastic than going down to London.*

This is ideal type free movement, opting for the international European move as an alternative to the standard provincial move to the national centre. Jonathan and Ellen are another good example. Brussels is the place where "their paths met". Both they and Rob and Rachel come from fairly average middle-class backgrounds, and all consider that their career development and quality of living in Brussels has been much higher than it would have been in London.

Spouses

The happy image of these couples coordinating might be thought to mask other pervasive social inequalities in gender relations, that typically play out in terms of career development – the frustrated choices when spouses are put in the disadvantaged "following" position. Much of the literature on married couples and mobility in professional life – especially the work on global expatriates – does indeed suggest this. Spouses might "choose" to follow their partners, and feel they are completely liberated from the usual discrimination in society, but their apparent agency is locked into a structured set of constrained options further down the road that produces the same result (i.e. life as a housewife) as if their choices had been deliberately restricted. More practically speaking, there is a massive human resources industry centred on managing the downsides of the following spousal situation.

Alain Verstandig, a consultant who specializes in just this issue in Brussels, points out to me psychological research that shows how the experience of the move diverges rapidly for the career mover and the spouse once they arrive in the new home. They may start out equally happy, but the spouse, who has none of the work place contact that the worker has, or who is forced to spend time looking for a job (after often having given one up), will find their morale going sharply down. Large corporations and personnel managers are desperate to manage the professional fallout from this situation for the employee well before it happens – and hence call in consultants like Verstandig.[6]

Spouses in this situation are usually women. But among the moving couples I met, just as many were men, and all appeared to have bucked the negative trend suggested by the expat literature. In fact, on the contrary, although their own choices had clearly followed those of their partner, they had used the freedom of not being the principle breadwinner to actually take time out and develop their own new career path. David in Amsterdam (see above, pp. 11–14) is a perfect example. Siofra, from the west coast of Ireland, would have been happy to stay there in the burgeoning start-up environment of a booming, tigerish Ireland, but when her husband got an academic job in England, she was able to shop around in London for a high-flying job in management in the pharmaceutical sector. She is confident that the moved enlarged her own opportunities dramatically, although she did have regrets at the time.

Clearly, it all depends on the scenario. Gunther (below, pp. 216–19) and Carmen in London had made it work very well for them. Another older migrant to London, Sandra, a Luxemburgher married to a German City banker, spoke very positively about her life and work as an artist in the city. Again, following here was in fact an advantage in terms of the lifestyle and opportunities it offered. Susan, the personnel manager, moved on spec to Amsterdam, when she met a new boyfriend in Bristol. She had just been made redundant, and thought she "might as well do something". She says the only Dutch she knew were the ones "you pitch your tent next to on holiday in the South of France". Annelis, like Susan, had only just met Marc in Bruges, when he was leaving for a PhD in the Netherlands. "We knew each other for one year. I was like 'If I don't follow it's over!'" She convinced her Dutch fashion retail employers – with shops all over the Benelux – that they might find a position for her in one of their Dutch shops. After a few months, she moved to work in Amsterdam, then Utrecht. At the end of his research, the situation was reversed. Annelis's designer employer asked her to manage a new shop in Brussels. This led to Marc establishing a new career in Belgium and the Brussels academic world. Now they have a house and children there, part of the vanguard of young open-minded Flemish retaking the city. Sometimes, the creativity and flexibility demanded of a couple trying to coordinate international career moves can lead to new opportunities turning up – or being created.

Networks and Systems

Rational actor assumptions about migration start out assuming individualism but, as can be followed, relaxing this assumption can still lead to rational accounts of how couples coordinate destinations, reconciling romance with career development. Pushing this further, it should be considered how such choices are embedded in wider relationships: with friends or family, or with social networks facilitating migration decisions. Rational choice would typically entail evaluating all possible destinations in relation to sending conditions: the assumption that apart from the key differential identifying opportunities as higher in one place or another, *ceteris paribus* the mover is indifferent about which. However, this neglects the possibility that there might be established patterns between particular places: for example, a cultural or historical "special relationship" that would facilitate more migration between the two places. Individual choices can thus be structured by a more systematic aggregate pattern.

This view of migration is one of movement governed by specific "migration systems": patterns reproduced by networks of individuals, that lead to trends of a more noticeable scale between two places. Such patterns are often institutionalized when states begin to politically or legally shape them. A protean migration system is the one developing between France and England. As a particular economic scenario endures – differentials in employment rates, which create stable job opportunities for young French to move to Britain – young pioneers establish the first connections. Entrepreneurs may step in to further encourage or capitalize on this movement (i.e. business consultants, relocation agencies, language schools); the media may begin to take notice (there has been much press in France about it); and there may even be an element of policy encouraging it (exchange programs, or para-public links). The end result is a sharp spike in numbers between these two locations, even if the differentials here are in fact less marked than those between other possible sending and receiving countries.

Migration systems also typically reduce the costs of mobility by giving individual movers access to the experiences of others, and social networks that encourage their movement by reducing transaction costs – put simply, helping you to find a job, a place to stay, and friends when you arrive. One of the most interesting migration systems within Europe is that of recent Irish migration.[7] The classic pattern, of course, is Irish migration to London. Siofra, who followed her academic husband to London, might stand in as an example of this.

> *I grew up in the Northwest, along with my husband. Very rural, a big emigration blackspot. You had to have qualifications to get a job. There was very high unemployment. I was sent to boarding school, then college and a degree at the National Institute of Higher Education, Dublin – an MIT sort of equivalent. Employment was the driving force in your choices. It was a biotech degree. It was new, interesting, the only place that did it.*

These rational education choices, following highly innovative vocational training – which Ireland has become famous for – set up a range of possible moves. I ask her what the big difference is between those that go abroad and those that stay, all other things being equal. A long pause.

> *Well, there might be a sense that they are more insular, that they are focused more on Irish issues, local issues, a bit more parochial. It's just about the environment you're in. London is more global. The other thing is, Catholicism is still such a big force in Irish life generally. It is an ingrained part of your family life. That can be a bit oppressive.*

She offers the legal profession in Ireland as an example of the parochialism.

Two things have happened to change Irish migration in Europe. One is a substantial return migration, that has followed the high-tech and finance boom in Ireland. The other has been a marked shift in the destination of Irish migration to continental Europe.[8] Ray, the independent businessman settled in Amsterdam, picks up the story:

> *The Irish went back when the economy came back in Ireland. Those that were working in construction, they went back. There's not too many of them left [here]. The people I know now among the English speakers here came to work in creative businesses, IT, advertising, banks, law firms. There's not so many barmen, waitresses, etc. There used to be Irish taking any kind of job. Now I find the people who are still here, have moved up the ladder, made some progress. The economy is going well in Ireland, so they just headed back. My generation [he is 40] was the last that considered that it had to emigrate. I think they waited until I'd left, and then said, "OK. Now we can deal with this economy. Get the money in from Europe!" [laughs]*

Amsterdam, Paris, and Brussels have now become big magnets for the educated. London has become less popular, partly because Ireland has come to see itself and its recent progress as part of the European project. It opted in to the euro, and has finally begun to sever ties and drift away from the old colonial British mooring. The young Irish are the conduit for this new, emerging social structure.

> *London was always easy because of the language. Also, the "island mentality",*
> *whatever. But now why go to London, when you can go to Barcelona or Madrid*
> *or Paris – there's a lot of Irish going to Paris – or Amsterdam, or Brussels, even*
> *more so than Amsterdam, perhaps? Yeah, London used to be first option. It was*
> *close to home, you jump on the plane, 45 minutes. Now it's not.*

I think about another Irish friend who moved to Italy some years ago. She had many stories about being hassled by anti-terrorist security every time she flew through Heathrow on the way home. Irish culture, on the other hand, is unequivocally adored and lapped up in continental Europe. Irish pubs have opened everywhere: even in the smallest provincial towns in Germany and Italy. Ironically, this mass produced and somewhat cheesy national self-representation – what Ray sarcastically refers to as "paddyish" – has become a universally effective social lubricant for Eurolife. There is "no way" Ray will be going back.

> *Ireland is kind of divided up between the people who can't wait to get out and the*
> *people who wonder why they're leaving.*

His family offers the typical Irish migrant scenario of an older era. Ray laughs dryly when he quips that they "have no choice" about siblings travelling all over the world. The experience of Michael, a marketing specialist in the Netherlands, even suggests that America may not even be what it was for the Irish. He very consciously turned down a green card he won in the lottery, identifying his determination to move abroad instead within an integrating and expanding Europe, that would keep him closer to home but widen his cultural and linguistic abilities. He ended up marrying a Dutch woman – a physiotherapist, of which there was a great demand in Ireland – and they moved back with the wave to his booming native isle.

Sinead and Tom are also typical of some of the younger Irish moving to Brussels, Paris, or Amsterdam. He comes from Dublin, with parents working in the public sector. Sinead's family are rural, a farming background. Brussels was a good coordination point for a move abroad. Tom had done some postgraduate studies in European integration and wanted to work politically in that field. Sinead saw it was a good destination for work in IT, after a postgrad degree in software localization. Tom already knew ten people in the city. The Irish seem to be particularly effective with this kind of network.

To the outsider it would look like a very casual system, but there certainly was in our case an older generation looking after people who are coming over and starting over. Doors are certainly open. From experience and from the way other nationalities behave, there is an [advantageous] *element here of "being English speaking but not of UK origin". Part of that is based on the perceived pro-European perspective of the Irish.*

Sinead established work through a different kind of network. Her highly specialized postgrad qualification turned out to be very sellable in all kinds of international locations.

I went to work at a Belgian company had nothing to do with the EU institutions. At the company I went to I was the first Irish person to go there. They have since hired other Irish people.

Sinead in fact became the entrance point for a new Irish network. She had studied on the first course on software localization, and she was the first to come to Brussels. She transmitted news of opportunities back to her friends still on this course and others at her home university in Cork.

In these and other ways their combined networks have facilitated life in the city. Getting housing, meeting new friends, hearing about new opportunities. Much of this passes through the network, word-of-mouth, which exists to smooth over the otherwise treacherous first arrival in the foreign city. Buses that arrive from Ryan Air's "Brussels" hub at Charleroi, in fact pull up in front of *The Wild Geese* pub in Schuman, a famous generic Irish pub that one friend refers affectionately to as "The Landing Strip". It's a place for *stagiaires* to pick up each other on a packed Thursday night; a place to (sometimes) catch former EU commissioner Neil Kinnock holding forth over a pint with "the youth of Europe"; and, anytime, a place where new arrivers can ask the barman about a job or somewhere to stay. It works. The Irish in Europe provide a good illustration of how to make European integration "from below" a functional reality.

An Estate Agent's Tale

The Eurostars of today owe their ease of mobility to the earlier pioneers of European integration who first began moving in earlier decades. Their stories are not so different, just all the more remarkable. To balance the bias in my sample towards the young movers of the present, I seek out some older

An Estate Agent's Tale—cont'd

Eurostars, some who might remember the Europe of an era before I was born. Such as London, already a Eurocity in the swinging sixties. The search takes me out into the less central zones of the city, out into the quiet suburban spread of North London. A ground floor flat, with a pretty garden. Giulia is ready for me, laughing, with an open bottle of wine. She is divorced, nearly 60, and makes her living as an independent estate agent. But that's not what we talk about. She is in the mood for reminiscing.

How did you first come to London?

I was very young, and I fell in love. It wasn't much of a decision when you fall in love. London at the time seemed the trendiest city in Europe – or the world – in 1966. I couldn't imagine any other place to go. I came from a small village in Sicily, and lived there until I was 13. From 13 to 18, my parents moved, I lived in New York. A big chunk of my growing up. Then my brother moved to Milan to study architecture. I'd fallen in love with an Italian from Treviso, when I was 16. So I crossed the Atlantic in the summer holidays, he was 24 and I was 16. That was it! As soon as I finished high school, I moved to be with my future fiancé. My "future husband" [laughs]… I went to see him again and … I didn't like him! But although I left Dino, I decided to stay in Milan, with the intention I was maybe going to enrol at the university there.

I lived with the foreigners in Milan. English, South African, American girls. One girl there is still my best friend, after more than 35 years. I spoke Italian, but Milan wasn't quite home. The Italians who were local stayed there. If you came from Milan, you very rarely moved away. If you came from other parts of Italy, then you had to move. Italians were great immigrants, but it was only those from poorer parts. Those from the richer Northern cities didn't move, except from Veneto, which was the poorest region [in the North]. If you look at American Italians, if they are from the North they are from Veneto, otherwise they are from Rome or the South.

I found a job with the American telecom or something – they needed an English-speaking girl, in those days it was much harder to find one. There was an English girl there, who knew this [English guy] Nigel, who was coming to Milan. I met him, and my life changed completely. I had no real idea about British culture. The only thing I knew was that London was funny [fun], and cold in winter.

London was amazing, but she still suffered the culture shock that many feel today.

It was an exciting time for lots of things, especially for a young girl. I knew about the music and that it was supposed to be swinging. You read about it, one saw films, it seemed like a great place to go. The Beatles, and those James Bond films, they were coming out. And the fashion industry – the girls were all wearing Mary Quant mini skirts. So anyway … when I came before I married to meet my future family, and also to see [the place], I did have a bit of a culture shock. My English wasn't like the English, I found it very tough to understand people. I was fluent from the USA, but people spoke different with various accents and a way of speaking. The other was the food, which plays a rather important part

An Estate Agent's Tale—cont'd

in our lives [as Italians]. *You couldn't get a decent sandwich. Awful. I'd never drunk tea with milk before. The coffee was disgusting, like cough medicine. They used to make it with this liquid stuff. This is before your time* [laughs]. *Things have changed now.*

Reality perhaps didn't always match the image that London had.

The other shocking thing was fashion. People dressed so badly. I couldn't believe the way women dressed after Milan, or even New York. I mean average women [not fashion stars]. *It was freezing cold and they had no tights on. Girls with bare sandals in the winter! As soon as there is a bit of sun, even winter, even now, people start wearing shorts! Then the most fascinating, intriguing people would talk about the weather all the time! Well, these are all trivial things, you can take it or leave it. What I found more serious, more shocking, was the class structure and the education system – "public" schools that turn out to be private! That has taken me a long time to grasp all that. It took me a long time to accept it.*

Perhaps what is remarkable, in fact, is how little things have changed in this experience, including all the same complaints. Mobility of young people was a central part of the 1960s in London: foreign European nationals were part of what made it a swinging destination, along with all the other young provincials heading to the city. Were all your friends here in those days other European foreigners?

Absolutely. There were different types than they would be today. Italians, Swedes … All my friends in fact were girls like me, with very English guys who had happened to move to London. I didn't have one English friend in London, except for Nigel's friends, who we slowly didn't have much in common with. Most of the friends we made were foreign. But they were integrated. They just got married like me. Or trying to find work, learning English. Some of the time you were not being accepted, but you were there and you were married … I think if I had to go to Brussels, I would not be able to integrate in the Belgian bourgeoisie. That goes for Paris too. London is much better for foreigners, even in those days it was much easier to integrate.

So she got married to Nigel, moved into a tiny Bayswater flat, lived the life. The story then begins to sound like the Beatles' *She's Leaving Home* – in reverse.

Nigel was public school. His family were conservative and I was an Italian communist. So there was a huge difference! I encouraged him to become left wing [laughs] *and in some ways he did. The family lived in Surrey, in the suburbs. The father was an insurance broker, the classic English family. His sister went to a nice day private school, he went to prep school aged 8. They were very narrow for me … We got burgled, and moved to his parents' house, and I thought I was going to die. That really was an experience that I'll never recover from. English family life, oh my God! My mother-in-law had her coffee morning, and my father-in-law played golf and bridge …*

To the anger of his parents, Giulia was making plans for her husband.

Nigel went to university after he married me. He was working in the City as an insurance broker like his father. The contrast was amazing. It was his father who arranged that

An Estate Agent's Tale—cont'd

he went to work for an insurance company in Milan to improve his Italian. One thing about his father was he didn't think it was necessary to go to university. He had his public school tie, you wore your tie, you got a job there. You were part of the old boys' network ... His parents were very upset when he was going to university. And Essex University, when he could have gone to Cambridge! But not for the social sciences. Essex offered economics, politics, and sociology. It was so much more political there ...

So they moved on to another iconic location of the 1960s: Wivenhoe, the picturesque village in Constable country, an artists' and intellectuals' refuge. Although they never integrated there, it was another classic place to live out the sixties. Giulia's stories blend into several other academics' lives that I know from that period. It's another world to me, bohemian and radical in a way academia today most definitely is not. Before my time indeed.

Wivenhoe! That's a very different kind of England from London. I loved to cook, but I couldn't even find a green pepper or aubergine. I had to go up to London to buy it. But you were still not part of the society, not really part of it, at home. You had to rely on being married. For the one or two foreign friends who were not married it was harder for them to get through to be part of the English culture. I'm one of the few that have a proper English family. Not my blood family, of course, but they are like a blood family. They are really English, but London is not a place were you meet many English.

So inevitably, Giulia gravitated back to London. Her husband moved abroad. Her daughters went to an expensive private school.

The girls went to a convent school because it's a bit cheaper [laughs]. *Yes, all of a sudden they became Catholic!* [raucous laughter]. *Funny, there were even Jewish kids at this convent. Half of the kids has one of the parents who is foreign, if not European then Lebanese or something. When I meet up with the parents years later, and ask what are they* [the kids] *are doing now. Not very much! You remember how we struggled to have to pay the school fees. What for!? It wasn't always worth it* [laughs again].

But her daughters did turn into successful cosmopolitans, with multiple passports, fluid identities, and Italian boyfriends. They now work in the fashion and media industries in Milan, and her former husband also lives in Italy. The EU certainly made a difference for them.

Yes, it's easier to work in these places. The fashion industry in Milan for instance. The majority of them [designers] *are English kids who graduate from St. Martin's with English degrees. They take them young and they train them. Armani alone employs 600 people. I think probably 250 of them are English. They wouldn't have been able to get work in Milan before. All their friends there are Londoners, English designers for fashion houses. I think the integration is easier because the work permit is possible now. There's more communication in general since the common market. I think the kids, they don't see the difference between one country and another. It was so much more dramatic for me, even though compared to a lot of people my age, who haven't been abroad ever, I'm different. I crossed the Atlantic five times, and in those days you travelled by boat.*

An Estate Agent's Tale—cont'd

But in the end London is where she stayed. After all these travels, I ask her how she thinks of herself.

Primarily I think of myself as Italian. You can't get away from that.

Do you think of yourself as a Londoner?

That's a good question [more laughter]. *I definitely see myself as more of a Londoner than an English person from Colchester … Yes, I identify with London.*

6

Mobility (1)

The most obvious question sociologists would ask of the new European migration is to check the social background of movers and ask how their spatial mobility might be changing settled patterns of social mobility in the continent. Europeans are not necessarily interchangeable rational actors. All European citizens are free to move, but some are surely more free than others. Free movement of this kind might systematically correlate to being born lucky: into upper-tier class positions, endowed with family privileges that furnish the would-be mover with social and cultural capital facilitating mobility. The further suspicion is that there is nothing particularly European about all this. That we are talking here about a subset of the globally mobile: elites in their flat world without borders, hopping between global cities in a protected, golden space of flows, while the disenfranchised and disadvantaged masses remain trapped in their local, parochial environs, excluded from the world party.

Movin' On Up

The history of spatial mobility in Europe has in fact been intimately linked with the ambitions of the socially mobile, and therefore those ranked *lower* on the social scale. If you were a part of the ruling bourgeois elite in one of the rich European urban city-states – the "burghers" of say, Florence, in the time of the Medici – why would you ever move? For sure, you might travel around on the grand tour, to get a taste of the intellectual and cultural fruits of a diverse continent, but you knew where your heart and spirit lay: in your hometown. This has not necessarily changed. Only in a more redistributive, democratic Europe, the feeling of already living in the best possible place – the place you come from – is quite likely to be widespread across much of society, North and South – at least in those places which have the public wealth and cultural depth of a long regional patronage. When I was first driven up by *motorino* to the hilltop in Fiesole by a bunch of heavily accented working class Florentine *ragazzi*, the only thing they said to me while motioning to the panorama of the city below, was: "Adriano, guardi ... Il paradiso." These guys were not going to be migrating anywhere in their lifetime.

Historically, these young Italians might well have had to consider migration as a key life option. The history of European movement is one of various stages and types of movement that have propelled Europeans across regions, borders, and oceans in search of a better life. There is a long history of two types of migration in Europe that are not elite based. The extension of such opportunities down through society to ever broader swathes of the middle and lower classes is, in fact, a "massification" typical of European modernity. One, of course, is worker migration, from the country to the cities. Industrialization put factories and terraced houses in the cities, smog in the air, and workers on trains and buses. Karl Polanyi's famous description is a good reminder of what mobility used to be all about:

> *An economic earthquake which transformed within half a century vast masses of the inhabitants of the countryside from settled folk into shiftless migrants.*[1]

The phenomenal movements of the nineteenth century were internal as much as international within Europe, but they changed the social structure of the continent for ever. Cities grew exponentially, the extended family structures and close-knit communities of rural village life were ripped asunder forever. The large-scale South-to-North guest worker migrations of the 1950s and 1960s were the last big-scale manifestation of this kind of migration on the continent. A kind of migration that left – to give a poignant example of a place I have seen first hand – empty ghost villages in the hillsides around Parma, Italy, and ice cream parlours called "Contis ices" in the streets of South Wales mining towns.

A second form of European migration, however, was of a more upwardly mobile, "white collar" nature. The sons (and later daughters) of school teachers, clergy, and minor bourgeoisie would often equally set off from the peripheries in search of fame and fortune, adventure and romance, in the more metropolitan centres. These movements were driven by a paucity of work in the rural areas, and developing educational channels which were increasingly efficient in siphoning off the more talented into administrative, bureaucratic, and clerical work in the cities. It was also driven by the marriage market, and an often desperate lack of suitable boys and girls among the farmhands and milkmaids back in the village. In the fluid mid-to-late nineteenth century much of this regional movement crossed notional international borders in the economically interwoven central regions of the continent. Much of it could be temporary and circular, insofar as some of the work was seasonal. As a life option, mobility increasingly became a norm not an exception, as the industrialization of the continent proceeded apace. New train, road, and canal networks facilitated unprecedented mobility. And colonial empires and the new frontiers out west led to this regional migration stream bleeding into a developing global river of migrations around the world, to North and South America, and later East Asia, the Middle East, Africa, and Australasia.

The underappreciated part of this story was the relatively late development of the European nation-state as an effective container and political-legal regulator of these regional population movements. Passports and effective border controls only appear in the latter years of the nineteenth century as effective forms of population control. Emerging nation-states thus sought to contain the fruits of all this mobility, and hence monopolize its benefits, while controlling its unwanted dimensions. In particular, the notion of citizenship developed as states sought to build mass armies, moving more workers off the land. Education too was universalized to better harness mobile talents. Peasants were turned into Frenchmen, and by the same process regionally minded men and women from farms – or their children – were turned into nationalistically minded educators and bureaucrats. And to hold this all together, nation-states developed welfare institutions, to pastorally care for and manage the lives of their citizens from cradle to grave – particularly the women and children left behind by mobile fathers – giving them a passport and national identity in return for a lifetime's members' loyalty.

The citizenship offered by national welfare states was all about systematizing and patterning these processes. It offered what came to be known as social security over the life course – hence stable payoffs for the individual investments that one might make following a certain education, or choosing a certain vocation – as well as a safety net against the risks involved. These benefits were mobile within the bounds of the country, but never transferable outside. The nation-state model was institutionalized across all of Europe, varying only in time and speed of the process. Different kinds of internal systems developed in regionalized countries such as Germany and Italy, compared to centralized metropolitan nations like England and France. Some countries that have later gone on to epitomize the pastoral welfare state – such as Denmark or the Netherlands – didn't follow the same industrialization pattern as others. But all, in some shape or form, developed a pastoral notion of national citizenship – bounded and rooted in the idea of the territorial nation, with a distinctive language and culture – and centred on the idea of a welfare state.

Mobility and migration in Europe continued to cut sharply across this emerging container-based version of European nationhood throughout the nineteenth century. The international dimension of European mobility collapsed entirely with the world wars of the twentieth century, although mobility had already solidified before this. Internal regional migration remained a feature to some extent of European nations, but even this declined as the twentieth century wore on, as economic differentials between and within nation-states evened out. In the postwar era, Europe instead turned to immigration from outside. Southern European guest worker migration gave way to immigration from North Africa, Turkey, and former colonies, and when this stopped, at the end of *les trentes glorieueses* in the 1970s, intra-European migration fell to an unprecedented low. An image was cemented that somehow "Europeans don't move" – that they are predisposed not to for "cultural" reasons, or because they have "roots" that Americans don't have.

One rare counter-current to this solidifying immobility – prior to the possible emergence of significant cross-border movements in an integrating EU – was the emergent baby boom mobility inside countries during the fast-moving 1950s and 1960s. The new younger generations of these decades grew up into social environments that took care of much of the needs of life, with state benefits standing behind their increasingly affluent families. This affluence and security could potentially root all social classes as comfortably as the richer "burgher" populations of Europe's cities. However, the growing number of bright, ambitious, socially mobile working-class and lower-middle-class children, educated in expansive state schools and new universities, led to a bottleneck in opportunities, and a frustration with the limited local options on offer. The "angry young men" in the Britain of the 1950s, for example – who were typically provincial-origin, hungry for success, and not finding outlets for their education in their regions – were a new kind of restless mover turning to mobility.

These were the "social spiralists". Social mobility was blocked at home, in a self-limiting world where you worked hard, did what you were told, learned your trade, and got a solid middle-class living in a settled suburban world. Social spiralism offered an alternative: taking a risky move outwards, away from your home town to make a move upwards. In Britain the obligatory move to London was also a step on an upwards escalator. This was spatial mobility as social mobility; and social mobility as cultural dynamism. New universities, with radical new degree programs, thrived on the energy and activism. The cultural and political explosion of the 1960s was largely driven by innovation from the upstarts below. In comparison, the decades since have been less fluid. Looking back, the social spiralism of the 1950s and 1960s looks like a lost romantic stage in increasingly class-stratified European societies. The opportunities that these pioneers opened up seem to have shrunk again, and social mobility has lessened. The egalitarian drive of expansive public education has been abandoned; elites seem more able than ever to reproduce themselves. Mobility patterns are very settled across Europe again. With one exception: European free movement. For those that still want or need to be mobile, the horizon is as likely to be move outside the nation as within it.

Global Elites and Corporate Movers

So the question is: Has the form of spatial mobility offered by European integration made any difference to social mobility in the continent? Has freedom of movement altered the well documented rigidities of European society in some way? And who exactly has exercised this mobility opportunity, swapping a better European horizon for the predetermined career path and social position that their respective national social structures would probably have dealt them?[2]

Looked at quantitatively, the comparison of movers and stayers in fact reveals little change to patterns of social mobility. On the whole, free movers are more likely to come from professional and service class family origins, and upward class mobility is not greater among international movers than national populations, with the exception of Spanish movers. Only Britain as a destination offers a clear escalator effect.[3] European integration appears to be reinforcing, if not exacerbating, social inequalities. But the broad sweep of a quantitative survey may well be missing a lot of the real stories. A qualitative, contextualized approach offers a different view. The statistical marginality of European free movers is in fact highly significant. Clearly, some of the individuals I talked with were not upwardly mobile, but others were. The first step therefore is to distinguish who, among my interviewees, fits the bill in terms of social and spatial mobility. This subset of Eurostars might then be set apart from those whose mobility was clearly propelled by a more elite social background, and to distinguish a distinctively regional European mobility from a more obviously generic international or global mobility. Among these, certain types of free mover might also be distinguished.

Elite global movers certainly number among the people I interviewed. Nour, for example, a French permanent resident, was born in Algeria, but comes from a more international background, a family of diplomats and officials working for international organizations. London – "the best jumping board at the time" – represented simply the next nodal point in a planned-out global career that went from Sciences Po in Paris, to journalist school at Columbia University in New York, to Washington, DC, to cable news in London. Pointedly, unlike the five French nationals in London, she is *not* benefitting from European free movement. The consequence of Britain's non-participation in the Schengen Agreement is that she cannot work here without a work permit. Being a high flyer, the company has taken care of this, but she is convinced she has to work that bit harder for it. These barriers are not the same as those faced by European citizens. In fact, they are the traditional immigration barriers that require much more human, social, and cultural capital to overcome. Her own mobility has thus been built on the reserves of capital she could access through her international background, mobility experiences, and the global horizon of her career and lifestyle. The crucial vector was her education opportunities. Nour is the image of the global mover, but relatively few of the people I met fall into this category. There are a couple of others (Norbert and Franz are examples) from families with international organization backgrounds, who grew up as the sons and daughters of UN workers, European commissioners, or diplomats. As elites get smart to the benefits of international careers, the high probability is that the *next* generation of Eurostars, fresh out of expensive private international schools and global business schools, will be more like this.

A slightly different category of privilege is the traditional national elite or bourgeois background: Rainer, who comes from the high bourgeoisie of Hamburg; Philippe, who was put through the ultra-elite *grande école* system in France, and used connections to avoid military service and instead work abroad; Saskia from Belgium, who moved to get out from the shadow of her father. Notably, all three are blue chip MNC employees, on self-consciously fast-track corporate careers. This kind of capital is even more typical of Southerners, and is related to the observation that the more peripheral a society is to the rich Northwest the more you are likely to need it – Carmen, Eva, Maria, and Valerio are examples. These are Northern Italians, Portuguese, and Spaniards from the urban metropolis: the sons and daughters of surgeons, lawyers, or businessmen. It is not typical of all the migrants from Southern Europe: Donatella from rural Puglia (pp. 42–5), for example, and the Spanish movers from provincial regions – Galicians or Northern Spanish such as Isabel, Pedro, and Raoul, and the Basques, Carlos and Susana. Anastasia, from Greece, comes from a peasant refugee family. On the other hand, traditional bourgeois family capital is highly noticeable among the non-European migrants on the fringes of my study. Like Nour, their global mobility was linked to exclusion from the more open, egalitarian benefits that a European passport bestows. Maria's Ecuadoran boyfriend, Isabel's Mexican boyfriend, and Raoul's Russian wife all had to have very high levels of human, social, and cultural capital to be mobile internationally.

They are an example of how much more it costs non-Europeans to move internationally in the same way. It can be speculated whether the EU enlargement to East European countries, or even the *de facto* association of countries like Romania (pre-2007) and Turkey – whose highly educated have already been given some of the European educational opportunities enjoyed by EU citizens – might over time lead to a socially expansive mass-ification of opportunities to people of a more modest background outside Western Europe. For now, the East Europeans and Turks who are filling postgrad opportunities in Britain or Germany, or getting fast-track City jobs in London or in the Commission in Brussels, tend to be of a higher social background relative to their home countries than West Europeans in the same positions.[4]

The specific impact of European integration for elites – although it may still have mattered in many of these cases – may be less because of the presence of other forms of mobility capital. A similar question hangs over many of the corporate multinational movers, whose international mobility has been organized within a global company. On the face of it, this is not the same thing as "getting on your bike" internationally to look for work in a free-moving Europe. Career mobility within corporations is, however, often conveniently parasitical on European free movement laws, in that the corporation is spared the need to worry about visas and work permits when it moves managers within the European space. The emergence of other kinds of international regimes such as the GATS agreement in the WTO is increasingly facilitating mobility of this kind within and for big corporations – particularly in relation to service sector work when the person needs to physically move to do their job.

My investigations into the MNC world centred on a major food and household products multinational, Unilever. A highly European MNC based on an Anglo-Dutch axis, Unilever is an increasingly global corporation, with growing interests in the Asian, Latin American, and latterly, North American markets. A mark of the company's human resources concern with mobility was the encouragement it gave to my research efforts. The personnel offices in London and Rotterdam gave me excellent advice, and put me in touch with a range of contacts. They know how important these issues are to the success of their employees.[5] The Basque couple, Carlos and Susana, offered me the clearest view of the archetypal MNC situation. Their decision to move to London was entirely structured around Carlos's career as a special-ized engineer and technical consultant. His work had taken them from Bilbao – where they are still deeply rooted – to work elsewhere in Spain, then the Netherlands, then London. They were now contemplating a new scenario with Carlos working in Dijon, while his wife would return to Spain. It did appear however that their children might be taking up the free move-ment opportunity of staying on for university in England. Each move unfolded according to the career negotiation that Carlos pre-planned in great detail to take care of the happiness of the family: including housing, salary, distance to schools and airports, and social networks for his wife. There was a classically gendered division of labour, with Susana covering the family side of life. Even with all the help, the moves were still not easy, and it took remarkably open and flexible personalities, and a rock-steady marriage, to make it work. An individual free mover does not have any of these corporate structures to guide them.

One of the key aspects of mobility within multinationals that has changed has been the move to a more "supply side" mobility within companies.[6] The Rotterdam-based senior personnel officer for Unilever, Martin de Jong, talked me through the logic. MNCs are now less likely to ask people to move as a condition of career progression. Rather, they are conscious that such movers ought to be allowed to self-select – which a percentage still do – and that packages for mobility can be better tailored to individual circumstances. Companies are particularly sensitive to the fallout from this when things don't work out for following spouses. Young high flyers like Philippe in London and Axel in Amsterdam shopped around for the best career move, but it was notable that they opted in the end for European destinations where their wives could find work unproblematically, and where – with young children to think about – it would be easy to get home to family and friends. Neither would be interested in moves further afield.

Rainer, a slightly older and more senior audit manager with Unilever, had moved to London with his family from Hamburg. He stresses all kinds of specificities about London that made the move work, but above all its regional convenience for Hamburg. Their family and friends connections there are still very much alive. Although he has exercised a good deal of control over his own mobility, he is not convinced that mobility in the company is entirely supply side and voluntary. Senior management "taps you on the shoulder" to suggest you should be mobile; yet many of his peers are reluctant to move or sacrifice their private lives to their careers. Rainer's move was tightly managed – albeit not without problems – by the human resources people, who found a house and helped with moving in. He recognizes that their corporate experience was quite different to some friends who came to Britain by their own means. The horizon in the country is quite short – a few years – although their son is now established in school. He has had to fight to maintain his expat status, which offers higher remuneration to offset mobility costs: the company seeks to phase out the benefits by "localizing" you. Prestigious corporate destinations in Asia or Latin America are ruled out because of security issues or family concerns. In particular, ageing parents are a factor. We talk at length about his family's embeddedness in the local bourgeois social world of Hamburg, of the disruption it caused when they moved, and the disbelief that family and friends expressed. This situation took a lot of skilful PR – particularly with his mother-in-law. They invited her to help with the move, and since then she became the biggest supporter back home of their relocation to London. Rainer's move – that in every other respect was straight out of a human resources textbook – was, in the end, a specifically regional European move. That's why it worked. In this respect, Rainer's experience is a lot closer to that of a more obvious free mover. It is doubtful whether outside of the European possibilities he and his family would have really opted to go further abroad.

Eurofamilies

Minus the global elites or multinational movers, at least two thirds of my interviewees were not movers whose mobility could be accounted for by elite or upper-class capital or by a structured corporate environment. They came either from average middle class backgrounds, usually provincial, or from clearly working class or rural backgrounds. For example, among the 13 "tales" I feature as archetypes of the new European mobility, David, Helen, Dario, Hedwig, and Dave fall in the former category; Donatella, Giulia, Federica, Laure, and Valérie in the latter. And, as has been shown, even among those from a metropolitan elite background or privileged corporate movers, much of the experience still remains distinctively linked to the new regional European space for mobility.

Regional integration facilitates cross-border mobility, lowers migration costs, and reduces the human or cultural capital needed. Economic barriers are reduced as prices go down on airlines and new fast train lines get built. Communication becomes effortless with cheaper phones and internet connections for all. The opportunities thus get massified, and the mobile turn out to be more middle class and regional than global or elite in their background. The other aspect of this is the clear transformation in European family structures made possible by the new spatial scale. Cross-national family life is facilitated by regional integration – with family networks a more universally distributed form of social capital. Families themselves are able to stretch over a European scale, and not in any way be undermined by a daughter or son going abroad. Nina points out the difference between her family relationships now she is in Amsterdam, compared to when she was studying in San Francisco. It doesn't make any difference if she drives two hours from Amsterdam to Düsseldorf, rather than two hours from Hamburg or Munich, and they love to visit her. Her parents had pressurized her, however, to come back from America.

The London-Ireland relationship has always been like this, as Siofra stresses; only now as Tom and Sinead point out, Brussels or Amsterdam are just as easy, and nicer to visit. A little distance, after all, can actually be a good thing where family is involved. Rob and Rachel in Brussels point out that they are no further now from their families in Manchester, in terms of travel costs and time, than if they had been living in London. And they can pop over for an enjoyable weekend, without coming to stay for weeks – that would be "unacceptable", says Rachel, laughing. Siofra would agree: going back to live in rural Donegal is "just not an option", but "moving to Australia – that's a different kettle of fish". The capacious way Irish family networks manage the distance of children and relations is perhaps a good guide to the well-functioning spatial adaptation of European families more generally to European mobility, under the present easy conditions.

A mobile family background – which need not be of the elite global kind – also helps explain why some middle and lower-class Europeans are predisposed to move. Family in the armed forces turns out to be a common background. Alan, the independent businessman in Amsterdam, grew up speaking a German he has forgotten on a NATO airforce base. He was "dragged around all over the place". An only child, he attended eleven schools in different countries, the longest time he spent in England being eight years at boarding school. He says it's impossible for him to answer the question: "Where are you from?" Jonathan in Brussels also had armed forces parents, as did Janet, the trade journalist, who also went to boarding school. Other interviewees of different nationalities reveal similar background stories. Sophie in Utrecht had a father in the French army; Isabel from Spain, a father in the Spanish navy. It is typical among the mobile French to have had parents who served for French businesses in North Africa or other colonies. Guillaume, whose parents had lived in Algeria and elsewhere in Africa, comments that at least they share with him the idea that France is "not the centre of the universe". They "failed in their integration" back in France, so don't want or expect him to come back. The parents of Saskia from Belgium – one of them French speaking, one Dutch ("it's more common than you think!") – had lived in the Belgian Congo for quite a while.

One additional factor noticeable among Southern European families with mobile children is that they made quite an effort to "train" the children to be internationally minded, by getting the access at early age and frequently to foreign language courses, especially in English. This is particularly noticeable in Spain, a country that has embraced internationalism and Europe vigorously in the last twenty years because of its long political isolation from the continent. The families of Eva and Carmen from Spain were very proactive in pushing them to go abroad. Carmen says although it seems common, it was not the experience her friends still back home had – and that she has been the only one who was curious enough to be mobile, as a consequence.

The other very small subset of the my interviewees who might be thought of as endowed with a certain kind of family related mobility capital are the sons and daughters of successful migrant families. This is to say, their background one generation back could be very modest, but that they do have international mobility "in the genes" as it were, perhaps because of the dramatic ambitions and trajectory that their parents had. They are second generation migrants in the classic assimilation story, where the family's success is here transposed up and out into the international environment. For example, Dario from Rome (a Jewish Sephardic family, with roots in the Middle East), Giulia (Italian immigrants to the US), Joannet (Polish businessman father in Netherlands, highly assimilated), Rachel (Italian businessman father in Switzerland), Dominic and Valérie (Italian migrant families in France). You have a different kind of view on spatial mobility when you are from this background. Movement as a life option becomes more a matter of course, is expected and valued. Norbert – whose parents were German diplomats – lived in Brazil, Greece, and Japan as a child, and puts it nicely: they have been very supportive because "they can hardly demand anything else!"

Social Spiralists

One noticeable background that many of the Eurostars have in common is that they are from the provinces and driven to move – whether by ambition, frustration, or boredom. These are the new social spiralists. Among the parents mentioned are numerous farmers, engineers, and especially school teachers. They would not have moved were it not for the new open EU free movement opportunities. Instead, they tried to use Europe as an alternative trajectory to the classic one through the national capital – a route that builds on the energy of feeling an "outsider" with a "point to prove". Social spiralism against the new European backdrop is most marked among French and British movers – the two countries with the most obviously centralized social mobility structures. Europe is finally providing an alternative route for provincials who found the competitive route through the capital blocked – monopolized as always by the same national elites, going to the same elite schools and universities. Guillaume missed Sciences Po in Paris by a quarter of a point, but was happy in the end: "I would have become this self-centred arrogant monster like most of them!" He says he would have been forced to hide his lower social origins there, whereas moving to Strasbourg "everything became possible", especially opportunities to move abroad.

The leap abroad can make all the difference in terms of trajectory, acceleration, lift off. The careers of the French women in London again proves this point: Laure (pp. 165–8), Valérie (pp. 182–5), and Nicole. Some were encouraged by their parents to move away. Others have to fight. Jeroen was lucky. It wasn't his parents experience, but they encouraged him to have the independent experience abroad. He remembers friends at school who had to fight their parents to go away, who'd accuse them of thinking themselves "better than me". And others who instead got a job at 18, and end up driving around town showing off in their cars. The ordinary boys. The break can be rough: families can also be over-protective. A career move abroad – albeit not *too* far away – can provide the right kind of distance, especially for daughters.

Being born in the heart of Europe – the central regions along the Dutch-Belgian-French-German-Swiss axis of the continent – also generally predisposes people to think in more regional European terms. Sophie, the French scientist in the Randstad, grew up in Strasbourg, then built her career moving to Basel ("one hour's drive"), then Heidelberg, then Utrecht. One thing was always ruled out: Paris. Nationalized capitals like London and Paris still serve an "escalator" function, but now they also play this role for international movers opting out of the standard career plan.

The most useful way to conceptualize the migration of those looking for a new horizon to their lives and careers is in terms of an emergent European "field" of mobility. The logic of the rational actor approach to explaining the lack of intra-European migration suggests more account be taken of the specificities of migrants who do move. What kind of calculation do they make when they put themselves among the 1 in 50? Where the rationalist account runs into problems is over the kind of information about opportunities that is supposed to feed into the calculations of individuals, couples, or families. With the exception of developing migration systems that fulfil this function or offer examples of successful peers, many of the migration stories here seem to suggest that the moves were a "shot in the dark", adventurous, speculative, "see what happens" types of move that did not involved any particular clear calculation about consequences down the road. Much of it was spurred on by curiosity, of an openness to possibilities. Sometimes this feeling is associated with self-consciously internationalizing oneself, or in other cases, an explicit kind of European idealism.

Caterina is a good example. One of the older Italian movers, she left her small home town in the North of Italy for a very speculative move to Brussels. Brussels was not a specific destination: she was looking for "somewhere", but had not been interested in visiting before. And this was not a simple rational migration; rather, she came to "see how it was", knowing she could leave and "look for something else". But she did want to "challenge herself in a different environment … discover and enrich my life". Many of the interviewees express this kind of attitude. It is a kind of "pioneer" attitude: self-consciously risk-taking and unique, projecting a possible life onto a new European backdrop. The move abroad involves a break with the more definite, mapped out social trajectories that staying at home would give. It is often indefinite, both spatially and temporally. But it is not like going abroad as a tourist, with a clear, delimited expectation of return. Rather, it is seen as a genuine career move, although there may well be some vague longer-term plan to return.

Thinking of this European space as a kind of protean "field" helps draw the contrast to the more fixed national economy of established rules, values, or payoffs. The historical account of European nation-state formation underlines how modern national welfare states stabilize and structure mobility opportunities. They establish clear educational paths, institutionalize careers, offer welfare guarantees and benefits, and generally try to manage the trajectory of individuals through society. The national framework was also a guarantee of returns to effort: a guarantee that everyone is part of the same collective game, with the same (just and fair) rules. In part this is what the idea of democratic citizenship is meant to express. The European Union falls far short of the nation-state-society in this sense: European citizenship based on free-movement rights is a quite different proposition. The EU offers only a weak identity, and few of the standard pastoral guarantees or assurances of justice. However, it does offer an alternative context in which to project one's life, albeit a broader, less defined, and more unpredictable one. One can begin to see one's career in different European terms, and crucially one does not have to opt out of the national and regional benefits of being close to home either, or even having access to some of the benefits of national citizenship.

European pioneers thus are moving into a field in which the values, rules, and hierarchies are not yet clearly established, as they are in the national context. They don't necessarily move with clear information about the destination or the consequences for their careers. Nor do they have clear feedback about some of the barriers or dead-ends that they might face unexpectedly down the road. Under conditions of uncertainty, the emergent field may offer different payoffs. This is the game they are playing: *un jeu sans frontières*. Maybe if you change yourself, your location, and hence your position in society, you will find an alternative route. Eurostars project themselves into the unknown. The absence of clear information or any assurance of an alternative "European" identity thus becomes less of a puzzle. And opting out of a national system and national identity offers an immediate benefit in a liberatory, denationalizing sense.

European free movers are pioneers in this sense, particularly those not driven by an elite family endowment or an MNC framework – which itself functions like an alternative welfare state. The problem is, the pioneer mentality is not something that can endure indefinitely. Individuals in the long run do need the identity over time of comparing self with self against a stable background. Longer-term calculations based on stable returns do eventually become imperative. As with the deals that expats get when they move abroad, there is probably a "sunset clause" to the benefits of playing the field. Expats are eventually "naturalized" by their companies, and treated just like one of the regular "local" workforce. Similarly, any new European opportunities will solidify eventually into institutionalized systems, which will tend to go back to reinforcing the pre-existing order in Europe. You can only be a pioneer for so long, and when there are few other people doing this. Successful free movement thus inherently has to be a marginal phenomenon. This begins to explain why so many people do not move. It points to why free movement as a transformative force in Europe is a finite phenomenon.

This is certainly not how the economic Theory of European Integration is supposed to work, or how the European Commission imagines the future. A more dynamic Europe will not be achieved simply through more and more people moving. Dynamic people will only feel the benefits of moving when there are not too many of them. Highly talented and original people will only move as long as their originality is recognized. The system will stop selecting for this "unobserved skill" as soon as it is no longer a pathbreaking move. Mobility capital of this peculiar kind, in other words, gets devalued the more people pile into it. European integration opened a window of opportunity for a generation of social spiralists. But it is doubtful their movement prefigures a dramatic replacement of the stabilized national structures for a fully massified and thereby Europeanized system.

A Social Worker's Tale

I met Federica at a typical Brussels house party. While sitting outside *Café Belga* in Place Flagey, I'd run into a Croatian friend I'd known at university in England. She invited me over to her housewarming that evening. They'd just bought a great little converted place in a rough Ixelles backstreet, off rue Malibran, a somewhat liminal road lined with Halal butchers, cheap telephone and internet shops, North African *épiciers*, and thrift stores. The party was a mix of international types working for NGOs and longtime Belgian residents of the neighbourhood. The talk was all politics and cultural life. Federica was suspicious of my project, but agreed to an interview anyway. She reminded me of so many of the independent educated women I'd met in Florence, Bologna, and Rome: attractive, intelligent, articulate, a little gruff. We meet again in the archetypal cosmopolitan Brussels café *l'Ultime Atome*, one of those classy spaces where urbane Belgians, European residents, and hip students would eat and drink; it's always full. With the multinational chat around us, I struggle to make a decent recording of our conversation, that takes place in French, with a little Italian thrown in for fun.

I am a social worker. It has been five years now soon. I work half time by personal choice, specializing in domestic violence – working with families and children touched by it. I work across the whole city, or sometimes at a hospital. I came to Brussels eight years ago, and have been doing this work for five years. I did my studies here. University is shorter here than in Italy – it took three years. During my final stage [work placement], I had the luck to

A Social Worker's Tale—cont'd

be offered a job. I hesitated a lot. Do I stay, do I go home? But then I decided I wanted to do some postgrad studies at Louvain-la-Neuve. And then I had the chance to work for the city.

I'm surprised that social work could be a mobile profession in Europe.

Yes. In terms of professional equivalences, I needed to ask the consulate for official recognition. Everything can be equivalent apart from the law courses. I informed myself about that. For the rest it's similar. I always need to explain my work to people in Italy. The studies, the technical concepts [are different].

I wanted to do studies abroad, and I considered England, and French-speaking countries. But I knew some friends here from other countries. I hesitated a lot between Paris-Bruxelles, Bruxelles-Paris… For me the first few months were very difficult. After that I began to get to know the city really well, and I realized that I didn't really want to go. It would have been much more difficult to integrate in Paris. Big cities like Paris or London, these are cosmopolitan, for sure. But what I like about the Belgian context is that it is a small city, but a small city that itself is very cosmopolitan. In terms of the meeting of Belgians and foreigners, or Belgians and immigrants, it isn't always so multicultural – but I would call it cosmopolitan. Sincerely, if there had only been Belgians here I'm not sure I would have liked it! Because I like a lot the fact you can meet people from all kinds of countries. This wasn't necessarily the case in Italy.

Why was it so difficult at the beginning?

Because I knew a few people, but not many, and then the ones you get to know at first aren't necessarily the people you would chose. I didn't know the language very well, the climate was very different, and the way people live here. The rhythm of life is so different. I had travelled, yes, a lot, but to live somewhere, that was different. This is a city of the North [une ville du nord] and I was not used to that. I think I was quite young at that time, 22. Plus, the city centre, when I came here eight years ago, the neighbourhood where you have lots of cafés and restaurants now [Sint Katelijne], it was not like that at all. It was all demolished, wrecked buildings, and for me that was strange. In my native city and other cities, there the centre is beautiful and that's where all the life is: in Rome, other cities in Italy. Here nearly everything was destroyed, but little by little it has been restored. But at first you didn't know how to find yourself here, where to go out, what to do.

She lives with her boyfriend, Hassan, a Belgian-Moroccan.

My boyfriend didn't want to live in the centre, and me neither. My Italian friends live in rue Dansaert [in Sint Katelijne]. But I wouldn't want to live in Uccle [out in the suburbs], no way at all! Or any neighbourhoods that are just residential. We looked in three quartiers, in Ixelles, Etterbeek, and Saint Gilles. The trade off between quality/price is good, compared to Rome, Paris, or London. You can find things here, even on a modest salary – if you don't always look in the areas that are most popular with the eurocrats. We wanted a quartier with accessible shops, also at night. It's the first time I've lived in an Italian neighbourhood. There are cafés, shops, a restaurant. Thirty years ago, they didn't have pasta. I remember the first time I saw pasta here, I thought it was awful. You know, pasta with meat balls, overcooked and covered in Gruyère, horrible.

A Social Worker's Tale—cont'd

When I looked for myself – and not with a big budget – they always wanted to know if I was working. "Oh, you are Italian. How nice [doubtfully] ...." *That bothered me. Then when I looked with my partner, we were "less" foreign, and yet we had some resistance from landlords. Not only that they asked if we worked – which is normal if you've got to pay the rent every month – but also, "What is your origin?", "Where is he from?" We had some comments which were very difficult for him. It's true in social work, you get to meet people of a certain age, Belgians. There is some racism. But it's not really directed at Italians or Europeans. People would talk about Italians in the old days, and say, "Oh, we had to put a lock on the door". Only now when I say I'm Italian, they say, "How nice. It is super in your country". Italians were very badly received before. They came here to work in the mines, and it was very difficult for them. Now it's no longer Italians who bother them, it's non-Europeans.*

Have they thought about buying a house in Brussels?

We thought about it. At the beginning, that made me nervous, the idea of the idea of spending all my life in Belgium, that makes me afraid [laughs]. *Even if I appreciate all the aspects about living here, I was worried. It was ooh là là, that really is rooting myself. But then I've had friends, foreigners, mobile people. They've sold their houses quickly, and it didn't stop them moving.*

What about children?

We've thought about it too. But it's not for that reason that they will be Belgian, oh no! [laughs]. *I say to Hassan, "Well, if Belgian nationality doesn't matter to you, then they can be Italian!" Now that you can't have double nationality in the EU: you have to choose, one of the parents. It's not the father who determines it. It's all theoretical really. It might be nice to have an Anglophone school, learning several languages from when you are small. We'll speak French together, but I'll want them to learn Italian, and him Moroccan. It will all be a mix* [laughs]. *I don't speak Arabic, but Hassan is learning Italian. I lived there 22 years after all!*

Italia calling?

Si, péro ... When I talk about leaving it's not necessarily to go to Italy. I'd like to go elsewhere as well. I grew up there, passed my adolescence. It's there that you form as a person. You create your first links with society. It's very important, inevitably. I miss the Mediterranean side of things a lot. I'm much more at home when I'm in Mediterranean countries, and not necessarily EU countries – Spain, Morocco, Greece, even Turkey. Although I wouldn't want to live there for political reasons. I mean, you can see that I'm not Belgian from the way I look.

In other words, you can easily stay Italian without being there for many years?

Oh yes, I find it the opposite [to losing your nationality]. *On the contrary, in my life, until I was 22 years old, as a resident of Italy, I thought of myself as citizen of the world. I loved it: I thought I was more than just an Italian. But ... the more the years pass, the more I recognize my Italian identity. It's the opposite that is happening. I go there regularly. There are two chez moi. The chez moi I have created here, and the chez moi there. There was a path here that worked out. But the chez moi of the heart, that's when*

A Social Worker's Tale—cont'd

I get to Rome. I need to go see my friends and family, especially places that I miss. Staying in touch with parents and family is fine. But it's tougher with friends – that's one thing I regret. Maybe my family will ask the question differently as they get older. They are now retired. My father worked hard, he had health problems, and in those moments it is not so easy. If I was close I could telephone more often or go there more. When things are difficult you want people who are close to be there.

So, will they stay or will they go?

At the beginning we discussed it. As the time passes in fact I realize that for him it would be much more difficult. He is much more attached here, his family and parents are all here, people he is close to. He is a foreigner, but he was born here. For me it's not like that, there is an asymmetry [décalage]. *Sometimes I say to him, "You could find work elsewhere in Europe". He is an accountant, but working in the social field. We could go to Rome, but he says there's not much work for him there, although there might be for me. Then I say, Milan? And he says, "If it's Milan we might as well be in Brussels". But from time to time, I say, "Well, Milan wouldn't be bad you know!" From time to time, I regret it.*

Do you think of yourself as a migrant?

I don't know what it is exactly you mean by that word. But if I respond just like that, then yes, I am a "migrant", I have migrated, yes. It's not the same as other Italians fifty years ago ... But, yes, there is an immigrant's heart somewhere here [oui, il y a un coeur d'immigré quelque part].

7

Mobility (2)

Adrian: *Do you ever think of yourself as a migrant?*
Alan: *Not really* [laughs]. *I think of myself more as an alien than a migrant …* [pause].

Eurostars both are and are not true migrants. In international statistics, stocks and flows of international migration are calculated on the basis that a person has migrated when they move residence to another country for more than one year. All of my interviewees pass that test – although many of them do not show up on official statistics. Yet their form of movement – their mobility in this sense – is clearly very different to the standard migration/immigration story on which this mode of calculation is premised.

Human geographers, in particular, are alive to the many new dimensions of mobility in a globalizing world. For them, any spatial mobility of residence, whether it is permanent, temporary, circular, within a country, or across borders, counts as migration. Some of this gets fuzzy as temporary migration shades into other forms of physical mobility, such as commuting, tourism, cross-border shopping, multiple residencies, weekend relationships, and the like. But migration is a purely spatial movement from a to b, that only becomes formalized as im-migration, asylum, legal and illegal, and so on, by extraneous political and legal conceptualizations, that draw lines between types of movement that states want to classify, distinguish, regulate, and thereby control. In this sense, official statistics pointing to the low stocks and flows of such migrants are measuring the wrong thing.

Yet, in another sense, as Alan ironically suggests, most of my interviewees didn't think of themselves as migrants at all. Their mobility could be classified and counted in all kinds of ways, but they generally didn't see movement within the emerging European space as a form of migration.[1] Qualitative investigation allows for a good deal more exploration of these semantic issues. Describing who they are and what they are doing is an important issue for all the movers. So, many of them accented impermanence and flexibility in their self-understanding, even if for all other purposes they were settled "im-migrants" in the country – owning houses, sending children to school, claiming medical benefits, and so on. Since none had naturalized, their attitude of remaining "outside" their country of residence was as much a question of choice and lifestyle as their decision to move there in the first place.

Above all, it is important not to see these aspects of spatial and temporal volatility in a negative light, as is often the case when they are looked at from the classical nation-state centred perspective of "integration". This is the master narrative of immigration, wielded by receiving societies, which assumes that all legally welcome "im-migrants" must be on some kind of track to full integration: to inclusion, incorporation, permanent settlement, and one day becoming a citizen among others. The integration narrative imposes the idea that their relationship to the host society must be understood, measured, and valued in these terms. This is the process by which nation-state-societies have always constituted and reconstituted themselves in the face of mobile populations messing up their borders. The narrative dismisses and suspects foreigners who are only temporarily living in the territory, seeking to exclude or (at least) ignore them, as having no kind of meaningful interaction or engagement with the host society.

In fact, it is precisely in the provisionality – the temporariness and flexibility – by which the Eurostars express their mobility. It's where their "freedom" lies. This is what mobility is all about – for them. Regardless of how the state or official statisticians might want to classify them, what is needed here is an empirical phenomenology of mobility that captures the everyday sense that this mode of life has for these actors.

Are You a Migrant?

The most frequent answer to this question was an emphatic, sometimes bemused, "No!" To Southern Europeans, indeed, the question is almost offensive. Miguel in Brussels, who is Portuguese, scoffs irritably at my question. He will have nothing to do with the older Portuguese migrants you can still see in some neighbourhoods in Brussels, who came as guest workers in the 1950s and 1960s. Maria in Amsterdam explains the negative connotation of the word "migrant". In Portugal, migrants were the people who left the country and then came back as *nouveaux riches*, building gaudy houses in the Algarve. They "lost their identity". She said she'd have to add something to the word migrant to make it tolerable. "Oh, *free mover* sounds so much better!"

In part, these respondents are reacting to the pervasively negative discourse about immigrants in Europe, which always centres on the "problems" that their "difference" and "distance" from European culture poses – an inevitable consequence of the integration narrative. The self-distinction from such immigrants, articulated by these Eurostars, is in fact quite important to Spanish, Italian, Greek, and Portuguese professionals in Brussels and Amsterdam. Officially they are still counted with the *other* population of older immigrant Spanish, Italian, etc., who came as labourers. Amsterdam, peculiarly, classifies all Southern Europeans together as an ethnic minority in city statistics. Brussels, meanwhile, makes no attempt to distinguish between the types of nationals in each commune, such that both Anderlecht and Ixelles have high numbers of Italians, but that they are completely different populations in class terms.[2] Italian professionals and eurocrats are also treated differently to other Europeans by city officials because of bilateral agreements between the two countries going back to the guest worker programs. It is confusing and uncomfortable for the Southern European professionals in the two cities.

In fact, the only interviewees who answer yes to the question are the ones who for professional reasons know the correct technical definition of migration. Susan, the personnel manager in Amsterdam, did a degree in geography. She remembers the "right" answer – but she certainly doesn't feel like one. Isabel, the labour market economist in London, knows "theoretically" she is one. And Bernhard in Brussels has done advocacy work as a lawyer for migrants' rights, so he can "identify" in some way with his North African neighbours.

Avoiding being classified an immigrant can have practical consequences. Many countries force emigrants to give up residency, and lose rights back home. If you can, as a mobile professional, you might thus want to avoid these official migration classifications entirely. Danes, Swedes, and Dutch, especially, face similar problems when internationally mobile. These tightly coordinated pastoral nation-states, with highly developed welfare systems, track everyone through computerized personal identification numbers, and force non-residents to de-register and give up certain rights. They are also highly aggressive in hunting down taxation. Membership comes with a price – and free movers don't fit the nationalized system.

Another objection to being seen as a migrant is linked to the symbolic image of immigrants, who are moving permanently, to a new life, never to return. This is the "painful" idea of immigration to America, the long boat ride to Ellis Island, as Sophie, the French scientist in the Netherlands, says. She also doesn't like the terms "expat" ("certainly not") or "free mover". Temporary or provisional mobility is different in Europe because many things stay at home. You might move most of you life to London, but you always keep your dentist in Madrid. Or indeed even your bedroom at your mum's place. When I ask Jaime if London is "home", he grins:

It's "home" for now. It's never really home, because home is like my mum's place, 'cos I know I can always go there. It's my base.

The Eurostars have pioneered a new migration system in the continent that has emerged as a result of increasing regional integration – and enlargement – of the EU. Poles, Romanians, even Turks may one day feel and be treated as simply mobile European citizens, not immigrants. For the time being, only the Westerners can hope to enjoy this degree of invisibility and spatial flexibility. From a subjective point of view, being part of this system is expressed by the sense of not having crossed any borders. We are not "migrants", we are just "Europeans". Of course, they are right in formal terms, in terms of European citizenship. It is, unsurprisingly, a common reaction among the *Brusselaars*, residents of a self-styled Eurocity. But multinational employees in London and Amsterdam can be equally vociferous. Carmen and Franz, bankers in London, express this view strongly.

Adrian:	*Do you ever think of yourselves as migrants?*
Carmen:	[long pause] *No.*
Franz:	*We are Europeans.*
Adrian:	*How would you describe yourself? What term should I use in my book to describe people like you?*
Franz:	*Europeans.*
Adrian:	*You are not expats?*
Franz:	*No.*
Carmen:	[emphatically] *No!*
Adrian:	*Some people use this word.*
Franz:	*No, no, no.*
Adrian:	*Free movers?*
Franz:	*I just say: Europeans.*

For these Eurostars, their mobility has nothing to do with international migration. Europe is their home, and this is the European city they happen to be working in.

Weightless

Honestly, we stopped planning. It doesn't make any sense. Every time we started to plan something, we have been somewhere else within a month [laughing].
                    Axel, Telecommunications Manager, Amsterdam

Movement can of course become a permanent state of mind. The grass is always greener ... Maria, the high flyer at the bank in Amsterdam, has no doubts that she is still moving. "The more you travel [for work], the more you want to see ... Anywhere." Further professional movement is obviously on her mind – however much she likes her job in Amsterdam. She mentions the US, Canada, South America, Australia, in breathless succession. But there turns out to be not enough sun in London, too much concrete in New York, too much insecurity in Brazil and Russia, too much corruption in developing countries generally. Sydney "sounds nice". Maria, characteristically, links her success to her open attitude, and to the fact that most people don't want to live like this.

Real movers will always choose to move: at the drop of a hat. For example, Nicole in London. She says she would move to company's offices in Barcelona or New York "next week" – if they ask her. Beyond European regional mobility, there is a pure expat world, with no continuity at all. Alan in Amsterdam talks about all his acquaintances there, coming and going. Mobility is his business: courier and transportation. He gives me the image of the profession: all the expat managers meeting up for a beer at the departure gate, catching the last flight to or from Heathrow, packages in hand. They live the life that they work. International journalists are perhaps an even more extreme case of the mobile lifestyle. They too always socialize together, because nobody else can really fit in with their hours or their mode of living and working. This dictates the kind of interaction they have with the society around them, delineating a peculiar worldview, global yet insular. Nour describes her journalist friends in London, working for the FT, BBC, or CNN. They always complain that they never get the chance to see each other when they are in London. They have to make do with "hanging out on assignment" in Saudi Arabia or Baghdad.

At a less rarefied level, European integration has provided similar opportunities of mobility to a much broader range of young professionals. Nicole in London crisply summarizes the sojourner mentality: a way of life made possible for her by the European free movement provisions. Provisionality is the key.

> *Deciding to stay for two years was a bit scary. It's stupid, I know, when you've been staying each time "just another year". This time it's just two years, but it was a big step for me. It's funny. I like the idea of knowing that it's OK if I change my mind tomorrow.*

She says she does "feel kind of settled" while "still travelling". She'd like to meet someone who likes the same thing; live five years here, five years there. And she feels she still has her friends in France, as well as close friends in London. This weightless state of mind is wonderful – as long as it lasts. Those that are still in the first flush of free mobility also often link it to their career progression. Carmen in London says how she feels she and Franz have become "special people": able to move, adapt, move on. The flexible few. She knows they are not going to stay there forever. One of the main attractions of the cities they chose to live is their superficiality, as much as their cutting edge culture. Life in the city is indefinite, ever changing. People come and go, things happen. You might stay, you might leave. Caterina in Brussels enthuses about this aspect, linking it to the ever present exit option:

> *We just enjoy the surface of this town. I can't tell* [how long I will be here].
> *I could leave in three months, I could leave in three years. If something is coming up that's attractive, you just move away. I met so many people who just moved away. It's a different kind of life, it's really different.*

Easy come, easy go.

Mobile professionals deal with the downsides of superficiality and provisionality – the uncertainty – by setting year-by-year plans: a specific horizon, usually linked to the time it might take to get certain experiences or skills "under your belt". Clearly, this also imposes a limitation on the experience of settlement in the current city of residence. Susan in Amsterdam is very definite about this: three years to get enough experience.

A short, provisional timeline might be the factor that makes it possible to take the big step – to leave friends, family, a settled world – as it did for Valerio, from Northern Italy, in Amsterdam. He says that as an only child in a small family, he was "doubting a lot" about the move. But he thought: "OK, I'm not planning to stay here for the rest of my life". A year, maximum two, made it seem possible. Couples coordinate these kinds of plans carefully. Sinead and Tom in Brussels agreed on a "five year plan", which they jokingly describe as very "Stalinist". For Tom, the international trades union has a four year congressional period, and Sinead sees potential for software localization in the place to which they dream of moving next – South America. They don't think they'll be staying.

The experience of mobility within Europe for many is still tentative, a first testing of the water. It is particularly so when families and spouses are involved, who of course do not have the same individual career motivations that the head of household might be following. When I meet Carlos and Susana one Saturday morning in a noisy coffee shop outside North Terminal International Arrivals at Gatwick Airport, they don't talk about mobility and their family life in triumphant globalist terms, but rather in terms of the sensitive difficulties of maintaining family "borders" and "mental hygiene" of this "superlife", in the face of work pressures. Carlos is garrulous, funny, and very self-reflective; Susana equally talkative. They have been waiting for a chance to tell their story, and they both want to push the discussion away from professional issues or general reflections on migration in Europe, into highly personal territory. This is the core of their experience, what they have learned, and what they have seen. They depend equally on their marriage, regional closeness to Bilbao, and to carefully planning specific timelines and horizons to their family moves. Carlos, in fact, took a coach to help him work out these issues in this specially created personal support environment, and not bring the pressure home. Older movers like them are perfectly aware of how fragile their lives and well-being – and their family's – are.

Younger movers have not necessarily yet arrived at this more cautious position. The weightlessness for them is still generally a pleasant feeling: of freedom, rather than anxiety, a sensation of no constraints and little structure. Hence the frequent references in my interviews to "floating around in the ether", "rolling along in a groove", "bobbing up and down on a sea". If you see something interesting – as one of my cohort at the European University Institute once pictured it – then you can swim over and try that … Jeroen says he "could have been a backpacker for the rest of my life". Buying a flat has at least given him some sense of anchorage. Jaime in London, meanwhile, seems totally content with his cosmopolitan work and social life, but says he is not really a Londoner, just a "passer-by". He is about to go travelling again, and is anxious about having to put all his stuff in storage space. "Psychologically", he says, "that is not very good for you". He doesn't feel he has that "safety net in your life' in London, or anywhere in fact that "isn't your mum's flat". After six years in Brussels, Janet feels detached from "insular" Britain and "weird, kind of stateless". I ask her if the company replaces that sense of belonging, one of the common myths asserted about multinational corporate life.

> *Oh God, no!!* [laughs]… *It's a great company to work for, but in terms of it being my life, no … I think there is this space that is being created more and more by our generation. We are much more mobile, flexible. We are settling down much later. We were wanting to live things a bit beforehand, just create a new dimension in a way … By moving.*

She also offers a gendered spin on this "new dimension".

> *My mum said to me, "You are very lucky, your generation". You can move around, travel, especially women* [now]. *Job opportunities are opening up.* [We're] *still not equal yet, but still there are so many choices. It make things harder. You can go wherever you want, do what you want. You end up feeling dissatisfied. You end up not really knowing what you want. When all is possible, all these cultures, languages, whatever, a melting pot …*

In the end, for most of the younger moves, a secure family link remains a key background condition for their freedom. Axel, the Austrian manager in Amsterdam, also recognizes how everything he is doing is anchored firmly in family and friends back home. A self-made "free mover", he combines a busy career with very frequent returns home.

Axel recognizes that friends' lives change very quickly – certainly more quickly than family relationships – and you have to work to stay up to date. Under these conditions, weightlessness can be a pleasant feeling.

State of Independence

European mobility is facilitated by the porousness of living in large, international cities, in which one can often live and work in various conditions of temporary residence and borderline legality. In passing freedom of movement clauses via the European Union, the nation-state in Europe has receded a little from its territorial role of micro-managing the residency status and cross-border movements of its citizens. In a perfect totalitarian state, the state would know where all its citizens were all the time. Communist regimes, in particular, imposed very strict mobility restrictions, both externally and internally. With growing global paranoia and the ubiquitous "war on terror", there may still be a future to look forward to in which everyone is barcoded and electronically scanned everywhere they go – in the name of "freedom". The technology is getting there, through computerized personal identification systems and scannable bio-data. It has in fact mostly been developed by commercial means: through customer loyalty cards, credit card banking, and the ability to spatially locate anyone anywhere on the planet via their mobile phone. The US may now treat all foreign visitors as potential terrorists, but the truth is it is still very porous internally, as is much of Western Europe. Western European states have always been less free on this dimension. But freedom of movement, in fact, has in fact seen a dramatic move in the other direction, towards a dismantling of state surveillance: enabling a true, if possibly fleeting, freedom, in the gaping holes that still exist *between* the pastoral systems of Europe's nation-states. Eurostars are masters of beating this particular system.

Bernhard has been living over two years in Brussels, and working steadily as a lobbyist. But he is also still a lawyer – for pension purposes – in Germany. They don't understand that he is resident abroad. He has "double rights" and nobody seems to be checking.

You can't get away with this kind of thing forever, and not at all in smaller countries like Denmark, but Germany apparently is too large to live up to its tight organizational reputation. Bernhard points out that when the German capital was in Bonn, there were countless numbers of German lobbyists and officials living in Brussels but never registering there. With some clever legal and tax manoeuvres, even having a family, living and owning a house in Brussels, can be combined with a German business "base", mostly located in a commuting car or train – a situation described in detail by Gunther, a roving IT consultant (see his tale, pp. 216–19).

Brussels is legendary for its informality. One Irish friend lived and worked in the city for over six years without any kind of registration in Belgium, until he was forced to go to the commune to unlock a wheel clamp on his car that he received after accumulating too many parking tickets. The matter was resolved without too much fuss. Tom, a trades union organizer and fervent socialist, also embarrassedly owns up to avoiding the state for over three years. He was "left on the vine" after moving from one commune to another, and nobody cross-checks. A variety of different tax statuses sometimes allow people to be invisible in Belgium entirely. Many still file taxes in their home country, or benefit from special European or international tax rates when they work for international organizations in the city. It can be possible to live there for almost a year, with a temporary position and bank account organized through your employer, but no other registration at all – as was my case when I was doing research for the Region of Brussels with a "grant". This quite common practice also enables the state to avoid any social security responsibilities for the visiting foreign researcher. In other cases you can be paying tax and holding a social security number, but avoid any contact with local communes, to whom communal tax is owed. Police registration in the local commune is in theory mandatory after eight days in the country, but freedom of movement makes a mockery of this legal relic of mid-twentieth century fascist Europe.

There are of course downsides to this. In such an uncontrolled, libertarian place, when everything is going fine, nobody is worried; but when things go wrong, they really go wrong. The system lets you be, and lets you get away with many things; but when it decides to control, it is arbitrary and rough. The police are the public face of this negative side of Brussels. During a research visit to the city, during which I was borrowing a friend's flat, I came home one day from a trip to find the door locked tight with a special security lock. I read the note on the door. Bailiffs had broken in, not to look for me – I am, admittedly, living there unregistered in the country and commune – but for repayment regarding an insurance policy of a former tenant. After scrambling to find a local locksmith to let me back in, I discover that many of my *own* belongings are targeted for repossession in a week, if the person now living in another country did not pay what turned out to be a relatively trivial amount. Very few European residents ever declare themselves resident as they are supposed to do, but the police occasionally check. Joannet, and her husband Stephen, high earning long-term residents in the city, had both managed to get themselves "deported" from the country in this way. To get "deported" like this is of course somewhat absurd, given that in Schengenland you can just walk back over the border without being checked. Stephen was driven by the police to the border. He came back the next day. The perception is that the police in Brussels are strongly negative towards European residents when they get a chance to impose their authority on this "privileged" population.

Over drinks in the francophone hipster bar *Au soleil* in Koolmarkt near the centre, I put these issues to Saïd, the French North African. He had a whole list of such situations that had affected him. Unsurprisingly, these appeared to be of a racialized nature. He had chosen to get away from the usual European world in Brussels, and lived in a flat in a cheap immigrant area of Vorst, the other side of the tracks from the *Gare du Midi* in Saint Gilles. He chuckled about the typical everyday observations you see in the neighbourhood: Islamic schoolgirls taking their veils off when they get on the school bus, putting them back on again when they have to walk back home past the local boys. Amid his lucid, almost lyrical perception of Brussels – its weird spaces and underground cultures – he recounted some of his crudely discriminatory experiences with the police. He believes they started to watch him and his girlfriend after he had run into problems with the local commune over his registration as a foreign student. This is a typical problem for non-Europeans – but he, of course, is French. The police kept visiting the flat, threatening deportation. He felt the racial harassment he received was fairly blatant, perhaps all the more so, given he was not the usual home-grown "immigrant youth", but an educated, articulate, politicized – and therefore highly suspicious – North African. The authority's nightmare: one that holds a *bona fide* EU citizen's passport.

London is every bit as porous as Brussels: a similar combination of open economy and bureaucratic disorganization. The Netherlands, however, is a different story altogether. When you move to work there, getting paid is made conditional on getting a SOFI (social security) number, which first requires a round of hasty trips to local commune offices and the police. To do this, you need an official residency – which rules out "illegal" sub-lets. In the end this often means being legally vouched for as living with a friend, or in some cases parents of a friend – since many young Dutch themselves live in "illegal" contractual situations. It is all hugely complicated, but effective from the state point of view: all the computer systems link up and cross-reference to ensure efficiency and control.

Intrastate porousness in Europe can of course be used to great effect in terms of taxation, savings, and pensions. A small minority of my interviewees resemble more the "new barbarians": hypermobile individualists ready and willing to sanction corrupt and decadent national welfare states, by moving all their assets offshore. Alan, the businessman, has been thinking about this for a long time: he is not waiting for the EU to solve the manifold problems associated with pensions and international mobility. He is also not relying on the Dutch state scheme. Rob and Rachel, the English couple in Brussels, offer me a masterclass on how to deal financially with mobility. Their savings are all offshore, and their financial advisor – who Rob names as "Mr. Ethical" – made sure all their "packages" are transferable. A lot of people are impatient with the state, and are looking for an "individualistic" solution of their own. When I ask Miguel, the Portuguese IT entrepreneur in Brussels, about retirement, he tells me to read Ian Angell, the Nietzschean LSE IT professor, who coined the term "new barbarians", outlining his philosophy. His wife Claudia, who is Italian, fancies Portugal, by the sea. Miguel rules this out, but thinks maybe France. He sees Belgium in strictly utilitarian terms, and his links with Portugal are getting very weak. It wouldn't make any difference to them if they left, he says, except in cost-benefit terms. "I only see countries in terms of the [instrumental] advantages they can give you." It begins to sound like the philosophy of master thief Robert de Niro in the classic cops-and-robbers movie by Michael Mann. Just be ready to move in five minutes, with all you can carry, if you feel the *Heat* around the corner.

Mechanisms of Settlement

What is going to happen to these people down the road? In some ways, it is not that cities – these endlessly shifting, transient places – change so much, but that people do. The cosmopolitan, protean aspect of urban life is a constant backdrop. But none of the Eurostars can continue living the way that they do – indefinitely. So I ask everyone about their plans. Here, the variation in my sample is clear. My interviewees span a range of life-cycle positions, in which the distinction between temporary, short-term *sojourner* and established, longer-term *settler* is crucial. Many are caught in between, in the long drawn out moment of transition. It is here that I find some of my most revealing material, especially when talking to couples.

The long, tumbling interview with Jeroen, the Dutch scientist, and his French girlfriend, Nathalie, in his Paddington flat, is one of the last interviews I make – and one of the best. Jeroen is eloquent, ironic, and self-reflective. Nathalie comes in halfway through the interview, calling out passionate, critical interjections, while fixing a late evening snack in the kitchen.

> Adrian: *What are your plans?*
> Jeroen: *Find myself a nice Spanish wife!* [laughs]
> Nathalie: *No!*
> Jeroen: *I'm not alone at the moment, so my ideas are intended* [hypothetical].
> *I don't have a strong thing about staying here. I miss nature. There's*

> *an exciting idea, but maybe not practical, to work in Verona for a while, near the Dolomites. [It's] partially romanticism. I don't think that will happen. We are thinking of buying a farmhouse in the Ardèche to develop.*

Nathalie: *That's not to live.*

Jeroen: *But it's a reflection of our thinking, where it might go. How much we feel bonded to London.*

Nathalie: *The nice thing about London, for me, [is] I could set off. I feel in transit. I feel free to come and go, so I stay, because I feel free. If I have to make a choice to stay in London, I would say no. But I always feel the same way as I did in the hostel. I can go from day one to day two. I'm free. I'm not dependent. The job here [she whistles] … Yes, no, yes, no … In fact, when I remember it's five years I'm here, and I planned to stay a few months …*

So far, so mobile. Nathalie expresses the archetypal sojourner mentality. Others in London had said the same thing. Isabel thought she was coming for one year; it was now six. Norbert says everyone thought they were here for a few years, but no longer. I ask how old they are? Jeroen is 35. Nathalie mumbles something about her age. She is "33 and a half".

> Nathalie: *I don't see myself going back to France for a long time. Also, I will not know where to go … Maybe [after five years] I am settling. Maybe it is that to settle. For me, it's OK. If for the next generation, if I have to be pregnant and have a baby, that I will have to think about, because I'm not sure I want to have children in London …*
>
> Jeroen: *That's funny … That's exactly what I said was a driver for why people move again.*
>
> Nathalie: *That's something that obliges you to think, so now what do you want? I don't think I really want to stay.*
>
> Jeroen: *But that's also part of your freedom [this flexibility].*
>
> Nathalie: *London is such a good compromise. Because you are close to everything, you can go [away] for the weekend. I've never seen so many people travelling just for the weekend. It's probably an escape. It's not a good sign. On the other hand, it's also the fact that it is possible. So I feel as if I'm in London I can go more to the Ardèche maybe than if I'm in Nice or Nantes or whatever.*

London encourages you to keep running, and think of escape. In fact, it is difficult to live any other way in the city. Jeroen is getting a little tired of the "compromise". Maybe one can live in some other way:

> Jeroen: *I am always aware that one can do more. One always has the tendency to limit oneself by the job one has, or the experience one has.*

> *I think there is also something interesting of actually saying, "OK. Here, I am going to live, and I am going to find something to do, and there are limits to this". I wonder how one can do that? It's a different way of living, to try something* [like that].

Nathalie: *Yeah. And right now I'm trying Marks and Spencer ...*

Jeroen: *I don't know. For me, that's a little bit a view of life. Sometimes more, sometimes less. I always had the feeling that I will never do what I'm doing now again. I think it could be very interesting to go to another place, and just live there ...*

But how does this happen? Jeroen and Nathalie point to a few of the mechanisms that can come into play: children, the body clock, age, fatigue, a different kind of horizon or lifestyle. As the Eurostars go through this transition, they realize – as Jeroen suggests – that there's more to life than professional career moves. Joannet, the Dutch political consultant in Belgium, is one of the younger interviewees. But she has thought very carefully about the settlement question, and realizes some things just happen that way. She says they are staying for now. She and her English partner have talked about it; they want to take "life step by step", stop "overplanning". Buy a nice house and work on their professional *and* private life. Their settlement decision will be linked to the regional scale of their lives there, as much as opportunity.

> *I'm a bit different there from my "expat" friends. They always have this discussion, "What city do you want to live in? Is London cool now, or Paris?" Now they want to live in the States, then Paris, then Asia, and they are really moving around. It's very nice for me, because I really don't have that. Brussels is far enough. I came here. I did not leave the Netherlands because I wanted to travel the world, or just to live somewhere else in Europe. I went because I'm northern Dutch and the European Union is here. We have travelled the world, we've seen people, nature, variety, it's good for you. But I just actually said to Stephen, "Why we don't we stop this discussion about moving?" Let's face the facts: we are very happy* [here]" ...

A job, a house, then children. Isn't that how it goes everywhere? Except you do have to decide to stop moving one way or another. Anniken and Dominic, in London, are mid-thirties, have a child, but not yet a house or fully established jobs. Dominic has a precarious but high-paying job at the London Stock Exchange. What exactly does it take to "settle" in London? I ask them about their future plans.

Dominic: *No future. I'm a punk, you know ...*

Anniken: ... [laughing]

Dominic: *With the job I'm doing, it's impossible to say* [the timeline]. *I don't know if I'm still in work with this company after four months.*

Anniken: *We don't really plan long term. We have some sort of plan for what we could do for the next year ... if everything goes well. If Matteo starts school, we buy a house ...*

Dominic: *Buying a house would be planning, but it doesn't mean we are going to stay here.*

Anniken: *We are quite aware things could change quite rapidly.*

For them, cross-national living is not a self-indulgent or quixotic option. It's the *basic condition* of their family life. In this sense, you can't stop being mobile, because it is part of the deal. This has to be reconciled somehow with the different life-cycle of a little boy who is growing up in a cognitively confusing situation. Anniken wants more stability for him, a house of their own, at least five years in one place. I ask if they would consider going to another continent. This sows further confusion.

Anniken: *No.*

Dominic: *We could try going to Asia ...*

Anniken: *Some things can happen.* [To Dominic] *You can get a phone call for a job in New York ...*

Dominic: *It depends what happens. You judge every two years with a job. That's how it is.*

The social theorists of global mobility have it wrong. There are human limits to flexibility, movement, and transience, as these intimate negotiations illustrate. Ultra-mobility is not a stable long-term option for real people, however high powered, who have ordinary family lives behind their mobile careers. It takes personal experience to understand this. And notions of mobility and settlement remain very subjective. The mobile may always like to see themselves in mobile terms, but their lives are complicated and grounded like anyone's. Sophie, the French scientist in the Netherlands:

Oahhhh [she groans]. *I don't like the idea of "settling" somewhere. But, yes, if you want to find a bigger place, then you have to buy.*

Even with someone as close to being naturalized as you can get, she has a marked reluctance to see herself as settled. Movement is still a possibility – for now.

For the time being, I will stay here. If I get other opportunities, I am open. My partner too. He is an architect. It would be in Europe, yes, I think so [laughs].

Have they considered the question of children? There is more going on here than I am yet able to understand.

Yes. We don't have any … Not yet! [laughs]. *Actually, I'm expecting.*

I stammer in response that I didn't know that.

No, you couldn't!! [laughing]. *You don't have children yet …*

What happens next? Settlement of some kind may be a human necessity, but is it really possible in these ever-changing cities? Only a look at settlement issues will settle this.

For now, the final word belongs to Alan. We have talked about his business and his Dutch connections, his relationship and everyday life, his pension plans and retirement, of moving or staying. Mobility remains the bottom line.

I'm constantly thinking about leaving. It's the longest time I've ever lived in any one place. It's constantly on my mind. If I didn't have the company and the house, I would have gone. The thing I'd like to do is get rid of everything and go and live on a boat in the Mediterranean. I see myself just sailing around. I keep saying to myself: one day, when my pension plan comes in, I'll do that. I've no real desire to stay here. Or Britain. There's nothing for me there. My parents are dead. I've got no family, no children. I can move.

Mobilito ergo sum. I ask him what is the timescale for the sunshine option down south?

Five years.

A Landlady's Tale

Hedwig is going to be 50 next year, and she is planning a big party. It will have to be a big venue. If she invites all the people she has got to know while running the only German-style pub in Brussels – *Das Bierfaß* – it could run to about half of the city's European population. And that's not counting the Belgians. She has been running the pub for 14 years, even though she swore she would only do it for three. It's quite a story. "I am the only woman to do like this in Brussels", she says with pride. *Das Bierfaß* is a Brussels institution. A small, traditionally styled German pub, it sits on the end of a quiet side street, just around the corner from the more famous, and populous, *Wild Geese*. The Berlaymont is a few minutes walk away, and the road itself – *rue*

A Landlady's Tale—cont'd

Stévin – has been the site of some bitter city development struggles. Like many, I'd overlooked the bar, and when Bernhard took me there for a drink after our interview I discovered the joy of on-tap German pilsner and homemade food, no music or sports TVs, good discussions, and the perfect landlady.

How did you come to Brussels?

That is very quickly to say. I came with my husband and two sons, 19 years ago. My husband had a contract at NATO, for a maximum of four years, but nobody wanted to go back at that time. We had moved 12 times in 15 years within Germany, all military moves, and everybody wanted to stay here – even what is now my ex-husband. We tried to build up a life here. I bought this house, and opened the pub here. I thought it would be a nice idea to open a pub. It wasn't even my idea, it was my husband's. We thought, "When it doesn't work out, it isn't a problem", but after one year we split up, and I was there with my pub ... And I'm still here!

I didn't have to do anything much [to make it work]. *It was amazing how quickly people came, to this new German pub. Back in the 1980s. German journalists came here, they made their press briefings and came with the ministers. That gave me quite good people coming here. They come here to talk. It's quiet, I've never had troubles or have to ask anyone to leave. It's small, I know everyone's name. People appreciate that. They come here once or twice, I remember their name, and that gives them a little bit of home feeling. I didn't know at the beginning that the location was so good. I get people from the Commission and the German Representation. I send them my menu by fax. In the evening, I have the big* stammtisch, *people meeting at the same time each month. There's the agricultural people, then the environment people. That gives me more satisfaction because I know who is coming here.*

Is it all Germans who come here?

No, not at all. They are not like the Austrians. When they have something for themselves they go there. The Germans don't do it – it's the German mentality. They are very proud of that. There are thousands of Germans in Brussels, but it's rare they stick together. It's funny. If you go to Spain or Majorca, they want their German pub, German restaurant, Sauerkraut, *etc., but not here. The type of Germans in Brussels are different. So there are quite a lot of Austrians coming – and Belgians, Flemish, lots of English speakers. It's not just typical German food. People can come to my kitchen to tell me what they want. In my experience, running a German pub is harder than others. The Germans all go to the Irish pub. So to survive really it's very hard, especially the last few years. There are 30 Irish pubs in Brussels now, can you imagine?*

What is it like running a business in this country?

I tell you if I had known the truth before I did it, I would never do it again. You are really cheated here with running a business. I didn't get any money from my husband, so I had to earn my life. But when I would have known what they are doing with me all the time with the taxes and the controls [audits] *... I have regularly a control every second year. It's not normal.* [The taxman] *is not a friend to Germans – he's French speaking. I even do the books in French to make it more easy for him! My* controlleur *says, "Your numbers are not credible. There are all these Germans living in Brussels", and I say, "So what!? They*

A Landlady's Tale—cont'd

don't all come to my place!" As an independent, I have very high taxes, 55 percent, and you don't get back anything. I'm treated as a physical person, I'm not a société [business]. *It's a very hard life here. There are so many things you can't understand. It's crazy, everybody* [else] *works in the "black", but nobody controls it. Yet I'm controlled all the time, and I pay and pay and pay, and my pension is less than somebody who is workless* [unemployed] *for 20 years.*

Her complaints about taxation as an "independent" are a familiar refrain of entrepreneurs here.

[Sighs] *At least here you can find a compromise, it's more flexible. There's always a chance to escape here, if you want to you can. Sometimes I get very angry with all the laws they make and nobody obeys them. That is the Belgian mentality.*

But talk of Brussels, and her tone changes. What does she think when people make all the usual negative comments?

I get very mad about that. There was a fonctionnaire *in the pub, and she said, "I hate Brussels!" And I asked, "Why do you hate it?" And her boss, who is Dutch, says, "But how can you say this!? You are never in Brussels!" And she says, "No, I don't want to stay here at the weekend". But then how can you know anything here? You have to make an effort. I think it's the fault of a lot of eurocrats working here. First, they don't want to live in the town. And when they do, they think it's the fault of the Commission where they have their job. Then they have their own sports club, their own crèches, their own schools. They are obliged to live in a ghetto and they do it because it's for free* [Commission employees have a special tax rate]. *It doesn't cost much money for them, and they don't know anything about the problems going on here, because they are not touched by them.*

That's why I joined the Flemish Socialist party. You have to participate, otherwise your opinions don't count. Then you have a better view of things, you understand the mentality a little bit. I started this year. I'm the first "European" who joined. They were very proud. I'm not a candidate yet. It's a very small, interesting group, not a big lobby. The French speaking group have 300 members, we only have 40. But they are very interesting people, lawyers or in the administration. When they come, they really want to talk and not just to drink. And it's a very young group. Not just old people. The French speaking group is mostly old.

What about the linguistic struggles?

Yeah, language differences! I speak Dutch and French. Before we went to Brussels, I studied six months French, and learnt by speaking. In 1986, I started to learn Dutch and now my Dutch is much better than my French. It is closer to my own language. It's very helpful to speak both the languages. There's a lot of people speaking Dutch here. When you talk their language they smile, and you can have everything you want. But you speak to Germans who have been here for 20 years, and they don't speak a word of Dutch because they think French is more … chic. But Dutch is a more natural language for them here.

Tell me about the neighbourhood here.

I live in the same house [as the pub]. *I like the neighbourhood, there are all kinds of nationalities around you. I get given all the keys of the apartments, people always know I'm here if someone arrives to visit. The location is very good, and they start now to do it up a lot. But it's all Europeans now, none of the Moroccans still live here now. They sold up,*

A Landlady's Tale—cont'd

moved to the other side of Saint Josse. Their children grew up with my children. But now it's finished, it has got very very expensive. There was a campaign against this. People were occupying some of the houses because they didn't want to sell out. They didn't want it to get so expensive. It's OK for me, because I own this house, and I bought it at a very low price. I would like to live in a Flemish town around Brussels, like the Brits and Germans in Tervuren. Or Watermael-Boitsfort, with a little garden, or a nice terrace for flowers.

Hedwig is the classic regional European – at home in the borderlands, in the centre of Europe. Brussels makes perfect sense for her.

I come from Westphalia, near the Dutch border. I go quite often to visit my family. Münster, a small town. I don't want to live in a small town anymore. What I hate the most is Sundays in Germany. There's nothing to do [everything is closed]. *Here, there is more activity, and you feel more the life. At first I didn't like it, it took me one year to get familiar. But when you get familiar then you like it. But everybody who has stayed three years, they didn't want to go back. After five, seven years, I know a lot of people who went back to Germany, but they came back! You get the impression you can live more free here. You can live the way you want and no neighbour is complaining. No one is stepping on your nerves, tolerance is very high. It is also so much more open for jobs, there are so many possibilities. Working for the company here you are more free than working in Germany.*

My sons are 23 and 30. Not married. They have girlfriends, they are settled here. They both lived in my place with their girlfriends. I was really fed up! But now they have their own lives. One is an IT manager, the other in tourism. They don't earn half of what they could in Germany, but they refused to leave. We speak every day, they come by. I expect to retire here. I'd like to always have one foot in Belgium, and always one foot in another country. My friend has a house in Marrakesh. It's hot, beautiful … I can't be without work, for long. I think I will start to write. I used to be very active, but working here I don't have time for it. I'd like to learn about computers, find a good course … Time is passing too quickly. I'd like to stop, and start a second life. This can't be life, to sit in the pub and work all the time.

Three years later, I'm in the neighbourhood again and decide to swing by *Das Bierfaß* to say hello. But the house where the bar was is being torn apart and refitted for new appartments. Hedwig has kept good her promise to herself. A little investigation reveals she is working for the representation of one of the German *Länder*, as an events organizer. The perfect job in Brussels for the woman who knew everyone. Doubtless she was still enjoying life in her adopted hometown.

8

Settlement

Amsterdam, London, and Brussels are all undoubtedly multicultural, international, and global cities. They opened their doors to free movement, and generations of new Europeans have moved there. But the promise of European integration suggests something more: a place where residents might enjoy not only the sense of denationalized freedom that mobility across borders brings, but also which provides an urban context where a truly cosmopolitan life might be achieved – on a mass scale. Much has been written about the potential cosmopolitanism of the European Union by social theorists and philosophers; much less has been substantiated in studies of real living people. Sceptics, meanwhile, argue that cosmopolitanism is the province of global and transnational elites alone. Yet actual existing cosmopolitanism, on a socially diversified scale, was right under their nose, ethnographically speaking, in the major cities of Western Europe: in the increasing diversity and *de facto* multiculturalism brought by conventional immigrant populations, certainly; but even more so – because of the invisible ease of residence and employment afforded by European free movement laws – among the growing European foreign populations in all of these cities. The Eurostars could in fact be the true cosmopolitans: pioneering a realistic, attainable, and materialized kind of denationalized life, in the rare spaces opened up by the Europeanizing dimension of Amsterdam, London, Brussels, and other cities.

How do these cities enable these individuals to step out of their national skins? How might freedom of the denationalized variety be possible? And, crucially, can these cities offer possibilities of settlement open and affordable to a range of ordinary middle-class foreign professionals, so that mobility is not only attainable by rich transnational elites, or expats with lives tightly structured and insulated by corporate multinationals? Mobility, flexibility, the liberating sense of provisionality in itself is not enough. Moving on serially also in fact excludes you from establishing a cosmopolitan residency. As so many of the Eurostars testify, the issue is not that you are always free to leave, but rather that you are able to settle in ways that make sense to your own mode of living. How to combine that precious feeling of mobility with a functional social and cultural life beyond work; with a meaningful life in a neighbourhood; with social networks and a sense of locality; with finding a house and building a home; with children, childcare, schooling; and with all the other practicalities that everyday life poses, such as medical coverage, financial security, and long-term planning?[1] These questions demand the possibility of a new kind of identification: with the city as a cosmopolitan place, not just one where it is easy to find and stick with your own co-nationals, or live in privileged foreigners' ghettos. Questions, in short, that chart the process from mobility to settlement. It's a once in a lifetime kind of thing: the moment the rubber hits the road, and it is possible to see how cosmopolitan these places really are.

The key lies in transposing the international dimension of the city with one that is well known from studies of domestic urban middle classes in recent years. Across all of Western Europe, urban middle classes have been reinvesting in inner city living after several decades of one way suburbanization. For these populations in the city, life over time and in the medium to long run, is all about conflict and struggle over access to scarce resources, in which they try to square the attractions and pleasures of urban life with the difficulties of inner city residence, in terms of cost of living, housing, family life, security, and space. Average professional incomes only stretch so far; life in the city is a compromise. The question here is: How well do the international residents fare in this same struggle? Although their spatial mobility patterns are very distinct, their social backgrounds are not so different, and they may well have identical types of aspirations to the majority national residents in the kind of urban life they are trying to create. To succeed in building a viable urban middle class life, you need a high level of investment in place, great familiarity and know-how with how the locality works, social networks, capital of various kinds, and (increasingly) social and political organization. All this, on top of enough hard cash to afford well located housing in sharply rising property markets. Economic capital is not usually a problem to these foreigners, and with university educated careers, they are high in human capital. But other forms of social and cultural capital are not necessarily easily available to them. As their experiences testify, they often came to these cities socially isolated, and possibly culturally ignorant of the finer details of life there; and although they may be affluent objectively in terms of income, they lack many of the other social connections that materially reduce the cost of living for long-term native residents. Comparatively, the question becomes: How well does each city do in delivering "quality of life" in the urban environment? Surely, if they cannot access it – with their ease of legal status, middle class capital, and ethnic invisibility – it is much less likely that other foreigners, similarly or less well placed in social terms, will fare well as outsiders.

Quality of Life

Without prompting, the term "quality of life" is the term resident urban professionals most commonly use to evaluate the attractiveness of city life. Academically speaking, it is an elusive concept, open to all kinds of indicators, but its core meaning is always related to how well the cost of living trades off against the benefits and difficulties of urban dwelling; that is, in relation to the opportunities, features, and services a city residence may offer. Typical indicators include public and commercial amenities, entertainment, health, crime, schooling, employment, participation, and so on. Recent efforts by the EU to promote this issue have also suggested incorporating more "subjective" non-material factors measuring cultural life and diversity in cities, as well as factors related to new technology and the quality of political governance.[2]

Of the three cities, it is Brussels that scores highest overall. It is worth focusing a while on how, in these terms, it is an ideal type relative to the other two. Regarding quality of life, Brussels' respondents consistently, virtually unanimously, offered favourable assessments. It didn't matter whether they came from the North or South of Europe, or were comparing the place to small towns or big competitor cities. Respondents were consistently positive about its facilities, cultural life, public transport, getting to work, getting in and out of the city, and above all the cost of living in return for a pleasant, village-like, yet wholly urbane, cosmopolitan city lifestyle. For many, it had become quite difficult to imagine going back to a city like London, not least because the lifestyle they enjoyed in Brussels would be totally unaffordable on the kind of average wages they were earning.[3] Brussels is one of the most affordable major cities in Europe, and it offers these benefits on open, accessible terms to *all* residents. For example, Tom points out how Dublin is so much more elitist, compared to the quite egalitarian feel of Brussels, which makes high quality neighbourhood living, and wide cultural opportunities, available to people on much more modest incomes. Paris or Amsterdam are much more expensive, and other residents compare it favourably to life in Rome, Copenhagen, and Geneva on these terms.

It is here that the informal ratings of quality of life in Brussels – as reported by international foreign residents rather than native insiders – contradict some of the typical international ratings.[4] Top of international listings is almost always Zurich, the German-speaking Alpine city that epitomizes the affluence and urbanity of multinational Switzerland.[5] However, as with Geneva, which is an ostensibly even more international city, these are cities in which the inner, bourgeois elite circles are notoriously closed to foreign international residents – even German or French nationals from just across the border consistently complain about this. They are also fiendishly expensive cities. Residents who know both countries confirm that Brussels is an infinitely more open city than these Swiss cities, which remain archetypal of the traditional, sedentary, bourgeois Eurocity of historically accumulated wealth and regional identity.

Brussels' advantages are not lost on the ECOBRU regional office of business development, who put Brussels' high quality of life factors as a key element in their marketing of the city to potential business investors.[6] Crucial among these factors is the cost of office space and housing, which is remarkably low by European capital standards. In international terms the city in fact appears underrated by businesses as a location.[7] At the other end of the scale, a huge global city like London is certainly open in all kinds of ways to foreigners, and great for global networks, but no ordinary residents would seriously rate quality of life high in terms of ease of everyday living, public transport infrastructure, environment, local political governance, or bringing up a family. In London, these are all a struggle, the spectacular attractions of the city attained in return for tough everyday residential compromises. No surprise then that Londoners of all kinds, no matter how proud, complain continually about their quality of life in the city as the one major downside of living there. It is ironic that some corporate ratings continue to place London so high. The answer, of course, is that, yes, it has great quality of life *if* you are a foreign exec on a six digit-plus corporate salary, with the company taking care of all family, domestic, and welfare details. For elites, London can indeed offer everything and anything. But it is not a city that is easy for more average middle class incomes, and it is here that Brussels scores so much higher. European resident professionals in Brussels are often not in the high earning brackets, comparatively speaking, even if the lifestyle they can construct in the city gives them the look of an urban cosmopolitan elite. Much of this has come as a pleasant surprise to those who moved there. It is a good place for social spiralists to feel like they have achieved something more than they might have done if they had stayed at home.

Urban Tribes

The secret to the quality of life in a city such as Zurich, as in much of urban Europe, rests in its dense, long-established social networks, monopolized by locals. The image here is life in a city where, even if you are not so affluent on paper, you always have family and friends to call on, parents are intimately involved in the domestic economies of their children, and real estate or land passes from generation to generation. Clearly, this is a large part of the reason why Europeans don't move much on a regional scale. It is exactly on these terms where newcomers and the highly mobile face the most disadvantages. Much of European society works like a club, in which you have to prove you are sticking around long enough before you are offered member benefits.

These social networks for young adults often stretch back to school days, or the college years, in the many instances where people didn't move away far from home to go to university. London social networks feel slightly different precisely because they are often – although certainly not always – rooted in post-college social networks, formed around work in the immediate, usually tough, first few years in the city. Elsewhere in Europe, a newcomer can quickly feel like they can never really be part of a gang that might stretch back, in its relationships and interconnections, to the most formative years of adolescence. It can be easy to feel excluded from this as a mobile newcomer. It is not a problem of language, or culture, or know-how; simply one of time, of water under the bridge.

The secret of American urban fluidity, in contrast, is always said to reside in the interchangeable quality of urban life across major cities; the fact you can move professionally, set up and settle in any American metropolis very easily. Young professionals enjoying the city also quickly form what have been pointed to by American pop sociologists as "urban tribes", the kind of close networked, but self-consciously constructed social circles to help access quality of life resources and deal with practical challenges. This is the *Friends* phenomenon, as seen in the well-known, cheesy, but vastly popular US comedy show. The gang of intimate friends, who share the tribulations of work, relationships, and single life in the big city, moving on together towards the first mortgage, married life, and (eventually) children. Among natives, especially in London, being part of an urban tribe is another key aspect of successful settlement in the big city.

The accessibility of this kind of social network will, then, be a key part of the success of any foreign residents in constructing the cosmopolitan urban life they have in mind. The cliché in studies of foreign expats in big cities is that they only form quasi-colonial national ghettos: the English guys down the English pub, speaking no foreign language, having no native resident friends, and living in pampered corporate isolation from the real city around them. This is, for example, how the Irish pubs such as *The Bank* or *Wild Geese* are presented in francophone Belgian guides to their own city; as places where you can watch foreigners socialize together *in situ*, like in a zoo. This is a perfectly possible scenario, most prevalent in fact in Amsterdam. However, in both London and Brussels, one can see something else happening. It is true that in neither case do foreign European residents penetrate much the social networks of nationals in the city; in fact, across the board, very few of even the most settled foreign European residents reported many "local" English or Belgian friends outside of work. But those international friends that they did have had often developed into a genuinely strong, supportive, stable network of the kind that urban tribes provide. They stop socializing in obviously expat, transient locations, consciously rejecting these in favour of more mixed and diverse places in the city. And often, too, these were highly cosmopolitan networks, spanning a multiple of nationalities joined by the experience of international mobility. They also often included native nationals who themselves had lived as foreigners abroad, and hence now felt out of the loop with their own co-nationals. A good test of cosmopolitanism in fact is how far the foreign resident seeks to avoid – or at least cultivates indifference – towards their own co-nationals in the city.

Caterina, the Italian science administrator, had committed herself to a career and settled life as a single working woman in Brussels. She offered a broad analysis of her social networks in exactly these terms. Her multinational tribe had a regular weekly meeting, that might be in a café, a film, or dinner at someone's flat. She drew a geography very familiar to longer-term foreign residents, who have moved on from the expat bars and EU centred social events near Schuman, to seek out some of the city's more obviously urbane, cosmopolitan locations. Her friends are "her family", and with girlfriends especially it developed very quickly – because they "all came here alone", as single, independent professional women, whose trajectories intersected in the city. She points out how mobility causes these friendships to develop, but also cuts across them, frequently, given their fluid, moving careers. Managing the comings and goings is the difficult part of the equation in these kinds of urban tribes, which are often forced to stretch to accommodate long-distance spatial ties.

Rob and Rachel, as a couple, clearly link their happiness in the city to the social networks they have built. These now have a character very different to the easy socializing that all newcomers in Brussels find when they first arrive, relying more on an "inner circle" who stayed. We talk about their upcoming wedding that will be taking place at Ixelles' *Maison Communale* – a symbolic choice of place, about which they are delighted. It will bring together their Brussels and other international friends with their friends and family from back home. For single men, in all these cities, Sunday park pickup football is a classic route to a mixed social network – "just give a man a ball", as Carlos tells me in London. Andreas, the Norwegian economist, plays out in Tervuren each week. He points out the downside of these international urban tribes, which may dissolve as quickly as they form.

> *It's a little bit fragile, not very big. My French is improving, but if my wife had some serious problem, it would be a little difficult to deal with ... We would not be alone, but it's not the same as growing up in the same place for twenty years ... Not like it would be in Oslo.*

Andreas here offers a reminder that the cosmopolitan urban tribes that have flowered in Brussels and elsewhere are but an approximation of the rooted social networks that most native Europeans take for granted.

Well-Being

Other practical considerations linked to personal security and well-being are also important to the sense of a viable settlement in a place. Mundane as it is, medical coverage and provision turns out to be an important point – both positively and negatively – in the three cities. In fact, on this question, Brussels rates far better as a destination that either Amsterdam or London. The heavily financed public health service in Belgium, which is organized through contributory *mutuels* linked to employment, is in fact one of the best in Europe. Belgium enjoys excellent hospital and doctor coverage, putting a lot of the money it doesn't spend on other public services – notably the visual appearance of the country, which is much less clean and pristine than the Netherlands – into medicine. The Eurostars who have settled are very conscious of these benefits, and speak approvingly of the system. Andreas, the Norwegian, and Bent, the Dane, both rated it as better than at home. Dario, from Italy (where "everything is a problem"), laughed at the endless complaints Belgians make about the system, because to him it seemed like "paradise" compared to home. Janet – who is acutely critical of many aspects of Belgian life – had experienced both private work insurance and the *mutuel* system; she sums up what many said by describing it as "brilliant, streets ahead of the NHS in Britain".

The few negative comments centred on it being a "confusing" system, especially for newcomers. Andreas thought the "the whole *mutuel* system is quite weird, fragmented". But they had found their way around, and a good dentist, because his wife's brother had been here before. Other residents were confused by having to pay "money up front" for treatment – even if you get it back. The fact the system is work related can leave problems during periods of unemployment or withdrawal from the labour market. Ellen was "very annoyed" that their children were under her *mutuel* and had to move to Jonathan's when she stopped unemployment benefit. For a while, the children weren't covered. One of her boys cut his head and required stitches during this period. The solution found, according to Jonathan, was very "typical of Belgium": the doctor wrote it up as if *his* head was cut open. But in the end they agree they are happy with the system, and have gone so far as to do the thing that is always the last thing that expats do when settling abroad – to shift to a doctor in the new country, and then, finally, a dentist. This is a symbolic choice that says a lot about the settlement process. They laugh about how their family back home couldn't believe they were staying in Belgium to have their first baby; and an English friend – "with rotten teeth!" – who still goes to see his dentist in London after ten years.

Social Reproduction

In fact, no issue better crystallizes the viability – or not – of the cosmopolitan lifestyle than the question of having and bringing up children in the chosen city.[8] A major part of my interviews was spent probing intimate issues to do with family life in the city. By this, I include relations with family back home, knowledge about other families, future thoughts about family, as well as direct experiences with children.

A huge part of the expat personnel concerns of the transnational corporation focus on managing family related issues, an issue that can easily blow apart an otherwise meteoric corporate career, or successful marriage. Much of this effort is designed to insulate the resident corporate family from any interaction with the institutions and practices of the host country. Hence, there has been a substantial boom in private international crèches and schools in major global cities, catering to the isolationist tendencies of corporate elites. But what other, more cosmopolitan options are available to European families in the promisingly international cities of Amsterdam, London, and Brussels? The issue of bringing up children raises fundamental, almost existential questions about how parents secure the future, provide for long-term stability, and plan for the social reproduction of their own standard of living (or better) for their heirs. As an individual, the question of long-term expectations can easily be deferred or discounted against the benefits of mobility. This is no longer the case when a family and children are involved.

One first discovery is that the foreign European population in the cities are less likely to have children than comparable couples in their home countries.[9] The decision for many couples is linked to their sense of being outside "normal" nationalized structures, in terms of both career and lifestyle, and in terms of "welfare security". It is thus easy to get a distorted view of resident foreigners by focusing only on expat parents with children at international schools. Sampling family life in this way distorts the questions because it misses couples and individuals who do not have children, as well as those who have engaged with the national education system. Many Eurostars pioneer urban professional lives simply no longer dedicated to national norms of family reproduction. And where they do have children, they are also not guilty of the traditionally gendered corporate family roles, which often seek to reproduce a "homeland" cultural environment abroad.

Among those with families, Brussels rates highly on childcare and schooling questions. Take Gunther, the German businessman (see below, pp. 216–19). What turned him around was having children in the city. It forced him to reorient his career around living in Brussels, and to take an active role in the crèches and schools to which his children were sent. In the meantime, he started to see some of the comparative advantages of Belgium in this respect. The family settled. The localization of authority over public services is one of the reasons why Belgium specializes so well in childcare. The state-run crèches are rated better than private ones because they employ people with state-recognized qualifications – the reverse of England, where expensive private crèches dominate, and quality is very variable. Several couples stress how much easier it has been than it would be in London. International parents in Brussels can also benefit from the curious political division of the city, in which large amounts of funding are provided to sustain minority language crèches in Dutch, for Flemish parents. These crèches often have a very progressive reputation because they openly seek to attract immigrant parents under a banner of promoting open, multilingual multiculturalism.

When Gunther's children reach the age, they will go to the European School to which they have access through his wife's work. Bent's two children from his first marriage also went through the European School – which is mainly for people who work for the Commission – for which he had subsidized access through his company. He points to how the prices have gone up and now, looking back, somewhat regrets the decision. Had he known he would settle, then the savings and the integration benefits involved might have made for a different decision. He thinks a private international school education "is not the real world". The expat resident magazine *Bulletin* in fact stresses there are lots of good options in the Belgian system. Jonathan and Ellen echo these concerns and opted to avoid the British school. Their three children are all in a local, non-denominational Belgian school to which they voluntarily contribute additional funding. Belgian schooling is "traditionalist, but it gets results". The schooling is all in French and follows the Belgian curriculum, but has extra teachers and is open to foreigners, including quite a number of Greeks and several Anglo-French children. The school "makes an effort to work with international parents", but "doesn't compromise or allow children to speak English in class". I asked why they didn't send the children to the British school, which is supposedly what all expats and eurocrats do. They respond as good cosmopolitans. It was way too expensive, they don't want to be stuck in a British ghetto, and they want the children to grow up with three languages, not one. Like Jonathan and Ellen, other foreign parents I met in Brussels nearly all got involved in the governance of their children's schools as a result of the difficult choices that childrearing poses.

Houses in Motion

As urban sociologists and geographers continually stress, the question which preoccupies residents most, and which often links together the other quality of life issues, is that of housing. Urban studies has experienced a dramatic renaissance in recent years, driven by the reawoken dynamics of development and change in post-industrial cities linked to gentrification. Some of the most interesting cases focus on how a younger set of middle class pioneers have sought cultural diversity and urban lifestyles in inner city areas abandoned by a previous generation during suburbanization. This has led on to new forms of political activism and a dramatic cultural transformation of certain cities. Other scholars see these processes in a more negative light, pointing to how corporate interests have encouraged these trends in self-styled "global cities" in order to purge themselves of unwanted poorer populations.

Brussels offers a particularly sharp scenario of this kind, in that it faced one of the most dramatic processes of suburbanization, industrial decline, and renewal. Poorer immigrants have played a major role in rehabilitating abandoned parts of the city with commerce and street life. Middle class urban pioneers have then followed them back into the central city. What is interesting about Brussels is the not inconsiderable role of the foreign European residents in leading the gentrification process in certain neighbourhoods. This leads to a rather different kind of multicultural interaction than other forms of immigrant settlement – a combination of ethnic enclave and middle-class gentrification – with distinctive types of housing, commercial development, and street culture.[10] No other city in Europe has quite seen, as Brussels has, the emergence of distinctly Europeanized neighbourhoods within the mosaic typical of international cities, although instructive comparisons can be drawn between Ixelles or Sint Katelijne in Brussels and De Pijp or Jordaan in Amsterdam, Shoreditch or Islington in London, and Bastille or Oberkampf in Paris, sites where similar dynamics have emerged in the last decade or so.[11]

The middle class struggle for urban life is at it most intense and competitive over housing. So much else – from neighbourhood life to access to crèches and schools – depends on getting a house in the right place at the right price. The middle class shift in investment from stocks and shares to housing during the last decade, combined with low interest rates and a resurgence in forms of local urban governance, have pushed up housing markets across all of Europe's cities, both large and medium sized, to a dramatic and possibly unsustainable degree. House prices in London, Paris, Amsterdam, Copenhagen, and Stockholm have scaled incredible heights, squeezing every middle-class urbanite ambition. Yet oddly, and with the exception only of Berlin among major cities in Northern Europe, Brussels has been uniquely under-populated and hence undervalued in real estate terms. The destruction and exodus of the past has given Brussels an extraordinary advantage in the quality of life/settlement equation. The single most important factor in convincing foreign Europeans of the quality of life to be had in the city, and the crucial attraction that takes them from sojourner to settler, is the way the housing market – both rental and ownership – works there. In stark contrast, housing is the one thing most likely to cause people to give up and leave Amsterdam or London.

Perhaps the best example of a cosmopolitan Europeanized neighbourhood is Ixelles in Brussels.[12] The commune is a magnet for many of the younger Eurostars beginning to establish themselves in the city. It lies adjacent to work in the European quarter, and is characterized by both poor immigrant inner city areas and more affluent residential ones. Bisected east-west by the thoroughfare Avenue Louise, the cosmopolitan Place Fernand Coq and Place Flagey to the north are typical first-time residences for *stagiaires* and newcomers, while more settled residents often opt for the slightly more affluent neighbourhoods in the southern "triangle", especially around Place du Châtelain and rue Américaine. Ixelles has a remarkably large and diverse foreign European population, with uniquely high figures for the recent Eurostars rather than older European immigrants.

Recent arrivals in Brussels often quickly settle on Ixelles as the place to look for housing, either because of networks of friends who already live there, or the initial positive experience of eating out and drinking in and around its vibrant squares. The old town house buildings are full of attractive apartments, rehabilitated by landlords for these new populations. Finding a place is generally easy: through word of mouth, newspapers, or just wandering through the attractive *fin-de-siècle* streets at the weekend, taking down numbers mentioned on the many *te huur* signs you see in windows. Brussels is one of the very rare cities so flush with housing that this kind of informal market works. A mix of contract terms encourages people to opt for longer rental commitments, as this sharply reduces price. This is a problem for the serially mobile, scared off by the idea of longer commitment, who then end in a pattern of unstable accommodation that might affect quite strongly their experience of settlement in the city (as it did in businessman Dave's case; see pp. 132–5). But opting for longer can in fact anchor you. Janet at

Unilever was still thinking of global mobility, but her three year housing commitment in fact had led to a certain kind of stable settlement.

As these examples suggest, the structure of the Brussels rental market plays a great role in facilitating settlement and identification with life in the city. Unlike in other major cities, foreigners in Brussels can get access quickly and reliably to desirable, good quality, good value housing that immediately provides a springboard to an enjoyable lifestyle. Coupled with the multiplier effect of foreign Europeans clustering in certain neighbourhoods, and inspiring new services and commercial outlets catering to their (cosmopolitan) interests, housing becomes the key to Brussels' extraordinary capacity to facilitate the life of denationalized would-be Eurostars. The period between two to five years in the city is the crucial transition stage, in which the initial enjoyment of the quality of life benefits in the city might get translated into something more ambitious. Since none of the other factors that might weigh on the settlement decision are a struggle – the job market, the housing market, international social networks, cultural activities – many Brussels residents feel comfortable enough to take further steps. Their housing strategies in fact become a form of proactive economic participation in city life that belies the image of social and political indifference to the city around them.

Joannet and Stephen's decision to stop talking about mobility was made possible by the housing mechanism. They met while renting as neighbours in the city centre, and were "bored with the Schuman syndrome" – the ever-temporary life of eurocrats in the city. After marrying and boosting their high joint incomes, they consciously said that they were "here to stay", but were "too young" for the sterile life of expats in suburbia. Their strategy translated into a move to a marvellous apartment on the Ixelles lakes on a longer contract, found by chance while out walking one night ("the only time we ever dressed up for a housing appointment"), then a whole range of plans to buy in Brussels and the Ardennes at a later stage. The initial perception of extraordinary opportunities in the rental sector leads to a realization that settlement is an option in the longer run. The line between sojourner and settler is a fine one; many talk for years about leaving, or about how accidental it is they are living here. The good life in a good flat can make all the difference. In the early 2000s, the general monthly rent or mortgage in Brussels was in the €400–600 a month range, between a quarter and a fifth of typical household incomes – much lower, and a much better ratio than is usual in London or Amsterdam. I heard similar housing narratives from all the other settled couples I met in the city: Claudia and Miguel, Jonathan and Ellen, Rob and Rachel. Each talked me through the process of buying a house in Belgium, which they and others had found a fairly "pleasant experience", particularly financially speaking and in comparison with buying in Britain, a notoriously cut-throat market. The process is paced out, gazumping is not possible, yet obtaining a mortgage easy. Healthy competition between Belgian banks for expat business helps.[13] But the market is slow, largely due to the very high legal costs when buying, which can amount to a statutory 18 percent of the house price. Owners cannot count on recouping costs very rapidly. With rent low, several interviewees with mobility on the mind – such as Dave and Janet – had been put off buying. In countries where buying is easier – as is London and Amsterdam – the purchasing of property does not actually signal a commitment to settle, in that it could just be speculative.

Brussels has clearly benefited from the willingness of pioneer Europeans buying into older, sometime wrecked town houses in less affluent areas. The driving up of prices by the demand of these gentrifiers is in this sense merely the positive effect of foreign residents recognizing the opportunities that abandoned town houses represent. Rob and Rachel were part of this trend, having bought their flat on a quite run-down major thoroughfare on the poorest northern edge of Ixelles. The neighbourhood is a mix of North Africans, Portuguese families, and very old retired Belgians, still rather dirty, full of graffiti and unfinished buildings. An "in between place", as they put it, but one clearly now gentrifying. They have made their calculations carefully, and the very well located neighbourhood is now changing. In fact, the Eurostars often live in beautiful places, which they had acquired through only a fraction of the cunning, ruthlessness, or luck it would take to acquire equivalent property in London or Amsterdam – a good example being Gunther's extraordinary "signed" art nouveau house in multi-ethnic Schaarbeek. Enterprising housing pioneers have similarly moved into less salubrious parts of St. Gilles, and Brussels-Centre (especially near the Marolles market) and Sint Katelijne, where prices are lower and the old housing stock equally full of potential. Gunther's real estate *trouvaille* is by no means extraordinary, and will be repeated should these European housing pioneers begin to look in completely unexplored areas of the city such as Molenbeek, Bockstael, Koekelberg, or Anderlecht – as they might as prices push them that way. For now, these are still alien territories. On this account, Brussels would do well to encourage the dynamism that European residents have injected into the city's housing market, rather than moan about the rising prices and foreign takeover. Things are likely to change, even in the deprived northeast of the city. After much wrangling, and interventions from the likes of public philosopher Philippe van Parijs and former EU Commissioner Neil Kinnock, Brussels finally agreed to locate the new European school out near Bockstael, rather than opt again for the affluent suburbs. This may encourage some of the bolder European residents with families to explore new corners of the city. For an eye-opener, they ought to ride some day the famous Brussels tram 81 – the name of a free multicultural newspaper in the city – which goes all the way from leafy Montgomery, through Ixelles, St. Gilles, and the Centre, up through some of the most dramatic neighbourhoods between the Gare du Nord and the Atomium. Here they will see street markets out of a different world, with radical Islamists and poor immigrant families living in the uncharted multicultural spaces of this remarkable unstructured city of diversity. But they will also be able to eye many desirable properties *en route*, even if they need to work out whether these streets are still too edgy to venture into at night.

Further out, the housing market is more difficult in the most desirable suburban parts of the town, where a previous generation of European foreigners have settled. A francophone estate agent I visited confirmed the difficulties that both Belgians and others were now experiencing in finding affordable accommodation in suburbs like the "village" of central Watermael-Boisfort.[14] Some areas, such as Uccle for the French and Tervuren for the British, remain places with specific European enclaves. Belgians themselves blame the housing squeeze on the resident European population. Yet, on the whole, the evidence suggests an account closer to the optimistic image of dynamic city in transformation, rather than a bleak narrative of corporate exploitation and exclusion. To some extent these will also be two sides of the same coin: there are always winners and losers in the struggle for access and control of the precious urban quality of life. The eurocrats continue to be seen as remote invaders, driving around in expensive German cars, with no meaningful contact with the city. Yet as Janet quips when I mention the notion of resentment: "Yeah, and there's a lot of Belgians making a lot of money out of it!"

Brussels' housing scenario offers a unique context in which newcomers can quickly find a home in the city, as well as opportunities which draw them into longer-term settlement and identification with the city. In the process, they have helped transform the city materially, and given it back some of its late nineteenth-century cosmopolitan grandeur. The structural impact of housing is always fast moving and changing, however. With sharply rising prices and rising demand, it is possible that the highpoint of Brussels' cosmopolitan housing scenario has passed. As ever, this space or moment is a fragile one, only ever conjuncturally possible. With the end of Brussels' exceptional housing scenario, the struggles over monopolizing the good life in the city may come to resemble other capital cities where foreigners have none of the advantages and opportunities that Brussels' Eurostars have long enjoyed.

A Businessman's Tale

I'm thinking: Dave looks like one of my uncles. No, in fact, he looks *just* like Ray Winstone, the film about the cockneys, where he is Michael Caine's son – *Last Orders*. I'm waiting outside airport departures when he pulls up. A smart motor, coat and tie. If this had been England we'd have gone down the pub for a swift ale, but instead we drive round for a leisurely interview in his office, somewhere in one of the warehouse edge-city developments near Zaventem airport. This could be anywhere in the industrialized world. Dave has a business to run, and a new life to lead. There is nothing like getting this stuff from the horse's mouth. What is it like doing business in a foreign environment? Employing as well as being employed? Dave sees what he is doing as a more civilized kind of business, outside the boom/bust Anglo-American mode. A way of creating, sustaining, and spreading a good quality of life. The obverse of the French libertarians in London/Ashford, in fact. The tone of the interview is frank and funny, albeit a little wistful. Every now and then, he drops a phrase into the conversation in a self-consciously fake posh accent. Occasional telephone calls about work that's coming up also keep me busy on the on/off button.

The easiest way would be to talk about my reasons for leaving the UK. Back a few years now, at the end of the 80s. I was in the same profession, an international courier. I was Heathrow based and the company I was with had an opening in Amsterdam for an office manager. So I thought about it very carefully – for a few seconds [laughs] – I had no ties or anything. Amsterdam is such an easy place to go to, it really is. It was very easy to adapt.

I moved into a suburban area, Amstelveen. Luckily enough, British Midlands were just opening a route from Amsterdam to London, so I ended up sharing a house with four or five British Midlands stewardesses [laughing]. I was mothered to death for about a year! After that, I actually moved into Amsterdam itself, which was great. I was living very close, on a tramline: no need to get a car into the centre. After five years I moved on. The same company I was with then was expanding. In our profession, Brussels is well positioned for movements in and around Europe, so we needed to get a hub facility here. I came here with a view to being here two years. I was going to just like set up things and then move on, but there are things you never plan for. The first two years, I was here Monday to Friday, but still living in Amsterdam. By that time, I'd become engaged to a Scottish lady. She didn't want to move down here. She was enjoying living in Amsterdam too much. But after two years it became apparent that things were moving quite well down here. I couldn't live up there forever. Other expansion plans were on hold, and I've just kind of ended up staying. My fiancée, who then became my wife, came with me at that time.

A few years later, the company I was with sold out to a very large multinational, a big transport group. So what was a very small, friendly company, the whole flavour changed. All of us within the company, we'd been together so long, we all decided to get together and start our own offices. For me, it seemed logical it would be in Belgium. That's where all

A Businessman's Tale—cont'd

my customer contacts were. I mean, in commerce that's everything, yeah. We cooperated, not as partners, but with the same trading name. So I own my own company under the same name.

So the business is financially located in Belgium?

Yeah, totally. It's Belgian regulated, tax, registration, the lot. [Sarcastically] *Yeah, fantastic! There were certain expat deals, but they are all time-restricted. So after a while I came under the Belgian tax system and all its related disasters. The employee social security payments are really quite restrictive. With eight people here, we could have eleven and a half in the UK. That's quite extreme in a rather small workforce. The Netherlands is similar to here. They used to be quite liberal on some employment issues, but they are really cracking down.*

I thought in some ways Belgium is supposedly advantageous for business, vis-à-vis the Netherlands. This is what the regional officers tell you.

Certain cash industries have huge black economy potential. But not ours, I'm afraid. It's all invoices and strictly by the book. Luckily enough, with the experience I had opening up in the other country, it was a lot easier to do it coming at it a second time. It would be quite frightening, coming from completely the outside because there's all sorts of contradictory information that you get given. When you move, you tend to think that what you've been used to is the right way of doing things. It's difficult to have an overview and see that it's not always like that. Once you've been away a little time, you understand the local systems and perhaps even appreciate some of the stuff [laughs]. *Learning not only how to open up a company, but to look after yourself. You have to rely on good professional advice. The chamber of commerce in Brussels was horrendous. If you are lucky enough to have a good accountant, that just about counts for everything. And financial advice. The banks are quite open here. They look it from their own point of view. But the key to everything is to get a good insurance agent and a good accountant. Just employ wisely, that's the advice.*

Dave reaches for another cigarette. I remark he seems to like an old brand which I remember my father once smoking.

Yeah, Embassy cigarettes. That's a thing. I can't find them in Belgium. I stopped smoking for 11 years. I started again last year. I've got a particular taste for them. They're only available in Luxembourg, I drive there every now and then.

Cheaper cigarettes. One of the benefits of free movement. What about your social life?

Well, I am still married, but my wife has moved back to the UK last year. She found life in Belgium from her perspective a little restrictive, and from the point of view of my business commitments, I didn't have a choice. So, it was just a mutual thing, just one of those things.

Would you say Amsterdam is more international?

I would say, primarily, more English speaking… Oh dear! [laughs] *One thing I did notice in Amsterdam is just how transient it was there. Really, people are there, then gone … One thing I find incredible here. My customer base is almost exclusively Brussels and area,*

A Businessman's Tale—cont'd

*primarily French speaking, yet they're happy to phone up and speak in English. I can't see
that happening elsewhere. Nice bunch! I moved to Leuven a year ago. I was quite happy in
Stokkel, but we were separating, and when I looked in Schuman, I found that in three years
the prices had gone up enormously. So I decided to try outside of Brussels. I'd always loved
Leuven, but always found it a problem parking at night. But I found an appartment with
pretty much the price I'd been paying in Stokkel, with private parking. So it was an easy
decision. It's just as handy for Brussels, although the traffic is a bit of a nightmare in the
mornings. The Flemish are very cosmopolitan minded, I find. I have a healthy social scene
in Leuven. Yeah, it's the expat trap. With other English friends. A lot of them are on contracts. IT at the moment is particularly prevalent. Also the medically minded. Pharmaceuticals.
Telecoms engineers. There are all sorts of people in contracts with the airport. There's a bit
of variety, and not so many non-Belgian pubs. It's fantastic, a student town, a lively lively
place. One particular Irish bar which I was introduced to, the Thomas Stapleton. It's the
modern day equivalent of the Community Hall.*

Are you going to stay here? What are your long-term financial plans?

*I can't see myself relocating voluntarily back to the UK. No, I'm afraid there's noth-
ing I really really miss. I know it's always where your heart is, but no, I'm happy enough
with life, with Belgium, little things. Age is a factor. I can't see myself being FourOh
back in England. That changed when I opened the company. It really restricts your
options, you know, being so focused on a particular industry. I certainly wouldn't rely on
the Belgian system. From a business point of view, you have to look at it as needing to
be self-sufficient now and later. When I was working for the other company, there were
retirement schemes and so on but none of them apply now. Ultimately it depends on the
progress of the company. It's all a bit imponderable. Everything is going fine on the business side. If there were positive reasons to move back … Unfortunately, I can't think of
any! I wouldn't want to move back because of some failure over here. If it's retirement,
then I'd go for the sun.*

Are you integrated here?

*[Laughing] Not at all, not at all! Has anyone replied positively on that!? [More
laughter]… But I don't feel any restrictions. I don't think that the barriers are permanently
down for me – although my Flemish friends would argue that I'm missing out on a lot of
things not speaking the language. You can't be totally impervious [to it]. Trying to understand things like the statutory forms.*

Are you a migrant?

*[Long pause] Er …. I wouldn't … This not really being the country of my choice,
I wouldn't see it like that. It's more an acceptance of the fact that I'm here in Belgium.*

Belgians seem to often resent resident foreigners. A lot of it comes down to
the completely incommensurable scale of their earnings.

*Yeah, it can be totally artificial … All right for some! These independent contractors,
what they are able to earn is frightening. It's all about quality of life in the end of the day.
Everything's a balance, isn't it? When you haven't laid your roots down completely yet. You
wouldn't be able to do what I've done in Belgium in Germany or France or practically
anywhere else in Europe I'd suggest, Holland being the other exception. I don't feel any direct*

A Businessman's Tale—cont'd

prejudice against me as a foreigner doing business in Belgium. Perhaps I'm particularly thick skinned [laughs]... *I think particularly when people find out you have a business, and you employ local workforce, that's quite a positive thing, as I see it. As long as things continue to bring me up, that's fine. You can't really allow yourself to think about the downside of things. Nah, it's all about motivation to make things go right. Stop the knockers, and get on with the Belgian people. It's not a bad life.*

While driving back to the airport, we talk about cars. They say it's cheaper in Belgium.

Well, in terms of looking at things in different ways... It's cheap to buy in Belgium, yeah. But look at the road tax! Here, it's based on size of the engine, so you end up paying a couple of thousand pounds a year for a higher end car. Also there's the registration, it's £3,500 to register a car ... You can never compare like to like. For every apparent pro there's always something underneath.

9

Integration (1)

Brussels scores high in the quality of life equation because it has been so affordable for foreigners – and so accessible. It works for many residents because it is possible to settle and achieve a kind of functional integration into the city without in any way being integrated into the national culture around it. Elsewhere, this settlement process might not be so easy – because the nation can be so much more present in the life of the city.

The power of the modern nation-state-society lies in its ability to standardize and reproduce the lives of its population on a mass scale. To do this, it relies on norms. The modern national society is thus organized around and for the normal, mainstream way of life: the statistical average that allows the system to manage the present or predict the future; the median citizen that wins elections; the democratic consumer to which the mass produced product is pitched. Norms in this world are nationalized forms of behaviour. They are what allow everyone to speak with confidence about *this* nation or *that* culture, as if they were perfectly bounded, self-consistent entities, ontologically secure in a world carved up into similarly distinct nations and cultures. Norms are also what allow scholars to ignore the 1 in 50 as "statistically insignificant." Integration, usually, is about getting into line with these norms; getting in synch with the rhythm of the nation. They are about getting on the train that will take you as a first, second, or maybe third class passenger, along the long line from cradle to grave. In a Europe of nation-states, to integrate means to naturalize, to go native. Immigrants – foreign nationals changing country – thus experience the pressures and opportunities of settlement and integration as a process of *renationalization*. But the Eurostars are not immigrants. They went looking for something else: a denationalized freedom, a life beyond such norms. But is this really possible? If immigrants all around the world succeed by assimilating as best they can to the norms of the new society, the problem faced by the Eurostars becomes clear. To get access to the full range of payoffs offered to them by the social system they live in, they might have to engage in the core middle class struggle over scarce resources and the good life in terms that are usually organized by a national way of life – that they, by definition, never intended to be part of.

Why might this be? The answer lies in their curious membership status. Historically, the democratic nation-state-society is a club that not only protects the rights and enables the freedom of its members; it also contracts to treats them fairly. Some kind of notion of equality has thus also been a constitutive part of the nation-building process in Europe that has unified regions, classes, genders, and cultures in a single political body, often after protracted political struggles. Membership in this club entitles a kind of baseline for all citizens: that returns for individuals will at least be proportionate to their efforts in a competitive educational system and labour market; that successful social trajectories and better lives for your children are open to all with talent, irrespective of where they come from; that every citizen has a voice in the decisions that guide how this system functions and is improved. Nation-states have thus followed broadly inclusive trajectories over the past two centuries – albeit imperfectly – to defuse the kinds of social tensions that can pull nations apart.

International migration messes with the egalitarian social closure implicit in this notion of citizenship. It poses the question of what to do with new-comers who have not been socialized in the society, and who may not yet follow its norms. Historically, immigration has, on the whole, also been dealt with by means of inclusion, often after further struggles, offering to immigrants the same set of rights and benefits that citizens enjoy. In return for this, however, immigrants had to be renationalized to become full members: become Black-British, Asian-British, and so on. And herein lies the problem. For formal equality – minus some key political rights – was broadly extended to foreign European residents with the invention of the free-movement laws of "European citizenship". This is not a true citizenship, but it does bestow rights and benefits on the European residents that enable them to claim equal treatment in their host countries' labour markets, housing markets, education systems, and professional rewards systems. Yet, as Europeans, there is no need and very little pressure for them to renationalize as Dutch, Belgian, or British. The nation-state-society, on the other hand, has always relied, for its very existence, on its ability to distinguish and discriminate between members and non-members, between a national and a foreigner.

What use is a club that doesn't bestow any distinct benefits on its members? A club such as this would have to be disbanded. European law in theory has made such discrimination impossible; global convergence of markets too has had its own flattening impact. But, almost by definition, the nation-state-society has to find ways of distinguishing, discriminating against, and sidelining non-members: it is the most fundamental mechanism of nation-building, a *sine qua non* of nationhood.

The Eurostars moved to the heart of the most global and international cities; they know very well not to expect equal treatment out in the provinces. But even here they might not escape the subtle processes that are renationalizing the games that they should be playing on a level field. These are processes that can absorb those willing to go native, to naturalize – fair's fair – but will penalize those who don't really want to sign the national social contract. The internationalization of the economy, the law, even the state, has made formal institutional venues less and less a place where these processes of exclusion can take place; they have to move down, into the realm of social interactions and small acts of everyday social closure. The things that remind you that you are still a foreigner; that you don't really belong here. It takes an ethnographic eye to tease out the subtle and informal moments of banal nationalism still at work in Europe today. And, again, the degree to which these renationalizing processes are felt, varies from city to city, just as it does between inner city and suburbs.

In Brussels, nationalizing and renationalizing processes are weak. This multinational, multicultural, and multileveled political curiosity is in fact the exception. In London and Amsterdam, however, in the everyday lives of the Eurostars, it turns out that renationalizing processes are ascendant over the twin denationalizing processes of Europeanization and globalization. To succeed in these cities they find they have to do precisely what they came there to avoid: live like a national would; a standardized, nationalized life. And so they never settle, and they decide not to stay. It is the small, almost insignificant mechanisms adding up to this dominant outcome, that will be explored here.

Mechanisms of Exclusion

First, there is the obvious subjective experience of this. The feeling that, despite having everything more or less settled, of having done everything you can to make the place work professionally and personally, you still do not quite feel at home. As such acute observers, the Eurostars offer some of the best insights into the nationalist idiosyncrasies of their adopted nations. On this score, both the Netherlands and Britain can come across as peculiarly provincial places, for all their avowed cosmopolitanism.

Britain's relationship with the rest of Europe is a strange brew. Arriving at Stansted airport – a potent symbol of just how European London has become, with thousands of young Europeans coming and going every day to hundreds of destinations across Europe – you take the overpriced express shuttle into the City. No less than five European languages greet the happy traveller. In glossy brochures, London offers itself as the multicultural "Babylon of the Modern World": a European marvel. Can this really be the same country whose most popular newspapers daily print squalidly racist articles about refugees, fan hysteria about immigrant floods from Eastern Europe, or cake layers of xenophobia on every negative article about the EU or its closest European neighbours?

Even the Eurostars have been infected by that "Great" British habit of referring to Britain and then Europe, as if they were something different. How many time have I myself made that mistake? Referring to the "Europeans" in London, as if London didn't have ten million plus *native* Europeans already living there. During an interview in Kingston-upon-Thames, it happens again.

Adrian: *Are there many other "Europeans" in this building?*
Rainer: *No, there aren't … Well, I hope they're all Europeans* [smiles].

Now, I am the *last* person in Europe who should make *that* gaffe. This successful German manager at Unilever, unsurprisingly, has strong views on the subject. He was surprised about the British reluctance to adopt the single currency, and simply cannot understand why in Heathrow you see these signs that say "Transfer to Europe". "For God's sake, this *is* Europe", he gasps.

Being German, though, this rather subtle form of exclusion can also take a much cruder ethnic form. Some renationalizing processes are blatant and in your face. Don't just mention the war. Go on and on and on about it. Before his wife came over to join him, he told her to read a few history books. He says it's the only thing that has really turned him off living there.

I'd been to a couple of cocktail parties, and they nearly all ended the same way! Everybody asked me questions as if I would have been an entire witness of the war. I felt a little bit exposed. That I couldn't answer these questions, but that I had to. After a couple of drinks, you can't make jokes about it … It gives me a sign that we haven't realized in Germany how much an issue it is still outside Germany. It's a learning for me.

Very characteristically for a German, Rainer has internalized the message, and not taken offence. All the Germans in London have had some experience of straightforward abuse. The older they are, the worse they remember it.

The defensive adaptation to other nations' reactions to their nationality is a familiar part of "postwar" life in Europe. The typical attitude among Germans has been to use this negative identity as the leverage for creating a denationalized republic at the heart of a federal Europe. They have always tried to internalize the feeling of self-criticism, and self-awareness of the horrors of nationalism – and instead try to be good Europeans. To most English, most of the time, they will just be Germans. You get the feeling that Franz – married into and half-native Spanish, as Europeanized as it gets – has been internalizing the message day in, day out while in London.

> *There are certainly ups and downs, but you have that in every city…* [His mood darkens] *I can't start whingeing, "Oh the English don't like me, they're against Germans…" They know that you are German and sometimes they get a bit rude. When you know it, you can live with these facts.*

A good strategy (the "counter attack", as his wife Carmen suggests) is to deflect the issue into a harmless nationalized rivalry that can always defuse the question for most English – especially in London, where it sometimes seems like 90 percent of all office and pub conversation revolves around it: football, of course. That seems to quiet them down again. He says friends who are visiting from Germany for the first time find it incredible, and wonder how he can live with it. But he says: "It doesn't hurt … and it's open, fair, you know, when you think about it." Franz is here being extremely reasonable. Football, though, can just be another excuse for xenophobia. During the European Championships in England in 1996, the tabloids referred to the Spanish quarterfinal opposition as "wops", much to the distress of many Iberian residents. Dubious refereeing helped England into the next round – against Germany. Gazza (Paul Gascoigne) and Stuart Pierce were pictured on the front of *The Sun* wearing *Dad's Army* infantry helmets. It's a laugh, innit? Pure clowning. England lost.

Nationalizing relations with foreign European residents has the predictable outcome; they renationalize themselves, folding back into their core national identities as the default when challenged. Jaime sees the teasing and stereotypical as part of the "joke" culture he likes so much. But he can see when the joke isn't funny anymore: he notes that that they "wouldn't do that with Asian people" – it would be seen as racist. He likes *The Sun* newspaper, but was a bit shocked about how nasty they get about the French, recalling the infamous page one picture of Jacques Chirac as a worm. The stereotyping helps keep the foreign Europeans in their place. The obvious reaction to this situation is that nationalized groups form as a self-help, such as the Spanish group Jaime sometimes hangs out with. He says, as a result, they all rant and rave about how difficult it is to get to know English people.

Franz also points to a specificity of the way Britain nationalizes foreigners to include or exclude them. As in the US, the dominant pattern of assimilation passes through the "ethnicization" of allcomers along the lines of the main immigrant groups that have been absorbed into the country. To get a resident's status, Franz had to go through a testing interview with an Asian-British administrative officer, whose own conception of being a categorizable foreigner, and of processes of international migration, didn't include the free movement of a multinational couple with a European identity. The officer first insisted that his wife's name – which in Spain retains the two original parents' names – had to be changed to his – against Spanish practices and European law. And when Franz answered that he had come to Britain from Spain, the officer refused to accept it, declaring:

No. You are German. You have come from Germany, from Frankfurt. You took the plane and you came from Germany.

Franz found this all quite funny, but his bank's inability to recognize his wife's correct name, or in fact that they were married, irritated him intensely. Carlos and Susana, also high earning MNC employees, had the same experience. They were unable to open a joint account for months because the bank would not accept she was his wife. In the heart of global finance, it turns out that British banks are far from open for international business if you are a foreign European resident and you just want to open a bank account. Banks routinely discriminate on grounds of nationality – presumably arguing that these British residents might only be temporary. Nathalie, Pedro, and others had to be paid in cash by their employers for several months. Banks are much less flexible in London than either Brussels or Amsterdam. Phone companies often prove difficult for the same reason. The suspicion is that these long delays in recognizing European residents *as* residents, and not just transient visitors, links to a deeper resistance to their presence.

Other residents have observed how class can be used to code and maintain national specificities. Nour loves working and living in London, but of all the younger Eurostars she is perhaps the least impressed about what it has to offer culturally. A self-styled "classic" dresser, she is a firm believer in doing all her shopping in Paris, exchange rates permitting. She would join dozens of other people arriving back in London on the Eurostar train armed with top quality *foie gras* and wine that would have cost a fortune "at Harrods". What is interesting is that these basic elements of the good life get coded (and priced) as upper class luxuries in Britain, when they are in fact available to a much broader range of the population in France. Her colleagues joked that she was "being very snobbish".

> *People tend to identify you here by how you look, and they are like, "Oh yes of course she buys her clothes in Paris" … But it has nothing to do with that, it's because it was much cheaper* [laughs].

The class judgment was used to mark her out as a foreigner. This rather quaint "overvaluation" of thus designated "foreign" goods still goes on despite the ease of circulation of goods within the European free market. A similar thing happens with the snob value of certain foreign cuisine.

Guffaws of laughter regularly greet foreign errors about class or social position. The sound of ridicule and irony is one of the main markers of social closure and exclusion in European societies. When you are the foreigner, you don't get the joke – you have to just sit there and take the humiliation. Carlos has some interesting stories about his own "gaffes" in Britain.

> *The first thing your neighbours do is check your car, and which company you work for – then they have already classified you, where do you belong to. We went for dinner, and they are asking, "Which newspaper do you read? Which radio do you listen to?" It's after dinner, and I answer – not* Radio 4 [the serious BBC news program], *which in fact I do – but* Magic Radio [a trashy London pop channel]. *Everybody laughed. Then I realize that the question was not that one. They were asking about my politics …*

Carlos comments on how one of the things you learn in England is that knowing the language is not enough. Unilever has to combine both cultures: the difference here between two relatively close European nations is vast. The Dutch are famed for being brusque and upfront, if not rude. Conversely, you never know what English people *mean*, however much they are smiling. In Britain, access to the language has been made so easy by American globalization that the nation preserves its spell by the subtlest of means. It is the older, long-term residents in fact that make the most telling points on this question. Even they can feel excluded by these mechanisms. Sandra, the artist, describes it as an "invisible door that you sometimes break through but … is never completely open". Was the comment meant to be funny or was it an insult? She always felt it was like a little "slap under the belt".

For the younger residents, it is the inverted snobbery of working-class "cool" that trips them up. It is interesting observing the sports habits of young European foreign men in London. Not only is the international pick-up game the standard way of meeting people on a weekend. They also try to take on the domestic habit among middle class London professionals of obsessive debate about football in pubs, a trend driven by the universal adoption of a (usually) fake working class identity as the badge of belonging in the city. Highly intelligent, well mannered, and often deeply intellectual people cultivate the impression that they have nothing to talk about except the latest local derby between Chelsea and Arsenal.

Jeroen tried sports as a mode of integration. He avoided the Dutch pick-up football in Holland Park, and the Dutch-style *borrels* – "with *bitterballen* and all that" – at *De Hens* in Piccadilly. Local Sunday league football was too serious and violent. It was fun to be with the local boys, but he "didn't really relate". Working out all the signals from class and nationalism is not easy. Jeroen is impressed by the real London cockneys. I point out how they are the only people who are really from London. Everyone else is trying to be like them: the public schoolboy rock bands, the street fashion, the gangster films made by ex-Etonians. Authenticity is confusing: so many codes. Nathalie, his girlfriend, is less impressed. She complains that if you don't have the right kind of label or shoes, you are "not in", and they see you as a foreigner. She was made to feel by her workmates "like an old lady, dressed like a bag". France is not any better; just a different set of codes. The point is that this stuff is still incredibly important in the social order of any given European nation-state-society, and *even* in the heart of the "global" city of choice, London. We talk about the old and the new East End, the Shoreditch phenomenon. How working class London affections have become the social habitus of London as "cool Britannia". Nathalie finds it pretentious, everybody wanting to talk like that and look the same way. She points out how it is "trendy" in London to hang out in areas where there are gangsters or bandits, in the "nearly dangerous" places: like saying "Oh, I live in Brixton". Most of the foreign European residents' local knowledge doesn't stretch to knowing much about by-now solidly gentrifying areas like Brixton. They aren't *cool* enough to live there. And that's why they remain foreigners in the city.

Language Games

Language is the most frequently cited barrier to free movement in Europe. At first glance it seems a self-evident objection to any future United States of Europe. As experiences in London show, it is true that much of what is expressed as difficulties with living abroad is linked to not quite understanding what is going on, to some lack of linguistic know-how. But there are aspects to this that go beyond the mere fact that host countries' languages are different or difficult to learn. Learning a language is not a one-way interaction, governed only by the migrants' willingness and ability to be part of the host society. The language learning process – which may be a necessary if not sufficient part of successfully integrating – is in fact largely controlled by the attitude of host speakers; by those who command any interaction, towards those who are trying to follow it. They can make it welcoming and accessible; or they can withdraw, and make it purposely difficult. And even having the language in your grasp does nor remove the fact you are still an audibly obvious foreigner. Residual nationalized barriers in communication can persist even when the language interaction *per se* is not the problem.

A common remark you hear when talking about learning the language to a native speaker is: "Oh, but French (or Dutch/English/Danish/German/ Italian, etc.) is *such* a difficult language to learn." This is usually said by a native speaker in order to sympathize with someone audibly struggling to master the new codes. But there is also invariably a subtle note of caution attached to the comment; a reminder that no matter how self-confident you are, you are on disadvantaged ground, and can still be humbled or excluded by your limitations. None of these languages are particularly difficult, but access to learning them varies dramatically. The alternative, of course, is just to use English as Eurolanguage. But funny things have happened as English has become more prevalent as the second language across all the continent. On the one hand, ease of English spoken everywhere might be taken to be a sign of decline in the vitality of other linguistic cultures, as well as a clear indicator of the powers of the global hegemon. But viewed another way, speaking the old enemy's language need not be any indicator of decline in the resilience or power of the national culture in question – or the inverse. The linguistic ability of the British – once the most cosmopolitan empire on the planet – has withered like an unused limb.[1] Furthermore, in continental Europe, among the natives of the host country, what once seemed so dependent on asserting the local language as the exclusive medium of all communication within its territorial domain, now might hinge more on *who* has the power to decide *which* language shall be spoken and *when*. The French still appear to be nervous about this – as if they are losing something in any anglicized transaction. But even they are beginning to learn a new power: dictating when and where English can be used; and, on the contrary, when and where communication can be selective, coded, private, and exclusively national. Confronted by linguistically challenged Anglophones, one superior edge you can easily assert is to impose *your* English on all conversations whenever they might try to formulate something in your language. The Netherlands, in this respect, is a much better example of how to do it. The Dutch know they are a small country, with no illusions about their language as a potential international medium of communication. But they have long mastered a double game with English and their own language, that ensures that fluency in the former – that is fully functional, open, and automatic across much of society – while preserving an inner world of Dutch communication – to which it is extraordinarily difficult for foreigners to get access.

The topic is a central one of many interviews. Guillaume sees it as a key to understanding the discomfort of foreigners in this "open", "tolerant" society. "Yeah, you know *the system*", he says ruefully. He'd learned English and German before, no problem, but after seven years in the Netherlands still only speaks "some Dutch". It doesn't matter how good your Dutch gets, the natives have a way of imposing English on all situations as soon as possible.

I used to think it was my fault. But now I know it's not, it's something wrong with the Dutch.

Aren't they just being polite? Guillaume has his own theories.

For your ego, it's horrible. When you speak a little Dutch, but they hear you have an accent, they feel threatened because they understand that you understand something … And then they become very very bitchy about you becoming some kind of spy on them. They don't feel very comfortable with the idea. Normally, they master things …

Assuming that foreigners don't or won't speak the language is a double edged sword. It also justifies feeling critical or superior about foreigners who have somehow failed to do something they *ought* to be able do.[2] Who fail to integrate. "It's just a matter of intelligence", a native once told me. *Ja, dat klopt.* I got the message.

Some languages like English seem to have very wide margins of comprehensibility. You can speak English with pretty much any accent in London and people will at least understand what you are saying. EuroEnglish – as illustrated in my interviews – in fact is emerging in its own right, as Eurostars speak and write English among themselves with little or no contact with native speakers. Dutch, however, has to be pitch perfect to work at all – a factor linked to the very small number of non-Dutch who actually speak it well. French used to be like this. Ingrid remembers how in Paris "if you don't clearly speak French, they don't understand". In that context, the natives felt empowered to impose their standards on the communication, dismissing as "unintelligible" language that didn't make the grade. Brussels, far more cosmopolitan in this respect, has never been like that. In Brussels, the rule is everyone speaks their own language, so the speaker chooses, and conversations are often multilingual. In the Netherlands, expats complain that the only people who would speak Dutch with them were the little children at the school to which they send their own. It is the only level at which you are allowed to feel comfortable.

The exceptions to the rule really are exceptions. David, the integrated gay man, has an "unusual ability to learn languages". He did Chinese at university, three language "A" levels, and a Dutch "O" level at school. Yet even with his near perfect language abilities he can still feel left out and vulnerable. Dutch jokes can still catch him out: the room will fall about laughing, and he won't have a clue why it was so hilarious. Stefan has also crossed over to the other side of the language barrier, but he shares the same frustrations. It clearly also is a key to his feeling of integration; it's a whole lot less humiliating living in Amsterdam now.

Stefan, however, needs to watch his accent. His attempts at finding a comfortable denationalized freedom in the city might be thwarted by another form of heavy handed renationalization very typical in the Netherlands. Like a lot of people, I learned my Dutch after learning German at school. When I try to speak it, German words often come out, or Dutch words with a slight German accent. It turns out this is an unfortunate affliction to have in Amsterdam. I used to hang out with a German friend, who like many resident Germans, had a kind of unrequited love affair with this country. He had come to the Netherlands to work as an academic, and was enthusiastic about the houses, the canals, the people, the culture, the food, and (especially) Dutch women – everything in fact. He was laid back and forgiving about all the bad points. But just going round one evening in Utrecht, I realized that we were getting a series of hostile if not abusive reactions from people. He shrugged it off: it was always like this – and understandable really. It's the sound of old Europe again. The war replaying in grainy black and white. Amsterdammers tend to see the German tourists that keep the city rich as invading armies of the past. Long-term residents struggle to disassociate themselves. The British and Irish in Amsterdam face a parallel problem. Expatica, the leading website for Anglophone residents, sells T-shirts for the expats living here: "I am not a tourist."[3] The slogan has become a trade-mark of the company. The last thing you want is to be associated with a bunch of boozy London lads hitting the red light district as part of a big stag weekend.

When I talk with Nina we are sitting high up in the top-floor canteen of the ABN Amro corporate headquarters, next to Amsterdam RAI. Like all canteens in the Netherlands, it is clinical and rational – and far from appetizing. Lunch comprises, as it does everyday, some dry sandwiches, plastic cheese, boiled eggs, fried croquets, and above all, lots and lots of milk. The yellow NS trains snake by down below in the distance, and Amsterdam spreads out against the sky. In the other direction, you can see the edge city of Amstelveen, and beyond that airliners taking off and landing at Schiphol International. I ask Nina the million deutschmark question: Is there anything particular about being German in Amsterdam?

You can see she has been waiting for this question. Nina explains how she came to Amsterdam because she thought it would be the nearest thing in Europe to San Francisco, where she had worked as a legal intern for a couple of years. She loved the freedom and alternative lifestyle of Amsterdam, like many West coast Americans. The people seemed open minded, very relaxed and friendly. Couple this with the usual German holiday maker affection for Dutch urban architecture, the sea and canals, as well as the sense that the Dutch are close relatives, it seemed like the perfect destination. But two or three years living there have changed her mind. She is finding it very hard to find Dutch friends, with rigid distinctions between work and private life. She now avoids speaking German when out in the city, after noticing the reactions when her mother was visiting. Her Dutch is still poor. The experience reinforces her sense of not integrating, and encapsulates all the things that haven't turned out quite as she expected in the Netherlands. Germans often blame themselves for being German, and Nina blames the integration failure on herself. If only learning the language were as easy as riding a bike, I suggest. Unfortunately, it turns out riding a bike the correct Dutch way isn't that easy either.

I was cycling, the Dutch are so impatient, honking their horns. This guy was yelling at me. I understood him but I yelled back in English, and he was like "If you cannot ride your bike then you should go back where you come from".

These are the days when she wonders if she should go back. Other days it still feels like the "nicest place on Earth". There is something sad about her experience. Everything keeps going back to the misleading San Francisco-Amsterdam analogy. But there is another old Amsterdam, old Europe underneath.

Everybody said Amsterdam is the best choice [for me] *after San Francisco. But I know now that it's not better here, or greater, or more cosmopolitan, or more liberal, or more open minded. It's just normal, average ...* [laughing]. *In the end, an average Dutch person is similar I think to an average German person.*

Nina is atypical of the Germans in Amsterdam, in that she has never really mastered the language. Most do: a year is usually enough to be fully functioning. The German experience, then, is largely a litmus test for life in the city *net* of the linguistic barriers that are so often said to be why people don't move or settle. It is not the language issue that causes them to not feel at home.

This point is all the more marked when considering the very specific experiences of Dutch-speaking Belgians in the city. With cultural and linguistic differences reduced to a minimum, there is still an extraordinary game of nationalized exclusion going on. The end result ensures these Belgians are no more likely to settle than the despised Germans, or the linguistically challenged Irish and British.[4] The Belgians are, in a sense, the most privileged observers of the game, given that they have full comprehension of what is going on.

Marlena is a journalist who has been native in Amsterdam since she was 15, and has much to say on this subject. Even she still gets things wrong sometimes. The rules are complex, unspoken. Making appointments can go wrong if you are too spontaneous. Dutchmen think you are coming on to them if you ask a colleague for a drink; for a Belgian, this is very strange. She complains about the prejudice in Holland towards Belgians. They think Belgians are "nice, friendly – and stupid". They find their accent "cute". They are the butt of endless jokes. Belgians on Dutch TV are subtitled as if they are speaking another language. After a while, this all gets a bit boring. So despite the fact the language is the same, and the distance short, there are in fact very few Belgians in the Netherlands. The Belgian view of the Dutch, or of Amsterdam, is the complete opposite to how Germans or English initially see the place: open, attractive, international, cosmopolitan. The Belgians, she says, already have Brussels and Antwerpen. The ones that live there make copies of Belgian things, like the food, but don't really enjoy the culture. Few choose to come, and all the Belgians she knew who did went back.

One thing it proves is that the reluctance of Europeans to move is not necessarily determined by language barriers. In Marlena's case, it is revealing that even after half her life in the Netherlands, she feels – if anything – less and less at home. She is tired of adapting. For residents like her, there is no one-way settlement process. Belgians have a hard time in the Netherlands, but the reverse scenario also holds true for Dutch people living in Belgium. With the boot on the other foot, the Dutch can easily become victims of crude stereotypes, or hapless pawns in local tussles over language and culture. One Dutch friend, who works as an interpreter, has been living in Belgium for 14 years, and has left behind the Netherlands in many ways. She has a Belgian-Moroccan partner and lives in Antwerpen, while admitting her top three TV channels are all Dutch. She still fumes about how in Brussels they never let you forget you are Dutch. It's the first thing they notice about you, and the only thing they remember. She once worked for a marketing firm, and she can remember the kinds of reactions she'd get from Belgians on the phone. A child will pick up the phone and shout there is a Dutch person on the phone. If something is sold out in a shop, it is always because a Dutch person came and bought it. Joannet, the political consultant in Brussels, also has a "very Dutch" story about milk and catching the crossfire in a bilingual city.

In the beginning people were always upset with me in a shop. So I spoke French, because that's what Dutch people will do, trying to get integrated. I thought this shop was Francophone, went in, ordered milk in French. The guy there gets very upset with me, very angry. I didn't understand. I did my school French, I said "s'il vous plaît", I was being very polite … The problem was he was not Francophone!

He was very upset, told me that I didn't love my own language, the Dutch language, and that I shouldn't speak French. It took me a long time – I had to buy a lot of bottles of milk – before that relationship improved.

The Flemish expected her to "fight for her language". But being a denationalized European, the scenario just left her cold. These linguistic games and struggles reflect the constant microlevel processes of nationalization and renationalization used to police the borders of two countries that in many other ways should just blend in to each other at the macrolevel. Like the Scandinavian nations, the Benelux countries have had a free movement area much longer than the rest of Western Europe; and like the Scandinavian countries, the region is a group of close, interwoven neighbours who are obsessed with small differences of dialect and tradition, petty rivalries, and hard cherished national distinctions. It is these mechanisms that keep national populations where they supposedly belong, rather than allowing them full and easy access to territories that in the end share the same (or closely related) language and much of the same culture. It is mechanisms like these that keep the Europe of nation-states firmly in place.

A Graphic Designer's Tale

I'm looking for Eva's place in Shepherd's Bush. It's on the less glamorous western side, a semi-suburban street off a gritty urban thoroughfare. Typical London. Up narrow stairs to a small, converted flat. I know Eva through her brother, who is married with children and has been living in London a few years. But she is living in a very different world: the exciting but precarious existence of the London sojourner. Eva is 28, but looks a lot younger. She is quiet, and doesn't say much, but her answers are precise and well thought out. I'd known quite a few people like her, especially young French, Spanish, and Italians who'd just come to the city on spec after studies at home. I think about an old girlfriend of mine in Florence. Whatever happened to her? She had just dropped everything and moved to London after we split up. Scraping a living in some little office job, studying evenings at Birkbeck College. Last time I saw her, she had some dope-smoking English boyfriend who played in a band. She was surviving OK. Amazing. Young foreign Europeans now come to London like English provincials and kids who grew up in the suburbs always did. Moths to a flame, in search of the bright lights. But it can be tough. A life in the city's many shadows.

My boyfriend came a year before me. The relationship was getting difficult. He'd never had an experience of coming to England, and felt he had missed out. So he decided he should

A Graphic Designer's Tale—cont'd

learn English – "it's now or never" – and went for it. I was very badly paid in Madrid, and I thought it could be a good opportunity. I could take a one year leave in Spain. I did a year in Paris before, with Erasmus. I started going abroad when I was eight. Three months each year to learn English and other languages. My brother did this too, all the family. My mother was very concerned about us learning languages.

What did your friends back home think?

They thought it was a great idea what I'm doing. They won't do it themselves – because they don't know the language – but they are jealous. I know there's a lot of people coming now, but young people still tend to buy the house near their parents. If they are in Madrid, they stay in Madrid. The same neighbourhood, two roads apart from their parents. I'm strange. I've known the language since I was little. I've had this mentality since I was little.

Eva's father was a surgeon, and they had a very bourgeois, but cosmopolitan upbringing. It's not so surprising she should move – in Spain now they even have websites and work placement agencies for people to find service sector jobs in London.

Yeah, but the majority still stays ... People come for the language. They know with English they can move around the rest of the world. Those without a connection to university or Erasmus, they tend to go to England. At first I couldn't find a good job. I started working in Mango, a Spanish shop in Oxford Street. It was a temporary job, just one month. I didn't want to continue to work in this kind of crap job, because I couldn't look for work [while working all day]. *I started becoming desperate. I was working two days a week in Harvey Nichols selling hosiery. I enjoyed it because I had the opportunity to do things I would never do in Spain. But it was very exhausting, on your feet all day, tidying up clothes. I found these jobs by dropping them a false CV, telling that I'd been a shop assistant and all that. The second one was through an agency – I also used a false CV. Then after one month, I got three different calls for design jobs. I had done advertising and PR in Spain in university, and did courses funded by European Community in graphic design. I'd had four years' experience in Spain.*

Do you know many people who've come over like this, just surviving however they can?

No. Well, I just don't know many people here. My boyfriend, yes, he's surviving! When he came to England, he worked in a farm for two months. He moved to London, stayed with his cousin looking after his two twins. It was childcare, for about three months. He got sick of this, because they spoke Spanish, and he wasn't improving his English. He looked for a job and house, then worked for Café Republic for three to four months [one of the many duplicate Starbucks-type chains in London], *then a hotel – room service – then catering for a bank. Now he has been there four months. When I got my job, he decided to drop the catering thing. He has done studies in journalism. His English has improved, and he wants more qualified work – something to do with marketing. He had an interview today with easyJet, for their cabin crew. He wants to be an air traffic controller in Spain, but*

A Graphic Designer's Tale—cont'd

he is waiting for the exam to be published in Spain, and he needs to be able to speak English. So maybe he will try to enter in the aircraft industry.

We don't move around with Spanish people. Sometimes we have a drink. My boyfriend, he is not very keen to meet Spanish people. We are here to practice the English. We don't go out much. We don't have much money either [laughs]. *The thing is, one of the reasons to come here was I was getting very little money in Spain. I get more money here, even if I'm not earning what I should in comparison. I'm happy because in Spain I wouldn't be able to live away from home. I have independence and I'm doing some saving.*

What's your job?

I design a newspaper. It's the first black newspaper in England, The Voice, *in Brixton. Design and layout.*

Sounds interesting.

It's interesting in terms of working with other races that I haven't met before. But in terms of the work, it's not very interesting. It's not very creative, just laying out the pictures, the text. I wanted to look for something creative. That was another reason I came to London. [Sighs] *But, well, it's my first job ...*

How did you find your flat? It's not so easy in London.

Through a Brazilian friend. It was easy, we didn't look for anything. The rent is £750 a month. We don't pay the council tax. People say we've been quite lucky. In euros it's very expensive. In Spain, they go crazy when I tell them the price we pay. But that's how things work here. I managed to get housing benefits here, for all the expenses I paid in London. I am very attentive person. I went to the job centre and got all the available information, on health and benefits. I was amazed: that's impossible in Spain. I had only worked here one month in London. I got some help as well from an association called Op-Shop. I went there weekly, they helped me with my letters. I got a computer access for free, go in the morning for the whole day, sending out my CV. I'd talk to a person about opportunities, they'd give me ideas. There is nothing like that in Spain, it's very good.

Do you know any other people around here, any neighbours?

Er ... No. Not really [laughs]. *A few English people at work. That's it. We've not really made any friends. Other friends? Can't think of any. I go to ballroom dancing. And to yoga. I thought maybe that would help to socialize a bit, but no. But I don't really need to* [meet people]. *If I was alone it might be different. We don't expect to have the same kind of friends that we've got in Spain, friends that we've had for a long time.*

Do you miss it?

Yes, my boyfriend wants to get back to Spain because of that. I think what he really needs is a good holiday back in Spain. And I miss them too, but for the moment I'm OK. It's a problem of communication. I can say things, but when I want to express myself, I'm a bit stuck. To make jokes, that's a problem. If I didn't have that problem I would have a normal life. People in England, they enjoy their life as they do in Spain. I didn't find much difference. I mean, in London the pubs are full.

A Graphic Designer's Tale—cont'd

Did your experience of France and England make you feel more "European"?

Um ... [long pause] Not European. I feel more international, not more European. Yeah, I like the idea of Europe because it helps the movement of people, and you get more opportunities, but I don't know ... I feel more "open minded", not more "European".

Do you feel less Spanish?

[Brightly] Yes! Well ... Not less Spanish, but ... I feel more critical of my country, that's it. If I went back, I'd have to go back to my parents' house. There's not enough help from the government if I'm looking for a job, and then I would get a rubbish salary. In Spain, you need to know contacts [networks]. You need to be very sociable, be a person who knows how to play the role. I even work less hours now than in Spain: 35 instead of 40.

Do you think the experience is changing you in any way? Could it be difficult to go back and settle in again?

Um, yeah. The thing is, you're more independent here. No one knows you. There you have your family, a society that knows you. You have to give things. They ask you a question and you have to answer them. You always have to explain everything you do. Here, you don't have to explain anything ... I get used to places very quickly.

What are your plans? What do you predict will happen?

I'd like to stay longer. I'd like to change the job and find other things. Now that I've got my first experience, try to improve that. Stay another year maybe. But my boyfriend wants to go back to Spain ... I don't want to go back to my old job in the same conditions. I need more time. So, we don't know yet, it depends on how things go.

Would you go anywhere else?

Now that I've lived here ... I had a quite hard time in Paris, people were different. Maybe it was my age as well, I found it harder. I was alone. I was a student. I didn't have much money. People were colder. I was living in a foyer. I didn't have money for anything. Coming to London was a way of saying to myself, "Let's try another time". I gave me another chance to try another experience. Now I'm not a student, I've got money, so [the idea] of going to another place would be great, I'd love to. Even if I move to Spain, I'd love to live in another place other than Madrid – Barcelona, or somewhere near the sea, or have an experience in South America for two years. I would love to. I'm not afraid.

10

Integration (2)

Through force of clumsy experience, time, and persistence, foreign residents may get beyond many of the rather trivial everyday barriers to inclusion in the city. What's cool or not matters less as you get older, and the jokes will eventually stop bothering you if you are thick skinned enough. But traditional forms of ethnic exclusion are not the most difficult barriers. In moving abroad, the Eurostars stepped off their own pre-planned trajectory back home: the line of citizenship rights and benefits that was going to take them from cradle to grave as the comfortably middle class progeny of a wealthy European nation-state-society. On paper, as European citizens, they should be able to hitch a lift on the local system. But in reality it doesn't work quite as smoothly as that. Access to membership benefits in nation-states is in the final analysis about the big unknowables of life and death; of sharing the burdens that life in society raises. It is only to be expected then that it is over – literally – life and death issues that some of the strongest forms of renationalization appear. These cut to the heart of the deepest middle class worries about the good life: how to keep healthy and in good shape – i.e. *existential* concerns about medical protection and healthcare – and how then to preserve it for you and your family – i.e. questions of *social reproduction*, such as childrearing and future family life.

Still Ill

There is an endless debate in Britain about foreigners sponging on the National Health Service. Ironically, however, hardly *any* foreign European residents has anything good to say about it, and they will do anything to keep their own health care – both doctors and dentists – anchored at home. It is not uncommon for this to be the last thing that free movers shift to their actual residence; and this, again, varies according to the perceived quality and security offered by the local national system. In the end, the problem is one about the high level of trust you need in order to have faith in a foreign system where you don't speak the language. Talking to a doctor or a dentist about how you feel is in fact one of the most difficult things you might ever need to express. Hence it is one of the last nationalized bastions you would give up, no matter how mobile the rest of your life is. Franz is one of the most mobile in London, yet he is anchored in Germany, healthwise. Unless it's your "mother tongue", he says, it's very hard to "explain where it hurts". What he is getting at here is that your mother tongue is also the language you speak to your mum when you have a bad tummy or your teeth hurt. It's about as primary as it gets. So how does the British National Health Service – the surrogate mother nation – do in these terms? Franz grimaces. No way, with all the horror stories he's heard. "It's *my* health."

Clearly, to not move one's very personal health security to the place where you are living is a big issue blocking settlement. Brussels comes out quite positively on these questions; Amsterdam is more difficult. But in London, just mentioning health care questions opens the door to torrents of negative critique. The NHS is universally seen as one of the worst medical systems in Europe. The residents from France – Nathalie, Laure, Nour, and Philippe – all laugh bitterly, while recounting nightmare stories of their encounters with it. Nathalie couldn't believe the bad hygiene she saw when she visited the gynaecologist. Laure's daughter was wrongly diagnosed with asthma when they refused to do a routine x-ray on her lungs. Back in France she was correctly diagnosed with double pneumonia. Nour was refused routine tests and told she should just take liquids and her faintness would pass. A friend helped put her on the Eurostar train to Paris where tests showed all kinds of things wrong with her blood count. She says there is no philosophy of prevention or well-being in Britain. Philippe complains about "criminals" who tell you to take an aspirin when you are sick, or offer an appointment in three days for a baby with an emergency 100 and something fever. He hates the "communist" set up in Britain. And so on. The negative comments are much the same if you are Spanish, Italian, Irish, or German. Carlos and Susana have "fortunately very little" experience of the NHS. They have kept their insurance in Spain, have all their tests in Spain. Their dentists are also in Spain. It helps that Carlos has a GP brother in

Bilbao, who gives him a "health kit" while on Airstrip One. Carlos's brother in fact came to the UK twenty years ago to observe the British health service; it used to be the model in Europe. Now they would "take a plane back to Spain for sure". Carlos is in mordant good form:

> *That's why I say the healthy survive* [here]. *Because in the end there is no waiting list any more* [laughs]. *Natural cleansing!*

In the light of all this, it is surely a poor joke that British politicians still insist on playing the welfare spongers card, talking about NHS access as an argument for why migrants come to Britain (as opposed to elsewhere). This is nonsense: foreign European migrants maintain doctors and dentists at home. In fact, therefore, the reverse is true. The British labour market is getting a free ride on continental social security, social dumping the costs of maintaining a fit and healthy (and highly exploitable) workforce. Most would not be able to cope without some kind of access to health benefits "back home". But how sensible is it to make your most sensitive health care issues dependent on being able to arrange your holidays around doctors' appointments, or your ability to find a quick, cheap flight back home in case of emergency? And what if they tell you that you are no longer resident there so have no kind of rights to these benefits? One day they will, when their home countries develop the same efficient gatekeeping mechanisms that ensure the Scandinavian welfare state stays so pristine. One worries for younger Eurostars, like Eva, who really are just not covered at all for anything serious or long term. Health, though, is by definition something that people start worrying about more as they get older; the highly mobile think about it later than the settled. Some of these highly mobile residents are gambling with their health and well-being; putting freedom ahead of security. And mobility sometimes means you just don't get round to checking out the things that you should, medically speaking – like not making a dentist appointment, while the teeth are rotting in your head. This is the metaphor Jeroen, the Dutch scientist, chooses to describe his condition. How long has it been? He laughs.

> *Three years! And I'm still not registered with a GP … Well, at least I have health insurance!*

The national welfare state exists for good reasons; and this is why it is the hardest thing to reconcile with free movement within Europe.

Carry On, *Huisarts*

Switch to the Netherlands, and a similarly revealing picture emerges regarding foreign residents and the question of health care. Again, the potential life and death issues of physical well-being are especially "close to home" in most people's minds; an anxiety that sharpens their confusion and sometimes anger in the face of a difficult doctor's appointment. The upshot is an almost unanimous verdict across the board: it's a terrible system. This is certainly not true – if you are Dutch. For most of the foreigners, though, they never get to grips with it.

The first experience is the confused first visit to the truly Dutch institution of the *huisarts* (GP). When I ask Nina about her experiences, she falls about with laughter. She asked her colleagues where to find a doctor or dentist, and they reacted dramatically: "They are like, 'What!? Are you sick? Why do you want to know?" This is the first rule of Dutch medicine: it is not easy to get treatment. In fact, it is impossible to get treatment *unless* you go through the *huisarts*. As the Dutch keep telling you: "everything is the *huisarts*". Just finding one that has any space on his or her list already is a challenge. When eventually she found one, she didn't trust his antique equipment. "They are very, 'Nahh, you are not ill!'," she says.

> *I think Dutch people think it's a weakness if you go to a doctor, even if you have a pain. Unless you are almost actually dying, you are not going to a doctor. But if I have something, I just want it to go, take drugs or whatever and have it gone!*

Her colleague Maria gets similarly animated. Like Nour in London – a high flyer like her – she feels she has had serious medical problems that have not been responded to. She says she pays a monthly insurance which she can't use because the *huisarts* will not refer her. As in Britain, the medical approach contrasts vastly with the more preventative, drugs-led approach favoured in Southern Europe. Respondents from Greece and France say the same things. Guillaume, as ever, gives me the most dramatic story. He says he had an emergency which they didn't grasp, telling him he was "just a sensitive French" who "wants antibiotics all the time". He had to call in a pharmacist he knew to get the right treatment. Guillaume's way of dealing with the situation was to get mad, and then threaten court. This generally works in the Netherlands because the Dutch are highly litigious, like Americans – among the most in Europe. The national stereotypes that all too quickly get used to deal with the foreign interrelation imprison Guillaume and his *huisarts* in a no-win situation.

One problem is that the Dutch have strongly normative, even moralistic ideas about medicine – as well as a belief in the institution of the doctor as expert – that sets them against other European practices. It is not a patient-centred system. My research in the Netherlands includes a stay based out of Nijmegen, a pleasant and typical mid-sized Dutch city near the German border. My contact is Kees Groenendijk, one of Europe's biggest experts on EU free-movement laws and their sociological consequences. One part of the report I write troubles him deeply: the section detailing the near-unanimous criticism of the Dutch medical system. His wife is a *huisarts*, and he points out to me how their professional attitude is both a question of philosophy and organizational practice. Doctors see themselves as the "gatekeepers" to an easily abused social system. They are supposed to get to know their patients over a long period, and build a relationship of trust in which the patient confides responsibility for their health and well-being to the doctor. The problem, for him, lies not with the doctor but the foreigners, who just arrive, treat the surgery like a service station, and do nothing but demand things from the system. Their expectations don't match how the Dutch system works. From the Dutch side, all they can see is foreigners – frustrated with their GPs – cluttering up the emergency room of hospitals. As David points out, the perception often gets racialized into an anti-immigrant point – the kind of thing out of which Pim Fortuyn made his short but spectacular political career. The Dutch see lots of Moroccans and Turks, but he has the feeling it was more Americans, British, or Germans who immediately go there to get some treatment.

Valerio also gets animated on the subject. He too has unhappy stories to tell. He had an eye infection which several doctors would not treat, and gasps that one had a "machine made of wood". He went to the hospital and they told him "it would go away like it came". The story then takes a familiar twist. Again, when health is on the line, foreign residents look to what they trust – "home". He went and got treatment in Italy. Although easy enough to do, the reflex puts in question the whole viability of "life abroad". You end up paying twice for social insurance – something that would not be possible if you were seriously ill. It also reinforces the sense of being ill at ease, unsettled. Susan, like Nina, Maria, and Valerio, is clearly never going to settle in the Netherlands. Like all the archetypal expats there, it will turn into an experience of a couple of years. So many foreigners like them come to the Netherlands, but so many leave again soon after. Medical care is a crucial mechanism. Susan has heard all the nightmare stories and has avoided doctors, but she has had a bad experience with dentists. "Wouldn't touch them with a barge pole", she says. Dutch dentists don't give anaesthetic as a matter of course. If anything your teeth are even more sensitive than your body. The solution was to fly "home" to mum and dad for the weekend – even if Amsterdam to Bristol return can be a bit pricey for a series of appointments. In a throwaway line – that is in fact vitally revealing – Susan removes a few more of the foundation stones of her foreign life, when she talks about those times when "you are needing to go home – like for dentist's appointments". This is the moment the migration project begins to crumble. A threshold of non-settlement is crossed. Ray Bradbury's *Martian Chronicles* – an allegory about American migration to California – sees the migrants going home when there is a disaster looming on their own planet; a nuclear war, that leaves only a few "New Martians" stranded on the red planet. You would expect people to go home for a funeral or a family crisis. But dental treatment appears to be even more important. You are basically still reliant on the cradle of your own nation. It suggests you are really only a tourist or passer-by in a foreign land, rather than a resident in the Europe of the future. It's the same for Guillaume, as for these other transients:

> *I'm really not happy. When* [if] *I get a big disease, there's no way I stay here. I go back to France. I don't trust it.*

Bringing Up Baby

Old age and illness are still generally distant in the minds of the Eurostars; they are focused on travel, experience, careers, and the quality of life. But the biological clock for some is ticking fast, the question of reconciling children to the life they have chosen *is* vitally important. There is evidence that among this population there is a higher than average preference for being single, or for the life of a childless couple – with cats or dogs, perhaps, if they can obtain a pet passport and get around mobility problems associated with this because of rabies restrictions.[1] But still most people want children, and many of the people I met have them.

London is the most difficult of the three cities on this question; possibly the most difficult place in Europe to raise children. More than anything, more even than housing (with which it is interlinked), it is the most important element in the competitive struggle among residents for access to and control over scarce quality of life resources in the city. London is tough, and it is the kind of issue on which you would have to mobilize all your capital – financial, cultural, and social – to get what you want. The Eurostars rail about the extortionate price of childcare and the professional compromises it imposes on families. It is clear they would have it much easier in Brussels (where childcare is good) or in Amsterdam (where international school options are better). Paris, too, would have had more options, and would be half as expensive. So would Germany. There are crèches in London, but it depends on the area, there is no statutory right, and you have to be able to pay. The alternative is a nanny from London's booming *au pair* business – that is, predominantly young East European girls in London to learn the language. Parents end up working as double income professionals at full financial stretch just to pay for someone else to look after their children. Nour wonders, in that case, "what's the point of having kids?" It defeats the purpose, she thinks.

If you are Scandinavian the differences are huge, as Anniken points out. They really know how to do childcare in Norway, Denmark, and Sweden. These are welfare states primarily structured around facilitating young professional middle class people having kids. While it may be the future of Europe that the promoters of "flexicurity" are talking about, it certainly isn't how the British economy works. Back in England you've got to pay to create this kind of cradle of society. Of course, native residents face exactly the same questions, and there is little or no evidence that resident Europeans are discriminated against in any way on access to the services such as they are. They just have to pay like anyone else. But herein lies the rub. Why would Eurostars who have only come to London for professional reasons do what natives do? They have no long-term interest in compromising their London life for a cheaper life in the leafy suburbs or Home Counties new town. English mothers routinely give up their careers for full-time childcare; and English couples routinely give up on London for a quieter life outside of the city. But if that's the option, why stay in England? This is not why you came here.

Isabel likes her job as a civil servant economist, has bought a flat with her Mexican boyfriend, and would like to think about children. She is nearing 30. It scares her. First, she thinks that she should just live here without children, and go back to Spain later. Then she thinks about staying here, having a child, and bringing over her family. It all seems impossible: the flat is so small, it would be cheaper to give up work, you'd have to find a nanny, they don't want to move out of London, she doesn't want to give up her career ...

You can see the mechanism at work. The clock is ticking, and London just doesn't make it easy. She concludes that she'll put off deciding another year. Isabel's thought processes summarize the situation when you are 30. Donatella is 38, single, professionally oriented, wants to stay in London (or move on to a "global" job); she has made her decisions. She narrates her situation through her friends. Childcare has forced them to give up work; when the child is old enough they will leave London. They can move around Europe, and free education is so much better in France, Germany, or Switzerland. The British just assume you have to pay. She says she would definitely consider leaving if she had children. It's OK, though; her path is not the conventional one anyway. Her London is fun, full of opportunities. For her colleagues, it's just a struggle.

This is the dilemma of the ageing middle class foreign European professional in London – in a nutshell. Again, like visible clockwork, you can also see the thought processes of a young professional couple in London, as yet childless, and likely to remain so while there:

Adrian: *Have you considered the question of children at all?*
Carmen: *Oh yeah.*

Adrian: *Can you imagine it in London?*

Franz: *The first time it's possible. We talk about it with friends. For foreigners, when you think about it, you don't have this connection to...* [trails off] *In the beginning, it's maybe easier. Later on with school, it's getting more difficult.*

Carmen: *Up to now, we didn't think of it because we were so much concentrated on our work. It was not the time to really do it. Also, there's the feeling of being alone here, without friends and family. And having a baby is a big responsibility. With both parents working hard, it's very difficult. But now I think we are more settled in our jobs, and we are thinking about it. I would say the first child is going to be born here, hopefully, and we'll see after that.*

Adrian: *Is it at all linked to the settlement process? After a couple of years you can't keep moving around ...*

Carmen: *The child might be born here. But I don't know how many months we'd stay here ...*

Franz: *Two to three years is the time frame. Yes, we are certainly thinking about it. But schools ...*

Carmen: [firmly] *He won't go to school here ... But then we need to decide if it's the Spanish school, or the German school, or the French school ...* [laughs]

Franz: *Then we would go for the Spanish or German school. Other foreigners, people with our vision, our background. Again, we are not in the community. You are too far in the couple when it's difficult to get into this English community.*

Carmen: *Maybe it's easier if you are a foreigner married to an English person ...*

Everything, of course, is different if you naturalize. The children will grow up English, maybe just about with a second language and culture, if it is the mother who is the foreigner. But none of these residents are about to naturalize. What is striking is how continental Europe is seen as the place where the costs of childrearing and education can be borne, whereas London is a place to make money and have a career, here and now. These are some of the most talented and dynamic people in Europe giving their best years to London's labour market. Their careers are spiraling beyond what they could have achieved. They will have to bear the costs of deferring children while there; and later will also have to push the costs of having children later on to their families back home, and the welfare states they have left – but assume will take them back.

Some couples do stay. Let us assume that you are that foreign European couple, with two great careers in London. You have the baby, maybe two; babies are portable at least, even if they are expensive and require constant care. But children grow up fast, and you face a moving battery of new decisions about the child's language, culture, and future education. None of this can be taken for granted, or copied from your parents, your siblings, or your schoolmates back home. You are on your own. When Dominic and Anniken moved to London from Paris, Anniken was eight months pregnant and nearly ended up having Matteo on the Eurostar train. Fortunately, they delayed boarding, and he was born on French soil. I ask his parents another innocent question. Well, maybe not so innocent...

Adrian: *Is he going to the French school* [the international school in South Kensington]?

Anniken: [laughs] *After much discussion ...*

Dominic: [firmly] *When he is five years old ...*

Anniken: *As usual Dominic knows someone who can pistonner* [push it forward].²

The London situation here is leaving Anniken and Dominic chasing after very difficult and expensive international residents options, the options created for upper-middle-class global elites living in the city. Matteo might get into one of the junior schools that feed the later levels, but it will be a struggle all the way to get him into and through the French lycée in London, which has costs in the range of some of Britain's most expensive private schools.

Problematically, relatively average middle class professionals tend to take on highly elitist attitudes about schooling when exposed to the difficulties of the international scenario. It is as if they feel they need to pay even more in order to adjust for the difficulties of trusting the host environment. Philippe, like Dominic, insists first that it has to be a French school for his children, which would mean the French school in London. Cognitively, for him, the only acceptable parts of the British educational system are, of course, the famous, most elite ones: like many foreigners, he thinks the only decent education available is at Oxbridge. He gasps in astonishment that there are "still some places in the world where you can't get a French education". So when the child is five they'd better go back. He thinks his next appointment will probably be his last abroad. And so international mobility comes to end, and home nation reflexes take over. Philippe's answers are very much reflective of social reproduction; his father's example and his own elite *grande école* education – which, paradoxically, taught him to think internationally, while programming him to be consummately French.

London is also not seen as a good third country option for joint nationality couples for language reasons. Learning the global language as the dominant language actually might make the children *less* globally minded – because it neuters other languages. Norbert says if they had children they'd prefer to live in Germany or a Spanish-speaking country, to make sure the children learn at least two. This concern is particularly the case for British couples abroad; they worry about their children *not* having international opportunities and experiences through being brought up in England.

In the Netherlands, childrearing issues focus on two things: the very special attitude to childbirth techniques there; and the intense urban competition for childcare. Most of the interviewees, such as Anastasia from Greece, tell of their views through the stories of others. She had a friend who was pregnant, and had difficulties with the delivery. The Dutch hospital would not assist the birth with drugs. It has to come naturally, they kept telling her. Very late on, after four days' suffering, it was found a caesarian was necessary. Anastasia says they will remember the Greek mother of her friend in the hospital – who was there helping – for a long time. "She became completely mental!" The Dutch, however, are proud of their quite unique system. Most children are typically born at home, without anaesthetic or gas. To naturally give birth is also to nationally give birth, as a bestselling book in the country has it. But again, these issues touch on some of the deepest anxieties and insecurities of foreigners. If you come to the Netherlands single, or as a couple without children, you might think twice about staying, once these stories start to circulate – as they do. Susan, for sure, "didn't fancy it".

But the difficult adaptation doesn't stop there. Childcare in the Netherlands is also a very difficult question. Moving out to a new town suburb, as Ray did with his Portuguese-African wife and their daughter, is one of the only ways of solving it. But for those trying to compete over local quality of life resources with the native Amsterdammers, they may well find themselves squeezed out. As with housing, it requires insider knowledge, linguistic knowledge of the rules and system, and long-term investment in the place. After more than fifteen years, Marlena has all this. On paper she is in the same position as any Dutch resident, rushing to get their child's name on the waiting list before it is even born. But as she points out, you don't have the same resources to hand to make this difficult situation work in case you still have to wait: she doesn't have the social network of family around that her Dutch neighbours do, and you only get three months maternity leave. Because of this and housing, she and her Serbian partner are thinking of finally moving – back to Antwerpen. Most people's image of the Netherlands is of a sophisticated and advanced welfare state, closer to the Scandinavian "pastoral" model than the stripped down "Anglo-Saxon" one in Britain. But it turns out that the national system is actually premised on quite high levels of informal family help, and often requires independent financial means to really negotiate it. As in Britain, many Dutch women drop out of the labour force or take up part-time work as a matter of course.

In the end, of course, bringing up baby is anyone's guess. It's just more difficult in a foreign land. Even an MNC deal can't take away the difficulty, sometimes pain, of these questions for parents. Rainer, the audit manager at Unilever in London, starts talking about his son. You have your minutely negotiated contract, you've read all the books, and you made a move you think all of you can deal with. A couple of weeks in, their three-year-old boy is sitting on the bed. Out of the blue, he says: "When are we are going home?" His parents were totally shocked. A three year old is supposed to be happy wherever he is. "But, *schatz*, this is home now ..." Rainer says they immediately started a "recovery program". He took some days off work, took him to Legoland, all the treats he could think of. But his wife started to have grave doubts about the move.

Rainer had all the right intentions and all kinds of strategies to enable him and his family to experience the cosmopolitan freedom of global London. But the strong impression he gives is that getting through these issues renationalized the whole family experience. They also had problems with the nursery, after trying first to send him to an English one. The son got confused by ever-changing nannies, and was not picking up either language as he should. They moved him to a bilingual German nursery which changed everything in their social networks. They didn't want to live in a ghetto, and Rainer denies that they do, but he says 95 percent of their contacts are purely German. Now their son is at the German school. Rainer points out another downside of this special education: it is a thoroughly elitist experience. The unreal world of global elites. He is worried that there are 700 parents, and every single one of them earns more than the teacher. Without the diversity of social backgrounds in their experience, he is worried "about how the children can become good adults some day". Not easy being a parent. I ask where he think the kids will go to university after all this. Rainer can't resist teasing me a little:

Probably they would like to go to Los Angeles [laughs]. *No ... I assume a German university. I know someone who grew up with parents in Singapore. He has never been to Germany. But he is determined to return. There must be something there. Roots or something.*

Boys Keep Swinging

There is a subset of the mobile population who are not subject to the more traditional nation-building pressures that inevitably get felt once questions of family life and childrearing are broached. Among my interviewees are several examples of homosexual men and single unmarried women, who have used free movement in Europe as a way of making sense of their own personal life choices – indeed, as their own way of "coming out" of the mainstream. In a sense, this is the opposite of the other traditionally successful way of moving and resettling internationally: the heavily gendered path of women who move to settle with their foreign partners. It is no accident that the best naturalized, nationalized route to integration – marrying a national and having children in their country – coincides with a choice to live the most conventional, norms-bound, form of family life. Stepping out of the normal national life, on the other hand, can also coincide with stepping out of normal mainstream sexuality or heterosexual relationships.[3]

Amsterdam especially has longtime functioned as the San Francisco of Europe in this sense; the safe haven, and utterly exceptional place, that all those born into mainstream, straight, intolerant "middle Europe" could flee to – just as young gay Nebraskans, Ohioans, or Tennesseans always "go west" in the US. But the point about the destination, as Guillaume vividly stresses, is not necessarily that you go there in order to live out the kind of weird, outrageous, wildly alternative life that you could only fantasize about while growing up with your family. On the contrary, you go there to live normally – to live a socially integrated life impossible in that small town or backwards region you came from. David, obviously, is the model of the "normal" gay man, completely at home in Amsterdam. This feature of Amsterdam as a Eurocity is one that made it quite distinct in the past. This now appears to be changing as other gay destinations emerge. David's path to happiness and integration on his own terms doesn't work for everyone. Over a rather plastic canteen lunch with two gay friends at the Commission building on rue de la Loi, one of them tells me why he so much prefers being gay in Brussels to Amsterdam. It's simply a younger, more happening scene. He has finally just got a permanent contract in the DG he works for, and the two talk about settling down. This might mean buying a run down town house in St. Gilles or Schaarbeek and doing it up. The alternative appeal holds for many artists in various fields – including many Dutch – who prefer shabby Brussels to the glamour of Amsterdam's famous canals. My friends describe Amsterdam as the "has-been of gay Europe": Brussels, Paris, London have all taken a lead on it.

Gay women would have similar stories to tell about their lives in these cities, although it is noticeable in Amsterdam how much more ostentatious gay men are there. The free gay guide that you can pick up in the bars around Regulierdwarsstraat is overwhelmingly focused on gay male sexuality – of the old school clones variety – and the affluent, highly sociable lives of professional gay men. This could indeed be the Castro in San Francisco. But another parallel group to these are the determinately single, professional women dotted through my sample. This gendered aspect of European mobility is another important part of what a denationalized European space has facilitated. The choice to move coincided with a willingness to step off the path of standard career and family choices that friends back home have made, leaving behind relationships, and going "wherever you want" as a woman in search of fulfilment. Janet and Caterina in Brussels, Saskia and Donatella (pp. 42–5) in London, Helen (pp. 26–9) in Amsterdam relate similar stories about the life of the single professional woman on the move. All see the move into Europe as a potential step to places further afield. All have been professionally successful, although some might not be staying; the excitement of a bigger, global world is a temptation in lieu of a settled married life. But they are also aware that it is much easier to be doing what they are doing in Europe – professionally, socially, and in terms of (still needed) relations to friends and family back home.

For these women and men, the mobile, flexible, tolerant Eurocity provides the right environment for choices that might otherwise be viewed as unhappy failures in contexts back home, where expectations of normal, settled family life run higher. At the same time, the kinds of integration they achieve will never satisfy the national "integration tests" imposed by public debates on foreign residents.

A Media Manager's Tale

Over a quick fake Italian lunch, in a road off Oxford Street, I meet with Laure, a French woman in her early forties who works at one of London's biggest media groups. Laure laughs and jokes a lot. Her engaging corporate articulacy is peppered with socialistic, anti-materialist side remarks and self-questioning. She warns me early on that she is not "typical", but that shouldn't put me off. It doesn't. She has been in London a long time compared to many others. She came from a small provincial town in the north of France. I check the dates. This must have been well before the big rush of French people to the city?

Correct. I always say that I'm the first generation [laughs] ... *Yeah, I came in '89, when it was actually rather gloomy here. I came to work for MTV, right at the beginning, and then CNN before the Gulf War, before it was big. They were exciting times of building something. It's a bit different now because our industry is contracting in terms of the number of players, people, and economically viable services. There was a lot of money available* [then] *for investment and new technology, and everybody lost perspective a bit. The advertising is now shrinking ... Our income is going down and down. Job security is not good. After the internet turndown there was a bit of a reality check for everybody.*

I studied for a long time. I did an MA in economics at Sciences Po [the elite social sciences school in Paris, where many French politicians and civil servants are formed]. *I was postponing my entry into the job market. That was the crunch thing to do – and it still is, by the way. This is very detrimental. I wish those politically responsible would change that, make people get out of school.*

A Media Manager's Tale—cont'd

Was Sciences Po still very franco-français in those days?

Awful! I had a very bad time there because I'm a bit of a non-conformist [laughs]. *Really! The fact is, you get out of your own country as a young professional when you think the flexibility and opportunities are greater elsewhere. I'm sure everybody thinks the same. In my case, it was very specific at that time. The industry was also young here, but because there was this link with America and the TV industry is born and bred from the States you just felt this pool of expertise is going to come first to England, and then to the continent. Which in fact is what happened. I hate to think of that. The American influence* [laughs]... *But that's why I came. I come from a not very privileged background, I hadn't travelled. To pay for that, I used to make* crèpes *in the street* [laughing]. *It's a funny story: I bought a ticket, came here, and forced them to hire me.*

I think about how is it to grow up in London. It's intriguing. My formative years were completely different. First of all you have a much greater sense of space. Here, you contain yourself in the streets. You've never seen the countryside until university. You don't look for much outside of London or Paris, because it's all there. But people like us, we came here [to London, the big city]. *It's probably quite a nice thing to have done. It makes you more tolerant, stronger. You learn a lot of things. I really would like my children to have to do that leap, you know.*

Laure married an Englishman, a journalist, after seven years in London.

We wanted to go back to France, both of us. We had great jobs but we started to feel it was a problem...

The "keep moving" thing ...

I'm not sure ... I think it's every five years. At the beginning, for a year or two it's great, then you have that. Every five years, like cycles for sleeping. I really think it's the same. Like a biological clock. You can't get away from it. It's like the culture is in your blood ... But we are not great at making big bold moves. We had a child, and I went back to work straight away. A lot of English women, when they have a child, they leave work. I come from the feminist culture in France, you don't even think about it, you just cope. Two of us working very very hard. We survived. But it really took a toll on me.

What actually happened to stop you going?

I think it's the mechanics of a couple. It really depends if you have a partner who is risk taking and easily transferable. I had a job, had found a job which acted as a focal point. But, getting personal, as a woman you prefer to be proactive, but you like to feel it's not all on your shoulder. I had two children, a job in the media. I just felt that I couldn't carry it all. It was too heavy on me.

Do you wonder how it would have developed?

Well, we wouldn't be here now [laughing]. *I don't feel a great sense of belonging* [here]. *I have this really naïve, picture-perfect image of life in the French village, with a community. I wanted to be a mayor when I was a child. When I said "mayor", everyone thought "mother"* [laughing] *and I said "Non, non, I mean mayor". So you know, it's part of my sensibility to be looking for that. I like the people contact. In Paris, I lived 7 years,*

A Media Manager's Tale—cont'd

there was a baker at the bottom of my flat, we always talked. I have been buying my French baguette here 13 years, and you know it doesn't happen.

This *Amélie* type fantasy of Paris obviously isn't the whole story.

Yeah, it's very good [life in Paris], *but it's a bit like* la pensée unique [one way thinking]. *Everybody goes in the same direction, and thinks politically correct things, which I do find a bit oppressive. French people always think that France is the best. Which is why they don't get on with the English. Because for the English "being born English is like winning at the lottery of life". This is my favourite quote, someone at work said that … We have such a culture of egalitarianism, then you arrive here, it's all about money. If you have money, then you deserve it, and everything will get better.*

There is the extraordinary side of London, so many nationalities, communities, the acceptance of "the Other" … I think that the English are less neurotic than the French. In general, the English are perhaps less racist … On the other hand there are many problems in England, the kind of thing that is arriving in France. You have to deal with it. I arrived here in the Thatcher years. It was very hard. There was Major, then Blair. This affected me. I always saw the black side of England, not just the little cute birds. This hurt me. For example, the breakdown of the GP system. We always go back to France.

One aspect of the English which I don't like a lot of people that take a lot of advantage. "Rip off Britain." That something [i.e. a plumber] *can cost £90, it's disgusting, for nothing … There are shitty schools, lots of people making a quick buck … In France, we have more respect for* métiers [trades]. *You don't just become a plumber just like that. There is a respect* [for the trade]. *Here there's no respect. At last I understand after 13 years why it is that the trains don't work … It's because there is no respect for engineers. Intelligent people never study to be engineers, they go work in the City. I didn't understand that. I met this guy* [in the City] *and asked, "What was your degree?" "I was an engineer", he said. "But no way was I going to work as one!" Then I understood why the Millennium Bridge didn't work* [laughs].

And this, in the cradle of the industrial revolution!

Yes, it's a pity. The quick buck. OK, they're not racist here, but how people are exploited, that really shocks me.

And so, again, you start to think about leaving, wanting to go back… for your children, if not you?

Yeah, absolutely. You wish you'd never left your little town [laughs]. *I'm starting to analyze this from my children's point of view. One of the thing you never give up on in your life* [here], *is the idea to go back. It's particularly on the cards now, because of the house market* [in France compared to Britain]. *Also I don't have the same expectations in terms of work and career now, in terms of lifestyle, so it makes it a lot easier.*

Is it a question of longer-term commitments?

Although I don't like talking about middle class problems – at the end of the day we are so much more privileged than people who have *to move – I would still like to know why it is there are more and more people who make that choice of where to live, to move to new*

A Media Manager's Tale—cont'd

places … It's part of having more choices. There's a friend of mine, she's German with an English guy, they are telling us how much you can do without kids. In two weeks they had been all over – Paris, Toulouse, Montpellier, the Alps – seeing where they might live, all these places where they could project themselves. I said, "you are mad or what?" [laughing]. They were enjoying it. They're both self-employed. What we are all doing is forgetting is that the most important thing is involvement in where *we live, not* where we could *live. And I put myself in the same basket as well, because I ate my breakfast today looking at the map of France! But I think increased choice does come with the loss of involvement. There's always that little village, you know … You have this possibility* [to move] *but it means that you are going to put less roots, make less effort – unless you have a lot of time, when you are bored.*

Our conversation goes back to the problem of childcare and being a working woman, and how she has solved it – by employing East European *au pairs*.

Yeah, these girls, it's an amazing phenomenon … They are so different to the "golden youth" [of Western Europe] *– the childhood of young French, German, Italian, Spanish teenagers. Your studies are easy, you pay nothing, you live with your parents … And then on the other side, all these young East Europeans in England. It's really so tough in London, tough compared to what young people* [in West Europe] *have. Compared to my sister's or my brother's criteria.*

There is a lot of abuse [of the *au pairs*]. *It's pretty easy to see which of those are going to do OK, and which are not "s'en sortir". It depends unfortunately on the background they had. The girls that are a bit more polished, better brought up, they start as secretaries, then they move out. They have this possibility to be mobile. Then there are the others, from simple backgrounds, farms, factories, and it's so tough for them, they don't have the resources … They are extraordinary people. I don't want a little French girl "na na na"* [speaking like a French girl] *… In human terms you have amazing exchanges with them. That's only something I have here, not in Paris, where everyone would be just like me …*

These girls, it's OK at first, but they are going to arrive at the point when they need to leave, and they are not going to be able to do it. They've had no professional development. There is a gap. The curve is like that [hand goes up], *and they are like that* [going down]. *At the moment they want to have a family, when they are less fixed on personal achievement … They need to go back to their own country where they are needed … It's a horrible situation. To all of them, I say 'You've got to go back!' It's too tough for them. Bosnia, Romania, Czech Republic … These countries might develop if they return. They might make lots of money, accumulate things, but they are living a very unstable life. I understand them, I am a bit that way.*

It's time to get back to her office. I tell her she had better go back and make some money. Laure grimaces.

I'm not very good at making money. I'm not a convinced enough employee. I'm in charge of international communications. Developing new channels, you know. Giving them more spaceships, more connections, more communication, in a more caring world. Wow, it's a fantastic crusade! [sighs]. *I'm 42. You know, maybe I'm getting wiser. I'm an idealist. I want to return to idealism, not to the commercial world.*

11

London Loves

The success stories of this book are the pioneers and the outsiders – the statistical anomalies. No nation-state-society has been so successful at standardizing its population or imposing its norms that it leaves no space for people who just don't fit the mould. For the kind of life Guillaume and his friends are leading, the big porous cities make perfect sense. If you don't belong anywhere, why not go to the places where everyone, at least some of the time, feels that way? Where the *anomie* of modern urban existence is a way of life. The standard middle class family life in the same circumstance is in fact much harder to achieve. Quality of life in a distinct urban context is the elusive prize. But to get what you want out of the city requires struggle, long-term strategies, and a willingness to play the same game that domestic families have to play.

London Beat

Over and over in my interviews, it is striking to hear how much pressure the city puts on people to live there in a certain way. It is built into the structure of their daily lives, the infrastructure of getting around, the habits of socializing, and the compromises involved in attaining any sort of decent quality of life. Behind London's cosmopolitan front lies the blunt fact that anyone who lives there is forced to assimilate to the ways of the city. This fact – the pressure of falling in with London's singular, insistent rhythm of life – stifles the very diversity of lifestyle and choice that is seen as its hallmark.

On this question, it's the trivial, everyday things that reveal that most. Drinking, eating, meeting people, dating. London imposes its norms, and it's mostly a one way street. It is always fun talking to the Spanish in London, because they have learned the hard way that to become a Londoner you have to lose a lot of your core Spanish "luggage". Pedro, 35, working in finance, is by now a veteran of London life. He complains how socializing here is completely different, and how he was not used to it: "the liquid lunch, down the pub – as many pints as possible". You go back to the office and you cannot work – but you have to. Work and social life are intense, and you have to start early if you want a big night out. You go straight out after work, there's no point going home. A total rhythm of life is imposed on you. He found this shocking. It removes your private life, and you have no time as in Spain to relax first then meet later for dinner. Then at the end of the evening, there is the scramble to find somewhere open after closing hours to have a drink, or you have to pay a lot to get into a club. This is assimilation at work.

> *Once you see how it works, you decide to do as they do. The sooner the better. Then I think it's the only way. It takes a time to admit it, that you start doing things like the locals do. That is the way the system works.*

The irony is, it's the same even if you go out with a bunch of Spanish friends. The Spanish are a proud people, especially of their eating habits. But these don't last long in London's kitchen. He stopped cooking, started eating takeaways five nights a week, and struggled with the food habits when he went back to Spain.

It's an unhealthy, wearing lifestyle. You need a lot of energy. But, again, it is part of the rhythm of social life; a norm – with sanctions of exclusion if you don't follow it. Norbert, the German economist, points out how if you don't go to a pub, you risk missing out socially *and* professionally. He thinks it ridiculous the British "use far too much alcohol".

> *Hanging out in pubs easily gets on my nerves. [But] you have to do it with colleagues once a week to keep up with what's going on in the office, all the unofficial things. More than that I can't bear. Sometimes I fear for me mentally going to the pub is work time not leisure time.*

His resistance translates into ideas about eating and food. He eats differently to most of the locals, finding it "horrible here" unless "you have a lot of money and go to very good restaurants". Food in Britain is supposed to have improved amazingly – Jamie Oliver and all that. Most of the continental residents are sceptical about the hype. The problem is, if you go home to cook, you don't come back in to town – and therefore you don't socialize much.

Over drinks and some stale pub grub – in a typically sterile, corporate owned London "local", full of tacky mock Tudor décor – Carmen and Franz pick up this story. It's a quite acute analysis of how social inclusion and exclusion works for these young European foreigners in London. Everything happens over drinks. They complain that you only make friends if you drink like the locals. "Not only Friday, every day of the week." The alternative is to spoil the party – and become the outsider. Franz would have two rounds of beer waiting for him while he was still drinking the first. His colleagues couldn't understand why he was so slow. He found this "quite hard at the beginning".

> *There is a difference between the continental scheduling. On the continent, you drink and you enjoy drinking. Here I have the impression they don't enjoy it. That they have to do it. "Today I need to drink 15 pints" – it's unbelievable – so that tomorrow morning, it's like they can tell everyone* [proudly] *"I was drunk, I had 15 pints, I didn't know how to get home". Everybody is sitting around, and it's, "Wow, yeah, and we had to put you in the cab, you know", and it's like, "Oh I was so pissed" ...* [Exasperated] *Let me out!*

Carmen continues:

> *This is a silly example. When I go out with my friends at work, colleagues. We go out once a week, and we are laughing and talking, it's great, we all sit down, we're having a beer, having fun, being friends ... Then someone like me says, "Oh I don't want to drink beer any more, I'll just take a coke or something." And they all look at you, and they are like, "What are you doing drinking coke?" You are not part of the club anymore. And they actually try to convince you not to drink the coke. If you say "Oh, I just want a glass of water" ... It's not that they don't talk to you anymore, but they just close up* [she is laughing, but this is a serious point], *and it's like you are not part of the funny group any more, until you go and buy a pint. I find it quite unbelievable. It's a silly example, but it took me a long time.*

Carmen and Franz have reacted to the pressures by preserving a bit of their "European lifestyle", trying to eat properly at home. It puts them out of step with many of their colleagues, and leads to them not feeling like they have really settled. Franz draws a bigger conclusion:

> *It's something, when we think about the future. We certainly will not live our whole life in England. It's a great experience, certainly very interesting and we have had*

some good times here. But when we come on to our future lives, it's certainly not in England. It will be somewhere where you know that you will have lunchtime and a more regular lifestyle.

Office culture is also where the limitations of London life have become apparent for Jeroen and his girlfriend Nathalie. A classic example of an English ritual that excludes them – but which is seen by the locals as a good example of how relaxed and open their culture can be – is the Friday "dress down" at the office. Their story sounds like a nightmare episode in the excruciatingly funny BBC comedy series *The Office*. We are talking about the English sense of humour. Jeroen likes the sarcastic wit. Nathalie disagrees.

> *I thought everyone was like the Monty Python* [before I came]. *I was sure I'd love the English because they have such a good sense of humour. But where are they* [these Monty Python characters]*? It's so difficult to meet English people. It's not true that they are so tolerant. They are because they are* obliged *to be so. There is the "dress down Friday" … In my company, they come with the most ugly football shoes, with shorts and things like that, and it smells awful. Oh my God!*

As Jeroen points out, it's basically just a cheesy American idea that has really taken off in some organizations in recent years. Nathalie ran into trouble with the locals because she didn't want to dress badly. Her colleagues were all telling her off, accusing of her "being French" because she didn't want to dress down. Nathalie protests that she couldn't afford to dress like that, and that she couldn't go to work in her pyjamas. Jeroen laughs that he has an Italian colleague who refuses to wear a tie normally; on Friday he wears a jacket and tie on purpose.

> *What a silly idea, this "dress down" idea. Is it on Fridays you don't have to respect each other? I mean, if you're relaxed then be relaxed, not this.*

Nathalie always opts out of the drinks that follow. It's that rhythm of life again. Great fun, good for a laugh – as long as you don't step out of line. Jeroen also avoids it, but is conscious about getting out of step:

> *To some extent, I didn't fall into it. The people I go for a beer with are foreigners. I'm a bit stubborn, slowish. All this running in London, I don't like this. I do feel a little bit overwhelmed by things coming at me, a little slower.*

Donatella has gone through various cycles living in London, and now is happy to see herself as an expat living in the centre of a global city, without bothering too much with integration to the local life.

What I found with English people, either they are completely closed to the rest of the world, or they are very very very international. There's nothing in the middle ... The great majority are a bit suspicious of everything that comes from abroad.

She says this sounds strange to an Italian, because "speaking as an Italian" everything that comes from abroad is better. She thinks this is because Italians are not very nationalized – although it is not quite clear how "speaking as an Italian", you *cannot* be nationalized. Italians always exaggerate how little nationalized Italy is, how supposedly localized it is in terms of identities. In part, this is part of the historical pain and denial of post-fascist reconstruction, at least until Silvio *Forza Italia* Berlusconi came along. But her point is that London certainly does not feel denationalized. She too complains again about the drinking and eating habits, the stress of having to do socializing straight after work. If she goes out to a concert, she has to grab a sandwich. These "bad habits" affect her quite a lot. The mechanism it leads to is one in which people are forced to choose between a "young" sociable life in the centre, and an "older" suburban life, where you just go home and it's over, and you never do anything – except maybe have children. That's London. You accept the lifestyle as it is. Compartmentalized and ageist – with you on the wrong side of 30. A little out of step, and outside the norms. The rhythm of the city – which is not quite yours.

Now I complain much less. Italian people are used to complain much more. Now I'm much better!

Donatella has learned to win the victory over herself. To love the city, despite its stern face. Even to think like a native.

I find my way around myself. I'm ... it's good, I learned a lot. Really! I mean, coming from a European country [she sees my face] *– er, when I say, a "European country", I mean France, Germany, Italy – it was a huge huge shock.*

London is famed for its global openness and unlimited diversity, yet in fact – because of the way daily life and patterns of sociability are so inflexibly structured in the city – the kind of lifestyle it offers residents is rather standardized.

From West End to Suburbia

The first couple of years in London are tough – but fun. But things change. Your older English friends start talking about moving out of London, looking for a little suburban place with a garden. Laure, who has made this kind of move herself, comments on the turnover. It is hard that the local friends you happen to meet move in and out of London. There is more stability in her professional rather than persons circles, although it might be expected to be the other way around. Assimilation pressures thus increase over time. The trajectory of housing is a good example. A young mobile adventurer arriving in London for the first time might well be content with kipping on someone's floor or living temporarily among other foreigners in a hostel. Over time, they will want to graduate to a flat of their own, and enter the fierce and pricey competition with other young native and foreign residents for somewhere nice – or at least halfway decent – to live in the city. If they settle, and begin to think of their adult lives in the city, they will end up facing the same compromises that all Londoners do. Again, the structuring of the rental and owner housing market in the city affects the degree to which the foreigner is able to live differently to a native, in a denationalized way.

First there is the question of know-how. Books of advice on finding housing in London can be bought, but self-styled expat guides are generally behind the times and pitched to a readership relatively unlimited in their financial resources.[1] Housing ideas of this kind tend to be the most obvious, clichéd ideas of where it would be chic to live – Chelsea, Kensington, Notting Hill, Hampstead, Swiss Cottage – places that might have been bohemian once in the sixties, but are now among the most overpriced in the city. They are, unsurprisingly, full of very rich foreigners, often on paid company housing – an international population often pointed to as "proof" of how global the city is. But these are not the kind of places that average British residents look to, and nor are they the place that young Eurostars on modest wages should be considering – rationally speaking. Yet on housing, several of my respondents demonstrated the key lack of local knowledge, that left them renting in well trodden, higher price neighbourhoods in North and West London – as opposed to doing as British newcomers in the city would do and looking south of the river or in the East End for better value housing.

Anniken and Dominic knew to look west, and first lived in Holland Park before graduating to their current place near Hammersmith. They also point out another reason determining the expat West End drift – the international schools. They tried Pimlico, South Kensington, and Swiss Cottage but could not find a flat with a garden. Anniken admits that she "doesn't know much other than West London". Sashia, who landed in West Hampstead, also reveals a mental map that has nothing south of the river.

Typically, too, they reiterate the false perception that the south is inaccessible because of a lack of underground lines (in practice, the overland train lines are a near equivalent).

Grouping together in typical expat places – which is also where the hostels for newcomers are concentrated – the new foreigners in town are easy meat for exploitative landlords. There is no reason why foreigners should be less smart than newcomer natives in the city at understanding and acting upon local knowledge. Where they lose out is that their social networks consist predominantly of *other* European foreigners, who are reproducing the same set of stale information.

Nicole's ever temporary existence seems to be always rising in cost. She is having to move downscale now. She is not atypical in spending over £500 a month rent on a salary in the low £20,000 range, little more than the average British income. She moved every year, even though she wishes she didn't have to: first out west, then back to her current, still expensive, location in St. Catherine's Dock, near the Tower of London. She feels she is going backwards, to something cheaper. She complains that the salaries look high "on paper", but that "you only just live". Before, she "didn't know London well enough", and with all her movement she still has "no attachment to neighbourhoods". Her lack of settlement precludes the kind of more localized ties and networks that other residents use to make London liveable and affordable. Nour, meanwhile – who lives with even more professional mobility, and more like the image of global elites in the city – opted to ignore the prices, and buy into the most obviously accessible international area of London in Kensington/Chelsea, some of the most expensive real estate in the city. Although not at all in the highest earning categories, she invested everything she could in a nice flat in this classic expat part of town to make relaxation in her hectic mobile life easier. Something about these neighbourhoods – all the transient rich folk you see, who are clearly not English – makes it a comfortable place to live, given her work and lifestyle. On and off planes, working nights, and highly global in her orientation (when not back "home" in Paris), she admits to not knowing her way around London much, and is still not sure about where to take out of town friends when they come to visit. On a mid-ranked journalist's wage, she complains that she can't follow her super rich Lebanese and Palestinian friends – some of the most visible of the global rich in the city – and that, as a consequence, her social life had contracted. She now rarely goes out.

Donatella also typically paid high by following the expat trail, including a very expensive commute from Oxford for the first few months. Earl's Court seems an extravagant choice: it's more where you'd expect to find Lady Diana and company. Again, the answer lies in the poor diffusion of local knowledge among expats. Earl's Court is full of expat Italians, it turns out. She later bought in St. John's Wood, also pricey. These expensive choices are driven by the quite understandable, if incorrect, perception that to really live in London you have to be living in or around zone one. Postgraduate British coming to London for the first time would be much more likely to discover liveable areas in the city further out in the semi-suburbs in zones two and three, where in fact much of the "real" London is to be found. Donatella describes how she built up knowledge through her expat contacts first. Once you are in an area, it's difficult to think of other ones. She rules out Islington – "no, that's almost zone two" – as "too far out" (!). Where she lives now is a rich Jewish area: "like a village", she says, with a 7–11, a Starbucks, Regents Park, and Madame Tussaud's just around the corner. This is not a London that many resident British would recognize as a village or neighbourhood. Donatella is, in fact, just reinforcing ideas that an older generation of foreign residents, more linked to high class living in the city, take for granted. Sandra – the artist from Luxembourg, married to a German banker, living in South Kensington – still thinks of the East End as way off the map for the kind of people they know, when I ask her. She thinks Islington "might be OK now". Islington is an interesting case in point, well on its way now to being as overpriced and inaccessible as South Kensington and Chelsea, except for naïve expats with corporate cash arriving in the city for the first time.

The other expat trail leads out of the city into the few semi-detached, multinational suburbs of outer London that are clustered near one or other of the major international schools. Out into the leafy avenues of Respectable Street, Surrey, lined with privet hedges and company cars. As well as generic suburbs, there are dormitory towns like Richmond, Esher, and Cobham. Rainer is proud that their brand new suburban detached just about manages it onto the edge of the London A-Z. They have four bed-rooms, a garden, a lawnmower, and English neighbours to wave to – but they still are not quite neighbours like all the others, since they had to follow the common practice with mobile expats and rent a house that their company has bought for them. Carlos and Susana had to do likewise, and chose their house in Cobham for convenience to the American school, his work, and Gatwick airport. Carlos says it is 60 percent expats and you "don't feel the need to communicate with locals". The one downside they have found is that the quiet, affluent suburbs can be a rough and violent place. Teenage vandalism has become a problem, and a particular target are the many rich American expats living in the area. Susana did some English lessons when she arrived.

> *The teacher said, "The problem is, when you* [foreign Europeans] *come here to London, you think you are in a foreign country, you behave like foreigners" – I'm sorry about this, but that is what she said! – "… but when Americans come here, with their dollars and the same language, they think they come to a conquered land".*

Cars with the American school sticker, where their children go, regularly get smashed up in the public parking around Cobham. So much for the "special relationship" with the US. Maybe it's not so nice to feel colonized; the English, at very least, should remember this. Even Sandra, who with her German husband has gone a long way to becoming a real Londoner, found there was no way of integrating with people "out there" in the London commuter belt. They bought a house in Esher, not far from the German school in Richmond, so that they could have "fresh air, a dog, the countryside". The house was "gorgeous", but "the hedges were so high you couldn't see the neighbours". It was difficult to make contact. They were lonely and isolated, and within two years were back living in Chelsea.

This is what life is really like outside of the city. Multicultural, open-for-global-business, cool Britannia isn't in fact very multicultural, global, or international *at all*, once you get outside of zones 2 or 3 of London. Just English, and suspicious of foreigners. The experiences create mechanisms that ensure non-integration or settlement. Sometimes it's just easier to opt for the complete expat package: two jobs, a car, and a furnished appartment in a private gated compound somewhere out in the suburbs. Philippe, who works at Unilever in Kingston-upon-Thames, prefers this kind of life:

> *It's absolutely brilliant. We met our neighbours* [all foreigners]. *And it's Wimbledon, posh Wimbledon! Everybody drives German cars, everybody is well educated, with nice jobs, extra money. People in our situation.*

But the alternative, to play the market at market value, causes decisions and compromises that in a sense remove much of the point of being in London anyway. Norbert, the German economist, clearly has a better nose for what his British contemporaries might be doing, and did look south then east. First, he and his Mexican wife rented in trendy Brixton, but decided the rent was too expensive after a year or so. They then started to look east, to buy, but had to look to find something affordable, but liveable. They ended up in one of the least glamorous areas imaginable: Walthamstow, far out in zone 3. Commuting into the centre, and having friends dispersed across the city, Norbert finds the place is little more than a dormitory, where they can't relate to anyone around them. They are the only foreigners. He has had to compromise *his* London. Like many foreigners, he was also put off by Britain's peculiar leasehold system. Apart from understanding these legal peculiarities, there is no formal discrimination reported against foreigners. In fact, London's insanely tight and pricey housing market discriminates uniformly, regardless of nationality: against the poor, and against buyers in favour of sellers. It has always been this way: London after all was the first city in the world to grow up and expand on the back of rampant property speculation (from 1750 onwards). It hasn't taken long for the foreign European residents to assimilate the idea that, whatever the price, they had better forget renting as they might normally have done, and buy. As everyone knows, the market is structured to overheat and exploit buyer's desperation, working to create a permanent housing bubble. This is the time honoured London process, and has become the model for all of the Western world in the last ten years, as housing has held up the global economy.

A lot of people in London have come from the provinces of Britain, and they quickly identify with the place, often fiercely. But the difference is, they quickly get into step with the counter-urbanization processes once they have children. First they congregate into outer zones of the centre, recreate their villages and urban tribes. Then they buy houses. Then they get married and have children and move further out to the suburbs. The international transient population does not follow them; that's not their city. The exclusion they experience is, then, a subtle one: a structural and temporal "social closure" for reasons linked to why they are in the city and their chosen modes of living in it.[2] Jeroen and Nathalie broach this topic by first discussing why it is they don't really have English friends. Nathalie complains that she has been here five years, is a friendly and open person, but still would not have one English person's address to take home with her to France. Jeroen points out the "obvious dynamic": other people his age or younger have their friends already, their lives planned. Newcomers to the city meet newcomers – other foreigners. Their frustration at this "closure" links to their explanations for why there is no appeal for them in doing what other English of their age are doing and moving out of the city to the suburbs. Jeroen says he would have refused to move with his job out to Harrow-on-the-Hill; they don't want to live that life. It's not just because they don't have children, even though it's true most of his English colleagues his age do. But the suburban middle class option has been the routine way that native Londoners have, since the early nineteenth century, squared the circle between the impossibly competitive struggle over housing, childcare, affordable education, space, and greenery, with urban life in the city they love. Very few Eurostars in London want that; it misses the whole point of why they are there. As Isabel, the 30-year-old Spanish economist thinking about children, says:

> *You have England, and you have London. If I had to move out of London, I think I'd just move to Spain, to France or to another place.*

Many fail to settle in London for this reason. It is a clear limit to the city's cosmopolitanism. If you are a gay man in Amsterdam, or a single professional woman in London, the city can work for you in the long term. But if you want a house, a dog, a car, and maybe children some day, it's a whole lot harder. London does have some of the spaces that Brussels has in abundance for international families seeking to settle. As ever, they are only open to the most tenacious and affluent, but there are intermediate zones in London – places like Highgate, Stoke Newington, the grid of South Wimbledon, Greenwich, Brockley, and areas around Islington – where Londoners have been able to square the circle between city and suburbs, preserving something of both. Foreign families can be found in these places, becoming familiar faces in childcare centres and local schools. London does have the capacity, then, but the steep price that people pay in terms of capital expended to achieve this makes it a struggle to which most are unequal.

There are also one or two examples of foreign integration into London via gentrifying multiculturalism, parallel to the Brussels case. Laure bought early in multi-ethnic Golders Green and loves it there. Siofra, from Ireland, similarly feels they settled in London because they found an unusual suburban space in multicultural Northwest London that still felt comfortable. They moved out recently from a more typically multi-ethnic area near Kilburn. Over coffee in an Ealing Starbucks, interrupted occasionally by the sleeping baby in the pram, Siofra describes how they solved the big London question. They found a villagey area in Penner, with good schools, on the cheaper end where there are also many upwardly mobile Asian families. It was the multicultural dimension to this otherwise classic suburb that provided the key.

> *We didn't quite want to move into the mainstream … We laughed that we moved from London to England when we moved down to Penner, but it's still a good mix [ethnically]. That was one of the differences here [in London] to Ireland [which we like]. We are still bringing up children in a multicultural environment. That's very appealing. It's why we are tied to London. We are not going to transplant to somewhere completely English.*

It is London's multicultural environment that is the key too for them to resolving some of the difficulties inherent in the Anglo-Irish situation. They don't need to become British, like previous generations of Irish immigrants. They have retained an Irish core, and feel European: the children were given Irish passports. Could it be that those people who enjoy urban living – such as the Eurostars in London – might also be able to deal with the suburbs if they were all multicultural like this?

> *I guess that's it, I suppose. I guess where we live now, we've tried to combine where we grew up [the west coast of Ireland], which is as rural as it comes, and obviously London which is as urban as can be. We've tried to have a bit of both. It's a happy medium. There are trees, but there is railways line that's gets you to the city. I think it's a good balance we've managed to strike now.*

Siofra's definition is of course *the* classic definition of the suburb, the very thing that London invented in the nineteenth century. This was before suburbs became associated with conservative attitudes, parking lots and mega-markets, no public transport, and silent, ominous streets at night. Insofar as the suburbs too can be multicultural, the suburban life for Eurostars might work out too.

But Siofra is an exception, and a limit case. To be Irish in London is to be both a foreign European resident *and* a recognized ethnic minority. They are native English speakers, and the Irish are not even subject to the same free-movement regime as EU citizens. For most Eurostars, a viable suburban option never becomes apparent. Long-term settlement on your own terms remains elusive. The open city closes its welcome, and closes its eyes. They remain an invisible, albeit massive presence in the city. European foreign residents are not excluded by law, by race, by education, by income, or by culture. Yet they are somehow still not a part of the city.

The Old Main Drag

Back in the central city, the Eurostars are weighing up whether it is worth it. The typical complaints voiced, trivial as they often are, are good indicators of the low quality of life that you get for your high investment in the city. Amid effervescent enthusiasm for so much of what London life represented, the interviews were peppered with moments of harsh critique, where interviewees despair of the destructive quality of life that native Londoners put up with, and that London imposes on you as a resident. The contrast with Brussels and Amsterdam is stark: lousy services, terrible public transport, dysfunctional governance, violent and drunken streets, bad schools and difficult childcare, huge expenses for everything. A large part of the problem is that the inflated incomes and lifestyles of employees in the City set the levels for everyone else. Norbert puts it succinctly. For them, there is not much of a trade off in quality of life. I ask him when he thinks this trade off will no longer be worth it for him. There is quite a long pause.

> *It's not really that something in my life will change and I will be better off some-where else. What I think is that things that annoy me here will just annoy me more and more, and at one point I just will not want to stand it anymore. Not because they get worse but just because I will have had enough of it. Then I will want to look for something else.*

London can be the most exciting place in the world for work, but it can also be crudely exploitative for the same reason. A lot of people put up with this – simply to be in London. Laura is a long way beyond her honeymoon period: she laughs it was over childcare, for her, "when the train started to derail". Her bitter choice of metaphor is very telling. Nothing has symbolized the break down of London life more dramatically in recent years than the (occasional, but regular) disasters on public transport. Nathalie recalls often taking the very same train involved in the Paddington station train disaster of 1999 and how upset she was the following week at the station when she got into an argument with an unhelpful and uncontrite ticket conductor. Nobody else seemed to be complaining – they were all queuing politely – but she was outraged. Nour makes a similar point (about the managers of her housing block):

> *When I complained, they were utterly shocked. I think it's a British thing. They said, "Oh, you are making a bit of a fuss aren't you?"*

Can't complain, mustn't grumble. If you want to belong, you've just got to grin and bear it. *Take the rough with the smooth, mate.*

In the long run, why would you put up with something like this unless you were a native of the place? But then, an awful lot of the natives are leaving too. For the droves of young Europeans moving to this hub of Europe, there are equal numbers of Britons pouring out to take up resident visas in the US or former colonies, abandoned cottages in France or retirement villas on the Mediterranean. This dramatic, almost desperate, desire to leave the place has grown to almost epidemic proportions in the last couple of decades: 200,000 or more people a year are out-migrating, and this during a boom period in the British economy.[3] The Eurosceptic British are in fact the most active and numerous exploiters of European citizen rights.[4] What is happening? Where are they all going? Anywhere else it seems – as long as they can still speak English. Maybe Britain will just be repopulated by the rest of Europe. Jaime, the young Spanish man, is in love with London, but he is disturbed by this phenomenon. His "Essex boys" colleagues keep coming to him for advice about where to buy a house in Spain, a flat in Barcelona, or where there is a cheap flight. If it's not Spain, then it's France or Australia. They all think when their kids are old enough, they'll get away, pocket their assets, take a loan, maybe find a little job there. The offshore, barbarian life of the "sexy beasts" on the Costa del Sol.[5] Jaime says it's nearly every other English person he meets who talks like this: far too many.

> *Why should a foreigner who comes here* [to Britain], *who is talking to his English colleagues who all want to leave … Why should he settle? There's no reason to. You have to say something is wrong.*

A City Broker's Tale

My investigation of the adventures of the young London French takes me one afternoon to a recently built flat in Islington. Valérie shares the place with a young American woman, but has the place to herself during the day while she works on her CV and new job applications. She is talkative, open, a little flirtatious. The daughter of a mechanic and seamstress, themselves of Italian origin, Valérie turned thirty a year ago. Her words are still full of the excitement of her independent London life, but there is a hint of anxiety about what lies down the road. The interview takes place in French.

I do wonder if you come from a big city, whether you feel the same things when you arrive in London as someone who comes from a small town. I come from a really small town, 25,000 inhabitants in the southeast. The last town before Italy, near Menton.

That's funny. I come from a small town about the same size in England.

I arrived in London to learn English. I didn't know if it would work out. I'd worked four years in Monaco, and had had enough. I decided to do my studies here, a degree in Finance and IT. Then, after three years it was the same thing. Do I stay here or go back to France? I sent out a few CVs, and I was hired straight away by the Dutch Bank. I made big advances in English because it was all another style and rhythm so … [laughs] It feels like I'm doing the same interview again that I did this morning. I left my work three months ago. I've been travelling a bit and am now looking for work again in finance. I was a broker at the stock exchange before, but that was really demanding and stressful – all jobs in finance are. So I'm looking for job in which I can use my languages, my French and my Italian, be a contact point for clients here. It's not great for work at the moment, compared to three years ago.

But you have experience of immigration in your family?

For them, though, it was surprising at the time [when she moved]. *Now it's different, my mother has the impression I'm always there with the telephone or internet. I go back every two to three months.* [In the old days], *it was all by letter when you migrated. My grandparents, they had so many brothers and sisters, they were all supposed to go to Los Angeles and New York, but one of the sisters died, and so my grandfather stopped in France … Shit!* [in English] *… I could have been born an American!* ["alors que j'aurais pu être américaine, shit!"] *… My grandmother, she left when she was 20. She never went back to Calabria or saw her parents. There's perhaps that in me. It's that they don't have fear of abandoning everything in order to find something better. My father says, why don't you come back and get a job here? He was ill last year, and I thought maybe it was the sign … They are 74 and 70, I know that it won't be in thirty years* [that I go back] *… I went to Monaco for an interview, but I didn't like the atmosphere at work. It's like what my mother says: "I prefer that you are with us, but if I know that you are happy where you are, make your life there." It's the same with my brother, he's been in* la Réunion *for 14 years.*

They are quite possessive. It's for that reason that me and my brother left the way we did. Here they couldn't bother me. They come, but here the roles have reversed. It's me that plays the parental role, and they are the children. I don't think I would have become the person I have become if I had stayed at home. My parents are Italian, very smothering.

A City Broker's Tale—cont'd

They like you to stay where you are. Maybe someday I'll have to go into psychoanalysis for this [laughs].

Where did you live at first?

I lived in the hostel at Bayswater, and it's there I met my close friends. Before that with my French boyfriend. But it was hard with compromising and so on. So when we split, I went to the hostel for three years. I stayed there throughout my studies, and into starting work.

These hostels are incredible focal points in the life of young Eurostars in London.

It's really a family. Everyone knows each other. It's also a network for information, jobs, visiting places. The Spanish always know where to go out in the evening … They are not exactly spoiled by the mode of life here. That's the reason that the most go home. Most people don't stay. I had a single room, but not right at the beginning. The hostel is a great place for meeting people [she shows me a prospectus]. *You all eat together in the dining room, breakfast and dinner. A lot of people leave because they don't like the cooking. I'm useless in cooking, so not me. Plus it's quite cheap* [sic]. *It was £110 per week, £440 a month, with everything included apart from lunch. In an appartment, it is much more expensive with rent, electricity, council tax. Then you become really lazy* [très fainéante] *because you can't be bothered to meet anyone outside of the hostel. I have a Greek friend, a PhD here. She's been there ten years!*

Surely, this is quite a tough kind of lifestyle to lead after a while?

I had some savings so it wasn't like the people who have to work at Prêt à Manger *making sandwiches. There were several at the hostel who were doing that – those that had to get up at 5 o'clock to make muffins. Yeah, people are living hand to mouth there. I left two years ago, it was hard to leave. I had a close girlfriend, but when she left the world collapsed. But obviously if people are not happy they should leave.*

Why do you like living here?

In Paris, it's perhaps just as good for all that, but you don't feel that denationalized aspect of life ["la côté depaisée"]. *I'm a foreigner here, that's what I like. That gives me the right to be different, because I'm not from here. I'm different. But also I'm different now in France, because I'm not like everyone now, and I like this way of not belonging to anyone, of making myself distinct.*

You see there the life is less stressed, people are more calm. Take Milan, people move ["bouge"] *there, but there is an atmosphere which you don't find here. Back in France, I couldn't believe it. Just to buy something, I wanted to shout "Move it, this is incredible"* ["Bouge! C'est pas possible!"]. *I could do three tours of the supermarket while I'm waiting to pay at the checkout* [laughs], *but anyway, when I came back, relaxed, etc., I appreciated that* [their speed of life]. *Whether I would like that long term … *[shrugs]. *There isn't the same competition, like here. I'm always amused here at 11, when the bell rings* [in the pub], *people always take three or four pints of beer. In France and Italy, you taste life – although I'm just as crazy* ["folle"]. *It annoyed me a lot when I worked – my job was intense, 8am–5pm – and you don't eat, you just work. When I went to this interview at Canary Wharf today, there were all these sandwich shops and all that, and I said*

A City Broker's Tale—cont'd

to myself [in English] *"Ah, I don't want that!" I can't do fast food while I'm walking. That stressed me out because I'd forgotten that. That's what I call the* "non qualité de vie" [anti-quality of life] *– where you can't take pleasure in eating, when you don't take more than two minutes.*

What about social life?

At the Dutch bank, we all had the same age. There were lots of men, but most were in couples. One got married, then another, then another. It was contagion! So it was difficult to integrate in a couple. I haven't met many English single guys my age, some Scottish, yes. I prefer Scottish to English, they are more warm. I can't tell the difference between Northern and Southern English, but Scots and Welsh yes … There is also this difference in the culture of dating – which is flagrant. The one night stands and all that are not for me. Here they do that all the time. It's part of the way people think. The few English I've met in bars they are very "fast" in coming forward. It's not my style. So that's maybe why I don't make contact. And with girls, I don't like the fact that they drink so much. I have a hard time accepting drunkenness. OK, with my French friends, it's funny because they talk complete bullshit ["racontent n'importe quoi"], *but they always have a limit. I find all the drinking a sad part of the culture.*

My best friend is more integrated because she drinks. I don't drink. I don't smoke either. There was a TV program, a sit com, in which the foreign girl didn't smoke, so she didn't integrate. Because everything happened in the cigarette pause, or the drinks pause. I think for me it's the same. I'm [in English] *"quite boring".*

Do you think you will stay here?

London is perhaps beginning to lose its allure ["déchanter"]. *It's such an expensive place. When I arrived it was already a nightmare* ["un bordel", literally "a whore-house"]. *Now I'm looking for work, I don't want to arrive at the point where I ask, "Is this game even worth playing?" I might be able to earn a good wage, but there's appartment rent to pay, and the quality of life all the same is not fabulous either. For the moment, I stay because I'm still …* [long pause]. *I think I'm going to stay here. I'm very happy with London, for the moment, but we'll see. I can't see myself anywhere else at the moment.*

So what next?

I'm off to Switzerland for an interview, so there may open doors somewhere else. Or if I do find the man of my life – da-dah!! – and – hey-hop!! – he wants to go to the US, then maybe I'll go to the US … But a priori, *I will stay for the foreseeable future. At the beginning it was like that, "I'm just here for three months", and* voilà *it's six years now. Maybe I'll be here in ten years time, but I don't have a definite plan. I like to take opportunities when they arrive.*

In a sense I'd like to go back, but … [long pause]. *The more things go on here, the less I can go back* ["plus ça va, moins je peux rentrer"]. *That's the only thing that makes me afraid. In France, I don't really have links with people, all my friends who I knew are all married now, all settled* ["installées"], *while here we are all single – even if you have a boyfriend – so there's none of that sentiment of "OK, I'm married now, so I'm not going out anymore" – which is not necessarily a good thing, by the way. But maybe that's why I don't want to settle down, because I don't have any examples around me.*

A City Broker's Tale—cont'd

After all, I still rent my apartment. I can't really feel that until I'm in a couple. My best friend thinks she will return to France, because she doesn't think she is going to meet someone here. I think that is more of a girl's emphasis ["une chose de fille"]. *I know it's daft* ["débile"], *but ... I should have bought a house six years ago, now it's too late. I can't buy anything by myself because that's going to be broken up the day that someone comes into my life ... There are many girls that have said that to me, that girls often think about the future in terms of their future partner ... That's a difference here, the English are more independent, while the French do everything in a couple. When you're a couple, you're a couple, that's pretty serious stuff* ["ça se rigole pas"]. *I can't imagine constructing myself on my own something ...* [Laughing] *Yes, I am waiting ... for the messiah,* voilà.

12

Old Amsterdam

Amsterdam, like London, imposes pressures and constraints that were unexpected to the movers there. The easiest way to get a view of expat life in Amsterdam is to go online. A number of well designed websites broadcast for the foreign professional population in the city, but the market leader is Expatica.com. Some of their most popular and widely used pages are the chat rooms in which foreign residents write in and sound off about their experiences. As Maria, the corporate lawyer, points out, if I want to get some quotable views on life in the Netherlands for expats, my investigation in fact need go no further than these pages. They are full of angry and amusing diatribes about Dutch life.

> *Have you noticed that they criticize a lot Dutch people? It's unbelievable. Every point that I mentioned* [in the interview], *they mention there. In the beginning I thought I was the only one saying it … Then I open this site and everything is there. Every same thoughts I had!*

So while in Amsterdam, I spend a lot of time at the various easyInternetcafés, chasing down expat commentaries. I scroll through the colourful pages, posting my own requests for interviews and comments, and receiving quite a few messages back – mostly anonymous, and mostly full of vitriol about their life in the city. Making (and not making) Dutch friends; dealing with Dutch bureaucracy; getting used to their personal habits; facing abuse on the streets; getting ripped off by landlords, or scrambling with hundreds of others for non-existent accommodation; failing to learn the language; wanting to go home. The same complaints are all here, but they are also shot through the interviews I conducted, as a familiar refrain. Everyday life as a foreigner in the Netherlands, it seems, isn't so easy.

Tolerate This

No country has such a vast range of expat publications, written by Dutch people to explain to foreigners how to live in their country.[1] Usually amusing, even self-critical, these books portray the nation as a series of exasperating, peculiar, or downright weird habits, that you – the bemused foreigner – are just going to have to get used to. Part of living in the Netherlands is dealing in everyday ritualized clichés, of the kind reinforced by these books, as the dominant way in which life in such a small, tightly packed nation has to be organized.

Get used to it; get with the program. Carlos reminisces about life with Unilever in Rotterdam, when they first arrived. A friend told him he'd better get a diary. It was early September, and Susana came home to tell him they had a coffee appointment in late November. He said, "Well, I don't know if I'm going to be dead by the 28th November." Roberta, another Southern European who found organizational life there challenging, echoes Carlos's description of the "culture of long planning", when she remembers "questi olandese quaddrati" ("these square minded Dutch"). Numerous other residents complain about the lack of spontaneity and inflexibility in this planning. Southern Europeans in particular have a hard time with the mealtime and socializing customs. A classic gaffe is the evening house invitation that turns out to be a cup of tea, not dinner. Maria, the Portuguese lawyer, remembers taking a box of chocolates with her partner to her Dutch friends, and sitting there starving, eating chocolates for dinner.

Younger foreign residents often find themselves similarly alienated by Dutch "parties" – at which it is often extremely difficult to meet people as an outsider. Valerio can't stand these events, sitting around a table eating *kaasblokjes* and *bitterballen* with little fluidity or mixing possible. Everyone already knows each other – probably since they were at school – and the get-together is likely to consist of replaying songs, games, and jokes that knit the tribe together. Guillaume gets upset.

You can never be part of these things. It's very stressful for foreigners because you don't master any code at all.

When foreigners are present, the Dutch have often two modes. One is the native "peasant Dutch culture", as Guillaume puts it, the self-conscious traditional re-enactment of rituals designed to be impervious to outsiders and reinforce the Dutch idea of a *gezellig* (cosy) social event; the second is the highly Americanized, modern, international external image, often imposed on the foreigner by making sure everything takes place in standardized Dutch English. The two modes of social interaction "cohabit completely" according to Guillaume. Resident European foreigners may well find neither option very appealing.

Repeated experience of these scenarios quickly leads to the archetypal expat reactions, reinforcing their own apparently self-imposed exclusion from Dutch life. Valerio:

> *There is a common feeling that we are living in a place that is really weird, that people behave in a weird way. That we are more civilized. We call them barbarians* [laughs].

He says it's a joke, but that there is some truth in it. Marlena, from Belgium, has a more evolved settler's view of these problems. She points out that the Dutch themselves have travelled and know other customs; they are very aware that their habits and rituals are weird. But that in a sense is the point. It is a way of reaffirming your national culture in the face of foreigners who are mystified, and whose denationalized attitudes dilute the specificities of their own place and identity. So you self-consciously renationalize yourself with silly rituals, albeit in a very self-aware, even ironic way.

Perhaps more mystifying still to the foreigners is that amid this tribal behaviour, reinforcing insider and outsider positions in the city, the Dutch also seem extremely, almost aggressively individualistic in their attitudes to intimate friendship and preserving the sanctity of their own personal space. Guillaume rails against what he sees as the "selfish, über-individualism" of the gay world, where people have no family ties, don't like being in a relationship as a couple, and live "very very lonely" lives in their little individual appartments. He feels he is being "contaminated" by this lifestyle; it's the "dark side of freedom and individualism".

But adapting to the Dutch mode of socializing is a necessary first step to having any kind of meaningful contact. Nina, from Germany, deals with it, but thinks that it contributes to her sense of not feeling settled, or fully satisfied with her life there. She complains that although they've made an effort to integrate, they don't know anyone they can just call up on a Saturday evening and surprise them. Anastasia, from Greece, says how it is "a constant fight working with yourself to understand how people function [here]". She has had many good Dutch friends, also a boyfriend. But she still feels ill at ease where the individual limits on personal space lie.

People here tend to control their feelings. When you want to come closer with people there can be a conflict there. You might go too fast, or you might think that they go too slow.

Once again, the metaphor signalling that integration just isn't working is one about being out of time, out of rhythm. Guillaume also can't quite understand what the problem is. Is it because he is French or a foreigner; or is it something to do with Amsterdam or Holland? He too hasn't made friends there like he expected. But he suspects that there is something systematic behind his: a kind of "apartheid" for foreign residents. Like many, he ends by drawing harsh conclusions about his experiences there.

[shrugs] *Dutch people are just not interested in meeting other people.*

Homeless

The most abrupt shock that any new resident in Amsterdam is likely to encounter is the question of finding accommodation. The Amsterdam rental market is enough to strike fear into the heart of even the most hardened global sojourner. It is almost comically difficult to find anywhere to live. Sympathetic Dutch friends might offer a bed to sleep in for a while, or to put a word out among friends. You can post your request in newsletters, student unions, and online. But they know very well how futile the search is for an apartment by any regular means. As Guillaume grimly quips:

What I've heard it's a city of 800,000 people … and 600,000 are looking for a new apartment.

It's a good question for the interviews. The anecdotes could fill a book by themselves. Ray, the businessman, has a lot of experience stretching back.

You need to be able to register yourself [as a resident with the police] *and that's the key to the whole thing* [getting paid at work, a social security number, a *vreemdelingenkaart*, etc.]. *But most of the people who have got places that they want to rent, don't want to give up their own name on the place. So they let you live there, but it's not a safe way to do it. You can't register. You can only stay in these places for six months … I did this* [illegal sub-letting] *for six years. I've lived in eight or nine places, ranging from super places with super neighbours and super landlords, to places that I was really really happy to get out of. And rents ranging from very reasonable to extortionate, and landlords ranging from nice guys to complete bastards …*

This is, in fact, a quite typical housing trajectory for a foreign resident trying to settle. Numerous interviewees recount at great length their "disasters" and nightmare "room stories".

I get the inside scoop on how this market works from Annie, a Scottish expat, who came to Amsterdam five years ago while working for the now closed British Midlands airline office. She now runs her own housing agency company, which is apparently successful although she doesn't speak Dutch, and it is not particularly well integrated on a personal level. Housing agencies are a thriving industry, parasitical on the daunting experience faced by would-be residents, and fuelled by the large amount of money that MNCs in the city are often prepared to throw at the problem. Two of the more affluent MNC employees I talk to, Helen and Axel, for example, were both found places in this way, and both are very happy. Annie points to the typical bad experience of 30 people all showing up for the same single showing of an apartment advertised in the weekly listings newspaper *ViaVia*, and each of them paying €250 for the privilege. Another one is to find and rent something, only to find out a week later that the place is in fact sub-leased, and that you have got to leave or be thrown out. She argues that the agencies offer a service to protect them from this. Her agency, specializing in Anglophone relocations, also helps typical first time arrivers in Amsterdam with practical stuff like finding your way around, dealing with the foreigner's police, etc. She notes how de Pijp is now becoming popular with Europeans and Americans – before it was always the Jordaan. There are slightly larger apartments in the south of Amsterdam, but the prices – which, on the private market, compare to other major world cities – are now similar.

Expats familiar with London, New York, Tokyo, or San Francisco – or indeed, in more recent years, Paris, Copenhagen, Zurich, or Los Angeles – might not baulk at the prices typical in Amsterdam. But what is flagrant about Amsterdam is that the same poky, run down flat in de Pijp for which a manager at one of the multinational pharmaceuticals companies might be paying €2,000 a month, is being rented by his Dutch neighbour for perhaps €250–300 a month through one of the city's rental cooperatives. Long-term Dutch residents are usually able after five or more years on a housing list to get access to decent apartments in one of Amsterdam's desirable central or near-central neighbourhoods. Persistent and cunning long-term strategies are the way natives deal with the situation. Short-term foreigners can forget this kind of option, and long-term residents find it very difficult to get into any of the schemes unless their commitment to life in Amsterdam is absolute. Salaries on the whole are much lower in the Netherlands than in other major global cities; life there isn't supposed to be expensive. The overwhelming majority of the foreign European residents in my sample are simply not in the exclusive expat rental brackets. They have to find their own way around the system, at affordable prices, if they are going to stay.

This kind of *de facto* discrimination against foreigners is in effect routinized and institutionalized in the absurdly tight Dutch housing market, in turn fuelling a housing market industry that is a goldmine for unscrupulous landlords and agencies. Residents themselves have to learn to be just as "brutal", as Marlena puts it, to get what they want. This subject makes Nina furious.

> *They* [the Dutch] *always say you are all equal* [as a foreigner here]. *That it's very easy to integrate, you get the same conditions as them. But it's just not true. I earn the same as my Dutch colleagues, but I have to pay so much more rent. For that money you get a 250 square meters penthouse in the nicest part of Hamburg. When I think that, and I'm sitting here with my little balcony ...* [laughs bitterly].

The occasional good luck stories become folkloric in foreign residents' tales of the city. For most, though, it is the make or break issue.

However, compared to London, Amsterdam is a counterexample when it comes to the owned housing market. Suburbanization is in fact the solution to the impossibility of the Amsterdam housing market for those trying to rent – ironically because many of the housing hardened native Amsterdammers think it is social death to move out beyond "the Ring" (the inner ring-road of the city). Clearly, buying is not an option open to all; some would not even think of it given their sojourner attitude. As in London, the system seems to be forcing people out into a suburban life-style for which they certainly didn't come to the city. But nearly all of the (rare) "success" stories of people having settled in the Netherlands are of people who moved out of the pressure zone in the city, and settled for life in one of Amsterdam's new city suburb developments. The irony about Amsterdam is go to one of these new suburbs to the west or south, and it's foreigners everywhere, mostly non-white and non-European. These are the most multicultural parts of the city.

Organization Men and Women

Employment in the Netherlands has proven to be an attractive and open possibility in recent years. Yet the everyday *habitus* of these work contexts can over time prove to be one of the most challenging problems faced by foreigners. Organized in an ostensibly communal and relaxed way, hierarchies and formal rules are often hidden in the informal practices of employees, and the complex consensual way in which decisions are made – often outside of formal meetings in corridor conversations and seemingly insignificant discussions. These practices set a very high threshold for understanding, that is often no easier even when most interactions are taking place in English. It is very easy to feel shut out as a foreigner, and the organizational habits can be used to outflank outsiders in managerial struggles.

A story from Maria illustrates this nicely. She feels she is doing fine at the bank. She thought she'd like the Netherlands because they are "direct"; but it turns out that her way of being direct isn't quite so appreciated after all.

> *The other day I was told by a colleague who was passing by my office − I imagine on purpose − that I'm "so direct" ... We had the most perfect meeting, it seemed. But he says, "I'm sorry if I was direct but you are always so direct and my reaction is to be even more direct." It was funny because then other colleagues were saying "Yeah, you are so direct, you don't go [beat] around the bush, you take no hostages, etc". I was like "Oh, OK ..."*

Maria reads the situation positively, but the comments seem to be directed to censure her not for being direct − which is in theory fine − but for being direct in not quite the right way. The comments continued, with her colleagues openly debating her way of interacting.

> *Then the other day, I was told a funny thing. One colleague said, "Oh yes, you are very direct ... And on top you are so petite" [laughs]. "We don't expect that from a petite person", she says. I mean, "petite"!! That's a concept I never thought about. OK, I'm not that tall, but with my way of being − which has to do with my previous experience in life, travelling, meeting so many people − I don't get easily pressed by people. For me hierarchical positions are not something so important. I never had a problem before ...*

In describing her repeatedly as "direct" and "petite", one gets the sense that the office is struggling to deal with a young, Southern European woman whose professionalism, experience, and determination confound their expectations and stereotypes − while subtly trying to impose controls on her that will bring her in line with the informal hierarchies and rules in the office that she apparently hasn't yet fully learned.

In career terms, these misunderstandings can prove costly. Sophie, from France, has been in the Netherlands longer and understands more. She too is an independent, career minded woman. In her English, which has an unmistakable Dutch ring to it, she explains her own learning process in the office place, which involved realizing that it is vital not to get angry or emotional at work, as the Dutch are "very uncomfortable" with this and see it as being "too French". She has learned the subtle way hierarchy works despite informality − not to be "too German" by trying to impose decisions as a boss − and is no longer as "confused" as other younger residents admit to being. Larger Dutch companies such as Unilever or ABN Amro can have their own, more internationalized, organizational cultures − at least where international employees are strongly represented in that part of the organization. Whatever else happens in the Netherlands, work finishes at 5 p.m. and your colleagues go home. The Dutch like to retain rigid distinctions between work and family or leisure life, and appear to lack flexibility or willingness to meet, except for an occasional, semi-formal *borrel* (office drinks). You remain a "colleague", never a friend.

The System

But the confusion at work is mild compared to confusion in the face of what everyone refers to chillingly as "the system": the Dutch public bureaucracy that keeps this complex, densely packed society so organized and well functioning. Nina is not atypical in her complete disorientation in the face of the wall of official bureaucratic requirements, from police registration and signing up at the commune, to obtaining social security, or dealing with taxation and medical issues.

Sometimes I think I'm doing things wrong. The system is not clear to me. I called people when I moved here and asked what do I need. I went there, but then they said no, sent me to another office. And so on. Maybe I'm illegal here, I don't even know.

It's even tougher in Amsterdam, as one Dutch friend tells me, because the city "is a system within a system". Guillaume's tale is – again – one of "horror stories": with the bank, the telephone company, the police, the university authorities. He complains of a bureaucracy that is "Soviet" in style, but which unlike in Russia you can't try to corrupt in any way. The problem is that you get the worst of both worlds; an inefficient and arbitrary bureaucracy, but one also that refuses to "discuss" anything, as they might in a more flexible system. If you try that they accuse you of behaving "like the corrupted French". Things started badly. Because of his irregular housing situation, Guillaume wasn't able to register properly for the social security (SOFI) number. Without that he couldn't work or get paid probably. The bureaucracy quickly seals off into one big vicious circle.

Alan, the businessman, is at heart a barbarian. He has spent years trying to dodge the system, managing to live unregistered in Amsterdam for eight. When he wanted to buy a house, he had to pretend he'd just arrived. Somehow he had managed to get around the SOFI number problem, even though he was illegally sub-letting. With improved computer technology, and the increasing securitization of society, this is no longer possible. All the bureaucratic systems in the Netherlands are hooked up, so that you have to register correctly with all agencies to get access to any. The brute face of "the system" is often first encountered in the Netherlands, as elsewhere, with banks. The Dutch are straight and play by the rules; but they are also notoriously seen as "stingy". Ray, who started up his own business, tells his story graphically. Financing was difficult, banks informally (and illegally) discriminating against European foreigners because they say they are not sure they can get the money back if they leave. They were forced to run the company initially with complete liability. It "wasn't the best idea they'd ever had". They found they could be out of "the system", yet also in it; paying for all their own insurance and health coverage, and with no unemployment coverage.

We realized we were very vulnerable, especially as foreigners – that they would make mincemeat of us.

The business did OK, and after three years they were able to put it on a safer footing.

Ray talks about "the system" as if it is *The Matrix* and he has been trapped inside for years. He evokes the word repeatedly. It took them several years to get on top of the tax system, at great cost. As a foreign employer, he has to deal with understanding and implementing rules that are in many ways alien to him, and judging when employees might simply be using them to take advantage of him. The experience has led him to reinforce national stereotypes, as well as break a few European non-discrimination laws of his own.

We find that the Dutch people are a lot more aware of what their rights are and will tie you up in knots. We've had some very bad experiences with Dutch employees, over employment contracts and things like that, so we tend to stick with English expats if we can find them …

These gripes are the complaints of small and medium sized business employees the world over, but they are sharpened by the inevitable difficulties that are faced by foreign entrepreneurs in a complex foreign labour market. Both Ray and Alan have been successful enough, and are the first to point to the benefits of their secure, affluent Dutch lifestyles. But their difficulties point towards why there are still relatively few business people ready to take up their cross-border opportunities in an integrating Europe. The free movement in services has indeed proven to be an even bigger stumbling block in European integration than the free movement of persons.

One of the blocks to a more integrated market in services in Europe may in fact be the vastly different attitudes people have in different countries to providing them. The Netherlands is historically famed for its trade and sales prowess – particularly internationally – but it is not reflected in the everyday attitudes of people working in services, who are very likely to only offer their work to you according to the strict letter of labour law. In an informal social environment, the same people – here acting like rigid automatons for whom nothing outside their remit is possible – can be generous, open minded, and highly adaptable. Maria puts it this way:

> *There is something that is stuck here and it's the way Dutch people say so easily "it's not possible", "it's not possible"* [dat kan niet] ... *It's really appalling for me. It's like, when it's their fault if something doesn't go right in their office, like a package or whatever at the post office. It is their fault, but the lady keeps on saying: "I'm sorry, it's not my fault. It's not possible."*

Dat kan niet. This is an expression foreigners get used to hearing in shops, offices, wherever and whenever you are asking for something that is not in the rule book. Nina, her colleague, finds the rudeness in shops equally bizarre – and she is German. "They treat you as if they are doing you a favour."

Susan, the personnel manager, suggests it is because the Netherlands is caught between a Dutch way of doing things and the dominant American-style business ideas in the MNC world. Whatever the explanation, to the highly mobile in spirit, the Dutch attitude to services is perplexing. Something extraordinarily powerful seems invested in the rigid adherence to the rules regulating the labour market; as if the entire system might come crashing down if the shop or kitchen stays open an extra two minutes. For Alan, as for others who believe in Europe as a liberalizing force, the reference point on these issues is the US. He complains that the customer isn't king in the Netherlands, and that there is "no dynamic" with the sales people he tries to employ. He sighs.

> *Really, how they are successful at business in this country I do not know.*

I suggest to Maria it is because the Dutch have always been very good in international situations, at flexibly adapting to doing trade and business abroad. "*Ja*", she says, "it's true". At the very least, Maria pronounces her *ja's* like an *echte Nederlander*. Sharp, crisp, slightly exasperated. But she fixes on the story of a friend who went to a showroom to buy a BMW in the window, and was told brusquely to go away, and wait two years. 'I'm sorry, it's not possible", she repeats, in a lovely Dutch accent. "How can you afford to be like that as a seller?" Maria reads *The Economist* and has been trained at top business schools. That's how the world is supposed to work. Yet she is missing something. The business practices – "the system" – ultimately appear to be impervious to even the most successful foreign businessmen and managers in the country. There is something going on here that is resistant to dominant economic ideas about how business, trade, and commerce are supposed to work in an integrated Europe – or even a highly "open" and internationalized West European economy, rated at the top of most economist polls. Yes, it's a nice theory. But that's just not how Dutch economy and society work.

Everything in its Right Place

The Netherlands is rated routinely as the most open country in the world, and Amsterdam is widely viewed as the most liberal city in Europe. Countless numbers of international movers have been attracted to live and work there, with the promise of open employment and a vibrant, tolerant, cosmopolitan city on a human scale. Yet the stories have a repetitive ring. Very few people manage to settle and stay, and the turnover of expats easily exceeds the inflow. What appeared open and cosmopolitan seems also to be closed and ultimately provincial to many who tried to live and work there. Understanding this, it is easy and tempting to fall back on the same crude nationalizing stereotypes with which the Dutch themselves love to categorize foreigners. The Dutch are "double faced", "closed", "tight", "difficult", "not interested in making friends". It's their "culture", it's the "way they are". These kind of explanations go no further than the caricatures of the cross-cultural business self-help books, or the gloating Dutch expat guides. To explain the resilience of national "systems" or the barriers to free movement in terms of "culture" – as if European nationals have some kind of innate essence that keeps them tied to a particular territory and society – is to explain nothing. "Culture", for sure, is what actors see and feel; but it is precisely the construction of these social distinctions that needs to be questioned and unpacked.

Understanding and explaining Amsterdam in fact would take us a long way to explaining the resistance found in Europe more generally to mobility and mobile populations. That highly desirable, ostensibly international or global cities seem to cultivate a latent hostility to cosmopolitan forms of life, expresses something profound about European society. These cities are economically flattened by global connections and regional networks that seem to dictate openness and a dilution of particularism; yet their very strengths and distinctiveness seem to lie in preserving these very particularisms. So these cities need the commitment and engagement of stable populations who invest their lifetime in them as places of belonging – while casting out those who are just passing through. To echo Karl Polanyi again, they prefer "settled folk" to "shiftless migrants". In these terms, of the three cities considered here, Amsterdam is far more typical of the classic medium sized European city; Brussels is an unnatural, one-off hybrid, a city of mongrels and the displaced; while London is a would-be hub of global flows, yet to transcend some aspects of the provincial and local. In Karl Polanyi's book written over fifty years ago, about a nineteenth-century Europe distant yet somehow still very present today, the basic mechanism at work here was expressed very clearly.

> *While on the one hand markets spread all over the face of the globe,* [on the other] *a deep seated movement sprang into being to resist the pernicious effects of a market controlled economy. Society protected itself against the perils inherent in a "self-regulating" market system. This was the one comprehensive feature in the history of the age.*[2]

Amsterdam is a glorious city, with a wonderful quality of life; located at the heart of a country with very high provision of social benefits and some of the most progressive social attitudes in the Western world. The Dutch in Amsterdam have a lot to lose if the *dijks* give way and a free-moving economy is allowed to just flow over them. They remember very well one of the meanings of the city's three white-on-red crosses, seen everywhere on the bronze anti-parking bollards (*Amsterdammertjes*) lining the canal side streets. *You are now standing below sea level.* There are perhaps good reasons why Amsterdammers make it so difficult for outsiders to live there.

What looks cultural may therefore on closer inspection be rather more structural. Consider the extraordinary population pressures of the dense packed Randstad, man-made on reclaimed land from the sea. Pretty much every urban-minded young professional in the country – minus a few stubborn Rotterdammers, and those who gave up and went suburban – wants to be living in Amsterdam. Part of Amsterdam – North Amsterdam, unglamorous and cut off by water, the Dutch equivalent of Staten Island – is not desirable; Bijlmermeer and other remote parts of the city, with their large immigrant populations, are also discounted. These residents are even scrambling to buy houses planned in the IJmeer – on a piece of land that hasn't even yet been raised out of the water! That's just counting the native Dutch. Add in foreign international workers and immigrants. Tiny houses, tiny spaces, and tiny opportunities. Three quarters of the city, as Guillaume recalls, are looking for another apartment. The equation is daunting. There may be jobs aplenty on the labour market, and social attitudes may be laid back and easy going. But the structural competition for access to and control over housing – the key to quality of life in the city – is already set at such a high pressure, it can be no surprise that naïve newcomers and foreigners feel this "cultural" context is impossible to negotiate, hostile to their wishes, and exclusionary of their hopes to settle. To break that barrier requires extraordinary persistence and good luck. There's nothing necessarily discriminatory going on; it's just "the system". It's tough like this for everyone, and young Dutch Amsterdammers have been working on getting what they want out of this city for five, ten, fifteen years or more. The Dutch are great travellers, but they always know they are coming back. While backpacking around Indonesia, they have ten to twenty year housing plans in their back pocket for when they go home. The strategies they are following are thus temporal as well as spatial. They have no problem with the long run; they know where they are going to be. Commitment is everything. Dutch society is sometimes like a bigger, blown-up version of the fraternities that dominate university life and professional networks. *Bent u lid?* Are you a member of the club yet? Free movers move to a different rhythm, and have a different horizon.

Exceptions like David and Stefan prove the rule. Stefan, who has managed to settle in the city – as a homeowner, successful architect, and family man – confirms this. I say to him that the people who really belong here, who have what they want in this city, are obviously going to stay here forever. It is clearly a struggle to create what you want, but once you have it, it's just kind of there. You've made it; become part of one of Europe's dream locations. Congratulations.

> *Yeah! I have a lot of Dutch colleagues who can't imagine they could ever do any- thing else. It's exactly like this. They are travelling a lot. They are international minded, cosmopolitan. But it's their investment. Into the idea of Amsterdam. That's the thing.*

Across Europe – with the exception of Berlin, now touted as the last European frontier city, the Eurocity of artists and nomads in search of a viable alternative – the scenario is this. Whether it is Stockholm, Copenhagen, Paris, Milan, Barcelona, or Zurich, for young urban professionals the typi- cal European city – however international it is in other ways – resembles more the impossibly competitive scramble for housing and quality of life that is so characteristic of Amsterdam, than either Brussels or London. The threshold that make this a closed and exclusionary system was reached a long time ago here. International residents enter at their peril. At best, they are an irritant to the system; at worst, they are easily exploited outsiders, ready to be milked as over-earning expats, or spat out and sent back home when settlement fails. The intensity of the dynamic is a function of the size, density, historical allure, and contemporary dynamism of the city. Amsterdam scores high on all except size, which intensifies the struggle all the more. Its socially controlled mechanisms of allocation, meanwhile, ensure that outsiders cannot even get access through the workings of the free market as they might in other equally difficult or expensive cities. The processes of exclusion at work are not anything explained by culture; just basic social maths.

Amsterdam is the future of an integrating Europe, not Brussels. Even the big open market of London may well go this way, with more and more

Londoners realizing they have to stay at home, and work their way into the housing market using long-term strategies. As the cities improve, and central neighbourhoods become ever more popular, the overwhelming pressure of native middle class demand is going to squeeze foreigners ever more. It is no small paradox that this demand is driven by the cities' cosmopolitan attractions, that in part depend on the presence of diverse, foreign populations. As the cosmopolitan city attracts cosmopolitan-minded nationals – who have the benefit also of being locals, knowing their way around, and not minding the idea of a long-term life in the city – it reduces how cosmopolitan the place really is. As the competition for quality of life gets tougher in these cities, they are going to be renationalized. For sure, global elites who come and go will always be able to afford to live there. But the average middle class European professionals – the ones on whom theorists of European integration are depending to be mobile – will be shut out of the game.

A Journalist's Tale

My interviews take place all over Amsterdam, but at least one takes place in every young tourist's favourite image of the city, on Oudezijds Achterburgwal, in the sleazy heart of the red light zone. I have to pick my way over used syringes and condoms, while I seek out the entrance to an office somewhere among the open brothel windows. When I get upstairs, it's actually an attractive open plan work space, a smart collective for independent journalists. That typical cool, clinical modern Dutch style. A map on the wall reminds me that this is the Randstad global city. Agnes welcomes me brusquely to her end of the office. She had been sceptical about meeting me, but probably figures there might be an interesting story in it. Eventually she warms up, enjoying for once being the other side of the microphone. Agnes is a freelance German correspondent in the Netherlands, and also works as a "professional German" for the Dutch media.

How did you move here?

I fell in love with a Dutchman. It was a long distance relationship for some years, but came to Amsterdam seven years ago. I've moved around a lot. I covered the international tribunal in Den Haag, and Geneva at the UN. I also studied in the US and had my first agency job in Frankfurt. I've seen it all almost. In Amsterdam, I wanted to be very close to where everything happens. With my job you can't live outside [the city]. I'm a big city person. Now, maybe only Berlin could match Amsterdam for me. You are looking for everything you have now. I couldn't go to a small German city, that's absolutely out of the question!

There is a high level of interest for the Netherlands in Germany; more than, say, Scandinavia. Because it's a neighbouring country, and they are progressive in a lot of

A Journalist's Tale—cont'd

areas. They are so close yet so different. Right now, they are interested in Dutch politics. On immigration, it has become very hard line. That's what I wrote about today. I translate what is going on in the Netherlands for Germany, a lot of things about society and social policy.

It's a special, particular relationship, the Dutch-German one. Ja [in a very Dutch style], *you learn to live with this. It bothers me. The typical Dutch evening with my husband's family, that is really something that you have to get used to. At one point I refused, I thought I couldn't do that anymore. It's too much. These parties, their traditions. Here it always remains the same. That is one thing all the foreigners have problems with. I talked to an American colleague, this was one of the reasons for her divorce* [laughs]. *She had the perception that the Dutch and her husband were very open and liberal, then she found out it was so traditional and nothing could change. That was one of the major reasons, yeah, these differences in thinking and the way of values. You discover this later, and you are already stuck!*

It makes it really difficult for me to get friends. I really have problems to get close. Old friends from university, they have their own rituals ... Sometimes I don't understand them – and I'm afraid that I don't want to. Even with my good Dutch friends, they still give me the feeling that I'm not part of it. That I'm the foreigner, yeah. And I think that doesn't belong in a friendship. It happens in certain moments. All of a sudden you think, "Oh!" ... I saw quite a lot of similarities to Switzerland. It's a small country and actually a kind of closed society.

Has it been tough to establish yourself professionally in Amsterdam?

Ja. *I moved from having a job at an agency with regular hours, to being here, and having to find new clients, and build up a network. It's more competitive than in other parts of the country, but it's easier because the international community is that big. They all have the same kind of perspective on the Dutch and it's very funny. Then you feel like at home in the international community versus the Dutch community. That's fun in Amsterdam, it really is. As a journalist, you always have to keep apart, an outsider even. You can't get too close, because when you get too close that's the time when you have to move on, because then you are not objective any more. If you become part of it.*

Is the European Union as relevant to your world?

Generally, I'm enthusiastic yes. I think it's a good thing. The euro, it's really great. I turned down working in Brussels. I like Brussels a lot as a city, but I hate the work you do as a journalist there. It's just conferences and documents and lobbying and running after people and getting opinions. I think European politics are interesting when you see what happens in the countries, in the member states. Having the facts from Brussels, that's OK, but then you have to go to the members states and see what they do with that. How do they change their own rules and what happens then. That's interesting I think.

Of course, I am aware professionally of being a European citizen. As a citizen, I was really pleased when I learned I had the right to vote in city elections, and the referendum. I thought, "Yeah, I'm a citizen of Amsterdam". I always want to know what's happening. For example, the IJburg, building new houses out in the sea. They had the referendum on whether they should build there in this natural area. In Germany and in Switzerland, it's a

A Journalist's Tale—cont'd

big issue to preserve nature, and not to build houses. So it was quite clear that I would be against it. But then I read about it in the papers and I talked to people, and I was astonished it was not a left-right issue. It was more a question of "we need space for housing in the city". So then I looked at it differently. Also the privatization of the public transport in Amsterdam. There was also a referendum in May. We talked about this in the office. It was refused by the people, it was a big issue. Then again, sometimes I have the feeling, "Well, is that really so important to me?" As if I'm not convinced that I will stay here, you know.

What about life here as a parent?

I have one child, a son. Of course I know a lot of Dutch people from my son's school. We also have a lot of international friends, you find each other. You just meet when you are in the park, when you are there at the playground. When the children are playing and you hear English or French or German, and then you start talking. Then it's quite easy, as a way of meeting people.

What about childcare?

The system is completely different than Germany. No woman knows when they have a first child, how they can manage. "Can I work, etc.?" I didn't know the system and they have a lot of crèches and these are not very popular in Germany. There's a notion there that they are only for people who really have to. It's seen as bad – by the Germans who are stuck in Germany. So I'd never thought of doing that. I changed my mind having seen the system here. I needed someone because it was very lonely sitting at home. I looked for a daycare mother, then kindergarten. I was quite flexible, I could work at home. Then I got this office. The competition for crèche places is high and expensive, much more expensive than Germany. You just work [to pay] *for the crèche.*

Do you think of Amsterdam as home?

Home … um, what's "home"? That's where I live, but no. No, it's not really.

Despite having a family here, a child, a Dutch husband, a house, and a stable job?

Well, you say it's home, that you are going "home" … But I could easily pack my suitcase tomorrow, and move to … I don't know, New York, London, why not? It's interesting, you have two groups [of foreigners here]. *The groups of foreigners who have to move because they are sent by their company – and they hate it. Then you have the group to which I belong to, that just enjoys moving. I could settle all over, I think. It's more difficult with the child, but for me as a person it's very easy to move.*

When they ask where I come from, I say Bremen. That's the place I lived the longest period. Five years when I was growing up. I'm still supporting that soccer team. Apart from that, no, I don't have a home. But I do have that feeling, that comes stronger and stronger, that I'm a German. That heimat *feeling is strong, which surprises me. I never had that but you know this coming from history, the cultural background and this kind of thing of having the landscape inside.*

What about your relations with family?

The good thing is that you don't have the everyday quarrels. When I come home, it's always special because I don't come so often. What I feel is that that my parents, my sister

A Journalist's Tale—cont'd

and brother, they don't see that life is really different in another country. They are not open to that. They think that I am the same person that I was in Germany. It's strange. Sometimes I just have to remind them. I've lived 14–15 years in foreign countries. The family didn't come to visit in Geneva and Amsterdam, not often. I have to live with it. What also changes when you are abroad, the distances are not that important any more. I'd drive 600 km to a friend's party, if you value your friends. This is maybe also something I'm a bit disappointed about. I would like my parents and friends to have the same kind of feeling. They just stay there and think that it's too far away.

But there is the whole German thing. The one example is the [World Cup] *football championship. My little son got from his grandmother a German flag, and in the neighbourhood the foreigners all had their Danish flag, and a Turkish flag and so on. But he was very happy that he had a team there* [the Dutch didn't qualify] *... He had the German flag and he put in the window, and I was kind of ... er ...* [confused sound]. *In Germany, this is not done. You don't do that! But I thought well, he is six, he is new in the world, so we do it. Then this very good Dutch friend came to the house – the evening before the Germans played the Americans – and he said, "Well, yeah, tomorrow you burn your flag!" ... I thought this is an awful thing to say. You know my son is six years old, what shall he think? I mean he* [my son] *was really upset.*

This sounds like a great example of not-so-subtle Dutch humour.

Yeah, you could call it their "heavy humour" but it also had a deeper meaning. They would never say that to a Dutch flag would they? Then you have the feeling, "Oh!" – and these are supposed to be your friends.

So how does your son feel as a German-Dutch boy?

He is aware of it. He considers himself a real Dutch. I told him you have a German passport, but he says, "I'm Dutch, I was born in Amsterdam" ... When Pim Fortuyn came up, my son watched the children's news, and saw he was really a bad guy, against foreigners. But then this guy was shot, and there was all this commotion. He was watching the TV and said, "You know, if I could vote I would vote for his party". And I said, "Oh, you know what he stands for?" "Yeah, he's against foreigners." And I said, "And so who is a foreigner?" I had tell him, "Even you are partly a foreigner." He is aware that he's different. At my parents, he speaks German. The bilingual thing has worked out. He speaks German when I'm alone with him. If there are lots of people, then he speaks Dutch.

13

Anomie

Some paths come to a dead end in these cities. The future might not be European. What happens to the Eurostars – these incomplete narratives – if the path they are following is a road to nowhere? For every individual or family that settles, there are many more that move on or head back home. It is a given of migration research, though, that migrants do not admit failure. It is not part of the self-representation of their lives. It has to be inferred. Migration research also tends to study migrants who have stayed, and so not focus on one of the most obvious indicators of failure – of the migration project at least – which is return to where you came from. The other side of the story about freedom, adventure, and self-fulfilment – the dream home heartaches – have to be teased out from their words: from moments of doubt, glimpses of another life, bum notes; little inflections of darkness or discord in an otherwise sunny eurolandscape.

Out of Time

On the whole, Eurostars seem to manage quite well the challenge of family relations on a new European scale. The problem lies more with friends back home. The drifting apart from the key relationships of your adolescence, but not necessarily finding new friends to replace them, is particularly a problem for young women, who talk a lot about missing best friends and confidants.

This kind of thing is easily disrupted by mobility. Susan now looks back wistfully at her group of close friends in Bristol, realizing that something special was lost. She was the "glue" in the group of single girls, and it fell apart when she met her boyfriend and moved to Amsterdam. She complains that people only know her now "as a couple." Others, typically, have not found that one special girlfriend – the one who shares all your confidences and commitments – while living the life abroad. Anastasia, from Thessaloniki, would do it all again; but it has made her a different person. She can see the costs and benefits to mobility now.

> *Sometimes I'm thinking I'm making my life more difficult. If I was living in a place that I know, surrounded by family, I wouldn't have had such a struggle. You feel alone. You grow up faster. You have to take care of yourself. You have to go through things that you wouldn't even imagine in your own country.*

The subject forms the core of several conversations with the young French women in London. This is the city where the struggle is hardest, and where the difference between life there and the cosy life of the "golden youth" back home is at its greatest. Nicole identifies how out of time she is, compared to her friends, and points to the astonishment of her family about the life she has chosen. Her friends at university didn't go to Paris, but stayed in Lille or went back to the small northern town she comes from. They have jobs, are married with children, and have family close to hand.

> *They find it very hard for me not to be in a relationship. They feel very sorry for me. They think it's a dramatic situation! Some of them think that I just don't want to be an adult in a way.*

She does feel selfish, much more focused on "myself, my problems, my little things" since she lived in London.

> *Sometimes I wake up and I'm still complaining about things. I know someone working for Red Cross. But I don't have the energy.*

Nathalie says many similar things. She comes from the South of France, but the drama has been much the same. Like many, Nathalie spent the first couple of years living in a hostel. Although she misses the fun, she also recognizes that, once you turn 30, this kind of serially unstable lifestyle has parents and friends back home worried.

> *My friends don't understand, because they now have a three room bourgeois in Nice with a chimney ... And they see I live in 10 square meters [in a London hostel], and share my bathroom with thirty other people, and they are really ... Quoi!? ... And,*

no, I'm not married, I don't have kids. All the 33 year olds I know are more or less in the family life.

Nathalie is increasingly concerned. The consequences of her choice of lifestyle are becoming more apparent.

I sometimes envy people that are just content with who they are … Maybe it's just because I don't want to make a commitment. The only thing I'm really frightened for me is that I don't want to think what I'm really doing in terms of jobs, in terms of life … You can just forget to make decisions … I just grow old because I'm in transit. If I was not with Jeroen I'd still be in my youth hostel and I'd be very happy to be so. There's an old lady there who is 60 something, and each time I see her I think: maybe it's me in 40 years, because I've not moved on from here!

When I'm 65

The sense of unease expressed by these young free movers gets even more troubling when the question of long-term planning is raised. On this question, the costs and benefits of mobility are quite the reverse to immigration. Typically, the long-term benefits to immigration outweigh the often sharp short-term costs. A new life in a new country, social mobility for your children, citizenship and full integration, will one day offsets the pain of leaving, the difficulties of moving, or the downgrading of skills and social standing that is the most typical trajectory of immigrant workers. For the free moving few, however, mobility offers the reverse. Moving itself is an adventure, a positive change. You often arrive flush with capital, earning more than the locals, with much fewer of the responsibilities; there are all kinds of social and professional benefits upfront in your new life, that often arrive immediately in the first honeymoon period in the new city. The problems and costs of mobility only emerge slowly over time.[1]

A denationalized life means, to some extent at least, opting out of the social contract of the national welfare state. This is rarely a total opt out: everyone, it seems, keeps their doctor, dentist, bank account, and family connections back home as long as they can. But can one really go it alone? Does the new European space guarantee anything that the nation-state used to? The bottom line with "success" or "integration" might well shift when longer-term responsibilities, planning, and calculation kick in. The settlement question is dominated by access to housing, childcare, and leisure facilities. But the middle class urban scramble – the sacred turf of property and social reproduction – is no less contentious than the longer-term calculations about social benefits, tax breaks, and pension payouts that are deeply embedded in the democratic European middle class order of things.

It is these issues that lurk behind the EU's sharp concern, but relative impotence, in the face of pension mobility within an integrating Europe. The immobility of pensions has long been recognized as an obvious, residual barrier to European integration and successful, unproblematic mobility. All too often, pensions both public and private are embedded in nationally bounded schemes and guarantees, that prevent them from being moved to another place, or around Europe. Numerous reports, recommendations, and directives have been made in recent years, but little progress has been made.[2]

If you are in your thirties, and the topic of pensions happens to come up, it can be a good idea to listen to someone 30 or 40 years your senior. After meeting for lunch in his home town of Tervuren – a well-known high end European residential choice, just east of the forest of Brussels – Richard drives me back to town on the Brussels ring road. He is, quite frankly, concerned about my lack of pension planning, not atypical for a highly mobile and individualistic person such as myself. Richard is a veteran resident of Brussels, who wrote to me when he read about my research in the expat magazine, *Bulletin*. He has worked for multinational companies and for the European institutions, both at high managerial level. He is full of ideas and theories about my subject. That day, as we speed past the entrance to the Bois de la Cambre, he gives me a nice piece of advice. Even if I've been out of the country for years, it would be worth contacting British social security, and paying voluntarily into my national insurance account, so that I can at least claim some kind of pension from the British state when I retire. Later, when I get a letter from the DHSS forwarded by my parents, inviting me in the kind, endearingly amateurish tones typical of British bureaucracy to make voluntary contributions, I start thinking again about something I'd mentally shut the door on years ago. Who knows what it will be worth? I imagine barely enough to pay for the gas bill, television license, and the meals-on-wheels when I'm 65. But at least I'll get something …

Talking about pensions and financial planning is not an easy subject to broach. It is like lifting up an ornamental paving stone in the garden to look at all the creepy crawlies underneath. For some of my interviewees, it is almost the first time they've been confronted with the question. For others, they have done a little thinking, but they are not sure, and doubts easily rise to the surface. Valerio, for example, thought things would be fine with his pieced together funds in the Netherlands, but was having trouble with Dutch bureaucracy. He feels secure because his life is still somehow anchored in Italy – "and of course we are in the European Community, so something has to be done". I gently raise some scepticism about his confidence in the EU to sort all this out. I point out the mobility of some pension contributions can be difficult; you lose financially on tax refunds at home while resident abroad, and you can't remove things without paying a lot of tax. If you only stay a few years, a lot of what is paid into Dutch social security will never be seen again. The attitude of most people is that state pensions are not worth it, and they are dealing with the issue privately. But private funds are often less mobile and more nationally specific than state funds, where there is now EU-level coordination. Valerio stays very quiet through all this. He is looking uncomfortable; we change the subject.

Younger movers, who are going to live forever, have not yet really thought about it. Maria, at ABN Amro, doesn't know "what will happen to all that money" she is paying. "I'm not doing any planning", she says casually. But, turning 30, these questions begin to sound a bit less theoretical. Tom and Sinead laugh, because this is another "one of those things" you don't deal with while living in "the Brussels bubble". Tom wishes they were "a bit more responsible". Guillaume, in Amsterdam, panics a bit on the question. It's a queasy response:

> *Actually, I'm in denial about that. I realize I'll never get a proper pension if I stay here, and building one in France is way too expensive from outside. I'm trying not to think about it, I don't see any other way to solve it.*

Guillaume opted out of the pension system attached to his previous researcher position because it was too expensive, given the small salary. He, like many of my interviewees, know lots of people who are not thinking about the issues or planning anything. Giulia, nearly 60, in London admits that she has no solution. The real pioneers of European mobility – especially of her generation – went out on adventures across the continent, like homesteaders looking for the wild west, without any decent coverage at all. She says she is "an example – in a bad way". The problem is not about collecting retirement pension if you move to Spain after working a lifetime in the UK. That now works. Where there is a problem is for people who have moved around serially, paying different amounts of money into different systems.

Most are waiting for the European Union to sort this all out. In the neofunctionalist terms that make most sense to enthusiastic pro-Europeans, it seems inevitable that the member states will put their heads together and come up with a sensible single system that works for all citizens in the EU, however mobile they are. Janet, in Brussels, has a private pension which she is "not sure is transferable", although it would be if she stayed with the company.

> *I'm in this transient state. I've been here for quite awhile, knowing I'm not going to settle here. Perhaps I'm unique.*

Her situation is far from unique. The whole point of social security is that it is supposed to make you feel secure and anchored. To allow you to plan, calculate, and invest in the future. Not make you feel insecure and uncertain.

The more pragmatic respond by, in effect, anchoring their lives back in their home nation-states. Viewed from this point of view, it is possible to be mobile while free riding on your native citizenship. For the time being, inconsistencies and loopholes in European welfare provisions do still allow people to get away with non-resident welfare benefits that should not be possible. Axel, the telecommunications manager in Austria, still has everything back there. His pension is private, his whole family is there, and "somebody can take of it if I need something done". The other alternative is to naturalize in the country of residence. For the businessmen in the Netherlands, such as Ray, there was no alternative but to conceive it that way, given that contributions are obligatory. This is a clear barrier to further mobility. It took him and his co-director three years, and a big hit in their cash flow. They are now "embedded in the Netherlands" and the tax savings can't be moved. Working within MNCs, meanwhile, everything is fine – as long as you stick with the company. The company usually agrees to make up the difference and cover mobility costs. In this aspect, MNCs function a bit as an alternative transnational welfare state. Rainer was certainly concerned about the question when he moved from Germany to England. He realized that after a year, you start to lose rights and entitlements:

> *To be honest, I trust the company that it will be all compensated. When I asked for the exact calculation, I learned I should trust the company.*

Trust the nation-state; or trust the company. Outside of that, you're on your own kid. When the time comes, in the final frames, the EU is not likely to be riding to the rescue over the horizon.

Don't Look Back

Most people, when pressed, think that their mother nation is still there for them. The question is, though: Can you ever *really* go back? The endless expat talk of return is itself another pathology of non-settlement, the admission that you will never settle "here". It is especially prevalent among the Southern Europeans, whose desire to return home parallels the southerly movements of Northern Europeans in later life. Valerio is a typical case. When I ask him if he is planning to move on, his thoughts turn home – to Northern Italy. Are there opportunities in Italy? Is it difficult going back?

> *One of the main worries – why I don't want to wait too long before going back – is that they always ask for young people to be employed and I will turn 35 soon. It's the time when everybody should be settled, and I'm still an international bouncing person* [laughs]. *But I think where I come from is a rich region, a rich*

city with a lot of industries, also medium and small industries. [Brightly] *I'm still young, I suppose.*

Could the difficulties be more psychological? It can be difficult to "go back" on that level.

I always have the idea [that] *the later I will go back for sure I will find some problems. I talk* [about it] *because I'm here, but when I will be there maybe I will regret something or feel that because all my friends there are married and I'm not. Most my friends are not married here, so there is more a kind of social order situation there, and here is much more a changing thing.*

Valerio is strongly attached to his region of origin. He discounts other destinations in Italy as "being a little bit like being abroad". He assumes he can go back to his old "customs and habits" very easily.

I really can say I have a feet in every place, one leg here one there. It has been easier [the] *last few years. One hour and a half hour* [plane] *and you are in Venice, then I'm in my own bed soon after.*

It turns out, in a sense, that Valerio never really left.

When I say there in Italy, I mean at my parents, my house, my room. I have a complete wardrobe [there]. *For me it would be strange not to have it. I feel very comfortable* [with this]. *It is all connected with our culture, our way of being …*

Caterina, in Brussels, is thinking about it too. What happens when you get older?

I want to buy a house in Italy that I will rent. It's a place which I'm sure I will go back to. Maybe it will be to go in a hole [laughs, then pause] *… Sorry! … I don't want to be old and lonely in a foreign country. I want to be where I know people.*

Caterina is very sure of her attachment, and that she will go back. She would take a job in another country, but only a couple of hours' flight away at most. Her sense of return is something she protects and cultivates, and it anchors her otherwise very fulfilled and successful single lifestyle in Brussels.

Carlos and Susana, who are a little older, know that this idea of return is not so easy to preserve. They always had it in mind they would return, but they have taken steps to avoid some of the familiar pitfalls. They kept the house in Spain as a "fixed point", and took care that their children had a sense of "roots" there. They worry that "you can lose your personality" otherwise. Still, Susana points to some of the problems. You can idealize the place you came from. They go frequently enough, that they don't start "dreaming" of home in this way. But your life has been *here*, while people have gone on with their lives *there*.

> *It's OK, they welcome you home, but they are not wishing to listen to your stories about the UK or the Netherlands. Sometimes I have even felt … [pauses] … that it's, "What does she think? Because she is living abroad she thinks she's better than us?" So [when I'm there] I'm not going to talk about my life abroad. Because it's a feeling that for people who never go abroad, they think you are showing off or whatever. You have to very careful with that.*

But would being back in a place where you had to edit and truncate your life experiences really feel like home? Sandra is a little older still, and has been much longer in London. She has also lived in Switzerland and Germany and she feels European.

> *But sometimes you don't know what you are. You are a little bit nothing 100 percent any more. You think differently now from people in your own country. If we would go back, we'd have the same problems as English people who lived abroad [back here]. You see the difference.*

The younger movers, who are still following their careers and personal adventures, onwards, outwards, and upwards, might not yet see these problems. Guillaume has already seen through this kind of attitude.

> *You don't meet older people like that. At some point the system broke and they have to question it. You cannot go like that forever… In my case it's actually a disadvantage [for my career] that I moved. I think I become a lot richer and more interesting abroad. But in France, if you've been to Amsterdam, it's like, "Oh you've been smoking pot for two years" or something.*

But where next might Guillaume go? He feels "stuck" in Amsterdam. Being gay "you set the level quite high", and all other destinations for him would be tougher now. I'm thinking: maybe he should try Brussels. He continues:

> *Being a migrant is not as easy as it sounds. I always wonder when people say, "Oh these fucking foreigners who come for our money and that." I always think it's because these people have never travelled. If they knew how difficult it is to live abroad, they wouldn't think that. It's ten times as hard if you are coming from Africa. It's hard enough if you are German or a French person [here]. I'm white, male, educated and stuff, and still it's not easy … They must really want to leave their country. It's not only because they like Holland! People should wake up a bit … I have to say, it's nice to move, but sometimes it's very tiring and very*

depressing and very challenging. Sometimes I really envy people. You know locals and that. They don't have to worry about so many things that seem very natural to them. Sometimes, I'm really doubting [my life here]. *I'm thinking: I should go back to France. Everything can seem unbearable* [here], *there are so many things you don't master. I guess it makes me a stronger human and stuff, but sometimes I just wish it was easier.*

Guillaume turns on his campest voice.

Really!!

Ghosts

Mobility can get to be a burden, a pathology, even a disease. A life without norms can also be a life adrift, in fragments, with no social or spatial coherence; a shadow of the society around you, a ghost passing by. Over a number of phone calls, I piece together John's tale, a British telephone engineer working in the Netherlands. These are appropriately disembodied discussions, snatched by phone card or small change from one of Amsterdam's green phone boxes. John is based currently in Den Haag, working for Siemens, but has lived and worked in and around Amsterdam over a number of years. He is a GSM engineer, one of a new breed of high tech engineers that have emerged with the mobile telecommunication revolution. He is very happy to talk, have someone at least listen to his story.

John is 46, divorced, with three children "now living in the Midlands somewhere". They lived in the South of England, and he had a regular family and work life until his late thirties, when he started travelling and "got the bug" for mobility. He had never travelled before, but then in a short period of time was transported around the globe on the back of the burgeoning mobile telecommunications networks, in the first rush to wire the planet for cell phones. He went with Ericsson to Saudi Arabia and Israel. There were projects in Iraq, Kuwait, and Zambia. Each journey was a lucrative job, but also a mobility fix – while the wife and kids stayed home. There was also a spell in Germany, which he preferred because it was on a regional scale, and more manageable for family life. Things got difficult at home. He tried setting up a consultancy based out of home, but it still involved projects in Norway and Austria. Long days and weekends away; frequent flying; exhaustion and disrupted contact with home. It didn't work; the marriage fell apart.

John sounds jaded. Mobility has taken a toll. His home life in tatters, he has spent most of the last few years chasing after ever scarcer contracts in the Netherlands. He had known "loads" of British engineers that had been lured to the Netherlands, either as individuals or as families, in the first flush of the telecommunications boom. The technology was more advanced in Britain, he explained, and in terms of both training and on-the-job experience, British engineers were needed to fill a huge gap in the Dutch labour market in this sector. They came on "unbelievable" contracts, collecting a temporary worker tax break, and able to feed the profits back home – rather like the famous *Aufwiedersehen Pet* British construction workers in Berlin, before their jobs were taken by Turks and Poles. The problem was that many of them then got caught out by the change in fortune in the business. Suddenly, when the economic climate went bad, they had to "run for cover" back to Britain. Many of them ended up unemployed, as well as having to endure a great deal of strain on their personal lives. In fact, in the meantime, the Dutch educational system had caught up, and was starting to produce its own telecommunications engineers.[3] At this point, there was no need to employ expensive foreign contract labour, and very few of these workers had the know-how or language to compete openly on the local labour market. They began to be seen as "mercenaries" by their potential employers. John comments on how it was a quite brutal process. A lot of his colleagues suffered from the insecurity, and even if they had work, felt undermined by their lack of settlement in the Netherlands. Those that had made brave attempts to relocate their families abroad usually went back after the regulation 24–36 months' "experiment". It's a familiar story: the Netherlands hardly ever seems to work out for any expats beyond this stage.

John, who didn't have much to go back to, tried freelancing – to "go contracting" as he puts it – seeking a solution in flexibility. But, bitterly, he found that working for agencies was "basically working for pimps", and even less secure or satisfying than chasing after regular work. The prospects in the Netherlands were not looking good. There was still work for him with Siemens, but his timeline was short. He was hoping that the new 3G technology would kick start the industry again, and lead to new work. He sounds like he wants to be on the move again, score some new opportunities to travel. "I'm not too keen to return to the old life in Britain." The line is getting faint. I struggle to hear his next words while the trams roll by on Damrak. He's got to go. Running out of change.

Failure is not a word Eurostars mention. You just keep moving. But in interviews, their stories can be moments of reflection; of catharsis when they step back and summarize what has happened to them, and how it looks in comparison to the lives they left behind, or the paths they didn't take. My interview with Siobhan in Brussels takes place in a cavernous new office space, that she is setting up – on her own – for a new IT consultancy business. It's out on an odd American-style edge city development, called La Plaine, in outer Ixelles. It's a strangely desolate workplace for such a sociable and talkative personality. So she talks to me. She came to Brussels in the 1980s, and yet her words still reflect some of the typical "unsettled" expat dilemmas. It's strange: even her Irish accent has been modified by French and EuroEnglish sounds. But her story is still one less about integration, and more about anomie. I ask about her friends and social networks: a lot of Irish, some English, a few French, an Indian origin boyfriend and some of his friends since she got divorced. He lives in the States, and has a recruiting agency in IT. She complains bitterly about Belgian "racism" towards them when they go out. Her "only" Belgian friend is someone I know – who has spent several years studying abroad, and is "not like the others". The point is that even with her settled lifestyle – including children at school there – she has never fitted in to Belgian patterns or rhythms, whether Francophone or Flemish.

We have a very different life to them. The Belgians live here, they do everything here, they are very locally rooted. I stay away from them. I live my own life. My ex-husband and I we used to try, it was both of our frustrations … He is French and he felt it much more than I did. He was very much a person who tried to integrate and came up against a brick wall every single time.

Her former husband came from the North of France: Lille – a city and lifestyle virtually the same as parts of Belgium. They lived out in the suburbs, one of the *communes à facilités*.

You'd come home everyday and people would look at you, as if you were strange people who'd come from the moon. There were no other foreigners around.

The consequence is a life without norms; the made-up international lifestyle of a handful of unrooted individuals, who may have little more in common than their experience of travel. Again and again, the experience with Belgians reinforces this sense of not belonging, even for her two daughters (15 and 9) who have grown up in the country, and have been educated only in Belgian schools. But Siobhan has in fact been living in Belgium for 17 years, much more than half of her adult life. At an age when her peers would be planning for middle-age comfort and the ease of retirement, she still doesn't know where she is going; maybe the US, maybe somewhere in Europe. Siobhan is still *roving*, like she was still the open minded Irish teenager travelling around Europe for the first time. Ireland isn't really an option. She has no illusions there. She also points out how people back home typically resent their relations abroad as living some unreal, fantasy, Disneyland kind of life, of self-indulgent freedom unrestrained by any of the hard realities of everyday life. The same lunar metaphor returns.

Yeah, they tend to think you're from the moon when you go back. They tend to think, when you are abroad, you enjoy yourself all the time. That's the attitude. That you don't actually work, that you don't have problems like everybody has. A normal life.

In other words, you can find yourself living a life without norms, because that's the way other people see you living. This can be tough. But unlike many of the people I interview, Siobhan faces up to who she is, and what her life has been. As with everyone, I ask her the big question: Do you think of yourself as a migrant?

Yes, no problem. I'm not part of Belgium. I definitely do …

There is perhaps something in the Irish historical experience that makes this easier to accept, less easy to deny.

Scratch the surface of the most mobile of the people and you find a similar sense of a life adrift – from family, networks, places to belong. In their quiet new flat in Brussels, neither Miguel nor Claudia are very expressive. But beneath the short and simple answers, you get a sense of rootlessness. They do go home, and it is Claudia – the female partner characteristically – who feels more the need to be connected. She says she has drifted apart from her best friends in Italy: "We changed, they changed." Miguel picks up:

Change is all well and good. When you are together you see the change happening. But when you are apart the changes happen on each side, and then you realize that … [trails off]

But Miguel also thinks it's "completely excluded" that they would have any roots in Belgium even if it has "all the conditions for a good life". He thinks Ian Angell is right about the new barbarian lifestyle.

It would cost us to leave [and live] in another country, because there are many problems, but it wouldn't make any difference.

Indifference to place, to people. A life without norms. But where can you go to be alone from society these days? Maybe Alan, the self-described "alien" businessman in the Netherlands, has the solution. The subject comes up when I ask if he does not feel attached in some way after all this time in the Netherlands.

No [pause]. Neither does my girlfriend. I used to live with an English girl here, so there were no ties on that score. Now I live with a Dutch girl, so things have got a bit out of hand. I'm kind of stuck! [laughs] Her mother's still alive – she is here until her mother dies … She's ready to go.

So I ask what remains of his attachment to Britain. His answers thud to the floor, one by one.

Alan: *Nothing* [long pause]
Adrian: *Do you go back much to visit?*
Alan: *Errr ... Funerals generally. What's left of my family ... An uncle and aunt. My parents died 4–5 years ago. My family is getting smaller.*
Adrian: *Does that make you feel strange at all?*
Alan: *I was brought up that way* [an army base in Germany]. *That's me, I guess. It's not because I couldn't be integrated, it's just that by nature I'm a loner kind of person. I tend not to go with crowds and a whole lot of people like that.*

But there is a solution, like he said before. A boat on the Mediterranean.

I can't understand [staying somewhere] *because I've moved around so much. Staying in London for the rest of my life, that would be strange. There must be more to life than that ... That's why I like the idea of boats. When you fancy moving ... you just move the boat* [laughs]. *I'd like to do it before I retire. Sailing around the world. You'd be surprised. There's a lot of people doing that. Some of them are young, some middle aged, some old. There is no fixed age limit on it.*

Of course, one day there is. Just as there is always another side to the self-representation of migrants. There is the way you narrate your choices, your moves; how you rationalize them as a story of success, of destiny; of Europe in the making. Then there are private moments when you admit this mobile life isn't so easy or rewarding after all. I catch Valerio on one of these days in Amsterdam. It's a sunny autumn day; we are enjoying *twee biertjes* at a canal side café. In the beginning, for Valerio, Amsterdam was liberation, difference, romance, "a kind of fairy country" – as it is for so many people, the first time they cycle around those magical canals, or inhale the sweet breeze. But things change. That other "culture" now just seems like a set of closed doors again; a bad trip that reminds you, "don't go there".

For me there is not that much more to discover in a way. The culture is different and now that I'm living here and have to cope with everyday life, I can see that there are many things, attitudes, that I cannot really stand any more. I appreciate much more what I left in a way.

A couple of years later, I ask around, "Whatever happened to Valerio?" He had gone home to his parents in Italy.

An IT Consultant's Tale

Over several beers in the garden of his lovely art nouveau home in Schaarbeek, I enjoy an evening chat with Gunther – a roving German IT sales consultant with his base in Brussels. He is brusque and businesslike, but offers one of the most perceptive commentaries of my whole project. I'd met him while interviewing Siobhan at her office at La Plaine. He had dropped by to do some work for her company and readily agreed to do an interview. I find the address in a pocket of beautiful town houses next to the Josaphat Park, in the shadow of Brussels' largest high rise, an ugly block just over the train line in a predominantly immigrant neighbourhood. That evening, he'd forgotten they could have had tickets for a night at the theatre, but no matter: the appointment was made and the interview went on.

I came to Brussels because of my wife, who is Portuguese. We were on a "weekend relationship" for two to three years. I was in Czechoslovakia, then the Czech Republic and Slovakia, then Bremen. I used to commute every week, Monday and Friday. After three years of commuting, with two kids, we said "Now we have to solve it somehow ..." I was working for ten years for Kraft, a German food corporation. It was time I changed. I decided to become an independent businessman, it gives you much more flexibility.

My wife was working here, we got married. She continued to work here. Sound familiar to you? It's maybe the road map for you too? ... So the first child arrived and for maternity leave she joined me. I was working in Prague and Bratislava at that time. Then she restarted her job [at the European Commission]. *I continued to go around to other assignments ... The trouble is, getting two careers organized is a nearly impossible task. So at one point, one has to make a step somehow. You should not overstretch the relationship, you know. Once the ship is sinking, nobody will hop on it anymore. So I think we got the right timing on that side. Also businesswise I wanted to do something else.*

Now I'm half here, half in Germany, but my business interests are more in Germany, so I'm travelling still. The interesting thing is I'm not really here [officially]. *I'm most of the time, businesswise, in Germany, and my business happens in German. For all the legal and taxation issues, I'm located in Germany. My wife is in the Commission, so I can avoid it. It has its goodies and baddies. The tax burden is too high all over the place ... You need to understand what's going on, how to read things* [financially]. *How to structure things in a way that is legal, but fits with the possibilities that are out there.*

So Brussels started out as a romantic getaway?

Well, before I didn't know the city to start with, you know. I was very much in love, so you don't see it realistically. You don't come here to say you are going to live here, but you come here to visit, and people speak French, the restaurants are good, there's a different environment [to Germany]. *That's quite sexy! I had a nice girlfriend, and so I felt pretty good about it, even though you immediately see the differences ... I found it quite interesting, and my wife was very much into the environment. She knew lots of people, that helped. We make some tours, out in the country. But it was really visiting at weekends. Starting to live here is a different thing...*

For a certain period of time I was pretty famous as someone who hated Belgium. It was the time of the Dutroux stuff. They had these strange ways of organizations, high

An IT Consultant's Tale—cont'd

taxation, and you say, "Jesus Christ, where am I?" So I really started to hit on [sic] this country, but I must say, once you accept it, the way it is, it has a lot of goodies that are very worth to talk about.

Finding the house seemed to make a difference. What about having children here?

That turns out to be a major advantage here compared to Germany: the whole crèche thing, the maternal environment. This is a disaster in Germany. The system is not existing the way it is here — the number of places, the structure. We are very happy about this, the quality is very good. Then there comes another couple of other things — like the kids' education. They grow up with a couple of languages from scratch. They do it, it's no problem. It's a big advantage — also for myself, I've practiced my French. We are involved as parents at the [European] school, very much so. A major parts of the school are run by parents' association, not the authorities. I was elected as a parents representative. You get involved immediately. You meet all the mothers and fathers.

Is Brussels "home"?

My family is living here, and this is an important element. If you define where is home, I feel home in Munich and Brussels, I would say. Anyway, more and more I'm living in a virtual environment, so I'm two days here, tomorrow there, so it's sometimes difficult to say where is home. But definitely where the family is, I would define home.

How are you dealing with pensions and all that, given your complex work life?

Pensions! You only know when you receive them if they are really there. We've done a couple of extra provisions on the private side. I think the time when you could lean back and say, "well, the state is going to fix it", is over. You have to take care a little bit of yourself. Now, looking at how the age structure of the population is going to evolve …

I'm a poor guy, because I'm living more than half the year in Germany. I'm considered a single [there] so I'm hit two times. I'm separated from the family, have incremental costs, and have a very — no, extremely — unfair tax structure. This is very bad, this costs me a lot of money. OK, I know it, this is my life, that's what I'm doing. When you're young you don't think about these things — long-term planning, settlement, retirement. You enter in the next step there, when the kids come. These things get more complicated … I think there are tons of reasons why people don't move.

The impact when you move out of the social system in Germany into the social system in Belgium as an individual is an extremely big hassle. I was not aware [before]. The big corporations, they can handle it fine. They say, "You're an expat, you stay on the payroll in Germany", and they continue paying. As long as you are in the same corporation. But within Western Europe, companies will say less and less, "Ok, we will treat you an expat." Getting housing differentials and so on. They will want to localize you, treat you like a local.

No normal person understands how the reallocation works. It takes years to find out if it is possible, and how, if not why not. You have to bring this paper and that paper. It's too complex. The problem is sometimes you don't know. You only realize it on your first pay slip what happened. You don't know exactly what the impact is on your social security in Germany — that you've accumulated for ten years or whatever — when you move out and

An IT Consultant's Tale—cont'd

you move into the Belgian social security system. So that was not a very agreeable experience, in terms of "free movement". I think a simplification of that process is absolutely essential. The Commission tries to push it, but for the national states, it's just not important. "Do we care about 2 percent of the population?" The question is, who pays what, at the end of the day.

Even if the social security were mirrored across all countries, and there was no problem, even then I think the mobility in Europe would not grow substantially. People want to stay where they are. That's a simple fact of life. I know if you take millions of people, there would be some. But let's not talk about the exceptions but the rule. A German would never go there [to France]. *Why? It would be stupid. He doesn't understand the language, he doesn't understand the way people think, it only creates problems. I'm living in Bavaria, I like the beer here, I like the mountains, why should I work in France? Or Belgium? Why should I go to the country where Dutroux comes from? Think like this, and you are finished. As much as I like the idea of Europe helping us* [the mobile few] *on taxation, it's not going to happen.*

But what about the business gurus – people like Ian Angell and his new barbarians, or Thomas Friedman and his flat *world*? They see the future globe as one big open space where MNCs will move operations or people wherever it's viable with no frontiers. Nation-states are just going to have to please the companies and the mobile people working for them. It's very different to your picture of how Europe works. Think about the IT or telecommunications business, your business …

Sure, it's no problem to send an email from India to here. Many people dream here of a certain mobility, but at the end of the day it's not really there, and it's not going to be there. Because why do we have all this immigration? It's not because Germany or Europe is so beautiful. It's because the situation in their country is unbearable. If you were in Kosovo and you were surrounded by war for two years, what can you do? You have to leave your farm. The house of your parents and grandparents. They don't want to go, but they are forced to go. For us, it's different.

The multinationals, sure, yes, they have the leverage to say "We are building our factory wherever, we don't care. We are building it wherever they give us the most money." And yes they can build it. But this is not the whole economy. This is the big misunderstanding [in all the globalization talk]. *90 percent of the economy is the small and medium sized businesses. It's the doctors and the butchers, the small companies that drive it. That is the backbone of a GDP. So if a multinational walks away with its factory, it's going to cost 5,000 jobs maybe. It sounds a lot, because it's a lot in one shot. But in the total they have no weight. They have much more press coverage and visibility because of their brands and whatever, but the real economic power is not there. The other thing is: sure, you can go to India and produce cheaper stuff there, but many of them come back and say it didn't work. Because it sounds easy but in fact it's very difficult. I realize this selling stuff into Germany. If you come from Belgium, already they don't know anything about Germany. So if they come from India, they know absolutely nothing. They even don't know where Germany is.*

What would be an example of some specific product that is difficult to sell in Germany if you didn't know anything about the country?

An IT Consultant's Tale—cont'd

Well, you have to know everything is there already. If you have telecommunications software, like one of my customers – billing software, they are the market leader here in the Benelux – nobody in Germany knows them. So how can they sell something in Germany? If you realize that there are many other companies out there that do exactly the same thing already for decades … You have to know who are the competitors. How to position your product in this market, track the market. This you cannot do from India. You will never get a feeling of what is going on.

Even from Belgium, a few miles down the road?

Even from Belgium. That's why I started the business. The multinationals are over-hyped.

But the European Union is built on a philosophy of free movement, of capital, goods, services, and persons …

It sounds very easy, but it's not. Lots of factories were put in the UK, then the pound went through the roof. Now there, everybody is complaining about the pound. How it puts pressure on the UK economy and how they are going to have to shut down factories. But based on a cheap pound, they built all the factories. But this is not a business base. You can't build a future on currency movements. It's a very risky thing.

What are your future plans? Is mobility a part of that? The birds are singing in the garden of his beautiful house, and Gunther is philosophical.

We are pretty stable here, for a couple of reasons. Overall we feel good. It's an extremely complex project to move with two careers. Then there's the house, the schools, that all keeps us. But it's not just that. We have no plan to move in the short term. In the long, mid-term, who knows? Our children are growing up international, European. My wife speaks Portuguese, they speak French at the school, then German. They are aware of different languages, cultures, Europe. It's normal to all the kids here in this environment.

14

Europa

Dark café days. When I do the rounds of my favourite cafés in Amsterdam, London, and Brussels in the cold winter of 2005/6 – those wonderful urbane places, where my ideas took shape, interviews were planned, notes were written – I half expect them to have all turned into Starbucks in the meantime. It has been a long road. When this project was conceived in 1998–9, Europe was still flush with the expansive years of the 1990s set off by the Maastricht Treaty. The euro common currency was around the corner, and Europe was clearly integrating. These were still heady days of cheerful Clintonite liberalism, sweeping the planet with its brand of globalization. Academics were all debating cosmopolitanism. I was contemplating another move – this time "global", to Los Angeles.

It all seems a long time ago. The cosmopolitanism and hopeful liberalism of the 1990s died a death in the mouth of Monica Lewinsky, then came crashing to the ground when two planes flew into twin towers in the world's most emblematic global city. Europe caught a cold, then pneumonia. By mid-2005, it was contemplating the rubble of a collapsed constitution, after a *non* in France and *nee* in the Netherlands made it very clear that the still nationalized populations of Europe wanted to go no further down the road to denationalized freedom. There was too much mobility, too many foreigners, too many vital elements of welfare provision, social security, and economic stability that were being opened to the winds of the single market.

The *nee* vote in the Netherlands, following the rise and death of Pim Fortuyn, and a new tone of aggressive anti-immigrant politics in this most urbane of nations, shocked much of Europe. Europeans have been used to populist politicians on the rise for some time, but to see the Netherlands – the heartland of liberalism and tolerance – veering right, somehow hurt more than the reassertion of a depressingly familiar *Gaullisme* in republican France – however galling. Of course, to any foreign residents who have tried living in the Netherlands for any length of time, this new face of the Netherlands came as no surprise. Many of the outside world's perceptions of the Dutch – their liberal values, their tolerance, their militant progressivism – are true, but only superficially so. Dutch society always depended on these values being embedded in a strictly nationalized system, no less nationalist than any of its rivals. The Dutch love to deny they are nationalists, that they are superior to all that; but this is exactly how their nationalism is expressed. They hate flags, and their whole society is defined in opposition to Nazis. The French are nationalist bigots, the Germans fascist bullies, the English colonialist world dominators. The Dutch are tolerant, open, cosmopolitan, laid back – and militantly so. They are proud about not being patriotic, arrogant even. Pim Fortuyn thus made an anti-immigrant political career out of saying there was one thing the Dutch would not tolerate – and that was intolerance. In other words, that our values are superior to yours – and especially those of non-Western cultures. This is, of course, what modern nationalists have always claimed. That "our" nation embodies the best of civilization – for us lucky members of the club, if not universally for the world. The populist politics of the last few years have at least made it clear that the Netherlands is no exception in Europe. It turns out to be a European nation-state-society just like all the others, with its own means and ways of asserting its "inviolable" national sovereignty and "superior" culture.

Amsterdam, London, Brussels all opened their doors, but down the road those who have really turned European mobility into a viable design for life remain the exception. In part, it has to do with the changing history of Europe around them. The high tide of liberalism in the 1990s that swept a whole generation of free movers around Europe, in search of new opportunities and experiences against a European backdrop, has subsided.[1] The waters have flowed back, behind the national *dijks* again, leaving the pioneers of European integration high and dry. Stranded, in lives outside the national norms, out of tune, out of rhythm. At least, that's how it seems some of the time. Some of the time, maybe it's something else: just the usual story about young, hopeful lives getting old and realistic. That said, denationalized lives are more vulnerable in a Europe in which the structures of social care and social security are still basically nationalized.

These human dimensions of European integration matter crucially. Much more, in fact, than the free movement policies of the European institutions, or the single market theories of economists. The future of Europe's economy is never likely to lie in completely flattening the continent, or removing all its frontiers. Instead, Europe seems hamstrung between its sense of cultural diversity, the meaning that locality, place, and culture have for people – including the historical wealth concentrated in these locations – and the economist's dream of a new Europe, built on an all-American model. Nobody in Europe really wants the four freedoms to turn out to be an all-American future, but that's the only outcome that the "no" voting populations see the European Union as heralding.

The sclerosis of the continent is a consequence of the neither-nor situation it finds itself in vis-à-vis the defining global economic hegemon.[2] The United States of Europe was never a serious proposition. The economist's model is not even necessarily true of America, or the urban system of American cities. Location, place, class, culture, and identity can been shown to matter crucially to Americans. On the other hand, it is a whole lot flatter in the US than Europe. Scratch below regional affectations in the US and middle class life in America is generic, homogenous, and multipacked. The real boundaries lie only at the edge of the nation. America is one big, functioning nation-state-society; an assimilation machine that still works. Europe, whatever it may become, will never be that. Its countries and its cities are not interchangeable, its states are nations, and Europe is not America. This is no flat *world* on which to build the future.

So the myth of the free European market bumps up again and again to the residual power of national and local cultures. That stick-in-the-mud quality of European populations, who perhaps rightly value cultural distinctions, the quality of life it assures, and the sense of community that closes this off to outsiders. They hold back the boundary crossing freedoms and opportunities that would flow in a Europe in which social and professional currencies were truly mobile, interchangeable, and convertible from place to place. These are the two sides of modernity that Europe is struggling to reconcile. Diversity and freedom.[3]

There may be no magic political or economic solution to this. Europe may just continue to be dragged along in the wake of the USA and the world economy. The contradictions between the demands of economic exchange and the resistance of national cultures may well become ever more painful, if Europe is not able to reconcile the two. If there is hope, it has to lie with individuals; the stories of the very real people whose mobile lives and denationalizing projects have lived out some of these tensions and possibilities in the incomplete Europe of today. In almost every respect, their lives do not resemble the kind of thing that business school barbarians are taught if they want to be globally mobile. These elites – whether in the Anderson School, LA, the Saïd School, Oxford, or INSEAD, Singapore – are all being taught the same thing: how to be American managers in an American corporation in an American flat world. Of course, these schools also teach them how to survive in those weird European (and Asian) contexts, giving them the expat "culture" guides to mother them through the local jungle, while telling them to trust the MNC that will package and insulate their experience for them on an everyday level.

This is all so different to the sentimental education of the Eurostars. These pioneer individuals, who learn – while crossing national borders and making their way in strange yet familiar cities – to be able to see and use all sides, to adapt and change without ever losing that sense of where they came from. They run up against the informal barriers of residual national cultures that fear their presence. But the stubborn persistence and hard won victories of some, may provide the role model and pathway for others wishing to transcend European nationalisms. In their banal, everyday adaptations to the challenges of living in a foreign city, they are generating enough innovation to keep the dynamo of an integrating Europe alive. Pioneers of a better, more cosmopolitan Europe, they embody the kind of liberalism that is, in these darker days of the early twenty-first century, in danger of being lost.

Which brings me back to Richard. Richard, the retired business executive in Tervuren. After first hearing about my research in the *Bulletin* expat magazine and writing to me for a copy of the work on Brussels, he becomes a kind of distant and occasional pen-friend, commenting on my work and ideas or questions that I send him.

Tervuren, Monday 7th May

Dear Adrian:

I saw a soundbite of your work in Bulletin *in which you say, "There will never be a true United States of Europe … because less than 5 percent of Europeans live outside their country of birth". I have been doing a little work on something analogous, and come to somewhat different conclusions. It is based more on a mixture of reported anecdote and the work of the United Nations on the Minorities Treaty during the interwar period, which used Operational Research techniques.*

The OR technique essentially consists of noting that frontiers and therefore countries are not very reliable indices. For example, before 1989 was Germany one country or two? Was Czechoslovakia one and now two? Even Scotland now has its own parliament. An OR approach would suggest that we should not start with such fallible units but begin by laying down a few bits of arithmetic. Thus one would imagine that any entity (person, animal, or flower seed) which found itself within a larger geographical space would be less likely to move to another entity – whether or not it formed part of some larger grouping – than an entity that found itself in a very small space. This is the simple principle of inertia. One would also imagine that the nearer the entity in one geographical space is to the boundary of another, the greater the probability that the boundary will be crossed. Concretely, it is more likely that French people in Alsace will cross the boundary into Germany than people in St. Jean de Luz. Conversely the latter would move more easily into Spain. This is the principle of contiguity and is recognized in legislation concerning transfrontalier workers.

The second OR question is to ask both what kind of transfer is normal (easier for flower seeds blowing in the wind than for people, I agree), and what kind of transfer is necessary to create a significant mass across generations. In the case of the Boston Irish, for example, the reproduction of the Irish over generations seems to have been more important as a factor in generating the phenomenon of the Irish in Boston than the initial numbers. If as you say "less than 5 percent" flow across a boundary into another geographical space OR would suggest by the second generation there would be a minimum of 0 percent transfers (all the flower seeds have blown back again or have been eliminated by selective weedkiller) or a maximum of a new nearly 5 percent plus the previous generation which reproduced itself – meaning that some 10 percent are no longer "native" stock. When one considers the infinite number of paths of differential breeding rates, that means that, in classic stock and flow terms, a movement of 5 percent per generation is quite enough to develop significant mixing.

As soon as one goes down the path of anecdote one risks getting lost, but one can systematize to some extent by taking samples of staff in known mobile occupations. Thus before the First World War there were many German waiters in London (unthinkable after the post-Second World War economic miracle) and they have been replaced by successive waves of Italian, Spanish, Portuguese, Greek, and Indians ... They didn't all go home. Nor is it restricted to the bottom of the occupational heap. In manpower planning terms, when the Willink report suggested the UK was not producing enough doctors (meaning enough to guarantee good promotion rates through to consultancy) it was suggested that the easiest solution was to import (temporarily it was thought) doctors from the Commonwealth. Many of them thankfully stayed and provide the basis for the multicultural NHS.

In the end the easiest indicator of mixage is probably if a married pair of generation 0 has two parents each and they each have two, what is the probability, that of these 14 people, animals, or flowers, all were born in the same geographical space? All this is to say that I would have thought in stock and flow terms 5 percent movement is easily enough to generate considerable mixing of entities from different geographical spaces, although whether it will lead to a United or Disunited States of Europe is of course another question.

Any interest? Pleased to hear from you.

Richard Bridge

Intrigued by such a delightfully witty letter – comparing my Eurostars to flower seeds, and invoking the spirit of the classic Ravenstein Laws in population geography – I write back to the retired gentleman, later sending him a copy of the report about Brussels.

Tervuren, Sunday 20th January

Dear Adrian:

To thank you for sending me as promised a copy of your report. I found the report very interesting and I am sure that those who financed it must be pleased with the outcome.

As you may remember my own interest is primarily the question of the way numbers affect the world. In the case of Brussels the demand/pull, supply/push question seems very important at the level of middle class jobs. Since there is an adequate – some might claim an oversupply of talent – in the whole of Europe, the demand needed to pull people in seems limited. In the few occupations where there has been a shortfall – notably computer work – the demand has also been high in the home country and the need to leave home is therefore also limited.

The permeability across the generations of Europe is still, I believe, greater than the statistics suggest. I was reminded of this the other evening when I had dinner with two ex-NATO people – so British that much of the discussion centred round the Empire! Their daughter, however, has moved out of the multilingual confusion of Brussels and has just taken a job in the multilingual confusion of Marseilles.

I really liked the point about there being no necessity to integrate into the national culture because the crossroads nature of Brussels meant that one was free to integrate à la carte, so to speak.

I hope that LA is living up to your expectations and that you can continue to work in this area of research, which I guess will remain important for some time to come.

Regards,

Richard

A couple of years on, I write to again to see how he is doing.

Tervuren, Sunday 11th July

Dear Adrian:

Nice to hear from you. Well I'm still around. Since our meeting I did some work for the Cabinet Office on understanding the different cultures of the EU countries which was quite fun.

Life, of course, has changed a good deal since we met and the burghers have become more resistant to the immigrants, legal and otherwise, vide Vlaams Blok (I am writing this on the 702nd anniversary of the Battle of the Golden Spurs). The shadow of China is falling on much of industrial Europe.

On the other hand I recently went along to my bank. Waiting in the queue for some information a girl signalled she was free and I pointed it out to the man in front of me. "Merçi, mais elle ne parle pas français!" he said. She was Polish and spoke very good English and the old parochial bank had a new pleasant if slightly confused international atmosphere.

In the meantime my son is engaged (what an old-fashioned term!) to a Chinese woman from Hong Kong who works for a Japanese company in England, and I met an academic from Leuven who has adopted three Chinese children. Unscrambling the omelette is now happily a non-option.

Last week Elisa, my wife, and I, having eaten elsewhere, were looking at the menu of a Greek restaurant and the owner came out and insisted that we enter even if we had eaten and invited us to take a coffee or a brandy with him. Elisa got it right by insisting on Greek coffee and I managed to remember a few Greek words. The interesting point was that the restaurant was cleverly called "Philoxenia" – I'm sure I don't need to translate.

Regards,

Richard

There speaks an inveterate Euro-optimist, now in his seventies. Europe needs them. Last time I saw Richard, it was for lunch at *Pom Noisette*, a very nice restaurant in the shadow of the Berlaymont building. It's a place that Gideon Rachman, *Financial Times* columnist and former EU correspondent of *The Economist*, describes as "a good place for eavesdropping". The first thing Richard spots is my "Århus" T-shirt. I explain that my Danish wife has recently moved back home to take a job there, which was necessitating some personal rearrangements. He chuckles. We order food and drinks. *Spa rood* for me today: I had a good night out on the town yesterday. Richard reminds me a lot of the actor James Stewart. A moment of vertigo. Then I ask him: So what do you make of the state of the European Union?

I've always though that the European Union was the best way of slowing down the inevitable decline of European civilization.

He thinks the American model of capitalism is not a viable option for the future.

In twenty years time we'll be able to see. I think the whole Enron scandal will prove a huge turning point in American capitalism. It can't go on the way it does. Shares, futures, options … Nobody knows who owns what anymore, these multinational companies are not responsible to anyone.

Here speaks someone who spent half a career working for a multinational, in the highest ranks of management. He also worked for the Commission in Brussels. He thinks Europe will weather its current storm, and is confident that the experiences and decisions of the mobile in Europe are going to play a decisive part in anchoring the vision of a politically and economically viable form of governance in the future.

I'm not too gloomy about the future of the European Union. Although I think the British will never accept being "European". They may have to leave.

He launches into a nice story (he has lots of these) about an English academic couple he knew who had abandoned London and a position at King's College for a new job as a professor at Leuven University. The funny part of this was that he was a specialist in – of all things – the theology of St. Thomas Aquinas. The English professor, with the specialism in ancient Catholic texts, was the only non-Flemish person out of 60 people (almost all men) on the faculty. I laugh. Old old Europe.

We share one thing in common. Richard once worked at the University of Sussex, back in the 1960s when it was being set up. We both have fond memories of the stylish brick and concrete campus in the downs. He is still worried about my pension, and asks what I did about my university pension in the UK. It's a terrible pension scheme, and completely immobile, I tell him. After a couple of years you haven't accumulated anything, and when you ask to move it to another EU country, it isn't possible without losing three quarters of it in tax. So I left it there, locked in. It will be worth approx 50p per annum in 2033, when I'm 65.

When I left Sussex University in 1968, I got myself into a much better deal. Thank God!

He is very optimistic about the EU's enlargement.

This has been an enormous achievement. The Poles and Hungarians will be the acid test. The scars of history are running deep, particularly in Poland.

But as his story about the Belgian bank shows, the young of Eastern and Central Europe are now seizing mobility opportunities about which West Europeans, on the whole, seem much more reluctant and ambivalent. It will be interesting to see if their experiences and trajectories come to parallel the Western Eurostars, or whether they become a brighter portent for the European future. We talk about the failure of the politician Michael Howard in Britain. Richard puts it down to his hidden East European immigrant background.

[Ironically] *Yes, because after all, "He's still a bloody foreigner". That was the problem. It's incredible how insular the British still are. The UK might drop out of Europe, but all of the other countries still have too much to lose. Think about it: Britain is the only one never to have been occupied, or faced desperate political instability.*

Our main topic of conversation, though, is migration and social mobility in Europe. Richard is adamant that I am wrong. Mobility *is* transforming Europe, he says. The statistics about Europeans living abroad mask the deeper reality. He thinks the answer lies in mathematics – and in intermarriage. Mobile Europeans will change Europe from within, two by two, by intermarrying. He offers his own story as an analogy.

I was from London, and my wife was from Portland Bill [the almost-island peninsular just south of Weymouth, in rural Dorset]. *They said the same things to her at our marriage. Why are you marrying someone from off the peninsular? When the cemetery was full of generations of Taylors, with their tombstones and engraved names? They'd been intermarrying for centuries. It just takes time. Europeans are marrying each other. My son is marrying someone Chinese, my daughter is marrying someone from Spain. It's spreading out so fast in their generation. It will just take two or three generations to see it. Nobody understands the sweeping changes that have come from globalization.*

I say that he might be right. From my qualitative research, and the stories I've heard, I remain sceptical. I'd like to believe in the mathematics of intermarriage, but that seems like a very slow way of building Europe. As we leave, we walk along past the newly refurbished Berlaymont, which is looking a whole lot better after its asbestos-caused retrofit. At the Schuman *rondpoint*, we say goodbye. Richard points again to my Århus T-shirt.

Congratulations on the (probable) move back to Europe!

I receive one more letter from him, a couple of weeks later.

Tervuren, Sunday 22nd July 2006

Dear Adrian:

At lunch you mentioned that you wished that you had studied more maths. It reminded me that one possible technique to test whether mobility is higher on the basis of intergenerational mobility is the use of Markov chains in the context of matrix algebra. Fundamentally it asks the question: Is something more likely to happen in time period n+1, n+2 ... as the result of something which happened in time period n.

I remember using this technique – with the help of a mathematician – to deter-mine how significant particular experiences, i.e. during their first two or three post-ings, were in helping to define who could become Chairman of ICI. Stripped down, it came to the conclusion that those who started with high salaries got higher salary increases, which put them on a high flyer's curve that after a few years became a self-fulfilling prophecy. The Civil Service also uses a similar technique to predict who will reach the rank of permanent secretaries. In your case it would be the simple question as to whether the children of mobile parents/international marriages are more likely to be mobile than those of non-mobile parents.

The answer is obvious but it looks better dressed up in Markov chains.

Regards,

Richard

Yes, indeed. But the numbers of Western Europeans living and working outside their home countries remain low. In part, those that have success-fully moved around Europe have been successful *because* they were only pioneers. Recall Franz the banker's remark: that he didn't want to be one of 15,907 German business school graduates looking for a job in Frankfurt. He went to Paris, Madrid, and London instead, moving out to move up the career ladder much more quickly than he would have done in Germany. When you treat Europe as a field of opportunities, processes of distinction (the one person who has a different qualification) can be just as important in making success and thereby creating value, as processes of interchange-ability (everyone recognizing the equivalence of qualifications). The power of the Eurostars' tales lies not in their generalizability but in their exception-ality; their uniqueness as stories in a Europe quantitatively dominated by familiar national tales and national norms.

What this all adds up to – the macrolevel conclusion – might not be as dramatic as Richard's Markov chains – the almost unstoppable force of some intermarrying demographic chain reaction across the continent. One reason is that as soon as intra-EU mobility passes some threshold – which may be 5 percent or lower – the value associated with being a pioneer drops sharply. If it's no longer original, and people are crowding in as foreigners to the international cities, then host societies are very quickly going to react against it. The opportunities will close, hostility will rise, positions in the social structure will be again internalized for more local candidates. Every expat on a nice multinational deal fears the day that the company asks them to be "naturalized" as a local employee. You lose the special mobility allow-ances, or deals on welfare benefits or education for your kids. You have to live like a local on a local salary. Usually, the choice is that or lose your job. The Eurostars never wanted to naturalize, and most never even had a special deal. They were always looking for a different Europe, a new Europe. One in which their denationalizing projects would make sense as everyday life-styles and professional choices. The price to pay is that it is a rather lonely path to take.

Maybe I should trust Richard's analysis of the future of Europe. He's right that in the end the answers in social science must lie in numbers and not my evanescent stories. But, after five or six years, stories are all I've got. I keep asking the same questions, over and over again. Is there a new Europe emergent in the tales of the Eurostars? Or is this still an old continent in which the new cannot be born?

Postface

We are back in Århus again. It's a sunny day, and we meet at the cemetery gates. This is my favourite place in this city. You can almost see our house, and the view from up here takes in the docks, the big Mærsk container ships, and Mols linien ferries heading across to Sjælland. You watch them leave, across the calm blue waters of the Kattegat, out past Samsø, the little Danish island where my wife grew up. You can hear the pop of tennis balls in my club nearby, and we are only five minutes' walk to the waterfront fishmongers.

Hand in hand, we go inside and take a look at the stones. There they all are. The Jensens, the Andersens, the Rasmussens, the Sørensens, the Jespersens, the Knudsens. Then more Andersens, Sørensens, Knudsens … Cemeteries in Europe are different in every country. It is quite amazing how much the aesthetic varies. In Denmark, the people are buried in tidy little square plots with miniature privet hedges and ornate stone paving, like little sunken gardens. It's all immaculately maintained. There are lots of trees and empty green spaces. I see an old man crying silently; a couple walking a dog. Most of the people buried in here seem to have been civic figures from the late nineteenth century, when much of this old social democratic city was built. I wonder how it is you get in here. How do you get a plot?

The sky is crisp and clear, Nordic. I like this place. It feels like the best place to be in Europe right now … But there is a chill in the air; the first breath of winter. We shiver. Maybe it's time to go home.

fin

Brighton
Brussels
Los Angeles
Paris
Århus
1998–2007

Appendix 1

Summary of Interviews

Who are the Eurostars? Some brief portraits are in order. I start in Amsterdam and with the youngest movers first.

Amsterdam

My inquiries begin in the ultra-modern corridors of the Netherlands' biggest bank, ABN Amro. **Maria** (Portugal), 26, is a high-flying lawyer, dealing with international mergers and acquisitions. She is still getting used to the Netherlands after a couple of years. Her colleague **Nina** (Germany), 30, also has a legal background, but has been in Amsterdam a bit longer. In another office, I find **Susan** (Britain), 30, who works as a mid-ranked personnel manager. All three live locally with their non-Dutch boyfriends. **Anastasia** (Greece), 29, is single, came to Amsterdam about five years ago with a former Dutch boyfriend. She works in the technical support office of a major telecommunications company. In a rather more organized corporate move, **Axel** (Austria), 28, came to the city with his wife, and is a fast-track manager with another large telecommunications MNC. He has been in Amsterdam just two years. **Guillaume** (France), 29, is an immigrant activist and journalist, and is my introduction to the gay male world of Amsterdam. He shares an illegal sub-let flat with his American boyfriend, and is now quite familiar with Dutch life after five years. **Michael** (Ireland), 28, works as market researcher for a heating systems company. I meet him through friends in Utrecht, and is one of the few Anglophones to convincingly break through the language barriers. **Annelis** (Belgium), 31, is Flemish and has no problems with the language, but has had mixed experiences living there with her partner, an academic, while working in the fashion retail business. **Stefan** (Germany), 31, is a very successful architect with one of Amsterdam's hippest firms and is, after four years, a homeowner, with an Australian wife and one child. **Marlena** (Belgium), 34, has been in Amsterdam much longer than most, having moved there in her teens. She has a Serbian partner, and works as a freelance journalist. **Valerio** (Italy), 35, is single and has a nice job as the costume buyer for a theatre, but is dreaming strongly of home. **Annie** (Britain), 35, from Scotland, has set up an agency for expat housing in the city. The very internationally mobile **Roberta** (Italy), 37, has two difficult years to discuss as a research economist in the city. **David** (Britain), 37, a successful management consultant, has lived in the Netherlands 14 years and shares a beautiful flat in the centre with his male partner. Working in another professional niche for foreigners in the city, **Agnes** (Germany), 38, is a Dutch correspondent for German media. She is married to a Dutchman with a bilingual son, and has been in the city seven years. Another successful career example, employed as a logistics manager for a major MNC, **Helen** (Ireland), 40, is still settling in to Amsterdam after two years. I travel out into the Randstad to meet with **Sophie** (France), 41, who works as a biochemist for one of the Netherlands' leading research institutions. She is settled with a Dutch partner who is an architect, and they are planning a family. Back in Amsterdam, I also check out the lives of foreign business entrepreneurs. **Ray** (Ireland), 42, co-owns a transportation business, and is now settled with a Portuguese-African wife and child in a suburban village outside the city. **Alan**, (Britain), 45, who is in a similar business, has also bought property outside of central Amsterdam and lives with a Dutch partner, but talks a lot about leaving. Finally, **John** (Britain), 46, is a rootless telecommunications engineer working on temporary contracts with major MNCs in and around the city.

London

Because of their number and diversity, it is very hard to get a full overview of the foreign West European population in London. My efforts are thus concentrated on the obvious professional stories: a younger generation in service sector jobs, and the high flyers working in London as the European capital of finance and media. Among the numerous young Spanish residents, I interview **Jaime** (Spain), 27, and **Eva** (Spain), 28, both graphic designers, who have retrained in the country and have been in London barely a couple of years. Then there are the many young French in London, who in my sample are mostly women. **Nicole** (France), 28, is typical, just about getting by with work for a web design company. **Isabel** (Spain), 29, a research economist, is an interesting example of a foreigner working for the British civil service. She has been in England about six years, and is wondering about settling with her Mexican partner. **Norbert** (Germany), 30, also has a public sector position, in a quango, working as a research economist. Curiously, he too is a recent homeowner and is married to a Mexican national. I also develop links with a major MNC with headquarter offices in London, Unilever. At their offices in Richmond-upon-Thames, I meet with **Philippe** (France), 30, a typically ambitious manage fasttrack, with an élite *grande école* background. **Valérie** (France), 31, has been in London longer, nearly five years. She is currently unemployed, but has been working at the tough end of the City, as a broker. **Saskia** (Belgium), 32, is also a City slicker, a very successful young manager dealing with risk assessment for a major insurance company. She is enjoying her first two years in London. Another international high flyer, with a diplomat family background, **Nour** (Algerian, French permanent resident), 34, is a high-profile journalist with one of the leading cable news companies based in London. **Jeroen** (Netherlands), 35, and **Nathalie** (France), 33, live as a couple and are wondering about their future in the city after two and three years, respectively. He is a science-trained researcher for a major pharmaceuticals company; she is an administrative officer at the headquarters of a famous retail firm. **Carmen** (Spain), 31, and **Franz** (Germany), 35, both work for banks in the City. After two years, they are beginning to have grave doubts about the viability of their life there. Another couple I interview together are **Anniken** (Norway), 35, and **Dominic** (France), 36. She is a housewife looking for work after completing a PhD in political science; he is a mathematician working at the London Stock Exchange. They have been in London five years, and have a son – but not yet a house of their own. **Siofra** (Ireland), 34, a senior manager at a pharmaceuticals MNC, is married to a successful academic and meets me while on maternity leave with her youngest. They are settled in the multicultural suburbs of Northwest London. Back at Unilever, I meet a senior audit manager, **Rainer** (Germany), 35, who talks me through the ups and downs of a complicated family move with an MNC from Hamburg to London. **Donatella** (Italy), 38, works as a data analyst for a City insurance firm, after having come to London to retrain at a late age. After five years, she has her sights on a bigger world, and does not feel settled as an expat. **Pedro** (Spain), 39, has been working for the Spanish bank in the City for five years, and has gone native – but not without costs. He is single and unsure about the future. **Laure** (France), 42, a very successful media manager, has been in London well over ten years, and is feeling jaded. Although nominally settled with her English journalist husband, she still has one eye on a map of rural France. **Carlos** (Spain), 47 and **Susana** (Spain), 44, are veteran MNC movers, in London for a couple of years with Unilever, after being previously in Rotterdam. They have two children and a big house in Surrey, but much of their life stays back home in Bilbao. **Sandra** (Luxembourg), 55, is an artist and wife of a German banker. She loves London and is the most settled of all, as well as the most Eurosceptic. We meet for a chat at her Kensington home. Lastly, **Giulia** (Italy), 59, an independent estate agent, takes me back to the 1960s, and narrates her long and winding path toward retirement in London.

Brussels

My work on Brussels begins life as a report for the Brussels-Region. My overview thus works as a comprehensive portrait of the life of foreign Europeans in the city, who are much more diverse than all the stereotypes there about eurocrats and expats might suggest. **Bernhard** (Germany), 25, has been in Brussels two years, and is an enthusiastic resident. He works as a legal consultant for a humanitarian NGO. **Joannet** (Netherlands), 28, also works in the world of international politics, a political consultant for Dutch interests in Belgium. She is beginning to settle with her English husband after five years in the city. **Raoul** (Spain), 29, is married to a Russian woman, and making a career as an aeronautics engineer. **Saïd** (France), 30, is French of North African origin, and works as a social worker for an international charity. He offers an alternative vision of the city, that blends cosmopolitan surrealism with the harsh face of discrimination. **Sinead** (Ireland), 26, and **Tom** (Ireland), 30, like living in Brussels, but have lives that still revolve around the international world. He works for the international trade union federation, whereas she has found work for a Belgian company in the software localization business. **Andreas** (Norway), 30, like them, has only been in the city a couple of years. He works as a research economist at a think tank, but is settling in well with his Italian wife, who does similar work. **Rachel** (Britain), 29, and **Rob** (Britain), 30, after five years, think Brussels works for them. They are homeowners, about to get married. She works for a regional representation, and he is a mid-level manager for a logistics company. **Janet** (Britain), 31, is single and works in PR with Unilever. She is looking to move on, but already has firm connections in the city. **Federica** (Italy) is 32, and has nothing to do with MNCs or international institutions. She came to Brussels to train as a social worker, and is now settled with a Belgian-Moroccan partner. **Claudia** (Italy), 34 and **Miguel** (Portugal), 36, also came to Brussels through a different channel: they met as students at Louvain-la-Neuve. They have just bought a flat. She works for a lobbying firm, he for an international IT company. **Dario** (Italy), 37, offers me the inspirational story of a foreign architect who has made it in Belgium after ten busy years in the city. **Gunther** (Germany), 38, is also a successful independent businessman, who has settled with three children and a Portuguese-German wife, who works at the Commission. He splits his time between Belgium and Germany. **Dave** (Britain), 39, is another successful businessman based out of Zaventum, who has happily settled in Leuven, newly single again, after a few difficult years living in Brussels. **Caterina** (Italy), 42, has an articulate vision of life as a single, free woman in Brussels for five years. She works as a science coordinator in a medical research unit, but still has dreams of Italy on her mind. **Siobhan** (Ireland), 42, is starting again after separation, bringing up two girls and working at an IT firm. She has been in Brussels 17 years. **Ellen** (Britain), 42 and **Jonathan** (Britain), 44 talk me through a family life in Brussels with three children that has lasted for over ten years. They are enthusiastic homeowners and involved parents at a Belgian school. Both have worked in political consultancy. **Bent** (Denmark), 44, is a high-level management consultant, who has been in Brussels 15 years. He is a landlord, and has children from two marriages growing up in the city. **Hedwig** (Germany), 55, is the famous landlady of the only German pub in Brussels, who has seen it all in her 19 years in the city. **Ingrid** (Denmark), 63, looks back on over 25 years in Brussels, working at the Commission, but also raising children and getting involved in local politics. Finally, **Richard** (Britain), 71, becomes a frequent correspondent with his commentaries on my work, offering his reflections on over 25 years in the city, and his work for both international institutions and multinationals.

Appendix 2

A Note on Methodology

Eurostars and Eurocities is a narrative based on 60 long, oral history-style interviews with these individuals and couples living in Amsterdam, London, and Brussels. It is supplemented by extensive ethnographic observations during repeated stays and visits in the three cities, and numerous background interviews and data sources. I personally contacted, interviewed, transcribed, and analyzed all the interviews; research assistance was only used for background research and bibliographical work. Taking the foreign West European population as its target population, and the three cities as the comparative cases, it starts off from the premise that although everyone knows these people are there, very little precise information is known in each case of how many or who they are. I intend my "sample" to be representative, but with no overall idea of how many or who the population is in each case, no formal "sampling frame" can be used to select respondents. Other strategies have to be turned to. These questions call for a qualitative, investigative approach rather than any based on formal quantitative logic.

There are in fact many popular myths about the population in each case. In Brussels, for example, there is a widespread popular and official belief that the new foreign European population is only comprised of elites, and that all are either stereotypical "eurocrat" *fonctionnaires* or high paid "expats" working (probably temporarily) for multinational corporations. The Dutch have similarly jaundiced views about the expat population in their midst. Since it helps sideline these populations even more, it is a self-reinforcing perception. Most of the numbers talked about officially or by the media are also guesswork – as seen most flagrantly in London. As this case shows, European free movement has in fact made the simple question of numbers fraught with uncertainties and ambiguities. Most national population statistics offices and cities have some idea about the resident immigrant population in their midst, usually broken down by nationality or place of birth. There are also significant *visible* irregular populations in each case, migrants from Africa, Asia, Latin America, and so on, who have slipped through the official dragnet. For these, there are often reasonable estimates. But this is not the problem here. The problem is that European residents can move across borders unregistered, and live in these cities unchecked, *legally*. They are largely *invisible*. Some, most perhaps, eventually show up as resident foreigners in official statistics, but many do not. These others live there on a more temporary basis. Official residence in their home country can be maintained for a number of years, with few practical difficulties. Still others lead complicated split or commuting household lives, living in one place, but working in another, or paying taxation and voting in different places. Ask for the detailed profile (by age, class, gender, ethnicity, profession, etc.) of these populations in each case, and the question gets even murkier.

To start from official statistics in each case, then, would be in effect to introduce a big distortion into the study. I wanted to get at hidden, unknown, or unrepresented parts of these populations, as well as residents who would show up on the official lists. I also wanted to use the study as a corrective of commonplace views that have grown out of the inadequate official statistics and popular perceptions. My strategy thus uses a *constructivist* approach to the object of research – the West European population in each case – before doing any interviews. I build a profile of the population from the inside out, using "subjective" on-the-ground investigation, then match this to all the different, juxtaposed "objective" representations of the population available. To frame the profile, I switch between official, public records of the population in question, independent academic estimates, and those of commercial service providers – such as expat magazines who do surveys of their readers – who have a different constructed image of particular populations towards which they are marketing their products. Since the bottom line for companies is commercial, not political, they often have very clear and accurate views on who their markets are. All offer partial views; none by themselves are complete. It becomes clear, for example, that in London and Brussels there are much larger numbers of younger, less well paid, independently working residents, who are far from the corporate expat stereotype. Moreover, as lacunae in the official statistics show, a very large number of the new Europeans in Brussels do not work in jobs connected to the European or international institutions. At the same time, commune-level statistics show that they do live in the central urban areas and not in isolation out in the "Euroghetto" suburbs. Sampling only "expats" or "eurocrats" would not be enough.

Respondents were found initially via a method of snowball contact, starting from a varied range of key respondents, of different nationality, profession, and age. Some were private individuals, but I also pursued interviews via companies, relocation agencies, and expat publications and websites, as well as city officials. After an initial set of interviews, I began to match these against the rough sampling frame that I had constructed. This, for example, might reveal that I was short of people in certain professions, of particular nationality, or gender/age etc. In the second and third round of interview requests, I would specifically seek out certain types of interviewees to fill these gaps. It is, of course, only an approximate way of achieving representativeness. For Brussels, the method works well. My study conclusively shows that the foreign resident European population in no way lives down to the jaundiced stereotypes. A new view of the foreign Europeans in the city is made possible. In Amsterdam, the approach works to identify numerous interviewees who might number among the most transient, unveiling the mechanisms that lead them to leave; but it also reveals clear exceptional cases, which help identify the conditions of successful settlement. In London, the overview is less complete because of sheer numbers and diversity, so I focus on particular sections of the population that are most revealing of the London story.

Interviews took place in public places, cafés, or at the home, place of employment or business of the interviewee. Most were in English or EuroEnglish; a few used French or Italian. Interviewing followed a semi-structured questionnaire, although in many cases the discussion ranged far wider. I am very much also a research subject in this project; it would be futile and dishonest to pretend otherwise. This provides the study with its potential empathy and intimacy, which is reflected in the stories gathered and my own role in the book. Although academics often hide behind theory and jargon in their presentation of research, I have opted for a different, much more "raw" approach. My commitment is to give as much room to the voices of the interviewees themselves in a tightly packed manuscript.

A quantitative survey is, obviously, a different kind of beast altogether. The PIONEUR project appears throughout as a source of background data. It is the first large-scale independent survey ever conducted of the intra-EU migrant population in Western Europe. Five thousand intra-EU migrants from the five largest member states in 2003 have been surveyed residing where they live in the five largest states (minimum one year residency). This means, for example, that PIONEUR surveyed a total of 1,000 French residents, 250 each in Britain, Germany, Italy and Spain. There are reasons why there has never been a survey of these migrants before. Being much less than 5 percent in each country, the numbers are too small in average-sized random national surveys to reveal enough individual cases. On the other hand, even the very best targeted surveys of immigrants or foreign populations that have been done in Europe rely on small panels, or ad hoc sampling procedures. To make matters even more complicated, there are very deep differences in how nation-states recognize and count migrant populations, for example, in censuses. The PIONEUR solution was to turn to a telephone survey – with all its attendant problems – that could identify enough of these foreigners through telephone lists to make calling viable. To do this, it used the innovative technique of calculating the frequency of the most popular names for each sending country, eliminating ones that also appeared in other countries' lists of names, and then sampling for the most probable names of the target nationality in the receiving countries. The approach was successful in terms of rates of target population found, except in Britain where the number of mobile phones used by foreigners renders it more difficult. Naturalized populations with foreign names in France and Germany (principally of Italian origin) also posed some difficulties.

I played a free floating role in the project, helping with all stages through project formulation, design, implementation, analysis, and editing of the final product. As a network project, different members took responsibility for different areas of data-gathering and analysis. The project was directed by Ettore Recchi, who also did the analysis on social and spatial mobility. Michael Braun oversaw the technical aspects of the telephone questionnaire, and with Camilla Arsène undertook the quantitative profile of the population surveyed. Oscar Santacreu, Emiliana Baldoni, and Maria Carmen Albert looked at the motives of migrants. Antonio Alaminos with Oscar Santacreu designed the sampling methodology and completed the analysis on acculturation. Nina Rother and Tina Nebe ran the study on the European identity of movers. Anne Muxel dealt with questions of political participation, while Damian Tambini looked at foreign media use. Maxime Vanhoenacker wrote an additional study on language use, and I and Tina Nebe made the analysis of East-West movers from Poland and Romania. The findings for all the project are collected together in an volume edited by Ettore Recchi and Adrian Favell, *Pioneers of European Integration*. They can also be accessed via our website: www.obets.ua.es/pioneur.

PIONEUR is a parallel survey to *Eurostars and Eurocities*, but the two are strictly speaking not connected. PIONEUR casts its net wider: it profiles all kinds of intra-EU migration, not only the Eurostars I identify. It can fairly claim to be representative of its target populations, insofar as these can be accessed via random telephone methods. My goal rather has been to do a range of interviews that would be approximately representative, but that would also enable the profiling of "ideal types" of intra-EU migration, highlighting its self-selecting nature. Finding those movers who most correspond to the theories of mobility and European integration, and asking where they differ, it is possible to reveal the limitations with the economic model as well as get a sense of why most people in Europe cannot emulate these pioneers. PIONEUR's choice of comparative cases – nation-by-nation – also gives very different results and emphasis to one based on city populations. Because of its ethnographic methodology, my study is able to place much more emphasis on temporary, highly mobile and unregistered populations. It also has a broader range of nationalities involved, and contributes to the study of smaller countries – such as the Netherlands and Belgium – which are often overlooked in the dominant emphasis on larger member states in Europe.

Notes

1 See their website: ec.europa.eu/employment_social/workersmobility_2006. The European Union produces a massive amount of information encouraging mobility and promoting the application of European free movement laws. To access all the practical information for individuals and businesses about their rights and opportunities in the EU, see the portal: ec.europa.eu/youreurope. A typical brochure is *It's Your Europe: Living, Learning and Working Anywhere in the EU* (European Commission 2003). "It's no secret. Europe can change your life if you want it to. Mobility means competitiveness. The European Union is not just about free trade, open borders and a common currency. It also gives every EU citizen, regardless of age, the right to travel, live, work, study and retire in any EU country they choose. And there are plenty of opportunities."

2 In its *Action Plan for Skills and Mobility* (COM 2002 72 final), the European Commission spells out in detail the role it foresees for mobility as a crucial part of the 2000 Lisbon Agenda, as well as its policy agenda for breaking down remaining barriers to these goals. Skilled and educated workers on the move in a borderless labour market are, in particular, seen as a key part of the agenda's stated goal of Europe becoming "the most competitive and dynamic knowledge-based economy in the world, capable of sustainable economic growth with more and better jobs and greater social cohesion". The rights of citizens of the EU and their family members to move and reside freely within the territory of EU member states are formalized in EU Directive 2004/38/EC. These rights date

back to the original Rome Treaty of 1957, article 39 EC, and have been progressively expanded through case law in the European Court of Justice. *Free Movement of Workers: Achieving the Full Benefits and Potential* (COM (2002) 694 final) lays out these legal developments.

3   The qualitative strategy used in this book was complemented by a quantitative approach in the PIONEUR project (2003–6), "Pioneers of European Integration 'from below': Mobility and the Emergence of European Identity among National and Foreign Citizens in the EU", directed by Ettore Recchi of the University of Florence. See our website: www.obets.ua.es/pioneur. This EU Framework V funded network-based project completed a survey of 5,000 internal EU movers from the five (then) largest EU member states resident in the five largest member states (Britain, France, Germany, Italy, and Spain), asking similar questions to mine in a telephone-based questionnaire. See my note on methodology for the parallels and differences between the projects. In endnotes throughout, I use selected preview findings from the PIONEUR survey as background to my own individual research. The full results of the project will be published in a volume, *Pioneers of European Integration*, edited by Ettore Recchi and Adrian Favell. A summary of the main findings can be found at: www.obets.ua.es/pioneur/difusion/PioneurExecutiveSummary.pdf.

4   Some of PIONEUR's most interesting findings concern questions of 'European identity' among stayers and movers, a question on the whole I avoid posing. Using Eurobarometer (EB 58.1 and EB 60.0) and European Social Survey data, PIONEUR documents the basic quantitative problem faced by advocates of European integration: at most 5 percent of the European population self-identify exclusively as Europeans, compared to the solid 40–60 percent who see themselves only as nationals (the highest percentage in Britain); around 12 percent put European as their principal identity ahead of national identification, although a plurality of Europeans (just over 50 percent) will admit to feeling national and European some of the time. In all cases, the experience of European mobility leads to much more positive feelings about Europe and the EU; but in the large majority of cases, this feeling is achieved by combining it with the national identities of the country of origin and/or residence, rather than negating any national identity. The survey does not find much trace of the denationalized, individualistic Europeans prevalent among my sample – perhaps because it is very difficult to ask questions about negative freedom in a questionnaire context.

5   At the end of a busy year, the European Year of Worker's Mobility also produced a booklet of short portraits of free-moving European citizens, *Europeans on the Move: Portraits of 31 Mobile Workers* (DG for Employment, Social Affairs and Equal Opportunities 2006). Its website is full of interesting blogs and commentaries by movers about their experiences and problems. Another source for similar stories is the NGO European Citizenship Action Service, whose "Citizens Panel on Workers Mobility Rights" (2006) unearths a series of quite serious problems with freedom of movement, particularly as it is experienced by East Europeans. Cases are outlined and legal resolutions are proposed. There is evidence in the stories that the Belgian authorities can be deliberately obtuse and obstructive, and that Britain and Ireland are often exploitative of workers. See: www.ecas.org/file_uploads/1292.pdf.

Chapter 2   New Amsterdam

1   In a communication entitled "Stop brain drain now!" the EU proposed action
     to improve researchers' careers along these lines. It has set up a mobility portal,
     posts messages to EU citizens in North America, offers reintegration incentives,
     and claims that 12,000 researchers have benefited so far from its training and
     mobility schemes. *Communiqué de Presse*, European Commission 18/07/2003.
2   The English language magazine in Amsterdam, *Expat*, conducted a survey of its
     potential readership in 2001: 15 percent of the foreign workers (of which 56
     percent were West European) worked in the financial and management service
     sector, 13 percent pharmaceuticals, 12 percent IT. Around half were earning
     more than €80,000 a year.
3   87 percent of Dutch can hold a conversation in English, according to
     Eurobarometer 63.4 "Europeans and Languages". This is easily the best figure
     among EU15 members, and compares to the 34 percent French speaking
     English, or the miserable 14 percent of English speaking their best language,
     French – itself a likely exaggeration of their abilities.
4   One example is the analysis "Measuring globalization" by A. T. Kearney Inc.
     published by the journal *Foreign Policy* in 2001.
5   Population statistics quoted are from a number of sources, including the annual
     OECD SOPEMI report, the Eurostat Chronos database, the Centraal Bureau
     voor de Statistiek, and the Gemeente Amsterdam.
6   Eurostat data suggests at least 20,000 West Europeans flow into the Netherlands
     every year. Gemeente Amsterdam's own census figures only reveal around 3,500
     each British and German residents in the city, only 400 Irish, under 2,000
     French, and a mere 1,000 Belgians – out of a total population of 740,000 in
     2006. Only 3 percent of the population are foreign EU residents. Half the British
     live in the inner city (*Binnenstad*). A total of 5,000 West European citizens live in
     the *Binnenstad*, and a further 4,000 in the *Oud Zuid* (de Pijp). These figures are
     probably a poor guide to a transient population with such a high turnover.
     Moreover, accurate figures are complicated by the odd statistical groupings the
     city uses. It counts industrial nations together, of which there are approximately
     70,000 persons (Europeans, Americans, and Japanese lumped together), while
     "ethnic" Southern Europeans are counted separately, at around 17,000 persons.
     See the city's website: www.amsterdam.nl.
7   See, for example, the report by Eurostat and the Directorate-General for
     Employment, Social Affairs, and Equal Opportunities, *Employment in Europe 2006*,
     especially ch. 5, "Geographical mobility within the EU" (October 2006). This
     documents an average figure of 1.5 percent of EU15 foreign residents across the
     EU15 member states. PIONEUR also reports on these stocks based on Eurostat
     and European Labour Force survey data. The Dutch figures are among the
     lowest percentage. Even lower are Italy, with fewer European foreign residents
     than Ireland (which is nearly 15 times smaller), making up a tiny 0.1 percent of
     its population. At the other end of Europe, Denmark has a mere 50,000 EU15
     foreigners (1 percent). Belgium, twice as large, has ten times this figure, over
     560,000, around 5 percent of its population. Britain has less than 2 percent, still

well behind Germany, although it is one of the few countries to show marked growth in recent years. Nearly all the others have stable figures for the last two to three decades, as well as stable ratios of European to non-European migrants, whose stocks are always between two and four times larger than the number of EU15 residents.

8   The source for US mobility statistics is the US Census Bureau, which produces regular reports on geographical mobility by region, state, and county. About 32 percent of Americans live in a state different to the one in which they were born; and the annual rate of interstate mobility is between 4 and 5 percent. Even internal mobility *within* European nations is much less: only about 22 percent of Europeans live outside the local region they were born in.

9   Eurobarometer 64.1 (2005) on geographical and labour mobility offers further data on what Europeans think about mobility. See the European Year of Worker's Mobility report analyzing this data, *Europeans and Mobility: First Results of an EU-wide Survey* (European Commission 2006). 37 percent think they would be willing to move to work in another country that offered better conditions, 53 percent think the "freedom to travel and work in the EU" is the most important single benefit of membership – ahead of the euro (44 percent) and peace (36 percent) – and 57 percent have travelled in the EU within the last two years, yet less than 4 percent ever have lived and worked abroad.

10   See the Commission report on breaking down barriers to international mobility in the "liberal professions" (defined as "lawyers, notaries, accountants, architects, engineers and pharmacists"): *Report on Competition in Professional Services* (COM (2004) 83 final). On the mobility of pensions, see the Commission's *Action Plan for Skills and Mobility*, p. 16.

Chapter 3   London Calls

1   The chapters on London draw on material originally published in *The Human Face of Global Mobility*, edited by Michael Peter Smith and Adrian Favell, copyright 2006, by Transaction Publishers. Reprinted by permission of the publishers.

2   According to Eurostat NUTS2 data (2007), inner London in fact boasts a regional GDP per capita that is 300 percent of the EU27 regional average.

3   One in every seven workers in London is a foreign citizen, out of an official total population of 7.5 million. Half the foreign population in Britain is thought to be working in London, whereas only 11 percent of the British work in London; 92 percent of the EU foreigners are under 35, 55 percent between 18 and 24. "A new mix", *The Economist*, 24 September 1998.

4   European Central Bank statistics show that Britain accounts for 41 percent of inward investment into the Eurozone, and that Britain is the biggest export market for Eurozone goods.

5   See the website of the Urban Audit, "Assessing the quality of life in Europe's cities", a section of the EU DG for Regional Policy: www.ec.europa.eu/regional_policy/urban2/urban/audit/index.html.

6   There is no trace of the Eurostars in the Mayor of London's much fanfared *Draft London Plan* (2002); a recent major academic report on the city's economy – *London's Place in the UK Economy*, by a team from the LSE (London Corporation, October 2004) – also overlooks them. See the city's website: www.london.gov.uk.

7   Police registration in Britain is particularly lax, unlike in other European countries, where it is a mandatory step before obtaining a social security number and being able to work. The ten-yearly census is a crude measure for any except the most permanent residents. In 2001, it counted only 219,763 EU15 foreigners in London. The incoming Passenger Survey might give some indicators, but these are projections based on tiny samples. The British Labour Force Survey ought to be the most accurate source, in that it's more frequent and linked to work, as well as that it counts by region (London and Southeast). But its projections too are based on a sampling methodology that would miss nearly all more temporary migrants.

8   It also creates a lot of problems for independent surveys. In the PIONEUR project, of the national cases, Britain was the most difficult and problematic on this score. Random telephone sampling had to be supplemented by contacting agencies and organizations, as well as snowball sampling.

9   The French politician Nicolas Sarkozy held a presidential rally in London in early 2007, describing London as "one of the largest French cities". Covering the event, *The Economist* put the figure at 300,000 ("Sarko embraces the Anglo-Saxons", February 3, 2007). The consulate itself guesstimates 200,000. The truth is nobody knows for sure.

10   Their motto is: "La liberté trouve toujours son chemin". See their website: www.francelibre.org. See also the website: www.franceinlondon.com.

11   There has been much negative coverage of the phenomenon in the French press. In 2005, Jean Pierre Raffarin noted in talks with British Prime Minister Blair that: "We send you all our young people and we are getting all your elderly". The trend is certainly not limited to France. In "Little Germany in England" (October 10, 2006), *Suddeutsche Zeitung* estimates that 230,000 Germans work in Britain – mostly in London – and that numbers have grown fourfold over the last ten years. Similar growth could be noted for Danes, Dutch, Italians, or Spanish.

12   A number of British newspaper reports have picked up on this. See "London's comings and goings", *The Economist* (August 9, 2003); "Vive les Rosbifs", *Observer* (January16, 2005); and "London's allure: European arrivals find hope and glory in a global metropolis", *Financial Times* (October 27, 2005). *FT* Brussels bureau chief George Parker waxes lyrical: "London has been the biggest single beneficiary of the open door policy. The UK capital is a twenty-first century Europolis embodying many of the ideals of Europe's founding fathers in the 1950s: a place built on free trade, where EU citizens can live and work without feeling like foreigners and where talent counts more than nationality."

13   London grew by 4.8 percent during the 1990s while other cities in Britain shrunk. Two thirds of Britain's immigrants go to London. The net gain in 2000 was 120,000 people. Now 67 percent of new immigrants are coming from high-income countries – mostly Western Europe – compared to 30 percent and 24 percent in Germany and France. More have degrees than locals, and on average they

earn 19 percent more than them. "London's comings and goings", *The Economist*, August 9, 2003.

14 A report by the Austrian Federal Chancellery, *Cross-Border Mobility of Public Sector Workers* (Vienna 2006), explores the barriers that persist in this large employment sector across Europe.

15 60 percent of Pret employees are foreign West European; only 19 percent are British. In 2003, it was able to offer 250 positions after 44,000 enquiries – quite a healthy ratio of supply to demand. One Pret recruitment brochure encourages potential employees to join their "Fun Loving Passion Giving Money Earning Jean Wearing Early Starting Sandwich Making Coffee Serving Holiday Paying Party Going Career Building Pret Team Members". See their employee magazine *Pretstar* and their website: www.pret.com/jobs.

Chapter 4 Brussels-Brussel-Bruxelles

1 Population figures are taken from the Belgian National Institute of Statistics (2006). Out of a total population of just under 1,020,000, 275,000 are foreign nationals and well over half of these (approximately 145,000 or 14.4 percent of the total) are West Europeans. According to the Brussels-Europe Liaison Office, in their briefing *L'impact de la presence des institutions européenes à Bruxelles* (2001), 35,000 of these are accounted for by totalling eurocrats and their families or others working for international institutions. There are around 40,000 French nationals, 9,000 British, and 8,000 German in the city. Another part of the overall EU15 population is an old working-class population from Southern Europe, over 50,000. This leaves a substantial number of "other" resident foreign Europeans choosing to live in the city, including many newer Southern Europeans of a professional background. See the city's website: www.bruxelles. irisnet.be.

2 Apart from one article on German eurocrats, the foreign European population in Brussels – half the total of foreigners – was wholly ignored in materials celebrating diversity and multiculturalism at the festival.

3 An example of this was the KU Leuven study by Christian Kesteloot reported by the daily newspaper *De Standaard* as an invasion of the city: "Europeanen gaan in Brussel wonen" and "Van Britse school naar Ierse pubs: Eurocraten trekken van de rand terug naar Brussel", December 11, 1997.

4 According to Eurostat NUTS2 regional data (2007), Brussels-Region is in fact rated the third richest region in Europe, after London and Luxembourg, rated at 248 percent of the EU27 average. Part of this figure must also be down to low-cost living, in that it is a calculation of per capita purchasing power in the region.

5 The "Chabert report", *De Sociaal-Economische Impact van de Europese en Internationale Instellingen in het Brussels Hoofstedelijke Gewest. Verleden en Toekomst* (Iris Consulting, 1998), estimated that the presence of European institutions was worth 62,000 jobs in the city – or 13 percent of GDP – half of which are held by European foreigners. Another 20,000 jobs are attributed to foreign companies in the city.

6 Norway is not a member state of the EU, but young Norwegians enjoy free movement rights and educational opportunities within the rest of Europe via association agreements with the EU.

7 Documented in a report by the Brussels tourist office, *Étude sur les comportements culturels, de loisirs et touristiques des résidents étrangers* (2000).

8 This is also the strong impression given by two enthusiastic American reports about life in the city, shortly before the euro was introduced: "Fast Forward Europe", *Time* (Special Issue) Winter 2000/2001; "Generation Europe: Young and restless adults are reinventing the Continent's identity – and their own", *Time*, April 2, 2001.

9 Brussels' situation at the heart of Europe is rated as its number one appeal as a location for business by the regional business development office, ECOBRU. Its transport and technological infrastructure, multicultural diversity, political stability, and quality of environment are also cited. The fact it is Europe's political capital is only eighth on a list of ten such factors.

10 PIONEUR's findings on media use suggest movers use both country of origin and country of residence sources. An average of 47 percent would use country of residence sources to find out about a major world event, versus 43 percent who would use country of origin sources. About 50 percent of the channels on Belgian and Dutch cable are foreign language channels, whereas in Britain they are less than 5 percent.

11 Given their numbers and potential voice, the non-participation of foreign European voters in local elections in Brussels – a key right of European citizenship – is strik-ing. Less than 10 percent even register to vote according to official data from the Brussels-Europe Liaison Office. Given their enthusiastic participation in other facets of life in the city, the suggestion is that this is less down to political apathy and more to an expression of "new politics" – politics expressed through housing choices, cultural affiliations, and consumption preferences. PIONEUR's study of the political profile of movers documents a high level of political awareness and interest, but low levels of activism. Although the movers in general are left-leaning, the population of Eurostars is better characterized as distinctively liberal on both economic and cultural dimensions. I deal with the political participation of resi-dents of the three cities in work published elsewhere. See an archived working paper on the subject: www.aei.pitt.edu/3096/02/austin2.doc.

12 A distinguished international brainstorming group on the future of Brussels was convened by the then Commission President Romano Prodi and Prime Minister Guy Verhofstadt in 2001, concluding that the city's function was "not to reflect a single identity, but Europe's diversity". Their findings build on the commitment of the Brussels-Region to this idea, especially of the then Minister-President of the Region, François-Xavier de Donnea, as well as the findings of the Chabert report, which has guided progressive thinking about the city since.

Chapter 5   Migration

1 EU Labour Force survey data (Spring 2006) on intra-EU mobility does now show clearly that the education levels of EU movers has improved markedly over the last ten years. Cross-border labour markets, in other words, are increasingly

selecting positively by skill and education level. Ireland and Britain are particularly benefitting from this, while one of the biggest destinations – Spain – is receiving disproportionate numbers of older, well-educated migrants (retirees and pre-retirement movers).

2　The European Year of Worker's Mobility has explicitly tried to address the information problem by its creation of the EURES information network, which offers advice on mobility, online job and CV search facilities, and a job database, especially related to health, IT, and tourism sectors. See its website: www.europe.eu.int/eures.

3　www.ec.europa.eu/education/programmes/socrates/erasmus/statisti/table8.pdf. *Passport to Mobility: Learning Differently, Learning Abroad* (European Commission, 2001) is an EU brochure encouraging students to move. "Personal mobility in Europe is becoming increasingly necessary in the era of the internet and the globalization of trade."

4　One of PIONEUR's key findings is that "love/family" reasons (30 percent) outweigh "job/career" reasons (25 percent) for moving among Europe's mobile few, figures also almost matched by "quality of life" reasons (24 percent). Among women, as many as 37.5 percent cite "love/family" reasons for moving. If Europe is being built by mobility, it is perhaps because the emotional and romantic experiences of Erasmus schemes prove more consequential than the professional/career ones. The findings were reported by the European Commission in a press release, "Europeans move for love and a better quality of life", IP/06/389.

5　Nearly half the EU movers surveyed by PIONEUR had previous experience of living in another country to the one they are resident in, and over 20 percent in a third non-EU15 country. Given they are such a slight population, their "supermobility" emphasizes again the self-selecting dynamics of many such migrants.

6　See the website: www.netexpat.com. Managing director Verstandig co-founded the company, which has in recent years expanded its operation to around ten countries in Europe and the Middle East.

7　In an analysis of Eurobarometer 64.1, *Managing Mobility Matters*, Price Waterhouse document that 10 percent of all Irish have experience of living in another EU member state, compared to the 4 percent European average.

8　During the 1980s, about half a million Irish left the country, peaking at 70,000 a year in 1988/89. By about 1993, immigration was positive, and in more recent years (1986–2002) an average of about 20,000 Irish nationals a year have been returning. The figure of permanent Irish residents in Britain is generally over 500,000, but the figure fell from 559,000 in 1987 to 537,000 in 2002. The numbers of Irish in Belgium (3,400), Germany (12,000), France (5,500), Netherlands (3,900), and Spain (4,200) had in each case approximately doubled during the same period. Sources: Irish Central Statistics Office and Eurostat New Chronos.

Chapter 6　Mobility (1)

1　*The Great Transformation* (Boston: Beacon Press, 2001), p. 157.

2　PIONEUR provides a very good overview of the four main clusters of intra-EU movers in Western Europe today. One of these corresponds to my population of

Eurostars: educated, younger movers, driven by work and lifestyle opportunities in an integrating Europe; a second group are the "late traditional" guest worker-style migrants, who can still be found moving in numbers, from Italy to Germany for example, for low-level employment. The survey then distinguishes between two rather distinct North-to-South movements: one is straightforward retirement migration, which has grown enormously in recent years from Britain, Germany, and Scandinavia to (principally) Spain, Portugal, and France; the other is a younger group, pre-retirement age, cashing in on housing differentials or investments to move and settle in the South when their children leave home. Again, these are Northerners looking for the sunshine, but they are not all in the senior citizen bracket. The *Daily Telegraph* reports on PIONEUR's findings in "The many faces of the EU expat", March 28, 2006.

3   PIONEUR data shows that on average about 1 in 4 EU movers in the countries surveyed originates from the so-called "service" (upper/upper-middle) class, compared to about 1 in 6 of the native population. This is suggestive of the idea of Europe facilitating a new kind of elite post-national circulation, that does not extend to lower classes in society. Destinations also select by class origin: 35 percent of migrants in Spain and 45 percent of migrants in Britain are found in higher service and self-employed categories. Given London's centrality, this corroborates the idea of London as escalator region, confirmed most dramatically for Spanish movers there, of whom over 40 percent are upwardly mobile.

4   PIONEUR included a parallel survey of Polish and Romanian migrants in the five West European states. It finds that their experiences are very distinctive from West European movement, and much closer to traditional immigration patterns. Overall they come from a lower class background on average and often encounter crude ethnic barriers or formal administrative restrictions in most countries. When they are highly skilled or educated, they come from more privileged backgrounds, and often experience mobility as socially downward. Most migrants of all kinds enter exploitative work scenarios. The one area where their movement is pioneering a new system in Europe is in their marked tendency to engage in transnational and circular migration within Europe, often linked to temporary employment opportunities. For studies of the impact of EU enlargement on intra-EU mobility, see the reports by the European Citizenship Action Service, *Who's Afraid of EU Enlargement?* (2005 and 2006): www.ecas.org; and the report by the Academic Cooperation Association, *Brain Drain and Brain Gain: Migration in the European Union after Enlargement* (2004). See also my work on the subject: "After enlargement: Europe's new migration system", Danish Institute for International Studies Brief (December 2006): www.diis.dk/sw31237.asp.

5   Unilever's international assignment office in London provided me with two booklets detailing issues of mobility for employees and their families: *Bon Voyage* (June 2003) for British employees transferring abroad, and *Welcome to the UK*, for movers to Britain. The office manages about 230 foreign employees in Britain and about 350 British managers abroad.

6   Unilever's very smart recruitment material emphasizes individualism, creativity, and dynamic youthfulness in its images of high-flying scientists and managers. The booklet entitled *Be Yourself: Passion for Achievement* shows the working lives of many such employees, stressing with their portraits, "Don't be Astrid – Be Yourself. Don't be Thom – Be Yourself."

Chapter 7   Mobility (2)

1   In the PIONEUR project, I wanted to include a question that explicitly forced interviewees to say what they thought they were. You could tick one or more boxes: "Would you describe yourself as (yes/no)? (a) a migrant; (b) an immigrant; (c) a free mover; (d) a tourist; (e) a sojourner; (f) an expat; (g) a rootless cosmopolitan; (h) a European; (i) a global citizen." Alas, the question didn't make the final cut – too many lines in an already tightly packed 30 minute telephone questionnaire.

2   In 2000, there were 3,382 Italians resident in Anderlecht and 2,151 in Ixelles. Source: Brussels-European Liaison Office.

Chapter 8   Settlement

1   A major source for my research in the three cities has been publications for newcomers or magazines for expats and foreign residents. Insofar as these works capture and reproduce collective knowledge on the issues and difficulties posed by settlement, they offer a good reflection of the process. They also contain a lot of direct and implicit criticism by the residents of the system with which they are dealing. Brussels offers a good example of the range available, among the best known of which are *Newcomer: An Introduction to Life in Belgium, Brussels Insider,* and *Brussels Life.* I also collected extensive back editions of the leading foreigner magazine in the city, *Bulletin,* which enjoys a circulation of 13,565 weekly (2005), and which regularly produces special editions on housing, schools, culture, consumer issues, or political participation.

2   The report of the Committee of the Regions, *Evaluating Quality of Life in European Regions and Cities: Theoretical Conceptualization, Classical and Innovative Indicators* COR-Studies - 3/99 CdR 197/99 (Luxembourg: Office for Official Publications of the European Communities, 1999) offers an extensive overview of the concept of "quality of life" in a European context along these lines.

3   The *Bulletin* readership survey (2000) offers a portrait of the foreign European population in Brussels, albeit one slanted towards Anglophones and MNC employees. Despite much lower average wages than London or Amsterdam, they find that 42 percent have lived more than five years in the city, 35 percent are house owners, they take an average of 11.25 air trips a year, and a third would buy bottles of wine over €10.

4   The EU Urban Audit Eurobarometer poll of July 2005, for example, gives Brussels a rather poor rating on many points, close to London in cleanliness, pollution, and security, and behind Amsterdam on many indicators. But the fact it scores rather low on two questions all other evidence reports it does well on – ease of finding affordable housing, and opportunities for finding work – suggests that the very small random telephone samples (300 per city) is skewed towards national residents, who in Brussels do tend to be excessively self-critical about the city. See: www.ec.europa.eu/public_opinion/flash/fl_156_en.pdf.

5   The William Mercer annual survey of quality of life in the world's top cities is the most representative. It ranks 200 cities on 39 key indicators, including political, economic, sociocultural, and natural environment; medical and health facilities; schools and education; public services and transportation; recreation; consumer indices; and housing. In 2003, the usual suspects come out on top. Zurich leads the ranking most years, with Geneva second, followed by Bern, Vienna, Vancouver, Sydney, and Copenhagen. Twelve of the top 20 were European cities. London is the costliest city in Europe and ranked 34th, well behind Amsterdam (10th) and Brussels (12th). Both Amsterdam and Brussels come in ahead of Berlin and Paris. See also "Quality of life", *The Economist*, March 3, 2001.

6   Interview with Annelore Isaac, economic advisor, ECOBRU (April 2001).

7   For example, the survey by Healey Baker (2000) rated Brussels 16th on quality of life in Europe, well behind Amsterdam (11th), London (6th), Paris (3rd), and Barcelona (1st). Cost of living, compactness, public transport, restaurants, and access to housing – on all of which Brussels would rate very highly – have not been factored into this study. The study absurdly rates London's public transport as the second best in Europe after Paris. The Urban Audit survey reflects better the views of everyday inhabitants: in its poll of 2005, London comes bottom of 31 cities on satisfaction with public services, notably public transport, affordable housing, and general cleanliness.

8   *Bulletin* produce a very useful supplement on schools in Brussels annually.

9   The HRM survey by *Expat* magazine in Amsterdam finds that while 65 percent of expats are married, only 28 percent of them have children.

10 See "The geography of cool", *The Economist*, April 15, 2000, pp. 11–13.

11 Among the "hip" city guides I have been collecting for the cities, such as *Time Out, Rough Guide, Lonely Planet*, etc., it is the *Virgin Guides* that capture these dynamics best. The Brussels guide features St. Gilles, Ixelles, St. Josse, and Sint Katelijne; the Amsterdam guide has sections on de Pijp and Jordaan; and the London guide offers tips for Islington, Shoreditch, and Clerkenwell. Characteristically, the ultra-hip guides from *Wallpaper* – which are aimed at self-conscious global yuppies on unlimited budgets – completely overlook Brussels in the range of books.

12 Out of a population of around 72,000, about 25 percent are EU15 foreigners. Source: Ixelles commune population statistics.

13 Interview with Leo Verhoeven, expat banking manager, KBC bank (May 2001).

14 Interview with Sabine De Clerck, estate agent, Immo Look, Uccle (May 2001).

Chapter 9   Integration (1)

1   In preparatory work that PIONEUR did on language use in an integrating Europe, the project documents the strikingly high rates of English people with *no* interest in learning another language (nearly 40 percent) versus rates between 5 percent and 20 percent in the rest of Europe, as well as the much shorter time of compulsory language education English students have compared to their

neighbours (Scots in fact also have more). See the PIONEUR working papers, available at: www.obets.ua.es/pioneur/documentos_public.php.

2   The topic of expat foreigners having to learn Dutch has been the subject of a number of articles in Amsterdam's *Expat* magazine. In "Speak Dutch" (4/2001) it reports that 89 percent of Dutch think foreigners should learn Dutch, and 38 percent within one year; 40 percent, meanwhile, claim to respond in Dutch when they are talked to in English!

3   See their website: www.expatica.com. *Expatica* has now expanded to cover five countries, including Belgium, Germany, France, and Spain. Interview with Simon Payne, editorial director, Expatica.com, Amsterdam (May 2001).

4   The HRM survey by *Expat* magazine found that only 2 percent of its target population in the Netherlands were German, and found no Belgians whatsoever. In the Rotterdam office of Unilever, out of 250 foreign managers, only three were Belgian, even though Antwerpen is barely an hour away.

Chapter 10   Integration (2)

1   EU pet passports were introduced in July 2004. Britain, however, maintains more barriers, which puts off many British abroad from returning, as they can't take their dog or cat back with them easily. Britain's historical attitude to the "threat" of rabies – which is negligible and easily controlled in all of continental Europe by vaccination – is a peculiar facet of its island mentality. As with all aspects of the British opt-out of the EU Schengen Agreement on free movement, Ireland is coercively forced to apply the same rules in order to maintain its existing Common Travel Area agreement with Britain. As part of the EU PETS travel scheme, the treatment of ticks and tapeworms is also required.

2   Literally, *pistonner* means "to piston". It is an untranslatable French word, which means to get help for something in your life or career from someone you know in a position of power or influence.

3   A remarkable 6 percent of the PIONEUR interviewees openly admitted to have a partner of the same sex. Of this 6 percent, their reasons for moving were also more frequently linked to the quality of life idea of moving "to gain new experience".

Chapter 11   London Loves

1   Examples of archetypal expat publications in London are: *Living in London: A Practical Guide*, published by the Junior League of Britain; *Living and Working in London*, by Orin Hargreaves (London: Kuperard, 1997); and the *Routard guide de l'expatrié* (Paris: Hachette).

2   The standard pattern is shown very well by cartographic representations of the 2001 UK census, put together by Danny Dorling and Bethan Thomas in *People and Places* (London: Policy Press, 2004). As well as showing a dense concentration of professionals, managers, and foreign EU nationals, London has a dramatically

skewed age structure. The core of the population is 18–44; the city is almost devoid of people aged 3–17, or over 45.

3   "The exodus", *Guardian*, May 23, 2001 reports 150,000; "The pull of Provence", *The Economist*, April 26, 2003 reports 300,000. A YourGov survey found 54 percent of British would like to settle in another country, and three quarters of the would-be migrants think the quality of life in Britain is deteriorating. There has also been a sharp rise in the EU as a destination. From about a tenth of migrants in 1981, it now accounts for about 100,000 emigrants a year.

4   A popular BBC TV series, *How To Get a New Life: Moving, Working and Living Abroad*, focused on European destinations. The accompanying book of the series includes a chapter on EU free-movement rights, trying to convince sceptical Brits that "the EU is your friend".

5   These are the pre-retirement lifestyle migrants that PIONEUR identifies as one of the four major clusters of intra-EU movement since 1973. They are named after the mordantly funny film about retired London gangsters in Spain, starring Ray Winstone and Ben Kingsley.

Chapter 12   Old Amsterdam

1   A sample of these include: Jacob Vossestein, *Dealing With the Dutch* (Amsterdam: KIT, 1997); Colin White and Laure Broucke, *The UnDutchables: An Observation of the Netherlands, Its Culture and Its Inhabitants* (Lafayette, CO: White/Boucke Publishing, 2001); Han van der Holst, *The Low Sky: Understanding the Dutch* (Schiedam: Scriptum Books, 1996). After two years, my colleagues at a Dutch university bought me one of these as a *leaving* present, presumably to help me understand them now that I was on my way.

2   *The Great Transformation* (Boston: Beacon Press, 2001), p. 76.

Chapter 13   Anomie

1   At the closing conference of the European Year of Worker's Mobility in December 2006, one of the final reports offered a much more cautious assessment of the benefits of geographical and employment mobility, seeking to balance it with a sense of the damage it can do to social integration and solidarity. The authors leave it open as to what might be the optimal balance for an economy or society in the trade off between economic flexibility and social cohesion. *Mobility in Europe: Analysis of the 2005 Eurobarometer Survey on Geographical and Labour Market Mobility* (Dublin: European Foundation for the Improvement of Living and Working Conditions, 2006).

2   As always, it looks a lot better on paper, or in a piece of EU legal analysis, than it does in reality. The official booklet *The Community Provisions on Social Security: Your Rights When Moving Within the European Union* (DG Employment and Social Affairs, 2004) lays out rights and entitlements for the mobile that guarantee the transferability of social security, and supposedly remove the costs. This is backed

by EU law (which, again, has supremacy – in theory – over national law): Regulation EC 883/2004 on the coordination of social security systems, which extends the foundational EC 1408/1971 on the rights of free moving workers and their families. An attempt by the Commission to address the grey area of the immobility of private corporate schemes and other national idiosyncrasies, *Proposal for a Directive on Improving the Portability of Supplementary Pension Rights* (COM (2005) 507), stalled in the European Parliament. Moreover, the implementation and enforcement of these rights at the national member state level is very uneven, and often challenged or subverted by national practices that rest on very different institutional histories of welfare security provision. A very good source for following ongoing developments in this policy area and others is the independent EU news site EurActiv.com.

3   "Should we stay or should we go?", *Expat* magazine 7/2001 documents the downturn in the IT and telecoms industries, interviewing the HRM of CISCO who explains why they are localizing expats or switching to locals in the industry.

Chapter 14   Europa

1   Despite all the policy talk about mobility, the report by Price Waterhouse for the European Year of Worker's Mobility found that the use of internationally mobile workers within Europe has fallen from 21 percent of companies it surveyed in 2001 to 13 percent in 2005.

2   The most intellectually substantial reflection on the future of Europe and the necessity of economic reform is the Sapir Report for the Commission (2003), *An Agenda for a Growing Europe: The Sapir Report* (Oxford: Oxford University Press). The liberal minded committee laments Europe's low rates of mobility, and fully supports efforts to improve and extend workers' mobility rights, but recognizes the barriers posed by redistributive ideas of cohesion and autonomy preserved at the national level.

3   The most talked about solution to the dilemma of liberalizing labour markets while preserving the welfare state is the notion of "flexicurity": making it easier for employers to hire and fire, while ensuring a highly protective level of social security and a more proactive state role in retraining and redeployment of the workforce. Euractiv.com reports on December 14, 2006 that the Commission was starting a two to three month European-wide consultation on "adapting labour laws to ensure flexibility and security for all". It is no coincidence that the "best practices" models most often held up for all to emulate are the Netherlands and Denmark – the two West European nations with the toughest line on immigration and the lowest levels of intra-EU migration.

Bibliographical Essay

For reasons of space, I have limited citations to key works and fields that have most influenced my own. A larger, fully referenced bibliography is available on request.

The **sociology of European integration** is a small field. Unlike anthropologists and human geographers, sociologists have found it very difficult to empirically seize an entity that is not a nation, a state, or a society. Neil Fligstein (2008) *Euroclash: The EU, European Identity and the Future of Europe* is one author who has pioneered sociological work on the EU. Fligstein's work is informed by the analogy with US federal integration at the turn of the nineteenth century. He also takes Deutsch's classic (1957) *Political Community and the North Atlantic Area* as the starting point for documenting how Europe is being built by the density and frequency of cross-border interactions, particularly business elites. Juan Diez Medrano (2003) *Framing Europe: Attitudes to European Integration in Germany, Spain and the United Kingdom* is another rare work: a comparative multi-methods study that shares my concern with contextualizing and listening to the voices of Europeans, while asking bigger macro questions about national identity and the building of Europe. Patrick Le Galès (2002) *European Cities: Social Conflicts and Governance*, meanwhile, maps out the agenda in urban and regional studies for this work. It is a convincing account of how the commercial and political activity of the medium sized European city is the core of its economy and society. The spine of affluent, densely interlinked cities running up from Northern Italy, through Switzerland, up the Rhineland to Flanders and the Netherlands is also the core of European integration, as discussed by Charles Tilly (1990) *Coercion, Capital and European States, AD 900–1992* in his account of the struggle between independent cities and nation-states in European history. Another work inspired by Stein Rokkan's macro-vision of Europe is Stefano Bartolini's (2005) *Restructuring Europe: Centre Formation,*

System Forming and Political Structuring. Like many, he identifies the new mobile populations in Europe as a crucial empirical indicator of the restructuring. Most comprehensive of all, Gøran Therborn (1995) *European Modernity and Beyond* charts the
social-structural, spatial, and cultural trajectory of European society in the postwar
era. Of note too is Henri Mendras (1997) *L'Europe des Européens.* All of these works
owe something to the German social historian Hartmut Kaelble (1987) *Auf der Weg
der europäischen Gesellschaft: eine Sozialegeschicht Westeuropas 1880–1980.* I have also been
influenced by a paper of Alan Milward (1997) "The social bases of monetary union?",
collected in a volume by Peter Gowan and Perry Anderson (eds.) *The Question of
Europe.* As he argues, European integration – and its limitations – is all about the
middle classes. Therborn also has a key piece in this collection (1997) "Europe in
the twenty-first century: the world's Scandinavia?" He may well be right that this is the
best we can hope for.

More quantitative approaches to the question of European society are constrained
by the fact international datasets – even Eurostat itself – reproduce everything on a
nation-by-nation basis: as discussed by Richard Breen and David Rottman (1998)
"Is the national state the appropriate geographical unit for class analysis?" This
either pushes studies towards the question of comparative convergence, or into the
varieties of capitalism mode. Colin Crouch (1999) *Social Change in Western Europe*
offers a comprehensive analysis along these lines, as does Andrés Rodríguez-Pose
(2002) *The European Union: Economy, Society, and Polity.* Works in this vein are very use-
fully framed and summarized by Gianfranco Bettin Lattes and Ettore Recchi (eds.)
(2005) *Comparing European Societies.*

In **political economy**, the question of how European economy and society
compare to the North American and Asian alternatives leads to the larger issue of
comparative regional integration. The economic theory of integration dates back to
the work of Nobel prizewinner Robert Mundell and its translation into European
terms by Béla Balassa. Regional integration, a subject also close to the heart of
another key sociological reference in the study of the EU, the work of Ernst Haas,
has been revived by Walter Mattli (1991) *The Logic of Regional Integration: Europe and
Beyond,* and Peter Katzenstein (2005) *A World of Regions: Asia and Europe in the American
Imperium.* See also Neil Fligstein and Frédéric Mérand's paper (2002) "Globalization
or Europeanization? Evidence on the European economy since 1980".

Among **historians**, there is no better or more chilling work on Europe's twentieth century than Mark Mazower (1998) *Dark Continent.* Historians of European
migration in the modern age are well served by two works: Leslie Page Moch (2003,
2nd edn.) *Moving Europeans: Migration in Western Europe since 1650* and Klaus Bade
(2000) *Europa in Bewegung: Migration vom späten 18. Jahrhundert bis zur Gegenwart.* An
unavoidable reference is Alan Milward (2005, 2nd edn.) *The European Rescue of the
Nation State,* and (ed.) (1994) *The Frontier of National Sovereignty* on the origins of
European Union. Work by Federico Romero here details the political origins of
freedom of movement rights.

The **sociology of nationalism** is another key field. The big picture is laid out
by Michael Mann (1993) *The Sources of Social Power Vol. 2: The Rise of Classes and
Nation-States 1760–1914,* and his two essays (1998) "Is there a society called Euro?"
and (1999) "Has globalization ended the rise of the nation-state?" I have been
strongly influenced by John Torpey's account of the "state monopolization of the

legitimate means of movement" in (2000) *The Invention of the Passport: Surveillance, Citizenship, and the State*. Nationalism is much less studied at the micro-interactional level. Here, work by Michael Billig (1995) *Banal Nationalism* provides a start, and I am indebted in my approach to the recent work of Rogers Brubaker collected in (2005) *Ethnicity Without Groups* and (with Margit Feischmidt, Jon Fox, and Liana Grancea) explored in an East European context in (2006) *Nationalist Politics and Everyday Ethnicity in a Transylvanian Town*. His work on "citizenship as social closure" in (1992) *Citizenship and Nationhood in France and Germany* is another conceptual starting point. The concepts of "de-ethnicization" and "denationalization" are used in a distinct but related sense to mine in Christian Joppke (2005) *Selecting By Origin: Ethnic Migration in the Liberal State* and Saskia Sassen (2006) *Territory, Authority, Rights: From Medieval to Global Assemblages*, respectively. We disagree about whether denationalization or renationalization is ascendant in Europe.

The crucial **language** question is framed by Abram de Swann (2001) *Words of the World*. His famous essays on Amsterdam have also been useful. Similarly, I have been greatly helped by the work of Philippe van Parijs on the politics of language (2003) "Europe's linguistic challenge", and other unpublished reflections on Brussels. His **philosophical work** on "freedom" (2005) *Real Freedom for All?* is also relevant to my discussion, and two other works by philosophers are alluded to in the text: Derek Parfit (1986) *Reasons and Persons* and Charles Taylor (1989) *Sources of the Self: The Making of the Modern Identity*. My own thoughts on rationality and identity are also influenced by Alessandro Pizzorno (1986) "Some other kinds of otherness: a critique of rational choice theories".

Core to the study of European nationalism is the literature on **welfare states**. Historically, the work of Peter Baldwin (1992) *The Politics of Social Solidarity: Class Bases of the European Welfare State 1875–1975* has proven useful, as well as the Foucauldian touch of François Ewald (1986) *L'État providence*. Gøsta Esping-Andersen's (1999) *Social Foundations of Post-Industrial Economies* is my key contemporary reference, providing as it does the entire intellectual infrastructure for policy thinking on the "flexicurity" agenda. But – and it's a big but – he very symptomatically has nothing to say about spatial mobility and immigration disrupting the model. Squaring this circle is the biggest single key to the future of the European economic system. I am indebted to the theoretical insights of Michael Bommes (1998) *Migrationen in nationalen Wohlfahrsstaaten*, and two works that do broach the key issue here are Michael Bommes and Andrew Geddes (eds.) (2001) *Immigration and Welfare* and Carl-Ulrik Schierup et al. (2006) *Migration, Citizenship and the European Welfare State: A European Dilemma*.

The study of **globalization** is marked by an excess of what can be called "globaloney". At the popular end, Thomas Friedman (2006, 2nd edn.) *The World is Flat: A Brief History of the Twenty-First Century* fills the shelves of business students and airport bookshops everywhere. Ian Angell (2000) *The New Barbarian Manifesto: How to Survive the Information Age* is a hilarious (or frightening, depending on how you read it) Nietszchean take on this world. Pico Iyer captures the rootless lives of global yuppies in (2000) *The Global Soul: Jet Lag, Shopping Malls, and the Search for Home*. And life on a Saturday is just not the same without ex-*Wallpaper* editor Tyler's Brûlé's queasy "Fast lane" adventures around the globe on the back page of the *Financial Times*. I explore these visions elsewhere in my essay "The dream life of a global superman". Academic work is often not any more sober in its analysis of these trends. Following the theorizing of Anthony Giddens, there has been an outpouring of speculative social theory on the consequences of globalization. John Urry (2000) *Sociology Beyond Societies: Mobilities for the Twenty-First Century* offers a manifesto for the study of mobility in all its forms, and Zygmunt Bauman formulates the idea of spatial mobility as the new form of social stratification in (1998) *Globalization: The Human Consequences*. The other well-known theorist here, Ulrich Beck, is also associated with the notions of cosmopolitanism that became popular in the 1990s. Steve Vertovec and Robin Cohen (2002) *Conceiving Cosmopolitanism* offers a useful collection, and Robin Cohen and Paul Kennedy (2000) *Global Sociology* a comprehensive agenda. Although this is the future of sociology, not much yet has been achieved empirically. A notable exception is the impressive research program laid out by Michael Burawoy et al. (2000) *Global Ethnography: Forces, Connections, and Imaginations in a Postmodern World*, and Michael Peter Smith and Adrian Favell (eds.) (2006) *The Human Face of Global Mobility* is a follow up to this, focusing on skilled migration.

Some **popular works on Europe** should be mentioned. My own book is a distant relative of Anthony Sampson (1968) *The New Europeans: A Guide to the Workings, Institutions and Character of Contemporary Europe*. Richard Hill offers entertainment and practical business wisdom in (1997) *We Europeans* and (1998) *EuroManagers and Martians*. Every *stagiaire* in Brussels has copies of these. Just as Europe was hitting the rocks of the constitutional crisis, two highly optimistic accounts about the European future were published by American journalists: T. R. Reid (2004) *The United States of Europe: The New Superpower and the End of American Supremacy*; and Jeremy Rifkin (2004) *The European Dream: How Europe's Vision of the Future is Quietly Eclipsing the American Dream*. Europeans are never quite so optimistic.

On **post-nationalism** in Europe, the references begin with Jürgen Habermas (1992) "Citizenship and national identity: some reflections on the future of Europe". The social theory of the public sphere has inspired several research programs, for example by Erik Oddvar Eriksen and researchers at ARENA, Oslo, in work by Klaus Eder and Hans-Jörg Trenz at Humboldt in Berlin, and work on Europeanization and claims-making led by Ruud Koopmans and Paul Statham. A social theory agenda for this is developed by Gerard Delanty and Chris Rumford (2005) *Rethinking Europe: Social Theory and the Implications of Europeanization*. Very influential have been the work on citizenship and post-national rights by Yasemin Soysal (1994) *Limits of Citizenship* and David Jacobson (1997) *Rights Across Borders*.

From this, it is a short step to **migration studies**. I have been strongly influenced by the agenda for migration studies laid out by Russell King, for example (2002) "Towards a new map of European Migration". This encompasses student migration and retirement migration: i.e. Russell King et al. (2000) *Sunset Lives: British Retirement Migration to the Mediterranean*. Survey work by Ulrich Teichler on the impact of the Erasmus schemes has been useful, as well as various essays on European mobility by geographers such as Allan Williams, Tony Champion, Paul Boyle, Allan Findlay, and Peter Dwyer. Louise Ackers and associates have generated a great deal of interesting empirical research on facets of EU migration, for example (1998) *Shifting Spaces: Women, Citizenship and Migration Within the European Union* and (2004) *A Community for Children? Children, Citizenship and Internal Migration in the EU*. Another key reference in charting everyday gender and family issues is Irene Hardill (2002) *Gender, Migration and the Dual Career Household*. Eleonore Kofman (2000) "The invisibility of skilled female migrants and gender relations in studies of skilled migration in Europe" and (2005) "Figures of the cosmopolitan: privileged nationals and national outsiders" are two very suggestive pieces. On regional and internal migration, Philip Rees et al. (eds.) (1996), *Population Migration in the European Union* is indispensable, as is the work of Anthony Fielding on Britain and London as an escalator region. Rey Koslowski (2000) *Migrants and Citizens* is perceptive of the demographic changes in the European state system on the eve of enlargement. In migration theory, George Borjas is an essential reference, especially in relation to understanding the dynamics of selection mechanisms, and Thomas Straubhaar's reformulation of the migration question as one of "why people stay" is immensely important. His essay "Should I stay or should I go?" in Fischer, Martin, and Straubhaar (eds.) (1997) *International Migration, Immobility and Development* provides the model for my chapter 5. Three recent books offer comparable empirical studies to mine. Kathy Burrell (2006) *Moving Lives: Narratives of Nation and Migration Among Europeans in Post-War Britain*; Monika Zulauf (2001) *Migrant Women Professionals in the European Union*; and Roland Verwiebe (2004) *Transnationale Mobilität innerhalb Europas*, which quantitatively compares incorporation of European migrants of different nationalities (British, French, Danish, Italians, and Poles) into the labour market in Berlin. I have also been helped by Paul Kennedy's ongoing work about European professionals in Manchester, which suggests there is a chance of finding cool Britannia outside inner London.

On the standard model of **immigrant integration**, my (2001, 2nd edn.) *Philosophies of Integration: Immigration and the Idea of Citizenship in France and Britain* remains one of the few works to think carefully about the dubiously Durkheimian assumptions at the heart of endless moralistic policy debate on immigrant integration in Europe. Adrian Favell (2001) "Integration policy and integration research in Western Europe: a review and critique" extends the overview to policy models and survey research in all of Western Europe.

The literature on **transnationalism** is also highly relevant. Peggy Levitt and Nina Glick-Schiller (2004) "Conceptualizing simultaneity: a transnational social field perspective on society" is a good starting point at the end of a long line of studies; the agenda is also spelt out in Andreas Wimmer and Nina Glick-Schiller (2003) "Methodological nationalism and the study of migration". Thomas Faist (2000) *The Volume and Dynamics of International Migration and Transnational Social Spaces* and (2001) "Social citizenship in the European Union: nested membership" are key works in a European context. Ludger Pries (ed.) opens the field to the study of both lower and higher end migrants in (2001) *New Transnational Social Spaces*, and Nikos Papastergiadis (2000) *The Turbulence of Migration: Globalization, Deterritorialization, and Hybridity* challenges migration studies to come to grips culturally with all the new forms of mobility. Convincing empirical works, again, are less evident, although two key references from anthropology are Ulf Hannerz (1996) *Transnational Connections: Culture, People, Places* and Aihwa Ong (1999) *Flexible Citizenship: The Cultural Logics of Transnationality* on the trans-Pacific Chinese. Hannerz pursues this agenda into the work and lives of foreign correspondent journalists in (2004) *Foreign News*. The work of French anthropologist Alain Tarrius, in part on cross-border commuters and traders, has also been of inspiration: see (1992) *Les Fourmis d'Europe. Migrants riches, migrants pauvres et nouvelles villes internationales* and (2000) *Les Nouveaux cosmopolitismes: mobilités, identités, territoires.*

Thinking on **expatriates and transnational elites** is too often marred by an easy sociological judgmentalism: of looking "up" from the position of the dominated dominant, as Bourdieu would put it. Work on the subject is also too often easily dismissed for the same reason. Yet it is the key to understanding globalization at a human level. Leslie Sklair (2001) *The Transnational Capitalist Class* pioneers the study of Fortune 500 CEOs; Michael Hartmann (2002) *Der Mythos von den Leistungseliten* challenges the global credentials of the highest flying elites in Germany; Magdalena Novicka (2006) puts flesh and blood on *Transnational Professionals and their Cosmopolitan Universes*. I have learned much from the UCLA PhD by Ödül Bozkurt (2005) *Transnationality at Work: Highly Skilled Workers in Telecommunications Multinationals in Finland, Sweden and Turkey*. Others have looked at the peculiar place of expatriates in distant corporate postings, such as Anne-Meike Fechter (2005) *Transnational Lives: Expatriates in Indonesia*, or the work of Brenda Yeoh and Katie Willis on expats in Singapore, and Jonathan Beaverstock on Human Resources Management, and on international movers in the banking and finance sectors. Bastian van Apeldoorn, from the "Amsterdam school" of critical IR, narrates European integration as a conspiracy of corporate elites in *Transnational Capitalism and the Struggle over European Integration*, and Anja Weiß (2005) "The transnationalization of social inequality" seeks to operationalize the question of studying social inequalities on a mobile, global scale. Thinking of Eurostars in terms of global elites, however, can distort the picture. It is better to think of them in terms of middle class "middling transnationalism", the kind of agenda pursued by geographers David Conradson and Alan Latham in their work on Antipodean transmigrants in London. One highly relevant study to compare with mine is Anne-Catherine Wagner (1999) *Les Nouvelles élites de la mondialisation* on professional foreign residents in Paris. This work comes to quite jaundiced views of the migrants – as living only in national ghettos, reproducing traditional gender relations, and failing to integrate in France – largely because it samples exclusively parents of children at rich, elite international schools. Another study by Sam Scott (1996) "The social morphology of skilled migration: the case of the British middle class in Paris" adds further to potential comparisons with my Eurocities.

Social mobility research comes in both qualitative and quantitative versions. My starting point is the classic discussion in 1950s functionalist literature by Alvin Gouldner (1957/58) "Cosmopolitans and locals: towards an analysis of latent social roles" or Robert Merton (1957) *Social Theory and Social Structure*. W. Watson (1964) "Social mobility and social class in industrial communities" identifies the social/spatial dynamics of "social spiralists" in Northern England, a discussion also evocative of the literary genre of "angry young men", for example as defined by Colin Wilson (1956) *The Outsider*. The social history of the period is covered in Arthur Marwick (1998) *The Sixties*, and the social structural mismatches that lie behind these dynamics is explored by Louis Chauvel (2002) *Le Destin des générations: structure sociale et cohortes en France au XXe siècle*. Tim Butler and Mike Savage (eds.) (1995) *Social Change and the Middle Classes* collect together a variety of analyses of this core but understudied segment of the population. Daniel Bertaux and Paul Thompson (eds.) (1997) *Pathways to Social Class* pioneer the use of qualitative methods – particularly oral history interviews, as I use – in the study of social mobility. The work of Pierre Bourdieu is also clearly crucial to my analysis, both methodologically and substantively. (1964) *Les Héritiers* (with Jean-Claude Passeron) and (1989) *La Noblesse d'état* analyze the social reproduction inherent in national education systems; (1979) *La Distinction* offers a model for studying the social and cultural practices of the middle classes; (1993) *La Misère du monde* illustrates how the use of direct interview transcripts opens a new sociological window on the study of society; and (2000) *Les Structures sociales de l'économie* is a gripping account of how class inequalities are reproduced through conflict and struggle on the housing market. PIONEUR in particular offers a contribution to mainstream work on social stratification. European social mobility and immobility are analyzed in John Goldthorpe and Robert Erikson (1992) *The Constant Flux* and Richard Breen (ed.) (2004) *Social Mobility in Europe*. This latter work ends by suggesting that immigration may account for a considerable proportion of the (limited) social mobility found in Europe. Our work offers new data that speaks to this and other key questions in this field.

EU studies itself is dominated by top-down legal, diplomatic, and institutional studies. Simon Hix (2005, 2nd edn.) *The Political System of the European Union* is the best single introduction. A self-styled social constructivist approach has of late introduced a more "sociological" style of thinking, particularly on the socialization effects of the European integration process on European political actors. Good examples are Liesbet Hooghe (2001) *The European Commission and the Integration of Europe: Images of Governance*, and work by Jeff Checkel and Brigit Laffan. In fact, a literature largely invisible to English-language readers has long been developed in France, represented for example by Renaud Dorandeu and Didier Georgakakis (eds.) (2001) *L'Europe sur le metier: acteurs et professionalisations de l'Union Européen* and in Virginie Guiraudon (ed.) (2000) *Sociologie de l'Europe: élites, mobilisations et configurations institutionelles*. The earlier work of anthropologists in the Commission, such as Marc Abélès, Maryon MacDonald, Irene Bellier, Thomas Wilson, and Doug Holmes, is also mostly overlooked by political scientists. A good overview of anthropological approaches is John Borneman and Nick Fowler (1997) "Europeanization" in *Annual Review of Anthropology*. The EU studies agenda unfortunately has now veered away again from considering the sociological effects of Europeanization, defining the concept instead in terms of technical issues of implementation at national level.

On the question of **European identity**, Richard Herrmann et al. (eds.) (2004) *Transnational Identities: Becoming European in the EU* is a key collection, featuring useful quantitative analyses of Eurobarometer data by Jack Citrin and John Sides, and original survey work by Michael Bruter. Matt Gabel (1998) *Interests and Integration: Market Liberalization, Public Opinion and European Union* is the most useful study of this kind, establishing the role of spatial proximity to borders in determining pro-EU attitudes. See also work by Sophie Duchesne on the subject. The existing **European citizenship** literature on the whole is too driven by normative expectations, missing the point that freedom of movement rights are essentially about freedom of movement, not models of democratic participation, social movements mobilization, or classic notions of citizenship. Antje Wiener (1998) *"European" Citizenship Practice* puts more of an emphasis on the everyday dimensions of European citizenship, and a good recent history is offered by Willem Maas (2007) *Creating European Citizens*. A survey of political participation of EU citizens in various countries has been done by Sylvie Strudel. For legal references I refer to Elspeth Guild (2000) *European Community Law from a Migrant's Perspective*, and Robin C. A. White (2004) *Workers, Establishment and Services in the European Union*. Didier Bigo and Elspeth Guild (eds.)

(2005) *Controlling Frontiers: Free Movement Into and Within Europe* put the emphasis on the exclusionary as well as inclusionary aspects of the law.

Another key interdisciplinary field is **urban and regional studies**. The flood of work on world cities started by Saskia Sassen (2001, 2nd edn.) *The Global City*, is very well framed by Loughborough University's "Globalization and World Cities" project, led by Peter Taylor. See their website: www.lboro.ac.uk/gawc, which generates an enormous amount of data on the network and business connections of cities in Europe and elsewhere. They rank London, Brussels, and Amsterdam as alpha, beta, and gamma world cities in that order. Michael Storper (1997) *The Regional World*, and Allan Scott (1998) *Regions and the World Economy* pioneered these studies, emphasizing the social structures that lie behind regional economic growth. Mick Dunford (1998) "Economies in space and time: economic geographies of development and underdevelopment and historical geographies of modernization" summarizes the regional argument for Europe. Neil Brenner (2004) *New State Spaces* uses this literature to rethink the urban spatial order in Europe, joining work on scale and governance with work on "glocalization" by Erik Swyngedouw, and work by Manuel Castells, which identifies the "fading charm of European cities" in his (1993) essay "European cities, the informational society, and the global economy". The problem with all this field is its spectacularly faceless, macro-dominated approach to society. This has to some extent been remedied by a second generation of transnational/global studies, for which Michael Peter Smith (2001) *Transnational Urbanism* offers the central agenda. My work also speaks to the literature on the creative class and urban development that has become so fashionable in urban planning in the wake of the bestseller by Richard Florida (2002) *The Rise of the Creative Class*. He considers the impact of their international mobility in (2005) *The Flight of the Creative Class: The New Global Competition for Talent*. The concept of "urban tribes" is taken from another popular journalistic work, Ethan Watters (2004) *Urban Tribes*.

A literature on **gentrification** is the background to my thoughts on housing. Two key polar works are David Ley (1996) *The New Middle Class and the Remaking of the Central City* versus Neil Smith (1996) *The New Urban Frontier: Gentrification and the Revanchist City*. Tim Butler's studies of the upper middle classes in London are the perfect comparison group for my Eurostars there: see Tim Butler and Garry Robson (2004) *London Calling: The Middle Classes and the Remaking of Inner London*. Gary Bridge puts a Bourdieusian logic to work on the subject in (2001) "Bourdieu, rational action and the time-space strategy of gentrification", a kind of work that has been done in Paris by Michel Pinçon and Monique Pinçon-Charlot (2003) *Sociologie de la bourgeoisie*. See also Rowland Atkinson and Gary Bridge (eds.) (2005) *Gentrification in a Global Context*. Case study work by Jon May on Stoke Newington in London, Patrick Simon on Belleville in Paris, Matthieu van Criekingen on Sint Katelijne in Brussels, and Darren Smith on "studentification" has been useful, as has the critical view on these phenomena by Malcolm Keith (2005) *After the Cosmopolitan? Multicultural Cities and the Future of Racism*. Nigel Thrift's work on "soft capitalism" in (2005) *Knowing Capitalism* is suggestive of the social structures behind the world of finance and markets, and Linda McDowell (1997) *Capital Culture: Gender at Work in the City* offers a context for my research on young women professionals in London. Theoretically, Ash Amin and Nigel Thrift (2002) *Cities: Reimagining the Urban* goes too far off in a speculative direction for my taste, but it does contain a very useful discussion of Lefebvre's concept of "rhythmanalysis" and the way cities standardize human life. On urban dynamics in the US, I have also been influenced by Joel Garreau's (1991) *Edge City: Life on the New Frontier*.

There is of course much literature on the cities themselves. On **Amsterdam**, a representative collection is Léon Deben et al. (eds.) (2000) *Understanding Amsterdam: Essays on Economic Vitality, City Life and Urban Form*, and I have made much use of work by Sako Musterd, Philip Muus, Robert Kloosterman, and Jan Rath. On its history, there is Simon Schama's study (1987) *The Embarrassment of Riches: An Interpretation of Dutch Culture in the Golden Age*, and Peter van Kessel and Elisja Schulte (eds.) (1997) *Rome, Amsterdam: Two Growing Cities in Seventeenth-Century Europe*.

For the history of **London**, Roy Porter (1994) *London: A Social History* is simply wonderful. Key contemporary references are Nick Buck et al. (2002) *Working Capital: Life and Labour in Contemporary London* and Chris Hamnett (2003) *Unequal City: London in the Global Arena*. On the migration history of London, there is Colin Holmes (1988) *John Bull's Island: Immigration and British Society, 1871–1971* and Nick Merriman (ed.) *The Peopling of London*. Eve Darian-Smith (1999) *Bridging Divides* is a fascinating account of the Little Englander mentality viewed through the story of the Eurostar tunnel, and Steve Vertovec (2006) "The emergence of super diversity in Britain" captures some of the social changes associated with new migration in Britain.

In **Brussels**, Marc Swyngedouw, Karen Phalet, and Kris Deschouwer (eds.) (1999) *Minderheden in Brussel: Sociopolitieke houdingen en gedragingen*, and Marco Martiniello and Marc Swyngedouw (eds.) (1998) *Où va la Belgique?* were my starting point. A number of essays by Christian Kesteloot and Guy Baeten were useful on the background of urban development in the city. An otherwise interesting cultural anthropology approach to the EU, Cris Shore (2000) *Building Europe* is an unfortunate compendium of the mistaken eurosceptic views of the city and of the life of *fonctionnaires* there. From the other side, Bart Aerts (2004) *Hartinfarct Europa: Brusselse Gevolgen van de EU-Uitbreiding* is a tirade about the growing presence of European foreigners. Julie Cailliez (2004) *Schuman-City* is a study of the lives of British *fonctionnaires* in the city; in *De Europeanen: Leven en Werken in de Hoofdstad van Europa*, journalist Caroline de Gruyter (2006) portrays her own set of archetypal *Brusselaars*; and Eric Corijn and Walter de Lannoy (2000) *Crossing Brussels: De Kwaliteit van het Verschil* celebrates diversity in the city. My original report on the new Europeans in Brussels (2001) *Free Movers in Brussels* is available at: www.kubrussel.ac.be/onderwijs/psw/onderzoek/ipsomlezingen/rapportFavell.pdf.

Finally, on **methodology**, my work uses a mix of constructivist, grounded theory, and comparative strategies. On the constructivist approach to identifying and enumerating populations, French sociology is much more sophisticated than English-language variants. Pierre Bourdieu et al. (1968) *Le Métier du sociologue* is a key treatise on how the object of research first needs to be constructed, while Patrick Champagne et al. (1996) *Initiation à la pratique sociologique* was my handbook for constructing the populations I sampled in the three cities. Jean Schensul et al. (1999) *Mapping Social Networks, Spatial Data and Hidden Populations* was also useful. See the work of Michel de Certeau (1990) *L'Invention du quotidien*, Alfred Schutz (1967) *The Phenomenology of the Social World*, and Barney Glaser and Anselm Strauss (1967) *The Discovery of Grounded Theory* for sources of my inductive ethnographic approach to studying the "everyday" lives of my subjects in an urban context. I have also been inspired by Michèle

Lamont's work in cultural sociology. She uses semi-structured interview techniques and small-n comparative research design to great effect in studying race, ethnicity, class, and gender. See (1992) *Money, Morals and Manners: The Culture of French and American Upper-Middle Classes* and (2000) *The Dignity of Working Men: Morality and the Boundaries of Race, Class, and Immigration.* Further discussion can be found in Michèle Lamont and Laurent Thèvenot (eds.) (2000). *Rethinking Comparative Cultural Sociology.*

Index of Interviewees

Index